A RISK MANAGEMENT APPROACH TO BUSINESS CONTINUITY:

ALIGNING BUSINESS CONTINUITY WITH CORPORATE GOVERNANCE

By Julia Graham, FCII, FBCI MIRM
And
David Kaye, FCII FBCI MIRM FRSA

Philip Jan Rothstein, FBCI, Editor

ROTHSTEIN ASSOCIATES INC., Publisher
Brookfield, Connecticut USA
www.rothstein.com

ISBN #1-931332-36-3

ISBN #1-931332-36-3

PUBLISHER:

Philip Jan Rothstein, FBCI

Rothstein Associates Inc.
The Rothstein Catalog On Disaster Recovery
4 Arapaho Rd.
Brookfield, Connecticut 06804-3104 U.S.A.
203.740.7444
203.740.7401 fax
www.rothstein.com

www.DisasterRecoveryBooks.cominfo@rothstein.com

Table of Contents

PREFACE

The escalating pace of change, a rising tide of technological innovation, almost instantaneous transmission of breaking news and the globalization of crime and terrorism, all combine to provide a heady cocktail of challenge for today's organization.

Clear to all business watchers are the dramatic ways that businesses have responded to these challenges and reorganized themselves, as they have taken up the opportunities available. These include new uses for technology, faster and direct to customer communications, increasingly open foreign market opportunities, outsourcing and offshoring, harnessing the power of the brand, sophisticated supply chain management, just-in-time delivery cycles, the ability to mine huge databases in milliseconds, and new relationships with the workforce.

These elements of the modern business may offer great flexibility and a magnificent ability to relate precisely to the needs of individual customers and other stakeholders. They have, however, also given rise to critical dependencies and single points of potential catastrophic risk and failure. Organizations can upsize and respond to new selling opportunities very quickly indeed. If an organization is fighting though a crisis, its competitors will most likely be well positioned to seize any opportunities created by the distraction and diversion of attention that recovery can demand. Interestingly therefore, the risk of sudden destruction of today's modern organization, however huge, diverse, financially strong and multinational, is more likely than businesses using the models seen in the 1990s and before.

The most critical failure points are not financial. Company boards have long established financial risk measuring mechanisms but the response to these new exposures and the growing influence of regulators are driving boards increasingly to consider non-financial risk. This is tougher to quantify, harder to grasp and consequently can give rise to boards feeling less comfortable and in control and consequently, less confident.

Business Continuity Management is coming of age to respond to the new needs of its own stakeholder, the organization for which it carries the responsibility. It is indivisible from risk management and is an increasingly important tool of risk management. The Continuity Industry leaders are now looking well beyond technology and other infrastructure replacement, and see a crucial value for themselves at the very top of level of their organization's strategy setting. They set out to understand the importance of these dependencies, measure the risk and impact in its very widest sense, and then ensure resilience and an ability to respond and recover to a level that the whole range of stakeholders are entitled to expect.

This book is a must read for those senior managers, risk managers and continuity managers who have the vision to see both the new opportunities and the new responsibilities of business continuity management.

George J. Mitchell, Chairman
DLA Piper Rudnick Gray Cary
Former Senate Majority Leader and U.S. Senator for Maine
New York City, New York USA
December, 2005

PREFACE

At last, a book for those involved in risk and business continuity management that proves beyond doubt why the traditional 'silo approach' to risk management and business continuity management must be removed and replaced with a modern day 'joined up' approach to protecting a business and the interests of its stakeholders.

Today's business world faces an increasing assortment of risks and threats that can have devastating effects. However we should not lose sight of those day-to-day incidents that can ultimately result in 'death by a thousand cuts.'

This book, written by authors with acclaimed knowledge, experience and wisdom within both risk management and business continuity management, provides clear guidance supported with a wide range of memorable and highly relevant case studies for any risk manager or business continuity manager to successfully meet the challenges of today and the future.

Steve Mellish, FBCI

Chairman
The Business Continuity Institute
United Kingdom

INTRODUCTION

As business practices and sensitivities change, Business Continuity Management (BCM) is increasingly a central and crucial tool for the risk manager. Responses to the Bi-annual Risk Management and Risk Financing Survey by AON in 2005 amongst risk managers, insurance managers and finance directors of the United Kingdom's top 1,000 organisations placed business continuity as the second most important risk issue that concerns them. The greatest concern, protection of the brand value, and others in their top ten, (1) loss of reputation, (4) product liability/tamper, (5) regulatory/legislation (6) physical damage, (8) terrorism, (9) corporate governance and (10) professional indemnity, are all commercial survival issues and key elements of continuity management.

The consequences of damage by a risk incident might not just be quantifiable initially in monetary terms, such as in the loss of valuable assets or by destructive levels of litigation. The consequences might involve the loss of life or valuable dependencies that are necessary for the organisation's very survival. These include intellectual assets, brand values, regulatory approvals, legality, the confidence of its various stakeholders, and its ability to deliver urgent, contracted, products and services on time. Furthermore the consequence may be that the organisation has to step away from its marketplace for a period of time and give free reign to competitors to do lasting damage to the customer, supply or distributor base.

The damage, of course, may not only be within the organisation. There could be destruction of the legal or physical environment on which the organisation depends. An urgently needed "just in time" supplier or distributor might be the one directly affected by a disaster, but their failure to deliver as contracted may have an equally destructive impact on the production line of the organisation expecting urgent and key ingredients into their own products.

We set out to write this book because we have seen thinking about business continuity starting to evolve from its roots in IT back up and contingency equipment and facilities departments, typically referred to as "disaster recovery.". We believe, though, that these roots are still often the drivers for business continuity and its practitioners and that they, and too often their employers, remain within these narrow thought horizons. The modern business is much more complicated than this, is exposed to entirely new dependencies and criticalities, and, in spite of its wealth and scale is even more exposed to single, organisation-wide exposures to destruction than in earlier business models. This causes us great concern and we feel significantly exposes organisations to destruction and total failure.

In the same way that risk management has moved on from being the purchase of insurance products, business continuity needs to emerge from its silos and position itself as part of the much wider risk and strategic management framework of the organisation. This book sets out to take the reader forward and has, we believe, important messages for chief executives, directors, non-executive directors, risk managers, continuity managers, internal and external auditors, investment managers, compliance managers, finance directors, project managers, regulators, education programmes and others.

An important aspect is that different organisations – and even personalities within an organisation – can take very different views on acceptability and unacceptability of risk exposures. They will make these decisions within their different backgrounds and cultures, and also the quite different pressures upon them. A bank, servicing credit cards and cash machines 24 hours, seven days a week, will take an entirely different view on acceptable gaps in service than an organisation where customers could reasonable wait a few days for the contracted service, product or for another response. Some organisations, especially those using e-commerce distribution may have competitors who could upsize and respond incredibly quickly to any difficulties seen in another player in their marketplace. It is for this reason that the amount of time lost or "time out" from the market place is another vital consequence for the risk manager.

Equally an organisation cannot allow damage to destroy their financial and other business controls over their organisation. An insurance company may, for example, be dealing at any one time with current claims valued at many billions of pounds and will have reserved accordingly. To lose records and thus intellectual control over such a claims portfolio could totally destroy that organisation.

Options Available to the Board

As always, the responsibility for risk understanding and management rests firmly with the board of directors. The board may delegate the processes for achieving risk understanding and risk management, but it cannot delegate the responsibility. Once the risks and the potential consequences are understood, the directors cannot ignore them and must make decisions around the information obtained. This is not just a regulatory issue, it is simply good management.

The decision could be that the exposure is an acceptable one. This might be a reasonable decision if the potential worst-case consequences are clearly understood and the board considers that they could not possibly have an unacceptable impact on their own people, their stakeholders, balance sheets, controls, legality, market presence, brand values, revenue accounts nor cash flows. If the exposure, however, is deemed to be unacceptable then the organisation has further choices to make:

- The board can invest resources to manage the exposure or the potential consequences down to what is considered to be the acceptable level.

- It could, of course, decide to avoid the particular activity or environment altogether.

- It can enter into a contract to transfer the risk into an insurance product or to another counter party.

- It can prepare beforehand for the consequences of a risk incident; knowing that, with that preparation, that business critical dependencies are safe and that the strengths of the organisation can be used to manage through the consequences without unacceptable damage.

The risk manager could use one of the tools listed above, but in practice is more likely to use the most cost-effective and commercially realistic combination.

It is worth mentioning at this point the ability of the organisation's lawyers to transfer by contract the potential cost of risk to suppliers, distributors or other counterparties. There is no real value however, when a risk incident destroys a just-in-time and critical supplier or a distributor; and that it in turn by its failure damages or destroys the risk manager's own organisation's ability to remain in business. The lawyer's view needs also the additional and important dimension of business continuity. Furthermore it is interesting to recognise that the most destructive of risks highlighted by the AON survey are not insurable ones in the conventional insurance market. 'We didn't need risk management because we had insurance' is too often a cry from the corporate grave.

This book deals with the last of the four options listed above, i.e., business continuity management. The message of this book is that business continuity forms just part of a much wider and coordinated risk management programme that sets out critically to understand what the exposure is and the consequences of that exposure. We believe, in just one example, that there is a crucial role at strategic level for the business continuity manager when an organisation is considering, choosing and establishing contractual and operational relationships with a potential outsourced supplier. This book takes a view across the options available for managing any exposure, or potential impact that would be life-threatening to the organisation. It is important, though, that the reader keeps in mind throughout this much wider picture of risk and risk management that BCM as just one of the tools available to be used in isolation or in conjunction with the others. The existence of a business continuity manager, especially one whose task is only to 'recover' the organisation from a physical disaster, is very likely to be raising expectations of resilience well beyond the ability to deliver.

Continuity And Its Risks

We should begin with the rather obvious but important maxim that – if the organisation allows itself to die during the risk incident – the best continuity planning will provide nothing more than a mechanism for trying to revive an already dead horse.

During a potentially catastrophic disaster in a modern multinational, the board's attention is on the survival of the business. It is too easy to consider only the insurers' view and believe that the most important concern is the replacing of buildings and contents, or defending from litigation. The loss of physical operations; whether they be buildings, contents, equipment or similar are, of course, important. The risk manager's view on BCM embraces these issues but also needs to look way beyond. It is crucial to consider the foundation stones, and thus vital dependencies, that enable a modern business to survive. These can then be matched against stakeholders who, in their own way are critical dependencies. Only then, we suggest, can we see the real post-damage pressures, and what is needed to be done, before the incident too, to ensure that the organisation can be kept alive.

In recent years, there have been important changes in the way businesses deliver and market their own products; changes too in their relationships with their stakeholders, and in the risks themselves.

Many a modern organisation can fairly be described as made up of no more than a brand, miners of owned or rented intellectual assets, controls, and outsourcing contracts. These ingredients have become crucial, urgent dependencies and single points of risk for the very survival of that organisation.

Stakeholders

It is valuable to also consider organisations from the perspective of their stakeholders. We could recognise stakeholders simply as those organisations and individuals that have a "stake" or interest in the current organisation's affairs. The stakeholders demanding the attention of the continuity risk manager are not just investors; they include internal and 'outsourced' employees, customers, suppliers, distributors, financiers and their advisors, and the political, legal and natural environment. Their needs and demands are different and in some cases contradictory.

If these are not problems enough, in the real world of damage, the problems of a company reeling from serious damage, are just beginning. All sorts of new stakeholders emerge, identified by their abilities and propensities to react to damage. These stakeholders can shift the ground even further away from underneath managers in already difficult circumstances, to keep the organisation alive. These include competitors, the media as wholesalers of confidence, the brand values, bankers, credit rating agencies and regulators. Many organisations have, of course, their own unique stakeholders in addition.

This book sets out to look at these processes, stakeholders and dependencies and places them firmly at the strategic issue end of the Board's attention. Above all, this book sees business continuity not just as something to remove a threat, but as something that is as much about opportunities for development and for enabling the much wider objectives of the organisation.

The Evolution of Impact

Risks themselves, therefore, have not only changed, but also the potential for damage from these new risks is totally different. Furthermore, consider the potential for damage to the organisation that can occur from old risks. A fire or storm damage that that occurs in a building housing a group-wide computer system causes damage that is unrecognisable from the extent of damage we could envisage in past business models from a fire in one building.

So many of these risks are not physical ones. The loss of intellectual assets, the reputation, key stakeholders walking away, a drop in credit rating raising significantly the cost of capital and destroying dependant financial models, are just a few of the impacts that would cause so much more damage than the loss of buildings and their contents. This concentration of single points of destructive risk too can cause the skills of one individual or small team to be skills on which the entire delivery of a multinational depends.

Business Continuity Management

The issue we address is not just the individual continuity manager's own department: it is more than this. It is about ensuring, at the highest level in an organisation, that continuity is not something that is pushed aside as unimportant, but needs to be positioned, structurally, and especially in business understanding and skill levels, in the very heart of today's organisations. To do otherwise is just lip service, and creating a risk in itself, because it will raise expectations amongst stakeholders including shareholders, employees, customers and regulators, and as such is more dangerous than having no 'business recovery' position at all.

1

A Risk-Based Approach
To Business Continuity

Objectives of This Chapter

- Track the development of risk management from its roots of origin to modern practice
- Provide risk related definitions
- Develop the link between risk management and business continuity management as part of a risk management framework
- Introduce the theme of risk management and business continuity management as part of good governancd business management

Risk - a Moving Target

Ten years ago, if you had picked up this book, because of the reference to risk in the title, you probably would have been a finance director, internal auditor or treasurer. This statement should not come as a surprise to the reader. In the early 1990s Board-level interest in risk management and internal controls was largely focussed on financial and treasury issues, and although there were some organisations that took a wide-angle view of risk and controls beyond finance, even in these cases, attention was generally focussed on hazard-related or insurable risk. With broad insurance coverage at highly competitive prices freely available a decade ago, there were very few reasons for "insurable risk" to be brought out of daily financial management to the attention of the Board.

Many risk commentators mark the terrible events of September 11. 2001 as the date this all changed, but the roots of modern risk management are much older and were already deeply embedded in the management of many organisations long before that fateful day in 2001.

Man has striven to understand risk for centuries. Whether affected by storm, fire or flood, man focussed on the fear of potential events and the negative impact these might have on his property and his plans.

Attributed to the result of Fate or acts of God, risk was rarely projected, and only when records were kept did an opportunity present itself to interrogate these records and to offer predictions of the future. Peter Bernstein argues "the revolutionary idea that defines the boundary between modern times and the past is a mastery of risk: the notion that the future is more than a whim of the gods and that men and women are not passive before nature… until human beings discovered a way across that boundary the future was a mirror of the past." (1). Bernstein's book tells the story of a group of thinkers whose remarkable vision revealed how to put the future at the service of the present. By showing the world how to understand risk, measure it, and weigh its consequences, they converted risk-taking into one of the prime catalysts that drives modern Western society. Bernstein continues, "The essence of risk management lies in maximizing the areas where we have some control over the outcome while minimizing the areas where we have absolutely no control over the outcome and the linkage between effect and cause is hidden from us."

Whether one holds the view that the seeds of risk management were sown in the coffee shops of Liverpool and London and the early pooling of marine risks, or that the foundations were built by individuals such as Gustav Hamilton (1974) who created a "risk management circle," or the governments and authorities of the 1980s and 1990s such as Standards Australia, it has only been in the last few years that risk management has come of age and finally been accepted as an integral part of good management practice.

This book is not, however, a trip through the history of risk management and business continuity management. It is intended to provide those who have a responsibility for leading or practicing the management of risk to join us on a journey to unravel the relationship between these issues and to provide practical support to the manager, risk and business continuity practitioners.

Risk Managing Today

In the mid 1990s, when organisations were facing pressures on profit ratios and finance directors were seeking the means to reduce expenses and ways to transfer the more speculative risks, the insurance industry was in turmoil with premium costs spiralling and risk appetite reducing. Coupled with a dilution in insurer credit ratings, the spotlight turned on what had largely been a soft insurance buyer/supplier relationship; boardrooms everywhere sat up and took interest.

- One outcome of this attention was a diversion of some larger organisations away from risk transfer and insurance towards risk retention through higher levels of self-insurance. Why transfer risk to insurers which might have credit ratings less worthy than your own? Why subject your organisation to the volatility of the insurance market when the Board wanted smooth and predictable business results in an already volatile world? To give the Board peace of mind at a cost-effective price meant following these circumstances through, and an increase in demand emerged for greater emphasis on risk management practices, with an expectation of information arising from these practices to satisfy peace of mind. As a by-product of this scenario two things emerged:

- Organisations started to gain a desire to investigate how they might manage all risks across their business, coupled with a growing division in management priorities and approach between managing the more predictable and quantifiable risk and the unforeseeable and more intangible risk.

- Business continuity management, for so long a subject of response rather than resilience and typically lodged within the domain of the Information Technology or Facilities department, started to attract wider interest as a potential key control and alternative mechanism for risk mitigation other than transfer of risk by insurance.

This situation presented and continues to present new challenges for the insurance industry. While the insurers are still collecting the bulk of premiums for non-catastrophic loss, they face a call for the harder to price one-off catastrophic event solution, coupled with a desire from the customer for solutions that move away from pure asset protection to the protection of intellectual and reputation value. These are typically much more difficult to identify, quantify and manage by the nature of their intangibility. Away from actuarial principals and with weaker balance sheets of their own in an attempt to satisfy their customers, insurers have on occasion struggled and financially suffered as they have striven to meet this demand.

For over a decade corporate governance and risk management have been entwined and, to many, synonymous with good management and control. From slender governance tendrils such as Cadbury and Turnbull in the United Kingdom have grown powerful risk management frameworks comprising broadly standardised risk policies, practices and associated organisational risk governing bodies such as the Risk Committee and Audit Committee directly empowered by the Board. Consequently there is a risk red-line running through much of what we now see arising from a huge variety of rules and guidance-setting governance, legislative and regulatory bodies and in response a plethora of solutions from consultants, professional service firms and educational institutions.

The risk-based internal control system has become an increasingly significant regulatory object, notably with the passing of the Sarbanes-Oxley Act in the USA (2). Regulatory incentives exist to have good controls in all types of "infrastructure" or "operational" risk including health care, safety, environmental issues, and business continuity management. But caution ... control systems cannot alone provide consumer or Board level comfort.

There is nothing wrong with introducing relevant risk-related controls into the everyday business environment. However in an increasingly complex and uncertain world, full of unplanned failures, scandals and disasters, organisations must invest time and effort thinking the unthinkable, considering domino effects and complex interdependencies, and a world where the principles of risk management and control are fine when the world is organised, but are suddenly very difficult to grasp and apply when it is not. Whilst we may be comfortable to accept that the controls environment has been re-engineered and re-packaged as risk management, and serves to extend the reach of risk management into every operational aspect of organisational life, a tendency to the tick-box approach with an inward looking focus of the controls system, however re-packaged, is not a replacement for effective risk management.

Today, in a fast-moving, changing, technology-driven, often insecure and unpredictable world, risk managers can have a tendency to try and organise what cannot often be organised because individuals, corporations and governments have little choice but to try to do so. The risk management of everything holds out a promise to do so even in situations when ordinarily this would be impossible. Whilst governments and regulators are increasingly forcing this position to be adopted, beware the organisation that wraps its approach to risk management around creating a position defendable to the Board which emphases as a priority the achievement of sound processes at the expense of intellectual consideration and content.

Risks are not always compliant: "Risk is like a tarpaulin flapping in a gale. As soon as one corner is secure another is up and flapping.." (3). Therefore, while risk *management and risk control* are related, they are not mutually exclusive and risk control should form part of a comprehensive or enterprise-wide risk management framework - more on which will be addressed later in this chapter.

Risk management may now also be put forward as a mechanism for organisational value management. In the public sector, in the absence of competition, risk management and risk metrics are providing a new focus for outcomes and performance, while in the private sector and especially in financial services, risk is increasingly used as a link between operational performance and capital requirements Given the range and stretch of risk perhaps risk management has caught on as a discipline ahead if its ability to deliver. In the absence of good definitional risk language, risk management professional capability and most importantly definition and measures of effectiveness, have encouraged a scientific approach to a subject sometimes more suited to the arts. Is this a risk in itself?

Whatever your view, there is a clear need to raise the risk practitioner game. Risk management should be practiced as part of regular strategic and operational processes. One route available to organisations is to improve integration of risk within the business and to bring risk management practitioners whatever their discipline and risk-related interest out of their back offices and into the business as a cohesive, professional team to better share and develop risk management capability across the risk silos that still generally exist.

There are opportunities for risk management principles which work in one risk discipline to add value in another and for risk management practices generally to add value to a business as a whole.

Risk Management Is a Balancing Act

Risk is the sugar and salt of life - too much or too little of either is unhealthy. And just as a good diet is achieved through a balance between the intake of sugar and salt, risk management is about getting the balance right between taking risk and avoiding it.

Too often the emphasis in risk management is placed on the negative or downside of risk and getting rid of it, and too infrequently on the opportunity or upside that good risk management can deliver. Risk management, and as part of this, risk control, can act as a mechanism for improvement, and differentiate an organisation from its counterparts and peers leading to real value added and competitive advantage.

More than half of Europe's top 100 companies now have a dedicated risk manager (4) As risk management continues to mature as a profession, many companies choose to focus on actively managing their risk rather than primarily concentrating on insurance buying and administration.

A variety of surveys, cast across risk managers in the United Kingdom, Europe and globally, noted that differences in risk management practice remain across the world. Although levels of government intervention in such areas as corporate governance will continue to influence the degree of difference, we can expect these differences to erode and greater consistency to emerge. The annual Centre for the Study of Financial Innovation Banana Skins Report (5) which, while focussing on the world of banking, includes risks that should feature on all risk agendas, including the spectre of the rising tide of governance and regulation and the risks associated with this. These risks feature in the survey for the first time, and are the most prominent riser, not solely because of repeated corporate failure, but also due to a fear of regulatory "overkill."

Three interesting features, common to most surveys, are:

- a perceptible escalation of the intangible risks in the league tables at the expense of the more tangible, quantifiable and transferable risks;

- continuing concern over the risks that are difficult to predict and consequently to plan for; and

- aggregation and domino effects in an increasingly interdependent and global business world

---

The Banana Skins Report reminds us that all businesses and industries are interconnected, and while one might postulate that a major banking failure is unlikely, the impact of failure of any major industry or industrial giant could create a huge fallout that might act as a tsunami which catches us all in its wake. This is a key consideration to bear in mind as we move forward to consider business continuity management.

Most of these surveys are not new and they serve to act as established and useful benchmarks and barometers to risk managers when setting their risk agenda.

Do we Live In a "Riskier" World?

Certainly business change is getting faster, technology more critical, terrorism increasingly organised and global, business interconnectivities and dependencies more complex and prone to failure - and, on balance, customers are more sophisticated and informed. When one adds consideration of the impact of mechanisms built by governments and regulators to protect their consumers and themselves - one could present a good argument to say that the answer to the question, *"is this a riskier world"* is probably yes.

Whatever your view and whether your goal is to grow for shareholder profit, partner profitability or social benefit, all business entities exist to provide stakeholder value. In an environment of intensifying competition, as markets and businesses mature internationally creating pressure on growth and profitability, the breadth of risks considered has increased and their severity become in some cases more acute, thereby changing the equation of balancing risk and reward.

> The role of management is to create an environment that facilitates the identification and tight control of the negative risks, while nurturing an environment that allows for the identification and conversion of opportunities, and their challenge to determine how much uncertainty an organisation is prepared to accept.
>
> The challenge for risk management is to provide the framework to help management deal with uncertainty, and the associated risk and opportunity to agreed levels of acceptability, with managing risk embedded as part of an organisation's strategic and operational management processes.

It consequently shouldn't come as a surprise to see a new generation of risk managers tasked with embedding risk management frameworks designed to address the spectrum of risks across an organisation, including boardroom-level strategic risk issues.

Risk management that stretches out across an organisation is not a new concept, but it is a poorly defined and articulated one. Essentially aimed at providing management with frameworks that allow them to deal with uncertainty and associated risk and opportunity, the goal in an enterprise risk environment is to:

- Enhance the opportunity to grow value and enhanced capability;
- Align risk appetite or tolerance to strategy;
- Link growth and risk with return;
- Enhance risk response decisions;
- Minimise operational surprises and losses, and;
- Provide integrated management and responses to cross-enterprise and multiple risks.

It's Risk But Not As We've Known It

The Committee of Sponsoring Organisations of the Treadway Commission (COSO) defines enterprise risk management as *"a process effected by an entity's board of directors, management and other personnel, applied in strategy setting and across the enterprise, designed to identify potential events that may affect the entity, and manage risks to be within its risk appetite, to provide reasonable assurance regarding achievement of entity objectives."* **(6)**. The components of the COSO framework are:

- Internal environment - management, philosophy and attitude toward risk

- Objective setting - connection of risk to objectives

- Event identification - determination of what risks an entity faces

- Risk assessment - severity (impact/probability) estimates of inherent and residual risk

- Risk response - actions to reduce exposure

- Control activities - measures to ensure responses are carried out

- Information and communication - sharing of risk information across the entity

To successfully apply enterprise risk management an organisation must consider the entire scope of its activities at all levels: strategic (top down), functional units or business streams (bottom up) and significant or "material" change (planned or unexpected).

Earlier in this chapter we explored the relationship between risk management, corporate governance and the control environment of an organisation. A cautionary word at this stage is to remind ourselves why we are managing risk.

There is an increasing temptation when led by legislative and regulatory guidelines and rules to overemphasise the value of the control environment at the expense of the risk environment. A control environment as a means to an end must be resisted. In other words the relevant businesses should identify and assess the risks, not a team isolated physically and intellectually from the internal and external business environment. The most fundamental alignment of risk management should be with the vision and mission of an organisation and while the regulator must be satisfied it does not expect to be the driver of why an organisation manages risk or what its priorities should be.

Any robust planning and performance management process will kick off with an organisation's objectives clearly established. Risk management should be part of the strategic and operational planning processes and performance management mechanisms by providing risk-adjusted measures. Without this how can you achieve integration of risk and reward - or risk managing what is at stake? Responsibility for risk understanding and management rests firmly with the Board, and a Board should only sign off a profile of risks that have true relevance to an organisation. Without a business enterprise-wide process embedded in these processes, the Board cannot be in a position to truly discharge its responsibilities.

Risk - the Journey

We have already drilled quite deeply into some of the paths that risk management has travelled but it is time to pause and ponder why risk management is where it is today and why practice can still vary quite considerably across industries and countries.

In the United States, while recognising the "COSO" model, John W. Schaefer, writing in The John Liner Review **(7)** discusses evolution from roots in insurance-and-risk management. He argues that recent increases in the cost-of-risk (primarily insurance) have raised awareness of the concept of risk management. While he acknowledges the relatively undeveloped terminology, tools and techniques, he urges risk managers to "... be active in shaping the future ..." and brokers and insurers to be "... ready to react to imminent change ..." In the United Kingdom, the Association of Insurance and Risk Managers (AIRMIC), The Institute of Risk Management (IRM) and the National Forum for Risk Management in the Public Sector (ALARM) have collaborated in the production of a Risk Management Standard (8). Drawing on a wide body of risk-interested opinion-formers, the rapidly developing nature of the discipline of risk management is recognised, while accepting that some form of Standard with supporting terminology is desirable.

The Standard recognises risk management as a central part of any organisation's strategic management. "It is the process whereby organisations methodically address the risks attaching to their activities with the goal of achieving sustained benefit within each activity and across the portfolio of all activities." With original roots in those who insurance-risk-manage, the Standard travels beyond the insurable risk agenda promoting risk management as "... a continuous process which runs throughout the organisation's strategy and the implementation of that strategy. It should address methodically all the risks surrounding the organisation's activities past, present and in particular future."

Work coming out of Australia and New Zealand (9) has as its roots an origin of health and public sector risk management with more than a flavour of engineering process. These standards actively promote the concept that risk management is an iterative process consisting of well-defined steps which, if taken in sequence, support better decision-taking by contributing greater insight into risks and their impacts. "Risk management is recognised as an integral part of good management practice. To be most effective, risk management should become part of an organisation's culture – integrated into the organisation's philosophy, practices and business plans – rather than viewed as a separate programme."

It is only a question of time before we see an International Standards Organisation (ISO) sponsored risk management standard.

The escalation in significance of risks associated with the rising tide of governance and regulation have already been referred to. It is fair to say that wherever regulatory developments take us, life for the risk manager will never be quite the same again. At the core of most regulatory change is the desire for a more competitive and dynamic marketplace, with greater transparency, and security for the consumer. Whilse there is a perception shared by many that the quality of risk management is improving, much of the improvements we are currently seeing are driven by regulatory pressure rather than a commercial desire to better manage risk. But the organisations that take a risk driven approach to regulatory compliance rather than a "tick box" approach driven by a regulatory rule book will be the risk winners. In financial services for example, Basel II banking regulatory requirements and the quality of response to these are already separating the laggards from the leaders. This point simply serves to emphasis the upside and downside nature of risk management, and the move that needs to be made away from purely serving the downside aspects.

Lord Levene, addressing the World Affairs Council in April 2004, (10) spoke of rising complexity of tangible and intangible risks faced by businesses and the challenges he considered business rise to face, in order to meet these as the new three Rs:

- Raise risk to the board room.
- Respond to a challenging risk environment.
- Return to strength and stability.

In a presentation to the Houston Forum in September 2004 Lord Levene added "in the world of risk, time never stands still and the threats and challenges which assault our businesses continue to emerge and evolve - from the faults in the earth to the fault in ourselves. Companies need to recognise that the risk environment has changed and that they cannot rely on 20th century management techniques to solve 21st century problems." (11)

Risk Management on the Board Agenda

The responsibility for understanding risk and managing it rests firmly with the Board. The Board may delegate the processes for managing risk to others, including a Risk Committee sponsored by the Board, but it cannot delegate the responsibility.

So how do we get and keep risk on the Boardroom table?

There is no magic answer to this question, but what organisations will benefit from is a simple mechanism that allows an organisation to articulate what it wants to deliver; to measure where it is up to in the delivery process; and, to facilitate effective and efficient communication of risk goals and achievements to an organisation's "risk managers" who are its employees and partners. Once risk and potential consequences are understood the directors can then make decisions around the information obtained. Otherwise how do you explain to a Board how well you are doing in risk management if you do not know where you are heading? How do you capture the hearts and minds of your employees and partners if they do not know what your risk priorities are, or why?

While open to the pitfalls already described by over-systemised use of controls and associated processes, a risk management framework can act as a vehicle for establishing the boundaries within which an organisation may position its approach to managing risk and the detail required for risk management delivery. There are numerous framework models offered variously by the large consulting houses, promoted within the rules and guidelines of regulatory bodies such as the Financial Services Authority (FSA) in the United Kingdom and "Basel" in Europe as well as those which have been developed down a more academic route.

Categorisation of risks is the bedrock of a framework in that it provides the basis for storing and then analysing data: for example, "if loss data is haphazardly stored, any values derived from the data will reflect its irregularity" (12). And importantly, categorisation provides the language for risk management and consequently a means of achieving the communication that is key to successful design and implementation of an organisation's risk management strategy and approach.

How an organisation categorises risk should be driven in part the nature of by an organisation's core business and in part by the complexity of its assessed internal and external risk environment. Accordingly a framework can only be designed and then embedded within an organisation after an assessment of risks has been undertaken and the risks clustered into categories in such a way the nature, culture, language, complexity and objectives of the organisation is reflected.

Typically an assessment might emerge into a half-dozen or so categories along the lines of:
- Strategic: strategic management
- Group: functional or geographic profile
- Financial: balance sheet management
- Operational: infrastructure
- Governance, Legislative and Regulatory: corporate governance and compliance
- Business: core business

For each risk category an organisation will need to understand what it needs by way of policies, tolerance levels (or appetite), processes, tools and techniques, management information and scenarios against which all of these might be stress-tested. Used as components these can then provide the building blocks from which a framework can be constructed. How complex and detailed components need to be should, however, not only be driven by the complexity of an organisation but also by its culture: there is little point having hugely complex and wordy policy statements, for example, if there is no appetite for complexity within an organisation. Better to have short and simple statements that get read and acted upon than award-winning tomes that sit unused on a shelf.

However, an organisation should avoid growing the seeds of an excessive inward-looking and self-referential set of practices. The potential to integrate the social value systems and ethical behaviour standards should also be considered; aspects of reputation risk management might provide a suitable channel through which to achieve this.

Once an organisation has a framework it can start to conduct a current-state risk management analysis using the framework as a benchmark, assess this against what is considered necessary for the future and then design an action plan to complete. The initial risk assessment should provide an indicator as to what the priorities should be. Given that risks are dynamic, risk assessments will require regular updating and priorities sense-checked against these.

Business Continuity Management – a Risk-Based Approach

Where does Business Continuity Management (BCM) fit into this type of risk management framework? The answer is *"everywhere."* BCM must overlay the risk management framework and dovetail into every aspect an organisation might need to risk-manage, internally and externally, as an enterprise-wide control mechanism. Only once an organisation has analysed its business and understood its risks, can it design and implement an effective approach to BCM then construct and implement effective and efficient business continuity plans.

As risk management can lead to a better understanding of an organisation and its business, so BCM can provide the strategic and operational framework to review the way an organisation provides its products and services - while increasing their resilience to disruption, interruption or loss.

In recent years, there have been important changes in the way businesses deliver and market their own products; this includes changes in their relationships with their stakeholders, and even in the risks themselves.

Clear to all business watchers are dramatic developments in the way businesses have reorganised themselves as they take up new opportunities to research, produce, market and deliver. These opportunities include new technological tools, wholesale data mining, new faster and direct-to-customer communications, increasing multi-nationalism, the sheer scale and strengths of merged companies, outsourcing and supplier dependencies, value chain management, and new relationships with the workforce.

Many a modern organisation can fairly be described as made up of no more than a brand, miners of owned or rented intellectual assets, and outsourcing contracts. These ingredients have become crucial, urgent dependencies and single points of risk for the very survival of that organisation. In other words, a sudden closure and/or removal from their marketplace is increasingly, not less, likely

The damage to an organisation may of course not be from within the organisation. There may be destruction of the environment on which an organisation or its customers depend. An urgently needed "just in time" supplier or distributor may be the one directly affected by a disaster, but their failure to deliver as contracted may have an equally destructive impact on the production line of the organisation being discussed. Think back to the Kobe earthquake and micro chips, US floods and key supplies for Nike or, perhaps, looking to the future, a major political or terrorist event in the country where your organisation has just outsourced a key service. Similarly, an organisation may be called into response by falling currency values of a country not even within their indigenous shores, failure of global or local oil supplies, a postal strike or an incident as local as that at a neighbour's property which results in denial of access to your business.

If an organisation is to effectively address the above issues then BCM must form part of the organisation's risk management, corporate governance and quality management systems. In the modern business, BCM is an enterprise-wide professional discipline embracing all strategic and operational aspects of an organisation: contributing to business reliance and long term business performance both during times of normality as well as times of extreme and unplanned response.

The outcomes of BCM today need to contribute a substantial benefit to the continuity of an organisation before a major disruption as well as following the disruption. *"As businesses seek to protect their employees, customers and facilities from threats there is no one-size-fits-all approach to preparedness and response, but a number of both general and specific guidelines are important to consider when company plans or validating plans already in place"* **(13)**.

The Business Continuity Institute and The British Publicly Available Standard on Business Continuity Management (PAS 56) **(14)** define business continuity management as *"A holistic management process that identifies potential impacts that threaten an organisation and provides a framework for building resilience and the capability for an effective response that safeguards the interests of its key stakeholders, reputation, brand and value-creating activities."*

That is quite a statement - so what does it mean?

- BCM is not just about response; it is also about building resilience to strengthen an organisation.

- BCM is not just about fighting fires; it is about understanding what might be at risk and developing strategies if things do go wrong.

- BCM is not just about having plans to recover a business that are over-elaborate; it is about having plans that suit the nature of your business.

- BCM is not an appendage to the business, and for it to be effective, it must be an embedded management process - as part of risk management, and in turn, as part of good businessmanagement.

At the risk and evaluation stage of business continuity management an organisation should *"Determine the events and environmental surroundings that can adversely affect an organisation, the damage that such events can cause, and the controls needed to prevent or minimise the effects of potential loss."* **(15)**.

> As with "enterprise risk management" BCM should consider all types of risk to an organisation, and action taken to improve resilience and plans built which are able to respond to any type of disruption, whether or not the material assets of an organisation are affected.

From roots grown in the 1980s, until the early 1990s, BCM was certainly around, but largely to be found in the domain of the IT department with a focus on recovery following disruption to technology-driven systems. The type of desktop we enjoy today was largely unknown and businesses relied on a remote box somewhere feeding "dumb" terminal technology. Business continuity was consequently largely about the backup and recovery of data stored in anonymous and usually off-site boxes which more frequently than not resembled vending machine technology in size and noise emission!

While you did not have to be affected by a terrorist act to suffer a disruption to an IT service (a workman can just as easily cut off power to your building and systems as a terrorist), it was to a large degree the terrorist activities of the 1990s which brought into focus a recognition by organisations of the wider business need for the ability to respond and recover following disruption beyond the IT environment.

CASE STUDY
The Manchester Bombing by the Provisional IRA, Manchester, UK: 1996

The incident affected a significant area of Manchester city centre and while there was no loss of life, over 200 people were injured. It is estimated that around 40% of the businesses that closed after the bombing never traded again.

Longridge House was the HQ to British Engine and Royal Insurance in the North West (now part of Royal & SunAlliance). 34 employees were injured and significant post-trauma issues emerged. The building was eventually demolished. 600 staff and businesses relocated to pre-planned temporary office accommodation. Customer service resumed on Day 1 and business re-established in the city centre eight weeks later. Key lessons learned include:

- *People issues were the most significant:* there is no blueprint for the recovery of traumatised people; use professionals you can trust

- *Security required extraordinary measures:* looting occurred on the site less than two hours after the bombing; use experts who can advise you and provide vetted staff

- *Re-engineer, don't reinstate:* replacement IT solutions used latest technology, and were quicker and cheaper

- *if the choice was between a good plan and an average team, and a good team with an average plan, go for the good team:* disasters never follow a pattern and an effective, local, empowered team should be able to enact decisions that did not necessarily follow what the plan said

- *Media issues were unfamiliar:* be prepared and use experts who can help

- *Communicate, communicate, communicate* with *all stakeholders*

Royal & SunAlliance turnover rose after the bombing as a well-recovered business retained customer confidence.

Around this time, the rising tide of corporate governance previously discussed in this chapter hit business shores, and as a consequence, alongside risk management, business continuity started to become a Boardroom topic. The Board had a duty to not only know that risks were understood and managed but that if the organisation faced disruption that its balance sheet would be protected.

Today, most regulated organisations (and those entities which regulated organisations deal with through supplier or outsourcing arrangements) are required by their regulators to have in place a risk-based BCM framework, including an appropriate business continuity plan. In the UK, this expectation is outlined in the FSA Handbook **(16)** and states that *"a firm should have in place appropriate arrangements, having regard to the nature, scale and complexity of its business, to ensure that it can continue to function and meet its regulatory obligations in the event of an unforeseen disruption."* The events of 9/11 heightened regulatory interest in BCM especially in the US, UK, Japan and Australia where further papers and guidelines were issued in the wake of the disaster.

"Private-sector preparedness is not a luxury - it is a cost of doing business in the post 9/11 world. It is ignored at a tremendous potential cost in lives, money and national security" **(17)**.

In the UK as the regulator makes "risk management due diligence" checks on those organisations that fall within their agenda, BCM features high on their agenda. Subsequent surveys of financial services organisations have revealed that they still have a way to go even having had the 9/11 wake-up call, before their regulator would consider plans fully up to date and fit for purpose.

The Bank of Japan **(18)** highlighted BCM as essential for three reasons:
- Maintaining the economic activity or residents in disaster areas;
- Preventing widespread payment and settlement disorder; and,
- Reducing managerial risks.

Their view was that prolonged suspension of operations in a disaster situation "makes it difficult for financial institutions to take profit opportunities, lowers their reputation among customers, and ultimately has a detrimental impact on their management." Of five key points identified by the Bank, exerting strong leadership is seen as key and requiring substantial investment of managerial resources and involvement, and also firm-wide awareness. Reflecting the external environment, the Bank goes on to state that in their view many risks and damage could be prevented or mitigated to some extent through prior measures including:
- Establishing facilities at or moving facilities to relatively low natural disaster locations (outside known earthquake hot spots)
- Anti-seismic retrofitting
- Installation of backup generators
- Enhancement of access control to restricted areas and strengthening of firewalls to prevent hacker attacks.

Importantly, the FSA, while highlighting the negative effects of disruption, recognise the upside of BCM in that any organisation which implements business continuity plans to levels of "good practice" can, in their opinion, issue a signal of confidence to customers and stakeholders that the firm is well managed and can deal with a crisis. This requirement is echoed increasingly by other regulatory bodies. For example, the Australian Prudential Regulation Authority (APRA) **(19)** set out a prudential standard for BCM in July 2004. APRA considers BCM an important component of a risk management framework and specifies that regulated organisations need to consider scenarios which include:

    I. Utility failure, e.g., electricity, water and telecommunications

   II. IT systems failure

 III. Compromised physical or IT security

 IV. Fire threat or damage

   V. Bomb threat or damage

 VI. Loss of key staff

VII. Damage or loss of critical paper and electronic records.

As with the FSA, APRA promotes an approach which should be tailored to suit the nature and scale of its operations and designed to increase "… resilience to business disruption arising from internal and external events and reduce the impact on the organisation's business operations, reputation or profitability." It also places responsibility for management responsibility and leadership firmly on the Board table.

CASE STUDY: Power failure in New Zealand (1999)

In February of 1999, the business district of Auckland faced an unprecedented disruption to power supplies. Although the Auckland concert hall continued to play to packed houses with an orchestra unconventionally attired without their formal dress, business elsewhere could not be resumed due to failures in building infrastructure systems such as air conditioning and water supplies.

Key lessons include:

- *Plan ahead:* emerging events could have been tracked, giving businesses time to prepare for disruption and their response

- *Consider different scenarios:* the scale and length of power restoration was much longer than anticipated resulting in some businesses being slow in response believing that power would be restored quickly

- *Consider the external environment:* disruption occurred during the height of summer which exacerbated the impact of power loss given that air conditioning units couldn't function

- *Think about exclusion zones:* many business in Auckland found that their recovery backup locations were inside the area affected

- *Take the office home:* recovery was effective in domestic locations using remote technology that was still functional; the lounge became the office

- *Think laterally:* one business used Auckland harbour ferries for recovery locations; commuters did not need the ferries and they had generators

---

The consequences of not building resilience and planning might include:

- Loss of work to competitors
- Failure within your supply chain
- Loss of reputation
- Human resource issues
- Health & Safety liabilities
- Higher insurance premiums

… and if you are unlucky enough to suffer more than one of the above from the same incident, then this may present a worst-case scenario and force you out of business. More than forty per cent of businesses affected by the Manchester bomb in 1996 went out of business, never to return. Since 1996 organisations have learned that BCM encompasses more than producing a business continuity plan. It is a proactive process that concentrates on critical resources required to continue key business processes, whatever the event.

The majority of disasters happen within an organisation or its immediate environment. It is fair to say that the events of 9/11 have forced organisations to widen their scope to include failure of national utilities, financial markets and structures. So it is perhaps shocking to learn that a survey in 2004 revealed that almost forty percent of Western companies still do not have adequate plans to protect them from terrorist attacks. (20) Could this be because of a failure to achieve top level buy-in and consequent management commitment and budget? This must be under suspicion.

Moving away from the tangible asset perspective, the need to think enterprise-wide both tangible and intangible is further supported by a raft of research, most notably that produced by Rory Knight and Deborah Pretty of Oxford Metrica (21) in their authoritative research on the impact of catastrophes on shareholder value. They argue that there is a significant variation in the long-term recovery capability of organisations in the aftermath of a catastrophe, the success of which would seem to be more down to the quality of management and their ability to manage a recovery than support based solely on the existence of catastrophe insurance.

They suggest that it is the *"… indirect factors which dominate the impact of catastrophes on shareholder value. The net financial loss has a relatively minor impact on the full change of shareholder value associated with catastrophes."*

Linking this research to the fact that around eighty percent of intangible risks are not transferable through traditional insurance mechanisms, coupled with the fact that a significant number of organisations have yet to design and embed effective business continuity management in place, the prospect for the recovery and survival of these organisations in the event of disruption does not look promising.

CASE STUDY:
Ladbroke Grove Rail Disaster, London, UK : 1999

The incident involved the collision of two trains on a busy commuter route near London, resulting in the loss of life and significant injuries. Although Thames' insurers paid for the company's legal costs as well as the civil claims made by those injured in the collision and the families of those who died, the cost to Thames Trains was significant in terms of:

- Management time dealing with the prosecution, the civil claims and the inquiry

- Disruption and distraction from the task of continuing to provide a rail service

- Additional stress on staff

- Likely increase in insurance premiums

- Bad publicity

- Loss of customer confidence and the possible loss of customers in the aftermath of the incident

In drawing this Chapter to a close we should not overlook the smaller organisation. In the UK 97 percent of businesses employ twelve people or less and across the globe most countries rely on this type of business for over half of their GDP. All authorities in this field support the view that the small business sector is critical to the health and wealth of a nation. If BCM should be concerned with external factors as well as the internal, BCM for the small business is a key consideration. So what keeps the leader of this type of organisation awake at night? From research commissioned by AXA (22) during 2004, smaller business put as their chief concerns:

    I. The threat of litigation
    II. The cost of compliance with regulation (and the cost of non-compliance)
    III. The threat of IT failure

And what of the potential impact of small business failure on the larger organisation? Many a disaster has been occasioned through the failure of specialist sole suppliers, be they manufacturers of microchips in Kobe, Japan or integral parts of trainers in the US midwest. AXA quoted their willingness to share their experience with clients to help them take a well-informed view of risk, and as a specific value-added service they promote is a guide to business continuity planning, AXA accepted that risk mitigation goes beyond spend on insurance.

"Expecting the Unexpected" (23) produced by the National Counter Terrorism Security Office (NaCTSO), London First, and The Business Continuity Institute (BCI) also focuses on the importance of the smaller business and provides a simple and easy to follow guide for the smaller business.

Risk Management, Business Continuity Management: Whose Responsibility?

Too often in organisations BCM remains in the domain of the IT or Facilities functions rather than embedded as part of a risk management framework. Often when risk and BCM are raised at the Board, it is assumed that insurance will solve any problem.

When we talk of continuing in business following a disruption, we should consider not only the impact of that disruption on a particular business, organisation or set of individuals, but also to the very fabric of the economy and society in which we do business. Grand words, but reflect on them: the suspension of financial institution operations, for example, could cause critical problems during and after a disaster. Residents in a disaster area might not be able to access funds and funds might not be transferable, denying access to salaries and pensions. Consequently, in addition to organisations suffering their own internal strife following disruption, society itself could bear the brunt of the suffering through loss of services just when it needed their support the most.

Summary

As Dwight D. Eisenhower said, "All plans fail at first contact with the enemy." There has been a growing realisation that businesses need to manage all risks, both tangible and intangible, and as a key control mechanism business continuity plans must rise to the challenge to respond. The silos of risk management are being drawn closer together into an integrated enterprise risk management framework. Whether the drivers for change are internal to an organisation or external through governance, regulatory or legislative pressures, risk management and business continuity management have come of age as united disciplines.

Business continuity management is about prevention, about understanding what might be at risk, about making judgements about criticality, and then developing strategies and solutions to reduce the severity of the risk and be able to respond to the risk with robust plans if it does occur.

The policies, procedures and structures in most organisations are designed for normal operations and in general are unsuitable for dealing with sudden and unexpected events. Although there is no such thing as the right time for a crisis, any time is a good time for developing even a simple approach to Business Continuity Management. But recalling President Eisenhower's observation, any approach to Business Continuity Management will only have a chance of succeeding if it has senior management buy-in and has been developed following a systematic management process in tune with an organisation's culture, complexity, internal and external needs, and is maintained and exercised.

Now let's continue the journey.

Bibliography

1. Peter Bernstein - Against the Gods - John Wiley and Sons - 1998

2. Sarbanes Oxley - info@sarbanes-oxley.com

3. Strategies for Risk and Balance Sheet Management - Chris Mundy - Marsh UK: 2004

4. The Aon European Risk Management & Insurance Survey: 2004 - 2005

5. Banana Skins: The CSFI's annual survey of the risks facing banks: 2004

6. COSO: Enterprise Risk Management Framework: 2004

7. John Liner Review - Winter 2004

8. Risk management standard: www.the irm.org, www.airmic.com, www.alarm-uk.com

9. Standards Australia - AS/NZ 4360: 2004

10. Speech to the World Affairs Council - Lord Levene - Chairman of Lloyd's: April 2004

11. Speech to the Houston Forum - Lord Levene - Chairman of Lloyd's: September 2004

12. Operational Risk Event Classification - Gene Laverez: Garp Risk Review: 20001/02

13. Committed to Protecting America: A Private Sector Preparedness Guide - 2005

14. PAS 56:2003 - Guide to BCM: BSI: March 2003

15. Generally Accepted Practices - Draft for Review - Disaster Recovery Journal (DRJ) and Disaster Recovery Institute (DRI) - July 2005

16. The Financial Services Authority: fsa.gov.uk

17. 9/11 Commission Final Report - July 2004

18. Business Continuity Planning at Financial Institutions - Bank of Japan: July 2003

19. APRA Prudential Regulations

20. CSO survey: Companies Lack Plans in Event of Attack - Paul Roberts IDG news service: June 2004

21. The Impact of Catastrophes on Shareholder Value - Knight & Pretty: 2001

22. AXA: www.axa4business.com: Mark Cliff - AXA: 2004

23. Expecting the Unexpected: brochure and CD: www.london-first.co.uk: 2003

2

Stakeholders

Objectives

The objectives of this chapter are to:

- Begin the process of understanding the operational risks to the organisation and, above all, the potentially destructive impact of some risks.

- Recognise the wide range of the stakeholders in the organisation; and understand their importance, their roles and their needs.

- Ensure sensitivity to these stakeholders' roles when undertaking risk assessments, business impact assessments, and any subsequent risk management activity.

- Understand both the role of the stakeholder who plays a part before a risk incident; and the potential additional impact of new stakeholders who emerge as a risk incident is unfolding.

- Set the wider scene for the risk assessments, business impact analyses and recovery planning subjects that are covered in later chapters.

The Organisation

The corporate model for a hundred years or more has traditionally "manufactured" the product or service from within the organisation's own production lines. Using its own employee labour force it has taken the raw materials though all of the processes necessary to deliver the end product or service, finally, to its waiting customer or wholesaler. These organisations had operational risks around the physical buildings, contents and machinery and around the workforce itself. They could incur legal liabilities to their workforce, product liabilities, or public liabilities in the event of a failure that caused loss or damage to another.

They carried exposures to fire, engineering failures, weather and the perils that are traditionally protected by off-the-shelf material damage, engineering and liability insurance policies. Infrequently they felt the need also to buy protection from the insurance market against "increased cost of working" while they set about rebuilding their operations. They were pretty confident, on the whole, that their competitors could only expand their own production lines relatively slowly; and thus enough of their customer base would still be around once their own rebuilding had taken place to make the reconstruction commercially viable. In other words, with some assistance from the insurance market in replacing lost capital and revenues, they could see themselves recovering the business in the longer term.

We have made reference in Chapter One to the dramatic changes in the way that businesses have reorganised themselves as they take up technological and other opportunities in market research, product development, and in the marketing and delivery of their products. The organisations taking us into the 21st century bear little resemblance to this erstwhile business model.

In the past decade or so, new processing and communications technologies have created different and cost-effective opportunities to communicate and to distribute. These technologies have brought the ability to mine huge databases wholesale and take that information directly into marketing or delivery processes. The technologies have enabled new, faster and direct-to-customer communications, often eliminating the intermediaries who were previously needed between manufacturer and customer. These technologies cross national boundaries with ease, and with the removal of more and more trade barriers have made multi-nationalism the norm rather than the exception.

Modern organisations may have huge turnovers and can be spread globally but are often made up of no more than:

A brand

Access to intellectual assets

Legal and regulatory approvals

Contracts with third party suppliers of a range of services and raw materials.

Contracts with third parties comprising a distribution chain

These opportunities and the mergers that came in their wake have created huge companies with a breadth and a scale of operations that have the strengths to ride through traditional risks with ease. National and international outsourcing, the management of a value chain management stretching from first supplier to final customer, and new relationships with the workforce, have all created opportunities to search out cheaper costs and be more precise in matching individual product to individual customers. Above all, these new business models enable flexibility to respond quickly to change; whether that change is based on the environment, politics, market place, labour skills or costs.

Relationships with stakeholders can be two-way. An organisation may outsource the manufacture and supply of an ingredient; but conversely one product may be manufactured and sold by many different organisations that apply their own brand name and distribute the product through their own sales channels. This is known as "white labelling" and could range from corn flakes to computers; or even, in the case of call centres – customer services. One call centre may act for many different customer organisations. The operator simply responds under different names and using different software; the software kicks in automatically based on the number the caller used to reach them. Thus, outsourcing has reached "front office" functions, not just the "back office", where it all began.

The multinational has become more the norm rather than the exception, enabling these firms to maximise the economies and values of different political, cultural, and regulatory environments. This has enabled them also to exploit the differing costs and balances of power, and between workforces and their employers that are found in different countries. Many a modern multinational has economic strength larger than some countries and has the power to hold some governments to ransom by simply moving to another base overseas into a "more business-friendly" environment.

There is some justification, therefore, in describing many of these multi-nationals as made up of no more than a brand name (implied in this is the ongoing support of a whole range of stakeholders; hence our agenda for this chapter), the right to access intellectual assets, and legality. You could describe as an intellectual asset or separately the contracts that place them in a value chain that stretches before them through suppliers, and beyond them though distribution channels. These contracts create the product ingredients and distribute the result quite precisely and exactly when and where needed. Further, within the intellectual assets are the entrepreneurs and the controls which bring it all together.

Such companies are sometimes know as "hollow" or "virtual" companies, reflecting that the core of the organisation has neither a physical essence nor a human workforce, but a series of agreements with other organisations feeding the parts of the whole.

This list of ingredients may be small in number, but they are very powerful organisational tools. The interest to the risk manager, of course, is that they have also become crucial and urgent dependencies. They have in effect become single points of risk that, should they fail for any reason, threaten the very survival of that organisation. In other words, an unexpected risk incident is more likely, not less likely to bring the whole organisation to a sudden closure or total removal from its chosen marketplace. The sheer scale of the organisation is no longer necessarily a defence against potentially destructive risk.

Indeed, these organisations may be huge, financially strong, superficially multinational and otherwise diverse. They are, however, increasingly dependent on these single points of risk, the consequences of which can cause total failure of the whole organisation. This recognition brings together risk management and business continuity management concerns and demands that the principles and practices increasingly diverge. This book sets out to explore this need in some detail and makes the point that business continuity planning without effective risk management of critical dependencies can raise unrealistic expectations about the resilience of the organisation to continue to meet stakeholder needs.

Furthermore, the speed by which they can bring the organisation to a halt is very much the concern of the risk manager. A manufacturer in the UK of motor vehicles sources its engines from Brazil and keeps just six hours stock on its premises. Metro International, a newspaper group, publishes 34 editions of its newspapers in 16 countries but it employs few reporters, buying not only the news items from news and picture agencies, but outsourcing printing and even most of the distribution.

> *A failure in the chain of supply or distribution, or in the technology and intellectual assets that make it all possible, can bring an immediate and potentially irreversible failure. This is particularly true if the failure brings irredeemable damage to the brand value.*

These same business models are used by competitors both at home and overseas and enable those competitors to expand production rapidly. This sheer speed of expansion can enable these existing or potential competitors to respond quickly to take away the customers of any organisation that has been weakened by a risk incident. If that business is in a "taste" product such as food, cigarettes, newspapers, supermarkets, restaurants, etc.,, the customers may acquire the taste of the competitor's products and never return.

Public service companies and monopolies also make use of these efficiency opportunities. Consequentially they are not spared the potentially quick and catastrophic damage by a failure to deliver. If a Government department fails in any way to deliver, for example, in the event of damage to a call centre, then their public will make contact using other phone lines, letter or by visit to departments that are simply not resourced for anything like the new demand on them. This can easily turn a crisis into a disaster.

Another change has been in the regulatory environment imposed on many private and public sector organisations. Adherence is not just a matter of legality; adherence is necessary to retain credibility with stock markets, regulators and customers. Company boards have long established financial risk measuring mechanisms, but Turnbull et al, in recent years, has driven boards to consider non-financial risk. These risks are much more amorphous, and as such these legislation and guides are taking them into arenas where they, quite rightly, feel much less confident. Increasingly these regulations demand, not only that organisations measure and manage their risks, but they report what they are doing within the published accounts and other returns another issue leading through to brand and confidence. The Operating and Financial Review (UK) and other trends show a trend further down the road of such requirements

Experience shows that the greatest potential for total failure is not in the area of financial risks but, on the contrary, in the area of non-financial risks.

**Case Study
Nonfinancial Cause of Loss**

At the beginning of July, 1996 a strong low pressure system (Xolska) developed over the Mediterranean, where it absorbed an enormous volume of water. It then moved over the former Yugoslavia, Austria, and Slovakia to the Czech Republic and Poland. Extraordinary amounts of rain were recorded (up to 570mm) in five days. Two weeks later there was anther flood wave after renewed heavy rain caused by the low pressure system Zoe, which followed the same track as Xolxsa. The catastrophe was thus prolonged considerably.

Some parts of Austria registered their highest rainfall in fifty years and there were flash floods that swamped roads and railway lines. Two people lost their lives. Slovakia suffered considerable losses to agricultural businesses.

East Bohemia and Moravia in the Czech Republic were flooded. Entire villages were washed away. 500 villages and towns were affected, 10,000 houses sank into the torrents and 1,600 were completely destroyed. Numerous factories, including major industrial plants suffered major flood damage which led to substantial business interruption. The infrastructures of telecommunications, roads, and railway networks were severely affected. The economic loss came to US$1.8bn in the Czech republic alone; of which only US$310m was insured.

Poland was mainly hit in the south where large towns like Opole (50% under water) and Odra (40% under water) sank in the deluge. 6,000 square kilometres were under water in fourteen provinces. 2,500 villages and 100,000 houses were under water. Furthermore 2,000km of railway lines, 3,000km of roads, and 900 bridges were damaged. Gas, electricity and water supplies were interrupted for weeks. Business and trade were hit hard and many industrial losses emerged from lengthy interruptions and problems with deliveries. The economic loss in Poland was US$2.5bn, of which only US$450m was insured. There was further damage and economic loss in Brandenburg, Germany, of which about 10% was insured.

"Return periods," i.e., an estimate of the history and thus likely frequency of such storms were regarded in Poland to be in excess of one thousand years. **(1)**

It can be valuable to begin our exploration of potentially destructive risk by taking a look at the various stakeholders in the organisation. We should begin by identifying who they are and measure their importance, their values and their ability to increase existing damage to an organisation exponentially.

Stakeholders

Our look at the role and needs of stakeholders is applicable to all types of organisations; public service, monopolies, competitive businesses, old business methods and new. Their importance may vary but they are the lifeblood of all manufacturing and service delivery businesses and organisations.

We could recognise and define stakeholders simply as those organisations and individuals that have an ongoing "stake" or interest in the organisation's current affairs. It is valuable however to have a wide definition and one that includes those who can become stakeholders, post loss or damage, by a reaction that could make a difficult situation even worse. The interest of either type of stakeholders is not always financial and we summarise them - and the nature of their importance – in the following paragraphs.

For the purposes of this chapter therefore we will identify and list the two types of stakeholder. First, there are the ones we describe as "ongoing" stakeholders who are a recognisable part of the organisation in good times; and secondly there are those who can emerge after a disaster to make the damage much worse and make recovery much more difficult or even impossible. We will return later in this chapter to each and explore the nature of the relationship and the potential for failure in that relationship.

Ongoing Stakeholders

Those stakeholders can be bracketed under the following headings.

Stakeholder	The Relationship
Employees	Employees and visitors have both a human and statutory right to be kept as safe as is reasonable possible from injury or death while in an area that is managed by the employer.
	Most employees have a crucial dependency on their work that enables them to provide housing, food and leisure for themselves and their families. They invest their personal reputation and self esteem in their relationship with a particular employer and its products.
	They bring skills based on intellect and experience and, while employer/employee relationships remain mutually positive, they bring those skills alongside the objectives of the employing organisation.
Customers	A customer will remain loyal only while there is confidence in the products or services sold and also in the future availability of services or supplies. In other words the "brand value" remains intact.
Distribution	For the purpose of this subject, distributors can simply be considered as wholesalers chain of customers. They bring and take away large numbers of customers in one decision. The comments above about the needs and reactions of end customers apply even more, so that the customer is just another link in the supply chain leading to an end product that is branded and sold by another named organisation.
Suppliers	The 2003 petrol strike in the UK brought home powerfully the point to which a whole range of very different types of organisation now depend on "just in time" deliveries to maintain their own services. The impact of this relatively short dispute was astonishingly quick, and was felt also across all kinds of organisations from supermarkets, manufacturers, emergency services and many others. The strike gained the status of a national emergency within days.
Financiers	Financiers come in many forms, whether they are institutional shareholders of quoted PLCs, individual shareholders of quoted PLCs, private direct investors, bankers, partners, government and quasi government departments, charities and

others. Whichever, their ongoing confidence and support are vital elements that can be too easily lost.

Business partners	Organisations and individuals often share objectives and responsibilities and indeed reputations. This sharing is mostly defined by contracts that establish the objectives and responsibilities.

If meeting these stakeholders' needs is not difficult enough, in the real world of damage, the challenges of a company, reeling from serious damage, are just beginning.

We have seen where existing stakeholders will respond to protect their own interests when faced by an organisation weakened by operational weakness. Entirely new stakeholders can emerge to play a direct role in the chances of recovery. They are, as discussed earlier, identified by their ability and propensity to react to a damaging incident. In this reaction they can shift the ground even further from underneath managers who are working, in already difficult circumstances, to keep the organisation alive.

Case Study
Stakeholder Reaction

Panic buyers drain stock. It is not just shoppers that clear the shelves when a whisper of shortages hits the streets. In fact the symptoms of this basic human impulse have been ably demonstrated by the big spenders in response to the appalling news flowing from New York over the past days (September, 2001).

"It was unbelievable, said the ITM Group. I called my regular contact at our supplier – the UK's largest PC distributor – and I was shocked to be told that it was no longer a question of what I wanted, but that I should take what was available. **(2)**

Emerging Stakeholders

These include:

Competitors	Whether current competitors or potential competitors, they will see the distress of another as an opportunity. They will be looking for opportunities to step into the damaged organisation's marketplace or other stakeholder support and take them over themselves.
The Media	William Randolph Hearst once said famously: "News is something someone does not want to see in print. All the rest is advertising." The importance of the role of the media is such that there is separate mention in this chapter and elsewhere in this book.
Regulators	It is no exaggeration to describe the regulators' role as one that simply enables the organisation to stay in business. They could fairly be described as "ongoing" stakeholders but we include them here because their potential reaction to operational damage or loss is an important concern to the risk and continuity manager. A wide range of regulators establishes the standards that an organisation needs to follow if that regulatory approval is to continue. Those standards may be about security of information, other business controls or a host of other detailed arenas.
The Environment	Other stakeholders will emerge. They can include tenants, landlords, neighbours or indeed the wider environment for which the organisation was carrying a responsibility as a "citizen" of the area or country.

Other
Stakeholders

Many organisations have, of course, their own particular stakeholders in addition to the generalised ones above. There are advocacy groups, unions, activists, environmentalists, local government agencies and indeed the wider relationships with employees that include their families and colleagues.

The Organisation Itself as a Stakeholder

The organisation considering stakeholders' dependencies need also to remember that it is almost certainly a stakeholder itself and may depend on the continuity of another organisation or market for its own survival. This reversal of stakeholder research may bring out new dependencies that the organisation itself may wish to protect in some way. Suppliers of car parts to Rover in the UK became aware of the company's difficulty before they hit the media's headlines and began to protect themselves by diversifying their own customer base and shortening credit terms. An organisation with fewer options was a luncheonette in Groton, Connecticut that suffered significantly facing the prospect of closure of a US Navy Submarine base.

The risk analysis, or indeed the business impact analysis, needs to seek out stakeholder dependencies that otherwise may be missed in less informal, more anecdotal, discussions.

The Critical Support Legs of a Modern Organisation

An unplanned, damaging incident can affect, to a varying degree, the ability of the company to deliver on its promises to any one of these stakeholders. The severity of any one type of failure will of course vary, incident by incident, organisation by organisation, and stakeholder by stakeholder. The impact can range from a level that is acceptable right through to damage that is irreparable in time for the organisation to survive at all. While we have a focus on the special criticalities and urgencies of a modern or "hollow" company, these support legs are by no means unimportant to any organisation that has a range of stakeholders to satisfy if it is to remain viable.

We need to look at these stakeholders again in more detail and now at their role as a critical and urgent dependency. In brief, these dependencies need to be considered against the responsibilities to:

- Keep people safe;

- Protect vital "assets" owned by the organisation and those assets belonging to others for which it carries responsibilities;

- Retain confidence in the business and thus the value of the 'brand name';

- Avoid litigation costs; and

- Ensure the continual ability to manage the organisation effectively and deliver on promises and contracts.

Before we do, however, there is value in bringing back into the discussion the few but crucial ingredients of a modern company. These were stated as:

- A brand name;
- Intellectual assets;
- Legality;
- Contracts that place them in a supply (or value) chain that stretches before them through suppliers and beyond them though distribution channels; and,
- Ownership and controls that brings these together.

Case Study

In August 2003 the backup power diesel generator that supported Air Canada's Control Centre failed. There had been a major power blackout and the Control Centre manages its flight planning and keeps track of all planes, fuel levels, etc. Air Canada had to cancel 500 of its planned 700 flights around the world and about 50,000 customers – or stakeholders – became increasingly frustrated as departure times were progressively delayed and they could not reach their holiday or business destinations on time.

A relatively small engineering failure had an impact across very large numbers of stakeholders around the world and caused not only immediate damage to the airline but longer term damage to its reputation and brand value. This is especially important as the airline industry is fiercely competitive and most times the prospective customers of the future have many choices in the airlines they can use.

The Brand

One crucial common denominator that is becoming clear throughout all stakeholder relationships is the importance of confidence in the organisation, i.e., that the brand name continues to have the "value" it has been promising. The brand or credibility throughout the whole range of differing stakeholder needs is a single, organisation-wide value on which the entire organisation depends for its survival; or at the very least for the current market position that it enjoys. Take this away and there may be no organisation left; as has been found too often the hard way.

To keep this value, the organisation not only has to deliver on its promises of quality and time, but stakeholders need to be confident that it will continue to deliver. An organisation facing a damaging incident not only has to deal with the consequences of the incident itself - it also needs to ensure that the confidence and trust of all its stakeholders remains firm. Stakeholders, as has been seen, are looking for entirely different things at different times and sometimes even have conflicting demands.

Management of the brand is often a quite separate and more difficult challenge in times of stress and damage. A famous incident saw a finance director, in the face of an ongoing major ferry disaster that was costing many lives, assuring the media that the stock market value would not be affected. He clearly thought he was addressing only one type of the organisations' stakeholders at the time.

Brand value can be lost, not least in an operational failure that causes a fall in quality or a unreasonable failure to deliver on time. Pan Am (Lockerbie), Perrier (pollutants), French wine (pollutants), Barings (internal lack of controls) and others, have seen the real impact of this exposure. Exposures of practices within Enron and Andersen Consulting have also had devastating effect on their stakeholder confidence to the point of total destruction of the organisation.

If the brand value can be maintained, the stakeholders are more likely to behave in a way that helps management have the best chance of rebuilding the damage, and thus return to "business as normal" as soon as possible.

Communication, therefore, is crucial; but different approaches and different messages are needed for each type of stakeholder. This needs targeted, clear and honest contacts with the specific stakeholders and their advisors.

It is more difficult to deal with the public at large who are forming their opinions on the organisation – and taking a view on the future of the organisation – based on what they hear and see in the media. The media has many forms:

- Local and national newspapers;
- Television and radio;
- Popular and professional magazines; and
- The Internet

At the time of writing there are some 350 radio stations, five terrestrial TV channels and countless satellite channels broadcasting within the UK alone, and countless other media organisations in America and other countries. Many of these, such as CNN and the BBC World Service are international in nature and footprint. A large number of these are 24-hour news channels. They are all in competition with each other, and often need their news programming to fit within their own commercial agendas and planned audience profile targets. The sheer weight of attack and potential for damage can be overwhelming. While this is perhaps an extreme example, there were 15,500 reporters in Paris immediately after the death of Princess Diana. There were even 600 members of the press in the Shetland Islands some hours after the 'Braer' shipping disaster. The media needs from across every country in the world following the World Trade Centre terrorist attack needed substantial energies and resources to effectively manage and deliver; quite apart from the task of dealing with the aftermath of the incident itself. Other organisational crises such as the sinking of the Exxon Valdez, the Lockerbie plane crash, the release of poisonous chemicals into the atmosphere at Union Carbide's Bhopal facility, floods and storms and countless other catastrophes have received a weight of interest from the press that can overpower managers already facing extraordinary operational challenges.

The media needs to be understood as wholesale distributors of the reputation of an organisation and its officials. If a publication is negative about an organisation much damage can be done. This is so whether the story reflects the truth, only part of the truth, or is even factually incorrect. The impact, therefore, is of significance to all other stakeholders.

Case Study

"We published a storey about Jas Mann of the Pop Group Babylon Zoo. The story wrongly stated that Jas Mann was depressed, had abandoned his career and joined a weird cult that practises exorcism and the ritual slaughter of animals.

In fact all Jas did was join a local community Group raising money for homeless children in India. He is not depressed and his career continues." **(3)**

Intellectual Assets

Modern organisations have dependencies on other intellectual assets other than brand values. It would be difficult to overemphasise their importance. They are much more than data on computer databases. These assets lie in licences, trademarks, computer software, paper files, and even in employee and management intellect and skills.

Resilience depends not only in ensuring that access and the usability of these assets are not lost or damaged and, once again, risk management and business continuity needs converge. They can be more difficult to protect than hardware by the very lack of physicality. Furthermore, if initially lost, the ability to regain access when needed can be a physical issue, an ownership issue or a legal issue. The Data Protection Act in the UK defines quite clearly who can use what personal information and for what purpose; this is supported by many of the contracts between, and right through the various layers of, the supply chain. An important question in difficulty can be who, within the value chain, actually "owns" and can use these assets. The middle of a potentially destructive crisis is not the time to begin to try to understand these things.

Legality

Another way of failing all stakeholders simultaneously is by the organisation becoming illegal. It can become illegal simply by working in such a way that contravenes the law of the country where they are operating or by failing to continue to meet the precise requirements of the regulatory authorities charged with policing the particular industry.

This exposure can be the fastest way to shut down an organisation. A regulator may decide that the controls and processes that were demanded to keep the organisation within the regulatory envelope have failed. The organisation is stone cold dead. Often this is in the area of information on which the organisation depends to deliver secure and effective control of the products sold. Even an assessed fine can lead straight through to a weakness in the brand value; leading in turn to loss of customers, share value, brand damage and costs of capital that is far greater then the fine itself.

The Value Chain

This lies in the contracts that place the organisation in a chain of deliveries that stretches before them through suppliers and beyond them though distribution channels to the end customers.

This delivery chain – sometimes called the "value chain" – is unrecognisable from the cosy, controlled, in-house delivery chain of yore. A failure, deep within a third party, just-in-time supply chain, can have catastrophic and immediate consequences on the final production line. A vehicle manufacturer is unlikely to try delivering new automobiles to customers with a note that the door handles will follow later! It is certainly cheaper to build and operate a call centre in Bangalore, Calcutta or Manila, but will the infrastructure, and the emergency response capabilities of those cities, be at a level needed to carry the organisation through difficulties?

Case Study
Supply Chain

There were deep sighs of relief all around at Land Rover's Solihull factory in the UK (and many neighbouring suppliers, too, no doubt) when it was announced that the company had reached an agreement with administrative receivers to end the deadlock over Discovery chassis supplies. Land Rover agreed to buy the chassis makers, UPF Thompson, for a reported £16 million.

Had the parties failed to reach agreement following UPF Thompson's financial collapse, Land Rover's chief executive, Bob Dover, had threatened to close Discovery production until a new chassis supplier could be found. The resulting job losses can only be estimated, but many thousands would have suffered.

Curiously, the receivers, accountants KPMG, suggested that Land Rover was in some way itself responsible for UPF Thompson's demise by driving down the price it would pay for the company's products. Land Rover had previously refused to pay out £62 million to take UPF Thompson out of receivership.(4)

It is not easy to understand the ability of a supplier to continue delivery; i.e., to quality check its own resilience and business continuity management. To do that with real confidence, one needs to embrace the critical suppliers to the suppliers, and the supplier's suppliers down the line. Risk and continuity practitioners have a healthy respect for whether their own in-house recovery planning will or will not work in circumstances that can only be presumed. Even exercising brings only a narrow level of comfort. Moving on into assuming confidence about a third-party organisation's planning increases the difficulty and exposure exponentially.

Supply chain management that embraces supply chain business continuity management has these difficulties to overcome.

> *This bottom line is that, however careful the continuity planning, it could still fail. If it fails, what precisely is the impact on the host organisation's own urgent processes and stakeholders?*

The recipient organisation needs to put itself, wherever practical, in the position that, whatever happens to the supplier, it can source what is needed elsewhere fast enough to stay in its own marketplace. Often of course that is not fully possible and business continuity decisions, just as with risk decision-making, have to be made about balancing risk and opportunity.

The Ownership and Controls That Brings These Together

The ingredients of an organisation – the ownership and the need for effective control mechanisms – must be brought together. Here is where the stakeholders and managers work in tandem to bring about the desired objective. From within these comes the initial vision to create the organisation and its values. Taking an idea through to a successful organisation is fraught with challenge and indeed operational risk can divert these energies from achieving that vision. Furthermore, when the organisation is in place, management oversight and business controls are key values that need to recognised as life forms of their own – and thus protected from harm or destruction. To fail here would fail all the stakeholders simultaneously.

Harold McMillan, when Prime Minister of the United Kingdom, was asked by a young journalist after a long dinner what can most easily steer a Government off course. "Events dear boy, events" was the reply.

The dependence on technology that often goes hand in hand with management, management information flow and business controls, brings its own risks. They are not just the obvious e-commerce exposures that we will discuss in a later chapter. A technological failure can often be the single point of failure that brings a multi-national to a halt across its entire organisation. That failure may not just be electronic; it may be security of information, communications, software or even the buildings and other hardware infrastructures within which the electronics reside.

Stakeholders in Their Role as Critical and Urgent Dependencies

We can now look back at the list of stakeholders and consider each in their importance as a critical ingredient of the organisation.

Stakeholder	The Relationship
Employees	Relationships with workforces have changed dramatically over the last 20 years or so. Putting much of the decisionmaking process into computer software has "dumbed down" many roles. It is a rare large company in the 21st century that has workforce relationships where the employee feels a permanent part of the scene. "Downsizing", "rightsizing", human resource management, or capability management, whatever name is used, reflects a devaluing of individual employees and reinforces the fact that enforced job change or redundancy is an ongoing part of the employee's life.
	Consequently neither the employee nor the organisation may expect, or be expected to give, loyalty above and beyond the call of contract. This can be a serious

exposure for the organisation facing an incident that has caused operational damage, and one that needs exceptional effort and flexible skills from the workforce to rebuild and keep the company alive.

It is simple reality that, in times of strain and/or lack of confidence, it is the best employees who are attracted away the quickest, leaving the poorer quality employees in place. The best employees are the ones with choices and may just walk away. They may see the weakness of the employer as simply a new environment within which negotiations can begin afresh. Furthermore, headhunters read newspapers, too!

Outsourced workforces will always follow the direction of their own employer. It may be that the outsourced service supplier may not choose – or be able – to re- deploy their resources to meet the extra demands of emergency situations in one customer. A direct employer may, in a disaster situation decide that priorities have changed and will move its workforce around accordingly. A contractor providing an outsourced workforce may not wish, or be able, to pull extra staff away from contracts with other principals because one of their customers has an immediate increase in needs.

Customers
If a customer loses confidence in the organisation, perhaps by hearing of an operational failure in the organisation, the customer (whether an end consumer or another business in the chain) has, almost always, the choice of moving away to a competitor's product. Often the debate – once confidence is lost – is around just how quickly, legally and operationally, that change can be made. With modern distribution channels such as e-commerce, customers can move away much quicker than before. Indeed, entire distribution channels can move away in minutes by the touch of a keyboard.

Even a public service organisation or monopoly needs to retain customer confidence. In the event of a failure in trust, or a risk incident that removes the ability to gain access by normal channels, customers may feel the need to search for reassurances. That search may be wholesale, exceeding normal workflow expectations and moving necessarily into parts of the organisation that are not resourced to cope with such a large flow of enquiry.

This can cause an impossible strain on resources bringing an already struggling organisation to the point of total collapse. An obvious example of damaging customer reaction is a run by customers closing accounts in a bank that has had questions raised about its financial strength.

There may be special requirements in some contracts to deliver. Contracts to deliver to the Ministry of Defence, for example, will have special demands to ensure security around the product information. An incident that destroys such special needs can bring the whole contract to a close. Some manufacturers, for example, in the defence, shipbuilding or airline industries, have single contracts that are so large that a failure of one contract can destroy the whole organisation.

Distribution
Chain
The impact and sensitivities here are of course much higher than those of individual customers. A failure to deliver can have an immediate impact on the others' own time-critical processes. Consequentially, a failure to deliver a tiny, and perhaps thought to be inconsequential ingredient, can have massive impact further up the supply line.

It is likely that the receiving organisation has contingency plans in place in case of such failure. They are likely to have other contingency suppliers ready to step in immediately; thus instantly taking away the damaged organisation's reason for existence and future marketplace. This will turn a failure, on the face of it a temporary one, into a total disaster for the supplying organisation.

Confidence in the supply continuing into the future is a crucial part of many just–in- time facilities management outsourcing schemes. The receiving organisation can - and will - move away should that confidence alone be damaged by a risk-based incident. Additional financial or other penalties, built into the contract, can be devastating to an organisation that is already reeling from an unexpected operational incident.

Another feature of a distribution chain would be third party distributors of the organisation's products and services. An example would be Independent Financial Advisors (IFAs) selling life or investment contracts on behalf of life assurance companies. Should a question emerge about the Assurer's ability to meet its promises, the IFAs have a wide choice of alternative products and suppliers to whom they could, and would, switch immediately. New cash flows to the Assurer would then stop immediately and there could, in some circumstances, even be a situation where the IFAs recommend to existing customers that they transfer their investments to other carriers. This would create a situation similar to a run on a bank. To meet such a demand for cash, the Assurer may need to realise assets quickly from a planned long-term investment portfolio. Very large volumes of shares placed together onto a stock market can, in themselves, cause a change in the demand and supply balance and cause the price of those shares to fall. Again, existing problems are exasperated.

Suppliers   The challenge with suppliers is two-fold:
Too many massive organisations find, in times of damage, just how much they themselves depend on the timely delivery of a particular supplier's ingredient, service or intellectual asset. This is of course the converse of the above paragraph. Loss of life and injury apart, many of the greatest problems facing large organisations after the September 11, 2001 terrorist attack was the realisation that a small but critical supplier; without the alternate resources of a multi-national, was destroyed.

An example could be a small software house that had been contracted to design, deliver and maintain software that is integral to the large organisation's own delivery chain. In the event of the failure of that software house, caused by perhaps a sudden and unexpected operational risk incident, the large organisation may find that it does not have the knowledge or skills to step in and continue to maintain the software. Furthermore, if the software codes – an intellectual asset – were lost in the damage, then they are unlikely ever to be able to get into the software and maintain it.

The second exposure is that the supplier, hearing of the customer reeling from serious damage, may simply feel uncomfortable with supplying further products without guarantees of the continuing ability to pay. These guarantees can be difficult or impossible to give at a time of wider crisis, especially while the damaging incident is unfolding in the public eye. There may be demands for payment prior to future deliveries, or shorter and more expensive credit terms.

Financiers   Investors in large companies are often guided by rating agencies, credit agencies and other wholesale advisors. The bottom line is that their support was provided in the good times. This was before any operational damage that leads to questions about the organisation's ability to deliver profit or dividend promises; or reduces the perceived financial strengths that were important at the time to invest. A change in credit rating can have an instant and simultaneous impact on the cost of capital from a whole range of capital sources.

Damage that significantly detracts from the business model is therefore a new environment calling for new decisions.

By definition, those decisions are likely to be less favourable and add further pressures. The investor may feel that the risk premium in the investment needs to be raised because the organisation, still reeling from unexpected damage, is less secure than before. As if the organisation doesn't have enough problems already, the cost of finance may therefore be raised dramatically, damaging further the pricing of the organisation's own products and other aspects of the business model.

A bank, for example can, within the terms of many contracts, demand the immediate sale of an asset on which a loan is secured. The bank will focus only on the need to ensure reimbursement of its loan. It may not wish to join in the gamble of the organisation being able to rebuild the business in the longer term. That asset may of course be a building or machinery that would be crucial to the organisation's chances of survival. The Bank may also have first charge on the insurance claims monies. We have two conflicting needs and the deciding factor may not be in the best long term interest of the firm but in the terms of the contract of loan between the bank, the company and its insurers.

One creditor with similar powers can be the tax departments; whether they are customs and excise, value added tax, corporation tax or any one of the indirect taxes that can be fed through businesses. The Revenue is within its powers to demand immediate payment of tax – even an estimate – if it feels that its future revenue has become at risk by the damage and the subsequently weakened organisation. It can take this step even if, by ensuring its own income stream, it damages the already precarious cash flows and the chances the organisation had until then to rebuild for the longer term.

Business Partners

Often there is a necessary sharing of brand values and reputation, and situations are created where each depends on the other to meet its own responsibilities and needs. Failure of one can be destructive to the other; hence there is an important stakeholder issue in the quality and delivery of the other organisation or organisations.

Competitors

We can now bring ongoing and resultant shareholders together. We have already illustrated how recent year changes in the way businesses produce and distribute now enable them to move, expand, contract, and change direction so much quicker than before. The flexibility of outsourcing, internationalism and electronic routes to market enables them to increase production much more quickly into new markets or new distribution channels. This much faster speed now from decision to market is a clear opportunity for competitors to take advantage of a temporary difficulty in a supplier and turn it into permanent damage.

A company in distress may be seen simply as a new business or expansion opportunity for a whole range of different companies. The new and existing competitors can equally be from foreign countries that have not before traded in the damaged organisation's market places. The opportunities created by the weakness of the damaged organisation can create a new business case to do so.

The Media
This subject has been addressed under the brand heading above. If a Board thinks it has problems, they may need to wait just a few minutes for the media to arrive en masse to then see what a problem really is. It is a very unpleasant experience is to see the brand – so often the single most valuable asset - in full freefall!

Regulators
We addressed this above in view of the impact of this exposure on a whole range of stakeholders simultaneously. Unexpected damage to the operations of the regulated company may cause them to fail to be able to continue to meet one or more of the standards set by a host of different regulators that can be industry specific or much wider in scope.

The regulator's own responsibilities to its own stakeholders will ensure that it uses its statutory powers to demand that the organisation closes down operations until it can illustrate the ability again to meet the requirements.

Until they can do so then organisation is stone cold dead. Becoming illegal, i.e., losing what is needed to remain within any laws of the country where the organisation operates, kills just as quickly.

The Environment
The wider environment within which an organisation needs to fit has many dimensions. As said, this "environment" can embrace the natural environment – often controlled by statute – through to the reasonable needs of tenants, landlords, neighbours or indeed any environment issue for which the organisation was carrying a responsibility as a "citizen" of the area or country.

Under modern guidelines, for an example, a fire brigade may wish to address a fire differently, if it is seen that the run off of water may cause unacceptable environmental pollution. Usual expectations of the service's response and reaction may not be realised, affecting such things as limits of maximum probable loss built into insurance protections.

"The environment" is a very wide subject not only covering pollution of the physical environment. Organisations may need to consider money laundering and insider dealing through to corporate manslaughter and other potentially criminal acts.

Other Stakeholders
Other stakeholders may emerge. They may be from their role within a trade body or similar organisation or the ongoing need to manage the relationship with industry pressure groups. They may be their sponsors, financial or otherwise, on whose continuity of confidence is a survival need.

Political bodies are one example. Another could be franchisees or other authorised users of brand names or other intellectual assets with contracted or implied controls around those assets that need to be followed. We mentioned earlier the wider family of employees, but also unions, government agencies and other organisations may wish to bring their own additional pressures on an organisation facing damage and even meltdown.

Summary

The purpose of this chapter has been to explore the relationships and mutual dependencies between an organisation and its stakeholders.

Using our wide definition of stakeholder we can thus identify them, in their different ways, as the end consumer of the organisation. They are the lifeblood of the organisation and necessarily the real beneficiaries in the work to be done in risk assessments, the business impact analyses and the recovery planning. Their roles and needs therefore will underpin throughout the agendas of the later chapters on these subjects.

They neatly bring together the fact that the business continuity manager cannot effectively promise resilience without a deep and clear understanding of the potential impact of damage right through to the different stakeholders who have demands on the organisation; and the power to make a situation much worse by their reaction to damage. The so called Business Impact Analysis needs to embrace also these dependencies. It needs to ensure that, where needed, there is not only effective recovery planning but also effective risk management of anything that, if lost, could make an organisation irrecoverable.

Bibliography

1. Munich Re. Topics. Annual Review of Natural Catastrophes 1997
2. Globalcontinuity.com September 2001
3. The Sun Newspaper April 2001
4. Richard Howell-Thomas; Land Rover Monthly April 2002

3

Governance, Good Practice, Standards, Regulation and the Law

Objectives of This Chapter are to:

- Consider the position of governance, good practice, standards, regulation and the law in the risk management framework
- Examine the relationship between governance, good practice, standards, regulation and the law
- Explore each subject in sufficient detail to appreciate the position of these in terms of business continuity management
- Analyse the global response of organisations to business continuity management regarding each of the issues

Taking Control - the Position of Governance

While the expressions *governance* and *corporate governance* are widely used, there is no generally accepted definition or model for corporate governance, although there are common themes which run through most governance models produced by industry and professional groups.

Governance refers to oversight mechanisms including the processes, structures and information used for directing and overseeing the management of an organisation. Most models and definitions of governance focus on organisational performance for the benefit of stakeholders and how organisations are directed, controlled and held to account. The simplest and least ambiguous definition is provided by the Organisation for Economic Co-operation and Development (OECD) which is: "... the system by which entities are directed and controlled" and which goes on to expand "... the structure through which the objectives of the company are set, and the means of attaining those objectives and monitoring performance are determined." **(1)**

Corporate governance more specifically relates to a risk-based approach to establishing a system of internal control and the review of effectiveness which companies are required to make to meet the rules of the stock exchanges on which they are listed, and increasingly the regulatory environments within which they operate.

While the concept of shareholders does not apply in the public sector or not-for-profit organisations, general principles of corporate governance readily translate across to these entities.

At a country level and within the scope of countries addressed by the most recent Aon European Risk Management and Risk Financing Survey, all included had a system of corporate governance in place - although some were more formal and embedded to a greater depth within organisational infrastructures than others. Around 87% of Europe's largest companies reported that they had undertaken a risk assessment in the last 12 months for corporate governance purposes (a significant increase over the last survey conducted). In the UK the number is particularly high - reported at almost 100% - while in contrast, just over half of Benelux countries have undertaken similar studies. These results might suggest that risk identification studies are driven by local corporate governance requirements, not because companies see much value in the results of these studies. **(2)**

Whatever the geographic, social or political environment within which an organisation operates , responsibility for effective and efficient governance rests with the board. But while a board cannot delegate this responsibility, it is nevertheless impractical and undesirable for a board to attempt to closely supervise every aspect of an organisation's operations.

In the UK, the Combined Code (3) sets out a number of good governance principles and practice with recommendations addressing:

- Director profiles and competencies

- Director remuneration

- Relations between companies and their Shareholders

- Accountability and audit

- Institutional investors

Successful governance is achieved through leadership cascaded from the top of an organisation supported by a visible commitment to good governance principles, demonstrated through relevant performance measurement and consolidated by communication at all levels and to all stakeholders. The board should ensure that their responsibility is delivered through the design and embedding of a policy which includes a statement of the organisation's commitment at the strategic and operational levels, supported by a series of broad governance principles such as those which might be derived from those of the OECD, namely:

1. The role and responsibilities of the board

2. Disclosure and transparency obligations

3. The rights and equitable treatment of shareholders

4. The responsibilities of shareholders

5. The role of other stakeholders in corporate governance.

The approach of the Institute of Internal Auditors (www.theiia.org) in the UK, Ireland and US is ahead of the internal audit game and through the production of specific guidance **(4)** promotes the following ten principles to provide a sound model for effective governance:

1. Interaction: between the board, management, the external auditor and the internal auditor
2. Board purpose: as well as understanding its own purpose to protect the shareholders, the board should consider the interests of other stakeholders

3. Board responsibilities: main areas of responsibility of the board should be monitored

4. Independence: the majority of directors should be "independent"

5. Expertise: directors should have relevant and up to date expertise to perform their role with a balance of expertise across the board i.e., finance, industry, governance

6. Meetings and information: board should meet as often as needed and have access to information required to deliver their responsibilities

7. Leadership: the roles of the board chairman and chief executive should be separate

8. Disclosure: proxy statements and other board communications should be reflective of reality and issued in a transparent and timely way

9. Committees: nominations, remuneration and audit committees of the board should be composed only of independent directors

10. Internal audit: all public companies should retain an effective, full-time internal audit function that reports directly to the audit committee.

This is a wider scope than promulgated by many other audit associations, and concludes that the board should set policies and internal control appropriate to the industry, scale, geography, external and internal environments, culture and risk profile of their organisation. With this in mind perhaps we are some way towards an explanation of the "Benelux situation?"

Business Continuity Management - Building Resilience and Customer Trust

An organisation should set out its approach to business continuity management as part of the overall system of control. Good practice might embrace:

- The position of risk management within the governance framework
- A definition of business continuity management in terms of subject matter, breadth and geographic coverage
- The position of business continuity management within the overall risk management framework
- The organisation's standards to which business continuity management should be delivered, the assignment of responsibilities and the organisational structure within which these are achieved
- The system for:
    - Assignment of responsibility and organisation
    - Policy and standards design, review and update
    - Plan development, capability, currency, budget, rehearsal and test
    - Compliance with internal and/or external standards, regulatory and legislative environments
    - Performance assurance and challenge
    - Internal audit

CASE STUDY:

An organisation should scope the objectives and purpose of its governance framework. Considerations for a business continuity governance standard designed in 2004 included:

Objectives:

- To ensure that there is a robust governance framework in place to ensure that there is 'fit for purpose' business continuity management capability in pace which is regularly maintained and tested throughout the firm
- To ensure that the firm can demonstrate compliance with regulatory obligations and legal requirements, relevant external standards and best practices adopted by the firm
- To ensure that robust management reporting and challenge mechanisms are in operation which collectively provide a credible and accurate view of business continuity management capability and compliance with relevant obligations, external standards and best practices so that informed decision making can be taken

Purposes:

- Provide an overview of the firm's business continuity management governance framework, highlight the key constituents and how they operate
- Provide clarity on the key business continuity management governance roles and responsibilities and requirements at all levels, across all risks and within all territories of the firm

---

Setting Standards for Governance

The governance regime that exists in the UK today is the result of a considerable process of evolution comprising principles and provisions published by the London Stock Exchange culminating in the unification of reports produced from committees chaired by Cadbury, Hampel and Greenbury in the 1990s, brought together in the Combined Code. Further enhancements to the Code followed through a variety of working groups and industry-led initiatives:

- The committee chaired by Turnbull commissioned further guidance on the role and effectiveness of non-executive directors.
- The enquiry led by Higgs in 2003 culminated in a report and guidelines on the effectiveness of non-executive directors. This report did not propose a prescriptive rules-based framework on the duties of non-executive directors but did provide guidance on the independence and effectiveness of non-executive directors. This included a view on the board composition and a requirement for the Chairman to perform an evaluation at least annually of the board, its committees and members.
- As part of the UK response to issues raised following a number of major corporate failures, a revised Combined Code was published in July 2003. Recommendations focused on the make-up and responsibilities of the audit committee including clarification on the audit committee's role as 'auditor of internal audit.'
- Most recently the conclusions of a working group led by Smith have led to further refinement of the Code involving the provisions for audit committees.
- The generic governance code agenda has been further enhanced by the development of industry- based codes of good practice for audit committees which have been produced for industry sectors tailored to meet different industry governance needs

But the objective of any organisation must be the level of management performance and not the observation of codes per se - and the means, by which targets can be set and subsequently monitored and performance achieved and declared, challenged.

A survey published by KPMG (5) in 2002 reported that 80% of fund managers would pay more for the shares of a demonstrably well-governed company with the average premium being 11%. This is key given recent examples of corporate scandal where whatever the code or practice might have been, clearly performance had failed.

Fundamental are the mechanics to ensure that an organisation's performance and compliance (and that of its directors and internal audit function) can be measured and assessed. Processes and benchmarks that state the organisation's current and future position should be developed and driven into existing quality and assurance management systems at the heart of the organisation, thereby ensuring a bottom-up as well as a top-down process. This serves to emphasise that governance, risk management and control are part of every employee's job and good management practice.

Further company law modifications are set to come - including those relating to company directors and the codification of their duties. Based on the belief that some companies are paying lip service to codes of governance, Douglas Flint (a member of the original Turnbull committee) will chair a working party revisiting the Combined Code with an objective to close the gap between what companies say they do and what they actually do. It is projected that revisions coming out of this work will be in place during 2006.

Governance in Practice

An awareness and consideration of these issues needs to be part of everything that an organisation does. How these components are drawn together, developed, documented and communicated should form an organisation's 'Governance Framework.'

The Canadian regulator of financial institutions OSFI (6) puts it this way, "Corporate governance refers to oversight mechanisms, including the processes, structures and information used for directing and overseeing the management of a company. It encompasses the means by which members of the board of directors and senior management are held accountable for their actions and for the establishment and implementation of oversight functions and processes." Further, the Canadian regulatory body adds that individual institutions will adopt different approaches to corporate governance taking into account the "... nature, scope, complexity and risk profile of their institution." (A 'red line' runs through most if not all of the many regulatory guidelines published globally.)

One governance size does not fit all, and it is important that boards seek to guard against adopting a tick-box mentality, where they seek to adhere slavishly to every directive and demonstrate their compliance through numerous checklists. A framework itself can become a risk. Once there is a framework with boxes, people will organise a line to tick them! Further there is no governance "blueprint." The concept of good governance is to promote broad principles that reflect the risk profile of the organisation and then to honour them, not to have an unnecessarily burdensome, rules-based approach designed somewhere else with regulations that sit on the shelf that nobody relates to and consequently sees fit to follow.

The creation of registered companies and the need to protect shareholders from debt beyond their investment led to the development of basic company law and corporate governance mechanisms. Sound familiar? These roots were sown in the 19th century and while there was a high level of interest in the regulation of the securities industry following the Wall Street crash of the 1920s, it was not really until the stock market crash in 1987 that there were loud and urgent calls for reform, especially from institutional shareholders. With failures continuing into the 21st century there has been a change in attitude towards and expectations of the quality in performance of company officers worldwide. A flurry of governance codes has emerged, developed variously by professional associations of internal auditors and company secretaries, stock exchanges, investor associations and the like. Generally, codes are not mandated by law, although aspects of codes may cross-reference into regulatory standards and handbooks and on occasion into associated law.

CASE STUDY

Standards Australia **(7)** has attempted to devise a generic governance framework suitable for a wide range of organisations: 2003

- The standard encourages a self-regulated approach and provides performance benchmarks. Comprising structural, operational and maintenance elements, the standard requires CEO-level commitment, policy, promotion and communication and a philosophy of continuous improvement. The standard loosely follows the OECD Principles of Corporate Governance and covers five areas: the role and responsibilities of the Board, disclosure and transparency obligations, the rights and equitable treatment of shareholders, the responsibilities of shareholders and the role of other stakeholders

- The principles do not advocate or prescribe a particular course but provide a framework flexible enough to reflect each organisation's circumstances. General principles are provided at the start of each section followed by others specific only to certain types of organisation for example, government bodies, companies, or not-for-profit entities, etc.

- To assist in ensuring that good governance is part of normal operations the Standard recommends that the requirements of laws, regulations, codes of best practice and organisational standards are integrated as part of an organisation's day-to-day procedures.

- Emphasis is made on the responsibilities and obligations of shareholders including a duty to make informed votes and where appropriate to provide reasons before casting a vote where this is against a motion.

- The standard will take a lead as part of a Governance Series comprising, fraud and corruption control, organisational codes of conduct, corporate social responsibility and whistle blowing systems.

Business Continuity Management and the Governance System

Business continuity management has long been recognised as part of good business practice and an integral part of corporate governance. While there are a number of sources of good business continuity management practice guidance, many take a narrow reactive information technology focus, rather than the holistic resilience and response capability which the discipline can provide. A board is charged with having a process embedded for the identification and control of all risks across an organisation and likewise business continuity management should rise to the enterprise challenge.

Today's view on business continuity management is it:

- Is about managing risk

- Is a powerful force for business sustainability

- Provides for business success

Following on from the position adopted in Chapter One, risk management and business continuity management are about managing *all* types of risk, building resilience into all aspects of an organisation, and having solutions in place that are able to respond when things do not go to plan. Governance codes and standards demand that all risks and controls are embraced and do not distinguish between one type of risk or control and another. Typically focused on recovery of critical operations, more recently the focus has widened to include a governance approach which should address the special circumstances which might prevail in the wake of an incident of the scale witnessed in September, 2001, together with those of a less tangible nature.

Risk concepts and management techniques are typically designed to support the management of the more tangible, asset-based risk. Management must rise to the challenge within their governance frameworks to address all types of risk, resilience and response including business-critical operations; those of their dependencies (including supply chains); wider industry and the community within which they operate; as well as those which may damage or even destroy their reputation. "An established and successful brand or public image, reputation and trust of either a private or private sector organisation can be destroyed in minutes, unless vigorously defended at a time when the speed and scale of events can overwhelm the normal operational and management systems." **(8)**

As with corporate governance guidelines and standards, the majority of guidelines and standards for business continuity management, while providing a generic and standardised approach, should remain sufficiently flexible to enable customisation to meet the challenges of scalability, different business profiles and priorities, various geographic and multi-jurisdictional needs coupled with governance, regulatory and legal regimes.

The Business Continuity Institute *Good Practice Guide* **(9)** establishes a process, principles, and terminology, together with a description of business continuity management activities and outcomes. As with industry-specific governance standards, the business continuity guidelines provide expert input to government, regulators and auditors in support of the delivery of their mandates and objectives, as well as for the organisation-based practitioner, supplier, outsourced provider or consulting practitioner.

But no good practice guidelines, however well drafted, can provide the governance solution for a specific organisation. To achieve wide recognition and appeal, guidelines can only be generic and must be adapted to suit the circumstances, vision and criticalities of each organisation's environment. The regulatory and legislative environment of the industry in which an organisation operates coupled with that of its stakeholders, and notably its suppliers and outsourced providers, will all exercise influence on the appropriate operating control environment. "A function of the differences between industries and within industries, the dynamics between risk management, business continuity management and corporate governance will ultimately depend upon the on the culture, maturity and strategic point of view of each organisation." **(10)**

Setting the Standard

Standards organisations feed off industry good practice. They are generally developed by committees of industry subject matter practitioners supported by relevant industry and government stakeholders and facilitated by one of the standards bodies, e.g. Standards Australia, British Standards Institute (BSI), American National Standards Institute (ANSI), or the International Standards Organisation (ISO).

A standard attempts to provide guidance on a governance framework and usually comprises a definition of the subject matter and a set of associated processes supported by a glossary of terms and referral points. Standards bodies do not hold themselves out as experts in the subject matter and they do not offer to police or enforce the standards which bear their approval.

Standards documents may be superseded at any time by the issue of a new edition or an update. Generally a standard at any time may be a combination of the original standard supplemented by updates - rather than a full reissue. Care must be taken by any practitioner using documents that they have the most up-to-date position.

A route of country-specific acceptance (ANSI - American National Standards Institute or BSI - British Standards Institute, for example) may be followed by wider lobbying and the development of an internationally recognised work (ISO - International Standards Organisation). On occasion, an international standard may be more generic than that of its country-specific relatives; although depending on the nature of the subject matter there are examples where standards provide virtual mirrors of one another (as with the information security management standard BSI 7799 and ISO 17799).

Standards may be developed as part of a series (as with the Standards Australia Governance and Risk Management standards) or require cross-reference to common language - as in the information management security standard ISO 17799 Section 11, *Business Continuity Management* and PAS 56, the Publicly Available Standard produced by the BSI on business continuity management.

Consequently, many standards have been through an evolutionary route:

- A standard may start out as a set of guidelines or handbook provided by a standards body (e.g. *Managing Risk for Corporate Governance* - PD 6668 produced by the BSI in 2000, handbook HB22 - *2003 Business Continuity Management* produced by Standards Australia)

- Guidelines may progress to become a Publicly Available Specification (e.g. *Guide to Business Continuity Management* - PAS 56 produced by the BSI in 2003)

- Following suitable endorsement and support a specification may progress to a country-specific standard (e.g., *Information Security Management* - BSI 7799) and subsequent internationalisation (e.g., *Information Security Management* - ISO 17799).

In the US, the 9/11 Commission's final report, published in July 2004, reported that given 85% of the critical infrastructure of the US is controlled by the private sector the first to respond to any future attack are likely to be civilians and private sector facilities. Consequently, private sector preparedness is not viewed as a luxury, "… it is a cost of doing business in the post-9/11 world." **(11)** The Commission's recommendations include an endorsement of a voluntary national standard for private sector preparedness - the National Preparedness Standard - developed by the National Fire Protection Association and approved by the ANSI **(12)**.

US NATIONAL PREPAREDNESS STANDARD - Headlines

- **Laws and Authorities**

The applicable legislation, regulations and industry codes of practice an entity needs to consider when developing a disaster recovery, emergency management or business continuity plan.

- **Hazard Identification and Risk Assessment**

The identification of hazards (e.g., natural, human, and technological), the likelihood of their occurrence and the organization's vulnerability to these hazards.

- **Hazard Mitigation**

Activities taken to eliminate or reduce the degree of risk to life and property from hazards, either prior to or following a disaster or emergency.

- **Resource Management**

The means within the organization to reduce or eliminate the hazards identified in the risk assessment phase.

- **Mutual Aid**

Agreements between entities to obtain resources in the event of an emergency.

- **Planning**

The process of developing advance arrangements and procedures which will enable an organization to respond to a disaster and resume critical business or service functions within a predetermined period of time, minimize the amount of loss, and repair, restore or replace the stricken facilities as soon as possible.

- Strategic Plan - A plan outlining decisions regarding resource allocation, priorities, and action steps necessary to reach the goals of the disaster recovery, emergency management or business continuity plan.

- Emergency Operations Plan - A plan outlining the response an organization will have to a disaster or emergency. This may include procedures or criteria for opening an Emergency Operations Center, the deployment of assets to meet critical needs and the description and assurance of a coordinated response to emergency situations.

- Mitigation Plan - The strategy and action steps to eliminate hazards or mitigate their effect if they cannot be eliminated.

- Business Impact Analysis - The process of determining the impact on an organization should a potential loss (hopefully identified by the risk analysis) actually occur. The BIA should qualify and quantify, where possible, the loss impact from a business interruption, operational, and financial standpoint.

- Recovery / Business Continuity Plan - The documentation of the strategies, procedures, resources, organizational structure, and information database utilized by an organization to recover from, resume, manage and continue operations in the event of a substantial disruptive incident.

- **Direction, Control and Coordination**

The ability to manage the response and recovery operations, as well as notify officials, emergency personnel employees and other personnel of an actual or pending emergency.

- **Communications and Warning**

The communication systems and procedures are to be established and regularly tested to support the program.

- **Operations and Procedure**

The implementation of all tactical operations at the incident, including response, damage assessment and recovery operations.

- **Logistics and Facilities**

Identifies methods and responsibilities for providing facilities, services, personnel and materials for the incident.

- **Training**

The implementation of a training / educational program to facilitate and provide understanding and support of the program

- **Exercises, Evaluations & Corrective Actions**

The evaluation of the program through periodic reviews, testing, post-incident reports, performance evaluations and exercises

- **Crisis Communication, Public Education and Information**

Procedures to disseminate helpful recovery information and respond to requests for pre-disaster, disaster and post disaster information including procedures for addressing media inquiries, as well as providing information to them.

- **Finance and Administration**

In July 2005, the Disaster Recovery Journal (DRJ) and Disaster Recovery Institute International (DRII) published Generally Accepted Practices for review and comment. **(13)**. Although these guidelines are an early draft and will require a great deal of refinement before sign-off, their goal is additionally to provide examples of best practice - a very high ideal.

Whatever stage of development – guidance document, handbook, publicly available specification or standard – the objective is to offer advice and to set out the basis for a subject-specific benchmark which is recognisable by stakeholders of the organisation which either promotes a basis for management or with regards to accreditation where available, as well as a foundation for the auditable achievement of a commonly agreed level of performance.

However, existing standards are not the answer for every organisation. By necessity, standards must appeal to a wide range of organisations and, consequently for many, the business continuity standards which exist have limitations. For example, PAS 56 is suited more to the larger business and lacks a degree of scalability; focus is clearer on the recovery element of the incident process but less so regarding early warning requirements and mechanisms and the process of invocation through to actual crisis.

BRITISH STANDARDS INSTITUTE - PAS 56 - Headlines (14)

PAS 56 comprises 10 sections, three Annexes and a bibliography, and spans 58 pages in total. The prime sections are as follows:

1. Scope

2. Terms and definitions

3. Abbreviations

4. Overview

5. BCM programme management

6. Understanding your business

7. BCM strategies

8. Developing and implementing BCM plans

9. Building and embedding a BCM culture

10. BCM exercising, maintenance and audit

An international standard for business continuity management will emerge in time. Perhaps the way forward for this has been set by the British Standards Institute (BSI), which announced in August, 2005 its intention to develop standards concurrently for risk and business continuity management. Those working on these standards should reflect that "one size does not fit all."

The Regulatory Response

A regulator is given a set of responsibilities under statute and its objectives are driven by the delivery of these responsibilities. Ultimately a regulator's brief is to protect the group of consumers that fall within its mandate and to ensure a sound and secure business environment within which these consumers are active.

However, regulators do not necessarily seek to operate a regulatory regime with zero failures. They accept that risk is a source of competitive advantage, if understood and managed by organisations within formally agreed tolerance or "risk appetite" levels.

Regulators express the opinion that regulatory guidance reflects commonly accepted practices already adopted at prudently managed organisations and that, consequently, the mere existence of a regulatory influence should not affect the way an organisation is managed. While governance codes and guidelines do not generally include regulatory considerations directly other than as a requirement within a risk-based framework, the reverse may not apply. It is common practice for regulators to make reference to corporate governance codes and guidelines and relevant industry or subject-specific standards and to embrace these within their arrangements for systems, controls and supporting handbooks. Many of the issues that keep the regulators of the financial services sector awake at night are common to other, if not most industries, including (1) automated and integrated technology that has the potential to transform previously minor processing errors into major systems failures; (2) the growth in e-commerce and the raft of new risks this brings; and, (3) the potential loss of control when organisations outsource and firms that take on the mirror effect by assuming risk through "in-sourcing" the activities of others.

In the UK the Financial Services Authority **(15)** has given great emphasis in their published guidelines to the importance of business continuity management, but permits regulated organisations to retain a level of flexibility:

"A firm should have in place appropriate arrangements, having regard to the nature, scale and complexity of its business to ensure that it can continue to function and meet its regulatory obligations in the event of an unforeseen interruption. These arrangements should be regularly updated and tested to ensure their effectiveness."

The FSA goes on to state that a firm should document its strategy to maintain continuity of its business operations including:

- Business continuity plans for short, medium and long term disruption
- Escalation and invocation arrangements
- Processes to validate the integrity of information affected by disruption

However, all is not what it might seem. There is an element of 'regulatory creep' in the UK environment evidenced in a number of advisory papers - not regulation - where FSA expectations of regulated organisations sets the pole much higher than might appear from reading purely the Systems and Controls set out in their handbook. While the FSA rules and guidelines are high-level, the benchmark they use to assess regulatory performance and compliance can be much tougher. There is an expectation that performance will be to industry standards and good practice levels as well as those published by, for example, the BSI in PAS 56, and those promoted by the Business Continuity Institute in their Good Practice Guide.

While regulators can highlight serious issues and enforce a degree of regulation in areas such as business continuity management, regulation per se may not lead to a change in practice, can be notoriously difficult to police when judged against high levels of rules and guidance and viewed as an imposed evil rather than a business value-adding benefit. Standards developed through industry-focused working parties fueled by competent professionals are probably going to achieve more buy-in from user group than regulation-imposed - so it really should not come as a surprise that the regulator keeps standards in his back pocket!. The FSA have stated that they will not take the same level of interest to the same level of detail in all organisations, adopting the principles of the risk-based approach they promote "... for major financial groups and other high risk firms we expect to monitor BCM as part of a close and continuing supervisory relationship." **(15)**

The regulator also has experience to share from a number of unique perspectives: following September 11, 2001, the FSA produced a working paper which captured the results of research they had gathered from the organisations they regulate, supplemented by the feedback they gained from contact with their counterparts in other countries. Views on why BCM fails were also offered:

- Roles and responsibilities: Comments range from absence of links between businesses and communication breakdown when plans are used in anger
- Communication: Failure to detect early warning signals and response to discontinuity and therefore a subsequent slow response and invocation

- Interdependency mapping: Interdependencies of key functions misunderstood failure to identify and back-up key processes

Regulators may take generic governance recommendations or guidelines and convert these into the regulatory environment for which they are responsible. Consequently, rules regulation will usually have some form of industry or consumer focus. The regulator's approach will be reflected by their terms of reference and these environmental differences and therefore their business continuity management goals and priorities will be designed with this in mind.

The main board of an organisation may oversee a business operating in a range of geographic as well as industry sectors, and while they may have one governance framework (with subsidiaries) they may have to deal with a wide range of regulatory requirements imposed by different regulators whose requirements may on occasion conflict with one another. Given the Aon survey findings and the differing risk regimes in the UK and Benelux countries, for example, one might predict that this situation would arise.

In regulatory handbooks and standards, BCM-related rules and guidelines will most frequently be found within the area of operational risk. In a definitional and qualitative sense, while operational risk is still finding its way in some industries, in the world of financial services (and in the wake of 9/11), this situation is much clearer and more consistently presented. Immediately after 9/11 regulators worldwide took time out to analyse the aftermath of the terrorist attacks with a view toward strengthening the overall resilience of the financial system.

CASE STUDY

An initial review by the US regulator concluded that few organisations had taken into account in their approach to BCM the potential for widespread disasters of the scale and nature that occurred in Manhattan:

- The impact of major loss and inaccessibility to critical staff had been underestimated

- Exclusion zones were often inadequate with backup facilities on occasion located in the same or nearby buildings - resulting in the loss of both primary and backup sites

- Very few firms planned for loss of multiple sites

- Key telecommunications requirement was for email

On inspection one might argue that very little change was subsequently required. Through an extraordinary level of cooperation among market participants, the financial system recovered remarkably quickly from the tragedy. "However, we cannot assume that the same combination will always work in our favour, and, therefore, regulators and the public have a strong common interest in learning from our horrific experiences of September 11." (11)

CASE STUDY

The US Federal Reserve undertook a review of the events of 9/11 and examined the impact on the financial systems of New York and beyond.

- The domino effect of the temporary loss of some market functions became critical to the resilience of the whole US economy and consequently had an impact way beyond the boundaries of New York.

- The events of 9/11 graphically demonstrated the interdependence among financial system participants - wherever located. Though organisations located outside New York City area were affected much less than those within it, many felt the effects of the disaster.

- The difficulty customers and counter-parties had in communicating with banks, broker-dealers and other organisations in lower Manhattan seriously impeded their ability to determine whether transactions had been completed as expected. There were situations where some customers were affected by actions of institutions with which they did not even do business, for example, when funds or securities could not be delivered because of operational problems at other institutions.

- During the week of September 11 liquidity bottlenecks at times became so severe that the Federal Reserve needed to step in to provide lending and credit while extending hours of operation to accommodate the backlog of institutional payments.

- From experience the Federal Reserve learned that institutions could not plan in isolation of their competitors, the market and the Federal Reserve itself.

- As a result the Federal Reserve believes that "... coordinated discussions of sound practices for business continuity involving the financial industry and regulators are an important part of our response to the events of 9/11." **(16)**

Looking outwards, business concentrations, both market-based and geographic, intensified the impact of operational disruptions. Loss of one critical market function impacted on another, making many market participants feel the effect even though for them business was otherwise open 'as usual.' Telecommunications vulnerabilities became evident when failures affected numerous institutions both within and outside lower Manhattan. Federal Reserve staff found themselves actually engaged in the recovery process, setting priorities for the restoration for key telecommunications circuits.

In a report published by PricewaterhouseCoopers, the concept of the "corporate reporting supply chain" was set out and how this model might be used to regain public trust in corporate reporting. A primary objective of the report was to identify and encourage certain behaviours by all key players in the corporate reporting supply chain that are intended to result in more reliable, timely, and useful information to assist stakeholders in their decision-making process.

This model serves as a useful tool to demonstrate how a governance framework functions where standards and regulatory environments are positioned - as 'red lines' running through the business' DNA. An organisation's governance framework should embrace all systems by which an organisation is directed and controlled.

So far we've examined governance, standards and regulation. So where does the law fit into this equation? The consequences of regulatory breach can be devastating. Many of the sanctions for breach are criminal or quasi-criminal with company directors and officers facing personal liability. Regulatory bodies now have more power than ever before - whether they be regulating the financial, taxation, customs, data protection, health and safety or environmental.

The Legal Environment - Evolution or Revolution?

There are a number of aspects of the law which overlay the risk management framework, and within these, elements which directly impact on business continuity management. This is not a book about the law, and so we just linger to consider where the law fits into the governance framework using a number of relevant examples and leaving the reader with food for thought.

There are two main ways in which the law impacts the governance framework - *evolutionary* and *responsive*.

Evolutionary Law

In an evolutionary sense there are laws which develop over a period of time stimulated by changes in social, cultural, political and economic circumstances and they are consequently going to vary from one country (and State) to another. The legal framework, and the law that sits within it, establishes the minimum set of rules for any governance regime, standards or regulatory guidelines. Whether this is law that impacts on the health, safety and security of employees and customers, their rights as employees or consumers, the environment within which they live and work, or the company laws that set the rules of corporate behaviour, this will form the minimum legal operational environment. Effective monitoring and assessment mechanisms must be in place to ensure that an organisation remains aware of and compliant with the legal environments within which it operates. Business continuity plans may require adjustment according to the assessment of the legislation and its perceived impact.

Reactive Law

Simultaneously, laws can be passed to respond to an immediate, perceived need. We cannot address all aspects of legislation in this book, but we will focus on three areas of responsive law which have had a recent and profound effect on our subject matter:

• US: The Homeland Security Act - 2002

From the morning of September, 11, 2001, the US had been engaged in an unprecedented effort to defend national freedom and security. In November, 2002, a new act was passed with the creation of the new Department of Homeland Security (DHS). The objective was to ensure that the defence of the US would be comprehensive and united **(17)**.

The department was charged with:
- Analysis of threats
- Guarding of borders and airports
- Protection of the critical infrastructure
- Coordination of the response of the nation for future emergencies

As the Act was signed, President Bush announced that, with the help of many nations, "We're tracking terrorist activity, we're freezing terrorist finances, we're disrupting terrorist plots, we're shutting down terrorist camps, we're on the hunt one person at a time. Many terrorists are now being interrogated. Many terrorists have been killed. We've liberated a country." The Act recognised that, as terrorists had targeted the US, the front of the "... new war is here in America. Our life changed, and changed in dramatic fashion, on September 11, 2001."

Setting up the Department of Homeland Security involved the most extensive reorganization of the federal government since Harry Truman signed the National Security Act.

The objectives of the new department were:

• To analyse intelligence information on terror threats collected by the CIA, the FBI, the National Security Agency and others, and matches this intelligence against the nation's vulnerabilities - working with other agencies, the private sector, and state and local governments to harden the US defences against terrorism.

  • Gather and focus all the efforts of the US to face the challenge of cyber-terrorism, and the danger of nuclear, chemical, and biological terrorism. This department is charged with encouraging research on new technologies that can detect these threats in time to prevent an attack.

  • Focusing of state and local governments to turn for help and information to one federal, domestic security agency.

  • To bring together the agencies responsible for border, coastline, and transportation security. There will be a coordinated effort to safeguard US transportation systems and to secure the border so that the US is better able to protect its citizens and welcome its friends.

  • Working with state and local officials to prepare US response to any future terrorist attack that may come. (The first hours and even the first minutes after the attack were recognised as crucial in saving lives, and the first responders need the carefully planned and drilled strategies that will make their work effective).

The overarching objective was to spend less on administrators in offices and more on working agents in the field - less on overhead and more on protecting neighbourhoods and borders and waters and skies from terrorists.

There was no desire to defend, predict or prevent every conceivable attack. The aim was to take every possible measure to safeguard the country and its people.

ANALYSIS OF THE HOMELAND SECURITY ACT OF 2002

Table of Contents

Section 1

Title 1 - Department of Homeland Security

Title 2 - Information Analysis and Infrastructure Protection

Title 3 - Chemical, Biological Radiological and Nuclear Countermeasures

Title 4 - Border and Transportation Security

Title 5 - Emergency preparedness and Response

Title 6 - Management

Title 7 - Coordination with Non-Federal Entities, Inspector General, United Sates Secret Service, General Provisions

Title 8 - Transition

Title 9 - Conforming and Technical Amendments

Section 2 - Definitions

This section provides definitions for a number of terms used in the bill. As provided in the definitions, 'Department' in the bill refers to the Department of Homeland Security, and 'Secretary' refers to the Secretary of Homeland Security. Other important defined terms are 'assets' and 'functions,' which are used recurrently in the bill in referring to the resources and operations that are to be transferred to the new Department of Homeland Security.

Many of the definitions in the section are borrowed from pre-existing statutes, such as the Robert T. Stafford Disaster Relief and Emergency Assistance Act, Pub. L. No. 93-288. Among such borrowed definitions are that of 'State,' which includes the District of Columbia, Puerto Rico, the U.S. Virgin Islands, Guam, American Samoa, and the Commonwealth of the Northern Mariana Islands, and that of 'local government,' which includes all non-federal public entities and Indian tribes and tribal and Alaska Native organizations and villages. Another borrowed definition is that of 'major disaster,' which includes natural disasters and severe fires, floods, and explosions, regardless of cause.

Section 3 - Construction, Severability

This section, modelled on existing law, provides an express rule of construction and severability for the bill.

Section 4 - Effective date.

This section specifies an effective date for the bill, which is thirty days following enactment or, if enacted within thirty days before January 1, 2003, on January 1, 2003

• **UK: The Civil Contingencies Act - 2005**

Following events including a fuel crisis and severe flooding in the autumn and winter of 2000 the Government undertook a review of emergency planning arrangements and current legislation. As a consequence a new framework for civil protection work at local level and a new framework for the use of special legislative measures were proposed. **(17)**

Throughout the process of developing and consulting on the new legislation the Government worked with an objective to codify existing good practice rather than develop a new emergency planning regime.

The Act's modernisation of local civil protection activities and special legislative measures to deal with incidents on a larger scale has meant that the Act has introduced a new updated definition of 'emergency' appropriate for the type of threats and risks that the UK now faces in the 21st century.

The Act is separated into two parts: local arrangements for civil protection (Part 1) and emergency powers (Part 2), but across both the definition is very similar. The new definition defines an emergency as: "… an event or situation which threatens serious damage to human welfare in a place in the United Kingdom; the environment of a place in the United Kingdom; or the security of the United Kingdom or of a place in the United Kingdom" **(18)** and is designed to include emergencies from local incidents to wide-ranging catastrophic events.

Part 1 of the Act covers the range of potential incidents which local responders must prepare for as regards their civil protection duties. Part 2 covers the emergency powers the Government may grant to facilitate the response to an emergency.

Part 1

Emergency responders are divided into two categories.

Category 1 Responders have a primary role in the response to an incident and include:

- Local Authorities
- Government Agencies
- Emergency Services
- National Health Service Bodies

They have the following duties placed upon them:

- Risk assessment
- Develop Emergency Plans
- Develop Business Continuity Plans
- Arrange to make information available to the public about civil protection matters and maintain arrangements to warn, inform and advise the public in the event of an emergency
- Share information with other local responders to enable greater coordination
- Cooperate with other local responders to enhance co-ordination and efficiency

A final duty applies to Local Authorities alone and that is:

- To provide advice and assistance to businesses and voluntary organisations about business continuity management. Category 2 responders have a supportive role in planning for and responding to emergencies.

Category 2 responders include:

- Utilities
- Transport companies
- Government (Health and Safety Executive)
- Health (The Common Services Agency in Scotland)

Category 2 organisations are placed under lesser obligations beneath the Act. Primarily their role is cooperating and sharing relevant information with Category 1 responders. They should be engaged in discussions where they can add value. Furthermore, they must respond to reasonable requests.

These are not definitive lists of category 1 and 2 responders as the Act is flexible in altering membership to take account of future developments.

It is required that Category 1 and 2 organisations come together to form "Local Resilience Forums" based on police areas to aid coordination and cooperation between responders at a local level. However, in London arrangements will differ, as a Local Resilience Forum based on a police force basis would be impractical; thus, Local Resilience Forums will be based upon local authority's mutual aid groups. For the City this would be NORMACE (Barnet, Enfield, Haringey, Islington, Camden, Westminster and the City).

Part 2

The Act permits the creation of temporary special legislation aimed at dealing with a serious emergency that fits within the new definition. Furthermore, it allows for the use of emergency powers on a regional basis. This enables any special temporary legislation to apply only in the part of the UK affected by the emergency, leaving the rest of the country unaffected.

There are, however, stipulations in the Act designed to ensure that emergency powers are not misused and are applied in a directed and balanced manner.

The Act also introduces the position of a "Regional Nominated Coordinator." This individual will be an experienced crisis manager with expert knowledge of the particular type of emergency in question who, if emergency powers are invoked, will act as the focal point for coordination of response efforts at the regional or devolved administration level.

The bulk of the duties of the Act take effect from November, 2005 with the duty on local authorities to provide advice and assistance to businesses and voluntary sector organisations in relation to business continuity fully in force from May, 2006. Local Authorities will face some tough challenges to maintain their current focus whilst rising to the demands required for further capability as well as offering advice and co-ordination of services to all of their critical stakeholders.

Civil Contingencies Act - Arrangement of Regulations

Part 1 - Introductory: Commencement, Northern Ireland and interpretation

Part 2 - General: Co-operation groups, discharge of functions, Category 1 responders

Part 3 - Duty to assess risk of an emergency occurring: Emergency types and risk registers

Part 4 - Duty to maintain plans: Communication, plans, escalation, training and exercising

Part 5 - Publication of plans and assessments: Alarming the public necessarily

Part 6 - Arrangements for warning and provision of information and advice to the public: Duty to have regard to emergency plans, arrangements to warn, etc.

Part 7 - Advice and assistance to business and voluntary organisations: Transitional arrangements, risk assessment, extent of duty, co-operation, activities of other responders

Part 8 - Information: Sensitive information, information sharing, disclosure, use and security of sensitive information, health and safety

Part 9 - London: Role of London Fire and Emergency Planning Authority and the role of other Category 1 responders in London

Part 10 - Northern Ireland: Duty to other bodies, joint discharge of functions, etc.

Schedule - Local resilience areas in London

- **Sarbanes-Oxley**

One of the most powerful pieces of legislation to affect organisations in recent years came with the passing of the Sarbanes-Oxley Act of 2002 **(19)**. Pressures to achieve business success were already high but passage of the act in response to a spate of corporate failures saw these pressures continue to mount, compounded by increased regulation, and a renewed focus on corporate governance practices, financial reporting integrity and transparency.

Fundamentally Sarbanes-Oxley introduces nothing new but it does add an emphasis in six key areas:
- Reporting: an upgrade of disclosures

- Roles: a strengthening of corporate governance

- Conduct: an expansion of accountability

- Enforcement: increased oversight

- Penalties: broadened sanctions

- Relationships: heightened auditor independence

Even organisations which thought they had good governance standards and controls have found the need to re-visit their practices in order to achieve the standards the requirements of the Act and its associated rules.

Rapid Regulatory Response

Regulation and the law demand treatment consistent with other risks in the organisation. When things go wrong response needs to be quick - many of those who police these areas have powers to call for documents, require answers to questions and enter premises under warrant. Just as with a fire or a flood, an organisation needs to have response plans prepared which may need to be swift to protect employee, client and shareholder confidence. And just as pre-prepared responses to personnel issues in business continuity plans might involve employee hot lines or counselling services, so now there are providers offering 24-hour crisis support and training in "dawn raid" and equivalent scenarios, tailored to suit the risk profile and response requirements.

Probably the greatest impact of regulatory or legal breach, other than the CEO or their directors finding themselves behind bars (a scenario which quickly focuses the corporate mind), is on reputation. Damage to reputation can be disastrous. Recent surveys indicate that FTSE and Fortune 500 companies have around 70% of their value invested in their intangible assets; ten years ago this figure was closer to 40%.

Reputation is much more than brand image and embraces issues such as trust in an organisation's integrity and how it will conduct itself. Damage to reputation consequently can expose an organisation to arterial injury - and if damaged more than once, the outcome can be terminal. A poor reputation can create a vicious cycle from which an organisation may fail to break free "... and minor events that might normally go unreported give rise to the opportunity for old stories to be revived and adverse publicity to continue" **(20)**.

Difficult to grasp and hard to quantify, reputation is rarely managed systematically and consequently the control environment, including business continuity management, infrequently joined-up. If passive box-ticking is a trend in risk management, then it is positively of epidemic proportions in reputation risk management. While a corporation may produce good financial results, if there is a perception that it has questionable principles in the profit and responsibility equation, effective recovery may prove more difficult when things go wrong as the organisation struggles to recover in an environment of negativity and mistrust.

Legislation, tighter regulation and improved industry standards are redefining the extent to which all organisations are expected to plan for an emergency. Simply having a business continuity plan may no longer be sufficient. Organisations should ensure plan are tested and refined, plans should account for availability and responsiveness of critical services and can be implemented from the Board down.

Turning back to market surveys, risk managers still consider discontinuity of business their biggest concern. "New legislation, developing regulation and new business continuity best practice standards means that organisations can expect to be under pressure from all sides to have effective business continuity planning that measure up to all these benchmarks." **(21)**.

Summary

A governance framework embracing good regulatory and legislative risk management harnessing standards as appropriate can be good and bad - both the facilitator of understanding and control - but also a major source of risk.

The answer is not more regulation and law, but an encouragement for organisations to develop and apply good risk and business continuity management practices with organisation-specific tailoring. Building resilience, not generic checklists, and testing the business continuity management product - the plan - are key. However, plans must be compatible with the regulatory and legislative environment in which they might be used. The way an organisation handles a crisis is not only dependent on the quality and timeliness of its response but on how this is conducted in the external environment.

The proliferation of corporate governance initiatives - from Turnbull in the UK to the King Report in South Africa, Brazil's innovative New Stock Exchange, and the World Bank's Corporate Governance Forum - all attest to rising expectations of corporate governance performance. There is no single model for effective corporate governance - as with all management capabilities, corporate governance must be flexible and adaptable. The OECD has said, "To remain competitive in a changing world, corporations must innovate and adapt their corporate governance practices so that they can meet new demands and meet new opportunities."

Organisations can be sound in strict legal and regulatory terms and tick the right boxes, but will they differentiate themselves in a governance or commercial sense from the pack? Will they recover effectively if they hit a problem? If they do not, their chances are less than break-even that they will not lose value in the event of disruption.

Bibliography

1. OECD

2. The Aon European Risk Management & Risk Financing Survey: 2005

3. Combined Code: Revised Code published for reporting on or after November 2003

4. A New Agenda for Corporate Governance Reform, Institute of Internal Auditors - UK and Ireland 2002, www.theiia.org

5. KPMG - www.kpmg.co.uk

6. OSFI - Office of the Superintendent of Financial Institutions Canada: Corporate Governance Guideline: January 2003

7. Standards Australia: Australian Standard - Good governance principles: 2003

8. Atkins and Bates - Reputation Risk - 2005

9. Business Continuity Institute (BCI) - www.thebci.org

10. Building Public Trust - The Future of Corporate Reporting - PricewaterhouseCoopers

11. Committed to Protecting America: A Private-Sector Crisis Preparedness Guide - March 2005

12. The National Preparedness Standard - National Fire Protection Association - American Standards Institute NFPA 1600 (endorsed by the Department of Homeland Security (DHS), the Federal Emergency Management Agency (FEMA), the Federal 9/11 Commission, the National Emergency Management Association (NEMA) and the International Association of Emergency Managers (IAEM)) - 2004

13. Generally Accepted Practices - Draft for Review - Disaster Recovery Journal (DRJ) and Disaster Recovery Institute (DRI) - July 2005

14. SYCS 3.2.19G Financial Services Authority: www.fsa.gov.uk; www.financialsectorcontinuity.gov.uk

15. FSA working paper on Business Continuity Management: 2002

16. Roger W Ferguson - Vice Chairman of the Board of Governors of the US Federal Reserve System - March 2002

17. The Department of Homeland Security www.dhs.gov

18. UK Resilience - http://www.ukresilience.info/home.htm - 2005

19. www.cityoflondon.gov.uk

20. www.sec.gov

21. Setting a new standard for operational resilience - Marsh Topic letter - XV 2003

4

Culture, Strategy, Performance, Risk and Business Continuity

Objectives Of This Chapter

- Examine the impact of cultural differences in terms of external and internal influences

- Explore how risk management and business continuity management can be embedded as part of good management practice

- Consider the position of risk management and business continuity management in the strategic and operational planning processes

- Review the risk environment in the context of what is at risk and what impact discontinuity might have on an organisation and its vision, values, culture and risk tolerance

- Consider business continuity at all levels internal and external to the business environment and in the context of enterprise risk management and enterprise business continuity management

- Examine how the board is engaged and attention sustained through demonstrating how value can be added to the organisation

Culture - Setting The Cultural Tone - The External Factor

Whilst it is the role of managers to carry through the strategy of an organisation and live the values and vision, it is the Board, the chairman of the Board and the Chief Executive Officer who lead the vision, the values, ethical positioning and overall culture of an organisation.

But the Board and Chief Executive are not the only drivers of culture. There are clear variations across industries and territories due to degrees of difference in industry, legal, regulatory, economic and social "DNA", and although these differences are eroding globally partly driven by convergence, they still play an important factor. The attitude towards the future and the response to future events varies across regions and countries and these differences will impact on the thinking and approach to the development and application of resilience and business continuity.

In late 2003, JR Consulting Partners (JRCPL), a Business Continuity and Operational Risk Consultancy, launched a survey through Intelligence On Line Survey Solutions (INONI) called "Attitudes to Risk" (1) in partnership with Continuity Central (www.continuitycentral.com). The survey set out to investigate the attitudes to risk and continuity that exist within and across organisations.

Conclusions were based on three indicators of *appetite, awareness* and *ownership*, and included significant regional variations:

- Eastern Europe exhibited a significantly high awareness but significantly low appetite and ownership of risk

- North America exhibited slightly above the norm appetite and awareness and below the norm ownership

- Western Europe exhibited slightly above the norm appetite, above the norm ownership but below the norm awareness

- Southeast Asia exhibited below the norm appetite, slightly below the norm ownership and slightly above the norm awareness

Results lead to a conclusion that a slightly above the norm risk appetite differentiates western and other economies. "This may be a function of competitive or economic maturity where a balance has evolved in favour of acceptable operational risk-taking to maximise profit or value." North America's risk ownership below the norm possibly reflects historical reliance on IT disaster recovery, but more likely illustrates the realised need for increased adoption of risk management by people in the wake of 9/11. "The outcome suggests a possible lifecycle effect as regions' attitudes to operational risk are borne of economic opportunity and then mature over decades or even centuries. This slow pace may disadvantage economies unless organisations intervene and kick-start risk culture."

What practical advice might an organisation take from this research?

- Those operating or planning to operate in regions where attitudes are at odds with traditional markets should be mindful of local risk cultural factors making risk behavioural training and alignment a strong priority

- Developing economies might accelerate their development by devolving their perceived need for awareness, reactivity and defensiveness to trained individuals

- Embed the view that however well-prepared or bulletproof an organisation might feel, normality will be disturbed by a severe event

---

Operations Away From "Home"

There is a view emerging that doing business offshore (away from the country of domicile) in unfamiliar territories with different risk profiles, results in a perceived loss of management control on the part of the outsourcing organisation. While some outsourcing providers dismiss these concerns, perhaps the sensitivities of organisations should be more sympathetically appreciated by suppliers where either key or high quantity processes are outsourced. If the supplier or the supplier's environment fails then how does the business recover a process for which it no longer has the capability or capacity in-house? There are often solutions available, but these may not be mature in their development nor within an organisation's current business continuity management tool kit.

Whatever the reasons for heightened concern and reaction, the regulatory experience and inspection of this type of facility are at an early stage, but indications are that they are in for a pleasant surprise. The risk assessment and business impact analysis processes have been consistently and thoroughly undertaken in these emerging environments.

Taking a converse view, some suppliers are growing in experience and capability using high-calibre employees working in purpose-built facilities with resilience frequently engineered to demanding standards independent of and mindful of potential disruption of local resources. For example, dual, uninterrupted power supplies and high quality generator backup capability are more often the norm than the exception. In some environments and countries, business continuity management is consequently overachieving and it could only be a question of time until this over-achievement is positively marketed as a business benefit for outsourcing and as a competitive edge.

There is no doubt that simply imposing business continuity management standards drafted elsewhere, taking into account external factors suited to another environment be that political, social or economic, is a high-risk strategy. It is essential that organisations continue to practice the basic principles of risk and business continuity management within the context of each environment within which their activities are transacted - by themselves or others. "Attitudes may be incompatible potentially resulting in misinterpretation of standards and increased exposure." **(1)**.

One of the most comprehensive recent reports concerning "off-shoring" was produced by the UK Financial Services Authority **(2)**. This report concluded that the main risk was the complexity of achieving suitable management oversight and control from a distance.

Culture And The Governance Framework

A cultural barometer of an organisation is the annual report or equivalent. The quality of disclosure this achieves, and what the board members say and the way in which they say it, is an essential source of information when setting out to assess or determine risk and business continuity management strategy. In addition to the transparency of an organisation the report can provide clues as to the tolerance and opinion on risk within an organisation and the statement on risk management activity; if it exists, it will provide valuable insights. If a view on risk or business continuity management is not in evidence this may be an indicator of ignorance, disinterest or absence of a view that these are important or value-adding activities in the eyes of senior management.

Getting the subject of risk and business continuity management onto a boardroom table where there is no appetite for the subject requires a very different approach from one where the need is understood and maturity of management is at a different stage.

Consequently, a thorough understanding of the values and behavioural expectations of an organisation and the external cultural context should be a priority for risk and business continuity managers. These will provide essential research on how they best approach the successful design and implementation of the risk management framework and as part of this, the strategy and delivery of business continuity management.

Within the management matrix the cultural perspective will be shaped by the political and economic state of a region, nation and even territory within a region. The ability or freedom to act or pay will influence the perception of risk: if a country is fighting for political or economic freedom this will dramatically influence and shape the risk profile. This may lead to a dilemma for organisations operating in extreme environments in this respect, as their vision and values as well as governance and risk framework will be shaped by a very different operational environment.

These dynamics must be understood and risk and business continuity management strategies adjusted appropriately. For example, highly structured but decentralised business continuity plans which are acceptable in one environment may or may not work in another with a greater degree of centralisation.

Culture should never be underestimated in terms of the influence it can bring to bear on an organisation in the context of the risk environment. This book does not attempt to provide an academic examination of cultural drivers and behaviour, but it is essential that cultural drivers and the effect of these within organisations are understood. These will influence the "DNA" of an organisation and what makes it tick, how it responds to risk, and how it will react when something happens that is not to plan.

A positive culture and a "can-do" attitude to making change work in an organisation can provide that extra factor that distinguishes the average from the exceptional. However, an organisation with a degree of self-belief that exceeds its capability to deliver can have a highly negative impact on the overall risk profile.

This negativity may result because of the nature of the business an organisation is in or the stage of development of the industrial sector. For example, in the initial phases of the "dot-com" explosion in the nineties, organisations that did not take a high-risk view of the risk/reward ratio probably would not have made the cut and survived. Similarly, in mature sectors where stability and a long-term view are key, an excessively high ratio is something shareholders will not tolerate. In publicly listed companies, the risk factor that shareholders are prepared to withstand will impact on the expectations of the share price and dividend returns: mature but safe stocks will suit the institutional investor and in turn one might expect the attitude to risk in such organisations is relatively conservative.

CASE STUDY

External circumstances may also impact on organisational culture and attitude to risk. An interesting case study in this respect dates back to the US space programme of the 1970s. The US was living through turbulent times of social change and racial conflict, including the impact of the assassination of President John F. Kennedy, Dr. Martin Luther King and Senator Robert F. Kennedy, coupled with the pressures of anti-Vietnam protests and movements supporting rights for women and ethic minorities.

This case study draws upon the book written by Diane Vaughan in 1996 **(11)**.

Against this background, the NASA programme became something of a national icon. It provided a symbol for optimism, an example of cutting-edge technology, adventurism and a vehicle for American pride and for international power in times of domestic turmoil. More myth than an actual example of success, opposition to the programme mounted during the 1980s. Spending money on space travel and building space stations started to look inappropriate in times of unrest, homelessness, escalating use of drugs and associated crime. The excitement of the heady days of the 1970s started to wane.

The arrival of the space shuttle reduced the idea of space travel to the point where ordinary US workers no longer left their desks to watch the latest launch. To provide the average American with a point of relativity with the missions, the "everyday" nature of each mission was tinged with excitement that was carried into homes by profiles of the astronauts and especially those that came from ordinary jobs that all could identify with.

This was especially true of Christa McAuliffe, a teacher, and a symbol of safeness, an example of the educational benefit of the programme (at a time when education budgets were being

---

slashed elsewhere) and of American life: the American public were given an insight into her family, their names and their everyday routine. On January 28, 1986, when disaster struck and the Challenger mission failed with the shuttle plunging to earth with all on board lost, many Americans felt personally touched and closely identified with the anguish of the families they had come to know.

To the credit of the investigating bodies, all recognised that the loss of Challenger was not one purely of technological failure. The NASA organisation was implicated. Initially the investigation focussed on facts that led to a conclusion that had middle management behaved differently then the disaster could have been averted. But this conclusion masked the facts:

- The powerful NASA hierarchy that took design and operational decisions facing commercial pressures imposed on them by the Government were distanced from the day-to-day risk assessors

- Faced with threats to their power base and institution, the NASA hierarchy altered the organisation's goals, structure and culture. This had huge repercussions and altered the consciousness and actions of the decision makers. It suited NASA to promote the routine nature of space travel at the expense of a level of attention to risk detail more suited to each mission - and encouraged the inclusion of non-astronauts in questionable circumstances

- Focus on management decisions took the spotlight away from the difficulty that the changed cultural environment at NASA had put on the technicians and the environment within which they had to operate: launch decisions became detached from technical decisions.

"The Challenger disaster was an accident, the result of a mistake. What is important to remember from this case is not that individuals in organisations make mistakes, but that mistakes themselves are socially organised and systematically produced." (11).

The managers and engineers knew that every flight was risky but they did not put Christa McAulife on the shuttle. They worked in a system that cut resources and reacted to political pressure to speed up the number of flights. And in such a complicated situation as the space initiative it is almost impossible to trace mistakes and ensure that further disasters do not occur. In such complex situation rules cannot be designed to address all technological and organisational situations.

Seventeen Years on Columbia

Foam which had dislodged and damaged a wing when the shuttle mission Columbia took off had not been considered a material incident. Yet this damage provided the hole through which superheated plasma subsequently entered the shuttle's structure and melted the wing, leading to disaster as the crew started their re-entry into the Earth's atmosphere.

Like the Challenger explosion, the Columbia disaster in an instant transformed the perception of the space mission. Instead of enjoying the reputation of an organisation which left the glow of man's ability to rise above his home on Earth, NASA adopted the guise of an organisation which had become complacent about risks.

Following the Columbia tragedy, NASA strived to do three things:

- Find out why Columbia had exploded

- Change its design so nothing similar could happen again

- Launch another shuttle to prove that the fundamental task of getting man into space and back safely could be achieved

---

Discovery - Before takeoff 2005

Prior to the launch of the Discovery mission in 2005, NASA stated it was confident that it understood how the Columbia disaster had occurred and that it could prevent a future, similar incident. "There is no magic spaceship that is 100% safe" said a NASA representative, "but NASA has decided that we understand the risks and that we are prepared to fly again."

The seven astronauts who flew in the successful Discovery mission knew that NASA has failed in three of its goals: to ensure no ice or foam would come loose from the fuel tank; make sure it anything did hit the shuttle that it would not cause damage; and if there were damage, find ways to repair it before the shuttle returned to Earth.

 The shuttle took off in the knowledge that these goals could not be met completely. Events proved that similar incidents might occur but on this occasion the shuttle and its crew returned safely - albeit following improvised in-space repairs executed during man's first space walk beneath the shuttle.

Postscript

Had the NASA culture changed during those nineteen years? Certainly, NASA is now upfront in stating that every mission carries risk. NASA accepts that Columbia disaster was caused by "a sequence of incorrect decision-making." It seems unlikely that such up-front comments might have been spoken back in 1986.

The power of culture should not be underestimated. NASA, confronted with clear warnings about shuttle technology, proceeded as if nothing was wrong when repeatedly faced with evidence that something was. The Columbia disaster was not purely a technological problem but rather a symptom of NASA's style of decision-making.

Strategic Management - Vision, Values And Setting The Scene

A few simple questions can help set the context for what constitutes strategic success:

- Why would any investor want to buy your stock? For example, what is the market perception of profitability levels, future prospects, confidence in product or service delivery and brand distinction and value?

- If an organisation has faced internal and external changes and events how has it fared? For example, what was the immediate and longer-term impact on stock value - did it quickly recover and prosper or stutter and look dull? An organisation prepared to respond to the unforeseen will have the corporate halo where it belongs - above the head and not around the neck.

If stock predictions are positive and the reputation "halo" (3) is in place, it is probable that strategic realisation will have occurred and/or expectations exceeded.

**An Organisation's Strategy Should Interlock All Aspects Of
An Organisation's Activities Including:**

- Objective setting

- Environmental scanning of external factors, economic, political and social

- A market position audit

- Overall strategic direction

- Choice of growth mode

- Competitive strategy

- Organisational structure

- People reward system

- Risk and control environment

Strategic Management: Good Management Or Pure Speculation?

While there are a number of ways in which an organisation can pull together these components into a strategy-building action plan, essentially there are three steps: analysis, development and implementation. Various arguments exist as to whether this is a linear process or whether these components all occur simultaneously, and whether these steps which imply a top-down, "baton-passing" approach are really how well-run organisations work in today's increasingly fast moving and complex environment.

Organisations may also approach strategic management from a market or a resource perspective: building strategic plans around perceived market segments and opportunities or around the resources an organisation already has in place.

An organisation may plan in a structured way or by experimentation and may be market or resource-led. The risk and business continuity managers must gain an understanding of how this works in their organisation to have a realistic opportunity of embedding risk and continuity processes within the overall planning and management processes. Even the smallest organisation will have surprising complexities when the layers are peeled away and in a larger organisation, even a minor internal decision or external change can have a significant destabilising effect and impact on the overall risk profile. Predicting the effect of decisions and change on short-term plans is well established risk management practice - but as one progresses further into the future, reliable outputs from modelling and scenario management become increasingly more difficult to achieve with any degree of reliability.

The tool kit for longer-term risk management has to accept that risk is difficult to predict. Risk is dynamic and we have already explored how the risks at the top of the risk manager's list of concerns have changed dramatically over the last ten and even five years. One of the strongest emerging areas of concern is the rising complexity of interdependencies. The smallest component or supplier can have the most profound impact on the product of greatest significance.

Risk severity can change rapidly and what was once an inconsequential risk buried at the base of an organisation's risk profile can rise through the ranks and outplay those risks at the top. And crucially for the mathematician, risk is nonlinear - the positive outcome predicted by "back-office academics" can suddenly transform into a negativity of devastating consequences. Once again this raises serious question marks against the "tick-box" approach to managing risk and the potential effect of insufficient intellectual consideration and investment into working out what sits inside the boxes.

If The Future Is So Hard To Predict Why Bother With Strategic Management?

If considered in the proper place as part of the management toolkit it has value - but it is not an end to itself. Good strategic management is about fuelling debate with high quality information. Modelling scenarios from different what-if situations and putting these on the board table can stimulate cross-organisational silos to co-function where frequently one will otherwise find different positions and solutions on risk. There is no "right" answer when looking three or five years into the future, but the better the debate and the better the challenge is that the understanding of the range of expected outcomes will improve, and with that the quality of decision taking.

And where does business continuity management fit into this picture? "Ultimately, modelling is one component of a risk management strategy - one that can provide early warning of hidden disastrous events." **(4)**. The better the level of knowledge about what might happen in an organisation, the better the understanding of the potential impact on the business, the better the design of resilience and the better the ability to create business continuity plans which will prove effective should the prediction prove right and the in-built resilience and other controls fail.

A survey undertaken by IBM and the Institute of Financial Services in the UK **(5)** examined the ability of the financial services sector to create and sustain operational resilience strategies and programmes.

The survey concluded that while the events of September 11, 2001 and regulatory pressures have been important drivers for change, many organisations reported that they are growing in their recognition of the importance of improving their operational governance and infrastructure environments as part of their drive to improve the consistency of the return that they deliver to shareholders through the realisation of their strategic and operational plans. "83% of the industry believed that improved operational resilience would be taken into account when assessing the value of their company." **(6)**.

Operational Resilience - a definition: "An organisation's ability to reduce and prevent any disruptions to its service and its corporate governance structure. It is made up of a number of functions and activities that together will help a company operate a consistent and secure service and prepare for both expected and unexpected change in its operating environment and business activities."

IBM and ifs (the Institute of Financial Services) joint research programme into the ability of the financial services sector to create and sustain operational resilience strategies and programmes (6)

A model offered by IBM to support the survey suggested that five activities, not always typically linked in organisations, should be positioned together:

1. Risk supervision and control;

2. Monitoring and surveillance;

3. Development of efficient and integrated business processes;

4. Building reliable, resilient IT infrastructures; and,

5. Protection and contingency.

Traditionally, the domains of risk, compliance, IT and business continuity management functions, the convergence of business need must inevitably drive a convergence either through a tighter managerial matrix or operating environment of these managerial silos.

Measurement and control must work together to mitigate risk; this is evidence of an increase of these responsibilities coming together under the umbrella of a Chief Operating or Risk Officer - taking these issues directly onto the Boardroom table. However, warnings raised in the earlier chapters of this book should be heeded in that these management processes must operate to serve and support an organisation, and avoid becoming a remote academic exercise out of touch with the business.

The Strategic Business Continuity Management Process

If the goal for businesses is to achieve end-to-end service availability, then strategic and operational planning and management processes must consequently identify what might threaten the delivery of the desired results. The criticality of business functions and records should be defined and priorities established so that strategies may take account of them. As part of this process the interdependency of key business functions and systems should be mapped and regularly reviewed - a crisis in one area may have a knock-on effect in others. This mapping process should include critical projects and the interdependencies between project deliverables and business unit plans. "This overall approach to constructing a strategy will provide the business continuity team with a sound picture of the organisation's critical and non-critical processes and enable them to prioritise critical activities and situations in any business continuity strategy." **(7)**.

Risk and business continuity management must consequently form an integral part of the strategic planning design and management processes. In many organisations, business continuity management starts at the wrong stage of the organisational "food chain." So often an afterthought to strategic and operational planning processes, project management and organisational change, business continuity management should, ideally, be an integrated part of all management practices.

Risk assessment should address the robustness of strategic plans and the confidence of the author of the plans in their ability to deliver the targets. If possible, such assessment should be aligned with risk assessment processes which otherwise already exist to avoid duplication, overlap and contradictory outputs. This will ensure that the process is truly embedded, not only within the management process but the intellectual consideration and boardroom and business debate and mutually reinforcing any "bottom-up" risk assessment processes performed at the business unit level.

Organisations vary in the level of integration and prescription offered for the risk element of the strategic planning process, but the essential component is that the risks should be documented and the Chief Executive or equivalent sign off the assessment profile noting the top ten or twenty risks as part of good corporate and risk governance. But the process does *not* stop there.

In addition to a description of the risk itself, a brief narrative on the effect the risk will have on any of the plan's goals, should it occur, should be provided. If a number of goals were to be affected, the impact against each should be noted. Importantly, and to ensure that the assessment is not merely an observation of an organisation's risk profile, a note of the risk controls either currently in place or which could reasonably be expected to be put in place, to minimise either the impact and/or the probability of the risk occurring, should be included.

Business continuity management plays a pivotal role in the overall control environment and should be in touch with the concept of enterprise business continuity management. The impact of these risks on the business should be assessed and suitable resilience considered and business recovery plans positioned. The management of strategic planning is in this sense no different to any other form of planning - other than, in this case, the future of the organisation and the realisation of its long-term vision and short-term future are at risk.

As we move deeper into the era of knowledge value and intangibles, conventional balance sheets and profit–and-loss statements, however, capture and reflect less and less of an organisation's true value and competitive potential. What is needed now is a new and more dynamic "iceberg balance sheet" approach, which focuses senior management attention on the 80 or 85% of an organisation's true value which cannot be explained by conventional accounting means. "It is the 'value iceberg' that contains the primary drivers of the company's future value-creation capabilities and unique comparative advantages." **(8)** By their nature of intangibility these factors are difficult to measure and to manage, but it is essential that the business continuity approach within an organisation embraces these within their scope, and that they receive an appropriate level of attention that the effect of failure may warrant.

The final stage in an assessment is for the management team to indicate their degree of confidence in the delivery of the plan, after taking account of the controls identified.

The management circle is almost complete. Once designed and signed off it is essential that the risk assessment is re-visited as part of the operational and risk management processes of the organisation; and that the assessment is not left on the shelf gathering dust, only to be taken down when the next strategic planning cycle kicks in.

Business Continuity Management - Opportunity Or Threat?

Practiced well, risk and business continuity management can add value to the running of an organisation. There is little doubt that, if focussed, properly resourced, funded and executed, risk management and business continuity management can enhance shareholder and stakeholder value through improved efficiency and competitiveness. Let's examine this close-up. The right starting position is to consider risk and business continuity management as part of good management - and not as management appendages that sit in silos managed outside of the business - as "somebody else's job."

When one examines risk and business continuity management lifecycles, they introduce into an organisation management techniques and disciplines that offer something beyond the traditional management defence mechanism frequently associated with business continuity. This results in a "product" - a plan. Approached from the top of an organisation as a Board-sponsored issue and from the front line of an organisation as an operational priority, and consequently an integrated management fashion, business continuity is a sophisticated management practice which starts with a requirement to understand an organisation, its operational environment and the potential impact of discontinuity in the context of an organisation's vision, values and strategies.

Measurement of business continuity performance success focussed purely on "after-the-event" economic loss of tangible, quantifiable assets post incident, rather than by use of metrics measuring the impact of pre-event avoidance, improved management performance or the overall resilience of an organisation, will provide inadequate indicators. Interest in business continuity management will become a feature of the "last big event" and consequently activity and budget become a variable element of the business, rather than a fixed investment.

While a Board may focus on the trading environment, product mix and delivery, research, market position and people and the business plan to deliver strategic and operation objectives, risk has a companion list of issues that ask questions, such as:

- "What are the competitive threats that we might be facing?
- What are the risks of the financial environment?
- What errors or omissions might cause damage to the organisation?

- What is the legal environment?

- Have we addressed regulatory and compliance issues sufficiently?" **(9)**.

What is clear is that the objectives of the Board, risk management and business continuity management are in harmony.

Business Continuity And Risk Management: Taking The Lead?

Most of the current debate centres on whether business continuity management is a subset of risk management. And while this book promotes this general view, business continuity management can act as the launch pad for risk management into the business.

Organisations can easily identify with failures in resilience although "... this assumes however that the firm has taken its BCP function seriously and elevated it to an appropriate senior and strategic level in business line and the corporate centre." **(10)** There are increasingly recognised synergies between risk and business continuity practices and processes, but whatever the approach taken, ownership for delivery of both rests firmly with the business.

For the sake of clarity and avoidance of overlap, increasingly risk and business continuity management work at least in parallel and, more often these days, in partnership. As organisations look to enterprise risk solutions, driven by similar risk profiles, enterprise business continuity must also be approached at all levels and across all risks in an organisation.

Performance Management - People And Performance At The Centre Of Business Success

Having addressed the top-down processes of management at the strategic level, let us now turn our focus to issues at the interface of the business with its operational stakeholders, and home in on the interplay of customers, finance, processes and people as key players in the continuity game.

If it is an accepted starting point that strategic management and planning provide an overall vision, direction and control, then performance management is one of the keys way of ensuring that the performance of the organisation is delivered aligned to business objectives. Performance management provides the means through which every individual within an organisation knows how they are engaged, what is expected from them and how well they are doing.

People success is equivalent to business success and most commentators today accept that people have a direct impact on the overall performance of an organisation. It is also a fact that organisations that "... use Performance Management Processes perform better financially than those that don't."

(12) Collectively the output from performance management provides the senior team within a critical feedback loop into the strategic and operational management processes and might be graphically expressed as the cycle below:

A report concluded **(13)** that staff commitment was highest when their work was:
- Focussed on set goals;

- High in volume;

- Against specific deadlines; and,

- Part of a smooth working routine.

Ideally, risk management should be viewed as a core management competence rather than as a separate process. Business continuity management should be considered a specialised capability within the risk arena. "Concern for risk, resilience and recovery" which, while qualitative, can be supplemented by quantitative targets developed along the lines of various Total Quality Management models, such as how targets affect people, processes, financials and customers.

In addition to targeting and rating performance, a core competency on "concern for risk and control" could be developed and embedded within formal job profiles. There are examples of "High Reliability Organisations" (HROs) such as power and utility companies; the military, where concern for safety is a core competency; and pharmaceuticals, where product problems, related errors ands losses have "zero-tolerance" ratings - and it seems to work.

There are few accidents and losses in such organisations due to their robust approach to safety and product-related processes, coming from the top where they are culturally embedded and given constant attention - "It's the way we do things here."

The issue, however, remains one of balance. If safety or product integrity is core to an organisation's vision and values, then the risk/reward equation must reflect that fact.

CASE STUDY

A major financial services organisation embraced risk-related targets as part of a SMART (Specific, Measurable, Achievable, Relevant, Time-bound) objectives:

"Develop a culture of greater governance, controllership, risk management and compliance and embed processes across the business. People will see greater management attention being focussed on these areas, there will be higher levels of visibility around issues and clear action plans to close gaps. Overall, the result will be fewer surprises and more positive regulatory approval rating."

This objective was accepted by the Chief Executive Officer and cascaded throughout the entire organisation. The collective effect was profound and probably achieved the highest level of focus on risk and control achieved. Given the organisation operated in a performance-related environment, risk and control became an integral part of the ongoing performance management process.

The key to the successful integration of competencies and risk-related objectives into performance management is to have "concern for risk and control" as competencies appropriate to the organisation. Targets should be set accordingly and evaluated at each appraisal, with a goal of having a measurable effect on reducing the number of surprises an organisation has to face.

This in turn could lead to quantifiable success seen to be adding real value to the organisation, leading to the embedding of a risk management culture, behaviour, framework, and associated core values throughout the organisation.

So, how can an organisation develop competency in the workforce for risk management? The first step is to define what is needed. Is risk management already one of the organisation's core corporate values? Is it a requirement of employee behaviour?

When reviewing core competencies the headings that appear for risk and business continuity management should adopt those more generally used throughout most businesses: strategic thinking; problem solving; relationship management and teambuilding. This will engender recognition that these are not different - but rather part of good management practice and behaviour.

CASE STUDY	
Business Continuity Management Performance Objectives can be designed at all levels:	
CONCERN FOR RISK AND CONTROL	**PERFORMANCE MEASURES**
CHIEF EXECUTIVE OFFICER	
Demonstrates leadership to the development of business continuity management as part of the overall risk framework	• Governance sign-off • Regulator risk rating • Internal compliance mechanism - i.e., emailbased voting complience system: functional/territorial score
MANAGER	
Demonstrates a strong awareness of business continuity management as part of the overall risk framework; identifies and communicates added value to the business. Establishes monitoring and challenge systems to ensure adherence to internal policies and regulations. Creates and actively promotes high standards of business continuity management to all key stakeholders	• Top-down risks identified and relevant controls in place • Internal audit report • Internal compliance mechanism - i.e. email based voting compliance system: functional/territorial score
TEAM LEADER	
Demonstrates a strong awareness of business continuity management as part of the overall risk framework; identifies and communicates added value to the business. Enforces codes of practice/rules with all employees, regardless of level. Complies with, and ensures that others comply with policies and practices. Takes personal responsibility for self and others.	• Employee awareness survey scores • Performance levels of plans used in anger • Internal compliance mechanism - i.e. email based voting compliance system: team score • Relevant targets set in performance appraisal at all levels

EMPLOYEE	
Demonstrates a strong awareness of business continuity management as part of the overall risk framework; identifies and communicates added value to the business. Takes personal responsibility. Recognises potential risks and takes action to report, eliminate or reduce them. Knows and adheres to relevant policies and practices.	• Relevant targets set in performance appraisal at all levels • Relevant performance target • Bottom-up risks identified and relevant controls in place • Internal compliance mechanism - i.e. email based voting compliance system: individual score
[ ] Always [ ] Mostly [ ] Sometimes [ ] Never	

In conclusion, a risk and business continuity management competency framework can be designed to align with the organisation's strategic goals without diminishing overarching objectives. On the contrary, it can also support those objectives - minimising risk and maximising success. Organisations are now under constant scrutiny by stakeholders; looking to see how they manage themselves and putting risk at the heart of a skilled workforce clearly shows good corporate governance. Today the risk management brief is widening to include corporate social responsibility, conduct, ethics, operational risk, reputation, regulation and compliance like never before. With a core competency evaluation of concern for risk, such things can be dealt with from the outset and be dealt with in the normal course of a business, rather than being major shifts in how it operates. The Human Resource function is an ally and there is an opportunity to be seized.

Getting Started - Persuading the Board and Your People

The first step is to understand what drives risk management within the organisation. Is the organisation:

- Committed to removing risk - with a zero or near-zero tolerance to risk?

- Financially-driven - committed to risk reduction or transfer?

- An entrepreneurial risk-taker - with "come back" plans?

- Facing risk head-on - as a competitive advantage?

- Fast moving and changing - risk is perceived as a barrier and might get in the way?

- Risk ignorant – "nothing ever goes wrong here" - "what risk?"

- Once the attitude to risk is understood, what risk strategy is adopted?

- Risk acceptance - change nothing

- Risk acceptance with backup arrangements - either with another in-house site, competitor, ally or third-party supplier

- Risk reduction - take measures to remove or reduce risk: perhaps through an exit strategy

- Reduce risk impact - a thorough business impact analysis will serve to identify and facilitate the improved resilience of key processes and dependencies

- Risk reduction and transfer - a combination of the above

- Reduce all risks to a level where the need for external assistance can be avoided

"Risk is an inevitable part of business, but not enough companies treat risk management as a strategic problem. The result is an increased cost to business from risk, an increased aversion to risk at every level, and an increasing number of nasty surprises. Reconciling the need for taking risk with the need for accountability is the first step to solving the problem." **(14)** The vision, values and culture of an organisation and the aggregation of the perspective of the functional departments from which it is comprised, and the environment within which it operates, must all be influencers on the overall risk tolerance of the organisation and on the business continuity strategy adopted. As the vision in any organisation comes from senior management, then so should the sponsorship for the strategy for business continuity management. This will have an influence on the plans which may need to be drawn into action in the event of an incident - triggered through an internal or external events or series of events.

In the UK Financial Times, November 25, 2004, Charles Tilley, the Chief Executive of the Chartered Institute of Management Accountants (CIMA) commented that CIMA has undertaken research with the International Federation of Accountants (IFAC) to develop a framework for "enterprise governance." This emphasises the importance of keeping corporate governance and business performance in balance. "At the heart of enterprise governance is the argument that good corporate governance can help to prevent failure; but on its own, cannot ensure success." **(15)** CIMA is in the process of developing a strategic scorecard. This will be designed to help boards challenge and test a company's strategic position and progress. The expectation is that the scorecard will help ensure that the board agenda is not crowded out by routine and compliance issues. Appropriate business continuity management - at all levels across a company to support resilience and recovery at an enterprise level - should be a key indicator on any boardroom scorecard.

Summary

The new Business Continuity Institute guidelines offer a view on "good," "best" and "excessive" practice and equates this in a cultural sense to "enthusiastic," "confident" and "blasé" - the choice of option being dependent on each organisation and its risk tolerance. "Each organisation needs to assess how to apply the guidelines to their own organisation. They must ensure that their BCM competence and capability is appropriate to the scale, nature and complexity of their business, and reflects individual culture and operating environment." **(16)**

Those who have been practising business continuity management for a number of years will have witnessed a maturing of their professional discipline. This has moved from that of a largely IT focus based on specific, one-off scenarios, to one demanding an intimate knowledge of an organisation, its vision, values, strategic direction and both internal and external operating environment. This has demanded a broadening in the business continuity manager's skills base, coupled with a growing expectation of the business continuity manager by senior management in the event of disruption. Not only must the business continuity plans of an organisation be maintained, developed and checked to meet the ever-changing complexities and needs of an organisation, but the competencies and performance of the business continuity manager must also keep up with the pace.

Bibliography

1 The INONI Report - Attitudes to Risk - Part Two - JR Consulting Partners – 2004, www.jrcpl.com and www.jrcpl.com/INONI

2. Financial Services Authority (FSA) Offshore Operations - Industry Feedback - April 2005, www.fsa.gov.uk

3. Atkins and Bates - 2005

4. Project Risk Management - Chris Chapman and Stephen Ward - 2003

5. IBM and ifs joint research programme into the ability of the financial services sector to create and sustain operational resilience strategies and programmes - May 2002

6. Operational Resilience - The Art of Risk Management - IBM/Financial World Publishing (the Chartered Institute of Bankers) - 2002

7. Governance and Risk - George Dallas, Managing Director, Standard & Poor's - 2004

8. Operational Resilience - The Art of Risk Management - IBM/Financial World Publishing (the Chartered Institute of Bankers) - 2002

9. Governance and Risk - George Dallas, Managing Director, Standard & Poor's - 2004

10. Managing Operational Risk - Douglas G Hoffman - 2002

11. The Challenger Launch Decision - Diane Vaughan - 1996

12. Who's the Manager? F Patten - report by Lathan & Locke - 1981

13 McDonald, Donohue, Shield and Smith - 1996

14 INFORM - Article by David Herratt - Risk Management, Lloyds - 2005

15 Financial Times, Charles Tilley, the Chief Executive of the Chartered Institute of Management Accountants (CIMA) - 2004

16 Business Continuity Institute - Good Practice Guidelines – 2005, www.thebci.org

5

Getting Started:
The Business Continuity
Management Cycle

Objectives Of This Chapter

- Consider how to engage the Board in appreciating the need for business continuity management

- Discuss the communication and embedding of business continuity management throughout an organisation

- Recognise the wide range of the stakeholders in the organisation; understand their importance, their roles, their needs and engagement

- Introduce the Business Continuity Management Cycle.

- Compare and contrast the Business Continuity Cycle to the Risk Management Cycle

Engaging The Board - Business Continuity Management As A Sustainable Investment

Many organisations make an error in judgement when trying to engage their board. That error is to capture the board's attention by setting out details of the most recent incident to affect the organisation and to use this as the reason for seeking their support for business continuity management. While this is one useful tool in the business continuity manager's toolkit, this approach in isolation is unsustainable, and could backfire.

A board will respond to the messages of a case study in the short term, but as their interest and attention fades the subject matter will quickly move down the scale of priorities on the boardroom agenda as other projects take precedence.

Nevertheless, case studies do have a place. Carefully constructed and based on an organisation's own experiences, those of its competitors, other industries and territories, or based on recognisable scenarios and key risks, they can make good sense. Additionally. case studies based on the experience of organisations that the chief executive and the board admire - whatever the industry - are especially powerful.

Opportunities to present case studies in support of a business continuity management programme include:

- A continuity programme kick-off,

- A major in-house policy and practice overhaul

- Contract renewal of a third-party continuity support supplier

- Purchase or upgrade of planning software

- A major new business venture where business continuity management plays a key role, i.e., when undertaking a major outsourcing venture.

On such occasions, case studies provide a graphic hook for board attention and interest. Supporting pictures, video and potential financial impacts can be more powerful than a lengthy report, however well drafted. (Such a report will probably find its way to the bottom of board papers on an agenda likely to be crowded with everyday routine and regulatory issues).

Sustainable Board Level Buy-In

As with any critical business process, business continuity management (BCM) should be approached as an investment with the issue pitched at the right level, using recognisable language and established business practices - including a cost-benefit analysis.

The board's key purpose is "to ensure the company's prosperity by collectively directing the company's affairs, while meeting the appropriate interests of its shareholders and relevant stakeholders." (1) Ultimate responsibility for the management of risk lies with the Executive, but day-to-day responsibility for the management of risk rests with the management of each area of an organisation.

A certain level of risk will be inherent within any organisation's activities, and it is the ultimate responsibility of the Board to approve the level which is acceptable. The level of risk accepted constitutes an organisation's risk 'appetite' or tolerance. Therefore, within an organisation the board of directors or the equivalent is the principal agent of risk-taking and the principal maker of commercial and other judgements. Pitching continuity in this context should strike a chord.

---

(2) Research and compile facts showing possible risks to the enterprise:

- Audit reports

- Regulatory and legal environment

- Past disasters

- Best practices publications

- Relevant regulatory Industry trade bodies

- Consulting recommendations

The board must be entrepreneurial while exercising control; sufficiently knowledgeable of the business to take informed decisions yet able to stand back; sensitive to short-term issues but able to take a longer-term view; able in parallel to think local and global; and be commercially focussed yet with responsibility towards employees, business partners and society as a whole. There are fundamental differences between a director and a manager and it is essential for the business continuity manager to understand and appreciate this when making the case for board support for business continuity management across an organisation.

"Early identification of clearly defined roles, responsibilities and authorities to manage the BCM programme and process throughout the organisation are key to success." **(3)**

The Institute of Directors in the UK summarises the key tasks of good board practice as:

- Establish vision, mission and values

- Set strategy and structure

- Delegate to management

- Exercise accountability to shareholders and be responsible to relevant stakeholders

The IoD Fact Sheet - 2004 **(4)**

Without repeating the ground already covered in Chapters Two and Three, good governance involves a set of relationships "… between a company's management, its board, its shareholders and other stakeholders. It also provides the structure through which the objectives of the company are set, and the means for attaining these objectives and how monitoring performance is determined." **(4)**

	Directors	Managers
Decision-making	Determine the future of an organisation and protect its assets and reputation	Implement the decisions and policies made by the board
Duties and responsibilities	Ultimate responsibility for the long-term prosperity of the company	Far fewer legal responsibilities
Relationship with	Accountable to the shareholders	Appointed and dismissed by directors and managers
Leadership	Provide intrinsic leadership and direction	Carry through strategy on behalf of the board
Ethics and values	Key role in determining values and ethical position	Must enact the ethos
Company administration	Directors are responsible	Can receive delegation to act but authority remains with the board
Statutory provisions	Face personal liability, criminal prosecution, disqualification and penalties if a company fails to comply with statutory provisions.	Many if these provisions do not affect managers

The IoD Fact Sheet - 2004

Taking The First Step - Understanding The Organisation's Environment

In most jurisdictions, regulators cite good governance behaviour as an illustration of good regulatory behaviour and as such should be a regulatory "given." While regulators will sharpen their focus on certain aspects of governance within their own business principles, these will generally be driven by their delegated responsibilities and the nature of the industry under regulation.

There are recognised differences in governance environments across the world **(5)**:

- Anglo-American:

    - Ability of dispersed shareholders to control management

    - 'Short-termism' stemming from continuous capital scrutiny

    - Weak internal controls and risk management

- Continental Europe/Developed Asia:

    - Less active market for corporate control

    - Influence of external stakeholders

- Emerging Markets (e.g., Emerging Asia, Latin America, Middle East and Africa):

    - Entrenchment of family members in management and board

- Transition Economies (e.g., Former Soviet block, other countries of Central Europe and CIS): structures:

    - Limited market for corporate control

    - Lack of effectiveness, definition and ownership rights

    - Influences of the state that detract from shareholder value

    - Weak internal controls

While all governance environments have their strengths and weaknesses there are two common themes: lack of board effectiveness and weakness of directors is a "red line" running through all country groupings, and no one system is without its flaws. And yet the Anglo-American environments which have the more mature governance environments have experienced some of the largest and highest profile governance failures. Governance 'complacency' is on the wane.

The Business Analysis Checklist

The business continuity manager has some key questions to pose before approaching the board table, which might include:

- What is the business of this organisation?

- What are its vision, mission, values and strategic aims?

- What is its geographic territory?

- Is the organisation a corporation wholly owned by shareholders, with subsidiaries and/or associated businesses, a series of franchises, a partnership, a private entity, a public entity, a not-for-profit organisation, etc.?

- Is management distributed or centralised?

- What are the legal, regulatory, political, economic and social external environments?

- Is there a governance framework in place? If so what is the attitude to risk and the tolerance towards risk and control, and the high-level risk profile?

- What is the risk management structure within the organisation - who are the key players, who do they report to and where are they based?

- What already exists in the form of business continuity management and what experience does the organisation have of using plans "in anger?"

- What are the time imperatives on the delivery of the products or services? (Which is specific to analyze for business continuity purposes).

- Who sits on the board and what is their background?

- Who might act as sponsor of business continuity management at the board table?

Equipped with answers to questions like these, the business continuity manager will be well positioned to consider the design and development of an approach for a business continuity framework. The policy, processes and practices which make up this framework, will also more likely meet the scale, nature, complexity and priorities of the organisation and achieve board support (coupled with that of other relevant stakeholders).

Answers to these questions will also provide the business continuity manager with good material for the development of relevant case studies to use in support of the overall continuity management strategy. For example, case studies that reflect the wider experiences of the non-executive board directors will strike a chord, as may those concerning immediate competitors. Risks which have been identified by the non-executive board members as key within their own organisation and industry (albeit they may not have been part of the organisation in question's direct experience), will provide recognisable scenarios. But while relevant case studies will prove powerful, visual and non-technical supporters to the reinforcement of the need for effective business continuity management, as previously challenged, they should not provide the primary driver in support of the chosen approach.

The Business Continuity Management Programme - The Boardroom Champion

Having taken that first step toward understanding the organisation along with its internal and external positions, the next step is to identify the relevant board-level champion. This will be the sponsor who will open the necessary doors into the board environment. The sponsor might be the immediate reporting line manager of the business continuity manager, or the end of the managerial "food chain" of the manager's department. Typical sponsors might include the Chief Risk Officer, Chief Financial Officer, Chief Operating Officer or the equivalent in larger organisations; or, the Principal, Managing Partner, Finance Director or Chief Executive in smaller concerns and partnerships. What must be made clear is that the role of the sponsor and his or her sponsorship does not stop at the design stage or the board table. "They need to be a champion on BCM from your planning work through to making sure that everyone in your organisation adopts the results as normal business practice." **(6)**

NFPA 1600: Standard on Disaster/Emergency Management and Business Continuity Programs - 2004 Edition: Extract from Chapter Four - Program Management (7)

Programme Coordinator:

- The programme coordinator shall be appointed by the entity and authorised to administer and keep current the programme.

Advisory Committee:

- An advisory committee shall be established by the entity in accordance with its policy

- The advisory committee shall provide input to or assist in the coordination of the preparation, implementation

- The committee shall include the programme coordinator and others who have the appropriate expertise and knowledge of the entity and the capability to identify resources from all key functional areas within the entity and shall solicit applicable external representation.

Increasingly as we see a general convergence between risk-related responsibilities, and the functions that deliver these across organisations, the sponsor may be the same individual as that for the sponsorship of risk management. This might either form a decision taken outside the business continuity manager's immediate area of control, or form an objective for the manager should they have the opportunity to exercise influence in this regard.

Whoever the sponsor is, if he or she already possesses the knowledge to effectively perform the role of sponsor the individual will require an awareness of the subject to promote to the board in an informed manner, and to engage proactively with the business continuity manager in the design and development of the relevant strategy. Further, it may not always be possible for the business continuity manager to be present to support the sponsor at board and other relevant senior management meetings where high-level discussion will take place.

Consequently, one-to-one briefing and consultation with this individual will not only reinforce the role of the sponsors but work to ensure that they lead the issue in an informed manner. There is a wide variety of senior briefing programmes available that can offer educational support in this respect. As an alternative, one might identify a friendly third-party organisation with a mature approach to the subject that the director has regard for, and which can provide independent experience, support and mentoring.

Practical engagement in business continuity management will also draw a sponsor into the subject. If possible, the sponsor should form part of the most senior team within an organisation's business continuity management response and plan infrastructure. This will ensure that not only is the sponsor academically involved in the matter but also underpins their involvement through hands-on experience during scenario discussions, plan rehearsals and tests, should the need arise for escalation and invocation processes. But the objective remains one of not attempting to convert the sponsor into an expert on the subject but rather to offer practical engagement.

The Business Continuity Management Programme
The Way We Do Things Here

Whatever analysis is undertaken and the results this reveals, and whatever the stakeholders and the influence these bring to bear, business continuity management should be considered as an integral part of good management practice led by individuals with relevant competence. It is not an appendage undertaken by a disparate team detached from the business.

Successful business continuity management programmes not only accept this approach but widely broadcast it. One route to underwrite success is for the champion or sponsor to promote their commitment and their expectation of others in a high profile manner and to reward good corporate citizenship in this regard and penalise poor or below par behaviour.

CASE STUDY

"The BCM capability that we are developing will deliver the above purpose, will reflect the nature, scale, complexity and geography or our organisation and be aligned to Industry 'Good Practice.' The BC Programme that Aon Ltd is delivering also meets Aon Corp's stipulation that Business Continuity is mandatory for all Aon operations worldwide."

Aon - Business Continuity - Getting Started 2004 **(8)**

The Business Continuity Management Programme - Defining The Subject

While it might be technically correct and in line with good professional practice standards and guidelines, it will prove a futile exercise to design and implement a continuity strategy that is at odds with the internal and external organisational governance environments. While one can promote a cutting-edge industry position on the subject, if it is counter to the organisation's culture then the potential for success will be severely impaired.

The business continuity manager equipped with knowledge from asking the type of questions posed above should consider the scope of business continuity management and work out a definition that suits the organisation's needs, its stage of continuity development and capability.

Industry definitions of what constitutes business continuity management exist and provide an excellent starting point. Further, definitional guidelines offered up by sector regulators, for example, should also be considered and embraced where relevant.

The Business Continuity Institute (BCI) defines business continuity management as "... a holistic management process that identifies potential impacts that threaten an organisation and provides a framework for building resilience and the capability for an effective response that safeguards the interests of its key stakeholders, reputation, brand and value creating activities." However, the BCI promotes that "... every organisation is different; it is run in different ways, is sited in different locations and it changes over time. Therefore it is not possible to be prescriptive about the solutions that an organisation should adopt. The approach of these [Good Practice] guidelines is to outline a process and to suggest methods on the assumption that an appropriate solution will emerge if the correct process is followed." **(9)**

Before embarking and agreeing upon definitional language for an organisation the following considerations should be borne in mind:

- What benchmark might an organisation use to assess its performance?

- What legislative and regulatory consideration should be made?

- If wider infrastructures might be involved in escalation and recovery processes following a major event - for example the UK financial authorities linking to the HM Treasury - how might their use of language impact on the meaning of yours?

- External authorities use different acronyms and expressions; ensure that these are consistent with those used in an organisation.

- Emphasis on certain aspects of business continuity management should be considered. For example, if an organisation operates in a time-sensitive environment, greater emphasis may be placed on resilience.

- And if there is a significant dependency on third-party suppliers and outsource service providers, what definitional language is expected to be embedded within their approach to business continuity - and what are their expectations of your plans?

Therefore, while a high-level definition should be adopted at an enterprise level, the nature of the business and territorial mix of an organisation may justify a range of definitional language at a division, function and/or geographic level. Such variations must be clearly communicated, albeit that the fundamentals of business continuity management are recognised and mandated from the top as a requirement for all operations.

Finally, and as with any aspect of business continuity, definition and the nature of emphasis within this will develop over time, and no definition should be considered as an engraving in a tablet of stone never to be changed.

The Business Continuity Management Programme - Stakeholder Influence

An organisation's network of stakeholders will influence the approach to business continuity management, either indirectly through the influence of the stakeholders exerted on an organisation's risk profile, or directly through service level demands imposed on an organisation by contract.

The subject of stakeholder management has been addressed in greater length as part of Chapter Two.

The Business Continuity Management Programme - Policy And Framework

"The BCM Policy of an organisation provides the framework around which the BCM capability is designed and built. It is a documented statement by the organisation's executive of the level of importance that it places on BCM." **(10)**

Generally speaking, a policy statement should be viewed as a relatively static document providing the overall vision and approach to the subject. More frequently, variable material that includes guidelines and associated processes should be included in a supporting "internal standard" which underpins the policy and provides the means for turning high-level policy principles into operational practice.

But every organisation will probably have an approach to the creation and dissemination of policy. Before stepping into the process of policy development, business continuity managers should familiarise themselves with how this process operates generally within their organisation. There is a need for consistency in decision-making, standards, quality assurance, risk management and people management issues such as recruitment role profiles, education and training.

Going counter-culture or against established business practice could serve to undermine the effectiveness in getting the continuity message across - and leave important information gathering dust on a shelf rather than absorbed into everyday management processes and behaviour. While any organisation's business continuity policy statement should contain a skeleton of common headlines, the degree of detail and style will vary from one organisation to another. The methodology for development will be more consistent.

Consequently, the business continuity manager should scope the overall requirements for a policy statement and supporting guidelines as a practice framework. This can then be dissected into components influenced by the organisation's overall approach and language for crafting policy and practice as documented within the wider governance framework.

Policy components might typically include:

- Aims and Scope of Policy
- Definition and Approach
- Risk Appetite
- Management Framework
- Roles and Responsibilities
- Assessment, Reporting and Performance Processes
- Management commitment and currency

Policy - Aims And Scope

A policy statement provides an opportunity to promote consistency of practice to agreed standards across an organisation - including that which might relate to associated policy, e.g.,in the practice of risk management. Shared aims might be to create an environment where management can take informed decisions which maximise the risk-return ratio, commonly held principles and mechanisms which should be applied when setting risk tolerance or 'appetite' levels, or in the assessment and management of risk and the control environment.

In order to achieve these aims, the policy should cover the structures, roles and responsibilities for business continuity management, thereby documenting the process of delegation from the chairman through to the grass roots of the organisation.

Finally, the policy should include a statement to the commitment of consistency in practice and implementation expected - and how this will be reviewed, monitored, challenged and/or internally audited.

Policy - Definition And Approach

Whether an organisation adopts a definition with industry, professional institute (e.g., BCI or DRII), standards authorities (e.g., ISO) or regulatory roots; or, in a language of their own, there is no "right" answer. A clear definition of the subject matter of any policy statement will serve to avoid ambiguity and provide the business continuity manager with authority, clarity in scope and area of responsibility.

Definitions should include useful details of the approach to the subject. Is the organisation operating with a culture of risk taking or risk aversion? Is the management approach centralised or decentralised? Does the organisation address all types of risk and function - or only those of a business-critical nature? And finally, where does ultimate responsibility rest? Whose signature appears at the foot of the document and when did he or she sign off their commitment? Of course to this latter question, the answer is typically the CEO or equivalent.

Policy - Risk Appetite

A certain level of risk is inherent in any activity, but the business continuity manager and those who carry out the role of managing continuity need to understand what approach an organisation takes to risk. Risk tolerance or "appetite" levels will influence the perception of a board towards disruption and the controls cost/benefit equation. If a Board has a high risk tolerance level this will influence the level of loss the company is willing to bear and how it might respond in the event of an incident. This must be a consideration when designing incident escalation and invocation procedures as part of the planning process.

High levels of resilience may not be interesting to a board with a high tolerance towards physical asset loss, or one with a weak understanding or regard to the potential impact of intangible asset loss, including damage to brand and reputation.

Policy - Management Framework

We spent some time examining the governance and risk framework in earlier chapters of this book. If a framework exists it is essential that the business continuity policy identifies where this issue sits in the context of the framework. This will be key when promoting business continuity to the board and communicating its importance across the business. In any framework, risk management will be articulated as a continuous process and mapping the business continuity process against the risk cycle can provide powerful arguments for leveraging business continuity onto the board table and for obtaining important initial and ongoing access to a dedicated budget.

Policy - Roles And Responsibilities

This is a particularly interesting aspect of the policy and one where some of the greatest variations might be expected between organisations.

Is an organisation orientated towards management by committee, empowering of its people and managers, centralised or decentralised in its style of control, fast moving and change-oriented or slow moving? Is the organisation regulated, and if so, by which regulator and what experience has the organisation of incidents - internal or external? All of the answers to these questions will have a differing degree of influence on the level of authority delegated to business continuity managers, their operating environment and that of the businesses with which they facilitate the management process. Whatever the operating environment, this must be clearly articulated in the policy statement.

CASE STUDY

Contingency Policy Statement

The Company strategy is to identify, measure and control any factors that are perceived to be threatening business continuity and the ability to access essential information. The threat of serious harm comes from people or from natural causes and the impact is likely to be on financial, physical and intellectual assets, processes, suppliers, distribution chains or staff.

The strategy is to identify and evaluate these exposures in a structured way and, where realistic and cost effective, to remove or at least reduce these risks. Where significant risks remain, the Company will put in place and quality check a recovery plan that is designed to meet all urgent and critical organisational and stakeholder needs, accelerate recovery back to normal working and, by doing so, minimise the impact on Company operations and control.

CASE STUDY

Business Continuity Management Policy Statement

Multinational Professional Services: UK based

(The organisation) is committed to the development and implementation of Business Continuity Management (BCM) appropriate to the scale, nature, complexity and geography of the firm, and the relevant environments in which it operates. (The organisation) believes that the way in which the firm plans, prepares and responds to incidents is key to its overall effective recovery and continuance. BCM is a specialised aspect of Operational Risk Management, and plays a critical part in (the organisation's) overall governance and control environment.

The Key Aims of the Policy

The key aims of the policy are:

- Protection of people, assets, earning capacity, information, reputation, brand and value of the organisation and its key stakeholders

- Compliance with the regulatory and governance obligations following an unforeseen incident

- Fitness of Plans through regular training, updating and testing to agreed standards

The Key Principles of the Policy

The organisation will:

- Commit to compliance with legislation and relevant regulatory requirements and deliver appropriate governance and reporting processes

- Provide adequate resources to achieve delivery of the Policy Statement

- Provide appropriate education and training in BCM to all staff to increase their awareness and to enable them to understand the Business Continuity Plans that they are part of and the role they have to play

- Embed BCM as an integral part of the business operation and good management practice

---

CASE STUDY (continued)

- Constantly review internally and externally key BCM Strategy and Good Practice and reshape and develop (the organisation's) BCM Strategy and Good Practice to meet the global needs of the organisation

- Develop systems to assess the effectiveness of Business Continuity Plans and carry out testing

- Develop systems to assess the effectiveness of Business Continuity Plans

- Carry out testing

- Communicate the results to the Board

..................................(Board Member with responsibility for Business Continuity)

..................................Date

Policy - Assessment, Reporting And Performance Processes

Having established a business continuity framework, an organisation needs to ensure that this framework is maintained and developed with an ongoing process for review and upgrade to reflect change. Changes may include those affecting:

- the business, business impacts (both actual and perceived), and those occurring following the experience of plan invocation and business recovery; and,

- developments in business continuity good practice and associated services (for example, in the provision of data storage solutions or the provision of work area recovery capability).

This will provide ongoing assurance of the organisation's control environment.

Ongoing reporting and challenge (that which is reported is an accurate reflection of actual performance) tailored to the nature of the organisation should be designed and installed - perhaps using an in-house or industry-wide benchmark and associated assessment tool. Whatever option for reporting and challenge is adopted should be communicated within the policy statement, thereby ensuring that the organisation is aware of the approach. This will also facilitate other interested business functions having an opportunity to consider, refine and dovetail their processes - for example, internal audit, compliance or company secretary functional areas that may have responsibility for quality assurance within an organisation.

Policy - Management Commitment And Currency

The policy statement should be signed and dated by the appropriate board-level sponsor, the Chief Executive or equivalent. Each time there is a significant change in organisational policy the policy statement should be reaffirmed by the Board, documented and published.

Entering The Business Continuity Cycle - Putting Policy Into Practice

Having identified the components of the policy an organisation should research which legislation, regulatory rules, guidelines and industry standards might be applicable for consideration and inclusion. This is particularly relevant if the approach to be taken for the policy is to be quite detailed and will form part of a business continuity performance benchmark or assessment tool.

Policies that already exist with industry peers, admired competitors, professional peers or those of organisations represented by board non-executive directors should be assessed as these may offer up good ideas and tactical advantage for inclusion. Whatever approach and draft is decided upon, internal consultation with the business continuity board sponsor and other interested parties is essential. For example, taking and applying views expressed by the Risk Manager or Officer (and notably the Operational Risk Manager if that role exists as a separate function), the Information Technology manager, Human Resources Manager, Security Manager, Facilities Manager, Company Secretary, Compliance Manager and Internal Auditor is an investment and can avoid reinvention of existing wheels or publishing contradictory advice. These players may also exert important influence over successful implementation of the business continuity policy as well as having a worthwhile and informed view on policy content and design.

Areas of potential policy overlap should be identified; for example, with IT or security policies driven by associated standards such as ISO 17799 (BS7799). These functional individuals are likely to form part of planning and response teams sponsored by business continuity and their input and buy-in is essential. **(11)**

Entering The Business Continuity Cycle - Establishing The Programme

There are no special rules for initiating a business continuity management programme, other than those adopted by an organisation for any significant programme or project.

The sponsor or champion at board level should appoint a person to lead the programme or manage the programme as head of the functional area. Appropriate professional experience and competence in business continuity management, preferably with a recognised accreditation such as Member (MBCI) or Fellow of the Business Continuity Institute (FBCI); or Certified Business Continuity Professional (CBCP) or Master Business Continuity Professional (MBCP) of the Disaster Recovery Institute International (DRII); or , must be embedded in the programme infrastructure to provide expert opinion and credibility.

Based on the assumption that the programme will have followed the steps already outlined in this chapter, where next? Mapping out a project or programme definition report (PDR) will provide the route map for sponsorship, development and implementation, the milestones for achievement, the foundation for budget support and buy-in as well as a communication vehicle for use across an organisation. A generic approach for the development of a PDR is set out as follows

A TYPICAL PROJECT DEFINITION REPORT (PDR) TEMPLATE

1.Heading

- Author
- Version number
- Date

2. Table of Contents

- Referencing page numbers

- Page numbering of appendices

3. Introduction

- Separate paragraphs for project background and document purpose

- Business justification, e.g., a cost/benefit analysis may appear here. If lengthy, set out separately and reference in this PDR

4. Goals, Objectives and Deliverables

- Separate paragraph for each

- Goals paragraph should describe the long-term strategic goals to which this project contributes

- Objectives paragraph should address the short-term objectives which will be achieved by this project

- This section may include a paragraph on Scope if this is not already clear. If so, break down into "within scope" and "out of scope"

5. Organisation and Responsibilities

- Place Project Sponsor, Project Manager, Sub-Project Managers in an organisation chart

- Set out reporting relationship for any other team members

- Set out any Steering Committee, naming the members (notably Chairperson) and describe the reporting relationship with the programme team

- Describe levels of authority of named individuals in respect of commitment of resources, sign-off of documentation, authorisation of changes

- This section may include a paragraph on Communication, if there are specific communication requirements, e.g., virtual meetings via teleconference/video conference

6. Chunking

- If the project is large enough to fall into discrete phases, set out what these are

- If the chunks are sufficiently large, they should be managed as discrete projects, the overall managing document becoming a programme

7. Milestones

- Show major milestones only – a more detailed bar chart, dependency network, etc. can be attached as an appendix

- Space milestones appropriately so that slippage can be addressed before the entire project is placed at risk

- If project has been chunked, show at least one milestone for each chunk

8. Success and Completion Criteria
- One paragraph for each. Set out clearly how the participants will know
- Whether the project has been successful
- When the project can be considered complete
- Provide at least one milestone for each chunk

9.Management Control
- Separate paragraphs relating to:
- The format, frequency, timing, recipients of progress reports
- How the plan will be maintained and reviews conducted
- If quality assurance or project assurance reviews are planned, they should be described here

10. Risks, Issues and Assumptions
(Risk is defined as an unplanned occurrence which could happen; an issue is an unplanned occurrence which has happened and which requires the project manager to take action).

- Separate paragraph for each.
- Risks should be rated on a matrix according to likelihood and impact.
- Risks paragraph should detail actions to reduce or eliminate each risk

11. Sign-off
- The PDR should be signed off by person(s) representing all those who will be committing effort or resources to the project

12. Appendices

The Business Continuity Management Programme - The Programme Outcomes

Programme deliverables will include
- Recognition of the importance of risk, identification of risk tolerance levels, assessment of risks with appropriate control treatment as part of the risk management programme

- A defined business continuity management programme agreed by the organisation's executive/senior management. This should be complemented by assurance reports produced at a predetermined frequency and delivered by a competent individual and (depending on the size of the organisation and approach) a support team. Expert knowledge of business continuity management will serve to underwrite a successful programme. Depending on the state of maturity and size of an organisation this expertise may at least in the initial programme phase be imported through the assistance of consultants - although management responsibility for the subject cannot be outsourced at any phase;

- A clear and documented strategy, with policy and standards embedded as a management process integral to the organisation's management and business continuity management programme and life cycles. (The development of the policy statement and a high-level "future state" benchmark are essential. These will provide the basis from which to conduct a "current state" capability analysis, examine the gaps identified and consequently design short, medium and longer term programme objectives, deliverables and timescales);

- Comprehensive and validated business continuity plans that suit the nature and scale of the organisation;

- An overview of the organisation's internal and external resilience and recovery solutions with suitable dedicated resources provided with an annual budget as part of ongoing financial management processes;

- Education, training and communication required to achieve programme implementation and ongoing success;

- Business continuity management established as part of the business planning and personnel performance appraisal processes;

- Metrics, indicators and supporting management processes including exercising and auditing that illustrate how well the programme is performing, and

- Ongoing management commitment and supporting evidence of this.

"Business continuity management is a major project that requires the substantial investment of managerial resources and a firm-wide awareness. Management needs to exert strong leadership and to become deeply involved in the process." (12)

Before we move on and enter the risk management cycle, it is worth dwelling for a while on the increasing pressures being applied to managers to be held accountable for managing their own risks by their business leaders, regulators and legislative change. There is a hypothesis that this pressure can result in a tendency for managers to attempt to manage risks across a broader base at an enterprise-wide level, but to a potentially narrower depth. The consequence is a desire to manage process at the expense of content and the adoption of a defensive preoccupation. At a time when risk should be seen as a competitive advantage, risk in itself can become a risk and lead to an organisation taking localised and insufficiently tailored risks. An intensified concern for organisational processes may incubate risks without seeing, imagining or acting upon the 'bigger' picture. (13)

It is essential that risk and business continuity managers adopt a management approach that allows them to see the detail and the wider view of risk and potential impact on critical business functions and processes. The possibility of "dumbing-down" the approach and intellectual content of risk and business continuity management escalates the need for balance in the need and demand for professional expert judgement. It also escalates the need to assess and take account of external and internal key drivers. Excessive attention to processes can turn a business inward and may mean that it fails to sufficiently address external environmental factors, the impact of aggregation and the potential of domino effects. Organisations must think the unthinkable and plan for the consequences.

One way in which an organisation may help externalise its approach and bring in current thinking on risk and good practice management is to consider the use of external assistance. Carefully chosen, the use of consultants can add significant value to the process - whilst retaining central ownership and control.

Understanding the Needs Of Others

The quotation by John Donne, "No man is an island, entire of itself, every man is a piece of the continent, a part of the main...." (14) serves to illustrate the point that people and organisations cannot act in isolation without due consideration of others. Just as an organisation must consider the risks and potential impacts associated with the supply chain, so too must organisations be mindful of the impact of their disruption or failure on stakeholders and the community as a whole within which they operate.

While the requirement to have plans is not new, the degree of cooperation expected and information sharing required is. "Firms can expect pressure from local authorities to provide evidence of suitable arrangements that will facilitate the continuation of their service following an emergency." **(15)** The greater the potential impact of failure, the greater interest one might expect from authorities in fulfilling their objectives.

Finally, an organisation should not overlook the opportunities available from consulting others and presenting the organisation as one that:

- Takes business continuity - and the customer - seriously

- Has a tried and tested plan with management support and employee buy-in al all levels, and

- Has the best chance of surviving an incident, to sustain delivery of commitments and be back in business in the quickest possible time

The Business Continuity Management Cycle

The first step on entering the business continuity management cycle (Figure 1) is to gain a thorough understanding of the organisation and its interactions, both internal and external. This chapter has already considered a general business analysis checklist The questions in the checklist are standard to business analysis, but the last one is specific to analysis for business continuity purposes.

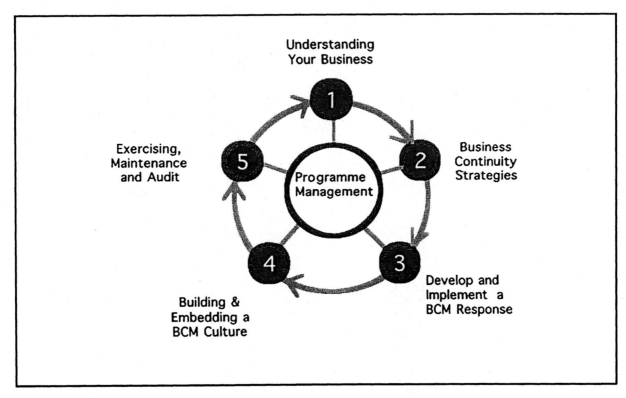

Figure 1 - the Business Continuity Management Cycle **(16)**

The understanding must be focused on the activities which most quickly threaten the achievement of business objectives. These tend to be the 'operational' functions, which interact directly with customers or other outside organisations. These activities may depend for their delivery on the 'support' of other internal and external process, which must also be analysed.

While not essential, certainly in the more complex organisation the programme manager should consider using one of the various software packages available to facilitate and record this process. Software packages are considered in greater depth in Chapter 18.

However well programme managers feel they know the business that they are working in, it will always help to talk with and consult others: and people generally enjoy talking about their area of business and their role. Face-to-face consultation is a powerful way to communicate the objectives of the programme and will:

- Ensure that all feel engaged and involved in the process and have the opportunity to contribute and ask questions

- Help to identify champions to act as focal points for future plan development and implementation

- Provide an opportunity to consolidate or transfer ownership for business continuity management to the business

- Open a door to access and take expert opinion. Whilst programme managers may be the experts in their own disciplines, they will not be the experts in all facets of the organisation or its stakeholders

- Facilitate a current-state check of existing plans and their general state of readiness to support the overall current-state against future-state review, and

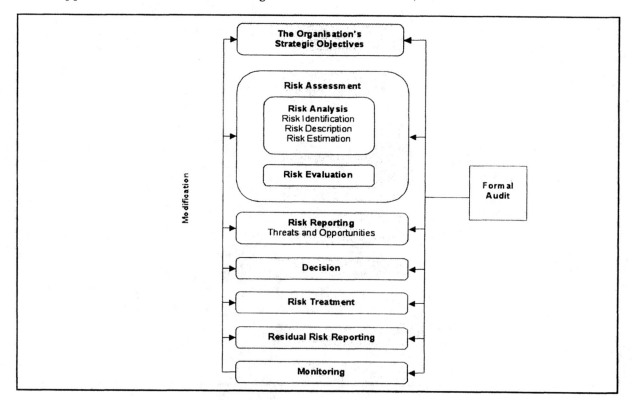

Figure 2 - the Global Risk Management Process **(17)**

- Provide an opportunity to reaffirm the risk manager's role: which is that of facilitator, centre of expertise, custodian of consistent policy and standards but not decision taker

- Before starting the programme, do go back and review the Stakeholders set out in Chapter 2. While the understanding of an organisation must be focused on the operational activities (and the suppliers to these activities) which most quickly threaten the achievement of business objectives, most stakeholders should still be engaged at this stage - it is too early in the process to dismiss potentially relevant players.

To help the understanding of an organisation for business continuity purposes, a **Business Impact Analysis** (BIA) and **Risk Assessment** (RA) should be applied.

The BIA identifies the urgency of each business function undertaken by the organisation through assessing the impact over time of interruption to this activity. This information is used to identify appropriate continuity and resumption strategies for each function. The RA as part of the risk management process **(Figure 2)** helps in identifying risks which might threaten the achievement of a set of business objectives and the inherent potential severity (before controls are applied) and residual potential severity (after controls are applied) of these being realised.

There is considerable debate as the whether a BIA or a RA should both be conducted and, if so, in which order. This book will explore each process in greater depth and leave managers to draw their own conclusions - albeit the view expressed here is that:

- Neither process is mutually exclusive

- Both serve an essential purpose in understanding an organisation, its exposures and in designing an appropriate control environment

- Elements of the methodology within each process are shared

There is a growing convergence between risk management and business continuity management and those who practice these disciplines within overall organisational governance and risk frameworks.

Summary

Risk management and business continuity management are complementary disciplines and neither is an optional process in a well-managed organisation. Both approaches require the adoption of structured and systematic programme management, which should adopt good programme management practice and be practised at all levels within an organisation.

The business continuity cycle sets out a process that if adopted should lead to the design and implementation of a business continuity policy and framework that is led from the top of an organisation, sustainable, fit for purpose, compliant with internal and external rules or guidelines, culturally suited to an organisation, owned by the business, exercised and maintained.

Bibliography

1. The Combined Code - www.frc.org.uk - 2003

2. Generally Accepted Practices - Draft for Review - Disaster Recovery Journal (DRJ) and Disaster   Recovery Institute (DRI) - July 2005

3. The Business Continuity Institute, Business Continuity Management Good Practice Guidelines - 2005

4. Institute of Directors - Information and Advisory Services - www.iod.com/information

5. Governance and Risk - George Dallas, Managing Director Standard & Poor's - 2004

6. The Business Continuity Institute, Business Continuity Management Good Practice Guidelines -   2005

7. NFPA 1600: Standard on Disaster/Emergency Management and Business Continuity Programs - 2004

8. Internal Guide produced by Aon UK - 2005

9. Expecting the Unexpected: Business Continuity in an Uncertain World - London First - 2003

10. The Business Continuity Institute, Business Continuity Management Good Practice Guidelines - 2005

11. SO 17799 (BS7799)

12. Business Continuity Planning at Financial Institutions - Bank of Japan - 2003

13. Risk Managing Everything: Rethinking the Politics of Uncertainty - Michael Power - Demos: 2004

14. The Collected Poems of John Donne - Wordsworth Poetry Library - 1994

15. Civil Contingencies Bill - a risk in itself? Gemma Rogers - Inform magazine - March 2004

16. Setting a New Standard for Operational Resilience - The Marsh Topic Letter XV - 2003

17. The risk cycle - the Global Risk Management Process - extract from the Risk Management Standard - FERMA [www.ferma-asso.org], AIRMIC, [www.airmic.com], ALARM, [www.alarm-uk.com], IRM [www.theirm.org]

6

Introduction to the Business Impact Analysis

The Objectives Of This Chapter Are To:

- Understand the role and the values of a Business Impact Analysis (BIA) within the business continuity management process.

- Understand the BIA framework, its needs, its players and its ownership

- Enable a consistency and clarity of objectives

- Enable a consistent, clear, and measured communication of risk issues

- Access and evaluate sources of information

- Consider the opportunities for decision-making around risk information evolving from the BIA

Risk: Definitions

A risk is the threat that an event or action will adversely affect an organisation's ability to maximise shareholder value and to achieve business objectives. Risk arises as much from the possibility that opportunities will not be realised as it does from the possibility that threat will materialise or that mistakes will be made. A risk is integral to all opportunity and is as much about opportunity as it is about threat.

This definition is in effect an enterprise-wide definition and takes in both speculative risk and operational risk; that is to say a wide definition that would embrace, for example, taking commercial decisions knowingly balancing risk and reward. Bringing opportunities for continuity planning into such a process is a useful enabler that could encourage an organisation to take a decision where they know that if the dice moved against them, they have planned an exit strategy with the aid of a reaction, or a continuity plan. While this is a real, added value of contingency planning for the board, most often the plans are developed to respond to an operational failure of some kind. Such an operational failure was defined by the Bank of International Settlements' Basel Committee (1) as follows:

"644. Operational risk is defined as the risk of loss resulting from inadequate or failed internal processes, people and systems or from external events."

With these definitions in mind we can move on to look at the business impact analysis itself.

The Role and Values of the Business Impact Analysis

We have, in an earlier chapter, positioned the BIA in the overall process of business continuity management. To reaffirm just how crucial it is, there is no value whatsoever in developing a business recovery plan when a risk exposure remains, that, if occurring, could destroy all chance of recovery. No amount of professionalism in building a response plan, response teams and their support infrastructure would be of the slightest use if the organisation has effectively died even as the incident is still unfolding.

> *Consequently, in the process of ensuring the resilience of an organisation, neither risk assessments nor business impact analyses are 'optional.'*

One example of such a situation could be when a critical, just-in-time supplier of a vital ingredient fails. Increasingly, the receiving organisation needs that ingredient quickly, and in time to meet its own critical service delivery promises. Furthermore, without pre-planning, the company may not able to source the part or service from somewhere else. It would certainly not be fast enough if the firm could not replace that ingredient within a time frame that would enable the receiving organisation to deliver on promises of its own and thus remain a credible player in its own marketplace. A failure of one delivery– in quality or in time - could mean, that the whole contract is deemed broken, with an organisation potentially facing hefty legal and financial penalties. The organisation may have individually large contracts on which the organisation depends for its very survival.

Furthermore, the first thing to be lost, and also the most destructive, is confidence in the organisation's ability to deliver into the future. This wider reputation issue is as immediate, if not more so, than individual, urgently needed deliveries, and can have a much wider and devastating affect on the chances that the organisation will survive into the future. It takes years to build a reputation and one poor experience to destroy it.

Another example of an incident causing unrecoverable damage is where the organisation manages to lose critical information without which effective recovery would be impossible. This exposure could be deep within a whole range of intellectual assets, such as computer software, employee skills and experience, and customer or design databases. That information may be held within the organisation, or within the offices or brains of a critical supplier. An example could be when a software supplier or software maintenance company closes down or otherwise fails. That supplier may be the sole owner of the computer software codes and thus they may become legally or physically inaccessible to the affected customer.

If the retention of information, safely accessible and able to be mined in a particular way, is a requisite of the organisation's particular regulator, and if that information in the format demanded is lost, the chain of events could quickly lead to the loss of legality and total closure.

In any of these circumstances, there would be very little opportunity, if any, for a recovery team, however skilled, to deliver the promises implied by its existence in a 'business recovery plan'.

The examples bring out the point also that too often the "devil lies in the detail" and that a failure in any one of these detail areas will bring about the total closure of the organisation or make it unrecognisable from the shape and value previously known. It is the job of the BIA to tease out and understand that detail and position its readers in the best situation possible to make decisions and deal with the risk issues.

The 'business,' therefore, of the Business Impact Analysis is to identify the exposures and to quantify, quite precisely, the potentially destructive impact which they could cause on the very arteries of the organisation. We have said that those arteries are not only physical ones. They can include 'soft' but difficult issues such as stakeholder confidence, wider brand values, intellectual assets and legality. With that clear and focused understanding, the risk/continuity manager can begin to encourage realistic decisions about balancing risk and reward. Furthermore the risk/continuity manager can also obtain decisions to protect, duplicate or otherwise manage any unacceptable exposure down to an acceptable level. A further value, of course, is that a clear understanding of the potential business impact emerging from a difficulty will be crucially useful information to continuity planners who are putting together the recovery plans. These plans, necessarily, should reflect decisions about urgencies and the positioning of resources to meet those urgencies.

In summary, a BIA has a clear and practical focus to its objectives, which is to enable more informed, and therefore better, decisions about risk, its acceptance, and its management. It is thus not an academic document but rather a working information tool and that must be trusted, as complete as it is possible to be, and constantly kept up to date.

Case Study:

From early in 1999 the Passport Agency had increasing difficulties meeting the demand for UK passports. They had a target of issuing a passport in 10 working days but delays occurred and were creeping up to 25 days, then 50 days and by June 1999 there were 600,000 applications awaiting processing.

How could this be, when passports had been successfully issued for the better part of a century? The problems occurred because the Passport Agency had embarked on a number of changes simultaneously and had not assessed the risks attached to each one and certainly not to the coincidence of problems occurring together. The Agency was simultaneously seeking to do three things. They were implementing a new policy of issuing child passports, introducing a new IT system and also relocating a lot of staff to new offices.

All this was going on without any pilot tests to see if the goals could be achieved without any training of the staff in the new IT system. They were doing this against a timetable that had been set for political reasons because the Secretary of State said that this was all going to happen by a specific date without consideration as to how long it would actually take to achieve.

Thus, a failure to assess the risks and the coincidence of the risks occurring together caused an enormous backlog, with a great deal of worry for the public and business trips held up, etc. What they also did not allow for was a 'run on the bank' because when people found that their passports were taking longer to arrive they all pitched in and created even greater delays. (1)

The Risk Assessment vs. the Business Impact Assessment

Risk assessments and business assessments often cover same ground but there is a fundamental approach in current practice. The risk assessment identifies the risks that may cause damage and it also considers the cost of the potential damage that that risk incident may cause. Furthermore, it goes on to consider the probability that the incident may happen at all. This balancing act of risk/impact and probability enables a risk manager to make effective cost/benefit decisions about risk management measures that can best be introduced. These measures may simply cost money; for example, in the installation of a fire sprinkler system, or may create diversions and use time and resources when security issues slow down otherwise straightforward processes. At the extreme end, the risk/probability assessment may encourage the organisation to desist from otherwise short-term, profitable activities.

In current practice the Business Impact Analysis concerns itself less with probability. This is because the objective is to tease out the potential for incidents that could totally destroy the organisation. When the potential impact is destruction, the board will consider less the potential frequency as it will most probably not feel able to accept any risks that could totally destroy the entire organisation. This latter view is reinforced by regulators such as the Securities and Exchange Commission (USA), the Financial Services Authority (United Kingdom) and others.

The BIA, in practice, as a tool leading towards business critical continuity planning, will concern itself with measuring the maximum amount of time during which the organisation can fail to continue to deliver on its promises to the whole range of stakeholders. Such a measure that factors in the potential impacts of these 'time-outs' will then enable the continuity planners to ensure that their work will enable the organisation to meet these urgent time urgencies and needs.

> *The Business Continuity Institute in its 2005 Good Practice Guidelines explains the concept of time out, or 'Maximum Tolerable Outage' (MTO) as follows:*
>
> *"Maximum Tolerable Outage: This is the timetable during which a recovery must become effective before an outage compromises the ability of the organisation to achieve its business objectives and therefore has the potential to threaten its long tem or short term survival." (2)*

This book sets out to look at business continuity planning through the eyes of the board, its stakeholders and all those in and around the organisation that are concerning themselves with risk of failure. It takes the view that potential 'time-outs' caused by damage are indeed an important business impact issue for business continuity managers but that it is also one of the most crucial 'impacts' that need to be considered by risk managers. In other words, we see risks associated with business continuity to be no different than risks relating to the business strategy. Further, we will not be drawing clear lines between the risk analysis and the business impact analysis. To fully understand risks it is crucial to know how quickly urgent services need to be reinstated and we urge risk managers to identify these needs. Similarly, we urge business continuity managers to understand the crucial dependencies of the organisation and ensure that these dependencies are managed so that they can be available during and after a crisis to the business continuity teams.

Business continuity managers, therefore, have an important need to consider failures in the outsourced supply chain as much as a failure emerging from within the organisation. Furthermore, there is an important need to plan to ensure that business and financial controls continue. It is also important that regulators can continue to be satisfied. One of the exposures not often considered by business continuity managers is the potential for a financial loss that can be so devastating that it effectively closes the organisation. That financial loss can be just as easily in cash flows as it can in revenues and assets, and if on organisation is promising resilience these risks have an equal need to be recognised, measured and prepared for.

We believe that the wider risk and continuity arenas are indivisible, and both equally are important areas of concern for both the continuity manager and the risk manager working as a team. We will develop this theme as the book evolves in later chapters.

THE PROJECT NEEDS, ITS PLAYERS AND ITS OWNERSHIP

1. An Understanding of The Business

A BIA and/or a risk analysis delivers value only where it has credibility amongst its various target audiences. These various audiences need to be assured that the author has not only understood the threats, but has also understood the organisation deeply enough to measure those threats and their potential impact on the functions and values that are the very survival ingredients of the organisation. Only then do we begin to see a useable business tool.

This is not as easy as it sounds even within a single-country, focused, service industry or product manufacturer. The challenge is even greater when dealing with a diverse group delivering products and services across many continents.

The potential for damaging impact does not necessarily relate to the size of the function being discussed. A manufacturer of nuts and bolts may, for example, distribute its product worldwide and through different distributors in different countries. The liability insurance programme may exclude the ultimate use of their products in the aircraft industry, and quite separately exclude any sales within America and Canada. If that was not a sufficient risk factor in itself, the policy may quite separately exclude any liability claims brought in courts that are subject to American jurisdiction. These are routine exclusions in many non-American insurance markets.

Without effective controls, one distributor may, unknown to the manufacturer, retail one set of nuts and bolts to an aircraft manufacturer in the United States. A potentially uninsured product liability claim could be so large that it would destroy completely the organisation's balance sheet and cash flows; leading through to loss of investor confidence and closure.

Business impact Case Study: Motor Insurance Industry

The Motability scheme in the UK enables disabled people to purchase and run motor vehicles, many of which are adapted for the individual person's remaining abilities. A motor insurer that is now part of the Zurich group provided motor insurance to the UK Government's Motability scheme.

Because of the nature of the portfolio it was handled using AS/400 computer technology in a separate operation in the South of England. The premium income was reasonably substantial, but not significant when related to the scale of the whole Group. A failure in this one business unit would not have affected the group's reportable financial position in any significant way.

A business impact analysis, however, recognised that a failure of this individual business unit to deliver could mean that a large number of disabled people would be unable to arrange or alter their motor vehicle insurance. Driving without insurance is not only very dangerous but it also makes the act of driving an illegal act. The impact could in effect make hundreds or thousands of disabled people housebound very quickly.

There is of course the human dimension to this exposure. Additionally, the situation would be a major interest story to the media. This is increasingly so as a very public figure, a member of the UK Royal Family chaired the scheme. This media interest would rapidly turn into frenzy – UK media style – and of course the usual hunt for villains and victims would be very easily satisfied, and quite rightly so.

The brand value of the company would be damaged very quickly and seriously indeed. This would be especially damaging in the business of providing the product of insurance protection, where confidence that it will deliver when needed and in difficult circumstances is a crucial ingredient in the decision to choose a particular insurer. Furthermore, that same brand name was used worldwide, and across a whole range of life insurance, pension, investment and commercial insurance products and services. The technological way that personal insurance is handled means, furthermore, that competitors can easily pick up large amounts of new business without having to retool in any major way.

The business impact analysis and the resultant recovery plan, for both human and commercial impact reasons, placed this business unit as an urgent and vital priority for protection and recovery. An opinion based on the purely financial cost of risk to the Group itself would not have done so. That opinion would have missed both these vital, urgent, and ultimately, business-critical impacts. A subsequent disk crash was recovered and service resumed with no noticeable break in service to the policyholders.

Subsequently, the contract between Motability and the insurer recognises the unique features and exposures of this relationship, and the contract itself demands continuity of service within very tight service and time parameters. These contractual demands make it unavoidable that the insurer has a contract with an external contingency service supplier. Only by the use of such a pre-contracted and standby supplier of contingency facilities could the terms of that contract be satisfied. This level of risk and continuity management is therefore an integral element of the wider contract. These contractual demands have continued beyond the Zurich relationship following transfer of insurer.

2. Credibility

A BIA is not just a document for filing. It is worth the time and paper invested only when it is a living document, kept up to date, and triggers effective risk decision making and real risk management and business recovery planning activity.

The BIA therefore needs

- Ownership and a clear place in the decision-making hierarchy of the organisation,
- Clear ownership separately of both the responsibilities and the tasks
- A clear agenda
- The ability to illustrate that the research is thorough and embraces all of the destructive exposures.
- Consistency in approach and measurement across all risks and across the whole organisation.
- To be up to date, and
- To be able to report in a way that often esoteric issues can be grasped quickly, and with real information that will enable effective decision making.

We will now move on to face and explore each of these challenges.

3. Ownership

The obvious statement is that the ultimate responsibility to understand the risks to the organisation and its stakeholders lies, quite simply, with the most senior executive of that organisation. This may be the board of a public company, the chief executive, or board of a private company, public service organisation or charity. Realism dictates that they must sometimes delegate the process down throughout the management teams, but they cannot delegate that final responsibility.

The risk manager or continuity manager, therefore, is not the one to make the final decisions about risks. Effective managing both in profit-making and in not-for-profit organisations is all about balancing risk and reward. This balancing act of any significant risk should be made by the business managers and ultimately at the highest management authority in the organisation. Realistically, some lower-impact decisions must be delegated because it is just not possible for the board to adjudicate on every single issue.

These decisions can be wildly different in each organisation. They will reflect such things as the culture of the organisation, the marketplace within which it operates, and the tolerance for risk among its stakeholders. The decision will also reflect the perceived strengths of the organisation to cope with a risk incident as and when it happens, with the use of its own inherent strengths and flexibilities.

A board will see the business continuity plan as one of the tools in the risk management toolbox. With confidence that a continuity plan will be effective, continuity planning can be an actual alternative or supplement to expensive risk management or a redesigning of processes to avoid risk. Such a careful and trusted plan may also be an enabler, giving the board confidence to move into a product or area that would otherwise be perceived as too risky.

The risk manager or continuity manager, therefore, should best be regarded as a centre of excellence in risk information and advice. By having a risk manager fulfilling a role of internal (or sometimes external) advisor or consultant, the Board has better quality information to enable them to make the best decisions that they realistically can.

An organisation may transfer the consequences of a risk by contracting to another party. They do not absolve themselves from any residual risk that may come back to haunt their organisation. Contractually and financially penalising a supplier, for example, in the event of a late delivery, does not in the slightest way help the receiving organisation whose very existence is at risk because it cannot complete its own urgent product delivery to others. The final recipient has no interest in where the failure was in the chain, just that there is a failure to its own requirement; and therefore places the blame firmly in the immediately previous link in its supply chain. The final supplier to that next recipient in the chain carries the responsibility and will no doubt have to face the response from its own customer for that failure.

Furthermore, an organisation may enter into a contract with a third-party supplier of contingency office workstations and technology. This is a common way to minimise the risk that the workstations and/or technology may become unusable or the site that they usually operate within is inaccessible. A contract with such a professional supplier will be for a defined number of workstations to be available in an agreed amount of minutes or days after the contract is triggered by an incident, for an agreed period of time. The organisation entering into the contract, however, retains the risk of that supplier failing to deliver on that contract (perhaps because of insolvency, or a wide-area disaster placed more pressure on them simultaneously from a wider number of clients than they had themselves planned). We have stated elsewhere in this book that scenario setting, for both the supplier and the client, is constrained by imagination and past experience. The quality suppliers will have their own backup facilities to offer in an unexpectedly wide disaster, and also some organisations will buy dedicated seats for operations identified as critical by the BIA, e.g., dealing desks. In risk management there are very few guarantees; just a significant reduction in risk – perhaps to a commercially acceptable level - by careful anticipation and preparation and planning.

There may be penalty clauses in the contract but none will adequately help the suffering organisation stay in business, nor are they likely to provide sufficient financial compensation to all stakeholders of the destroyed organisation. Again, the responsibility stays with the primary organisation and, however careful the choice of third party supplier and the contract wordings, there remains a need to be aware that there will be a residual risk.

We are totally clear, therefore, as to whom has the responsibility for risk. Hereafter it gets a bit murkier.

4. Risks and Threats

The murkiness begins with the very understanding of what kind of risk is being addressed; and also which manager is responsible down right throughout the organisation for a specific risk. The army of "risk managers" includes all those who carry the responsibility for their own business unit or function within the whole organisation. There is another army - risk specialists. They include the company secretary, the investment manager, the internal auditor, the external auditors, the audit committee, the finance director, the health and safety manager, the security manager, the credit control manager, the compliance officer, the internal and external lawyers, the insurance programme manager, the pension fund trustees, purchasing manager, engineers, IT security manager, continuity manager, fleet control manager, office facilities manager, the architect and others.

It is into this cauldron of skills and vested interests and skills that we need to introduce another variable. This is the subject of risk itself; with all its widely differing definitions, views and tolerances amongst these players. Simply listing risks takes us deeper into these differences.

One risk map may look something like this – or on the other hand an organisation may wish to cut the risk cake in an entirely different way! While increasingly in use, especially by regulators, the absence of this type of risk map and supporting guidance is an accepted weakness of many of the 'risk standards.'

From Ownership to Activity

Risk managers, tasked with understanding and delivering business impact analyses, need therefore to be clear with themselves, and must communicate to their audience the parameters of the task

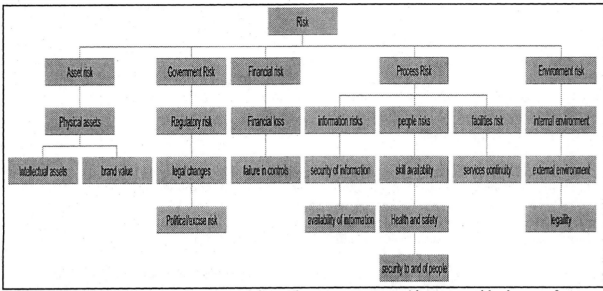

and precisely what they are setting out to deliver. They can move on with a reasonable chance of success only if this clarity is grasped first by the risk managers involved, then by their principals and also all those who will need to contribute. This range of people and their departments' inputs are critically important sources of information about the organisation and its risks; furthermore, these players and their individual risks are part of the decisionmaking and business continuity plans afterwards.

> *The continuity BIA needs therefore to retain clarity of purpose throughout, recognise these individual roles, take on board their contributions in a structured way, feed quality information back to them, and in return retain credibility amongst each and every one of these players.*
>
> *The metaphor best coming to mind is that the person charged with delivering a BIA is likened to an orchestra conductor who needs to recognise and respect all of the individual skills of the orchestra; may not be able to deliver each personally, but still needs to bring them all together carefully to deliver the agreed objective.*

There is another practical message emerging from ownership. The task is to get these managers to do something that may not come naturally to them. The managers are usually very busy people facing changing priorities which are already confronting them day by day and will no doubt be trying to deliver on the challenging tasks set by their own line managers and individual stakeholders. The need of the BIA is to get them to stop doing this for a while and divert time away to think about not what is happening, but *what may or may not happen.* Aggressive, self-confident, career-building managers may find it difficult to admit that things could go wrong "on their watch."

The process may not always be grasped with enthusiasm. The requirement may not be given the urgency of other time-driven tasks like year-end figures or preparing for a particular appointment with a colleague or a client. A promise to 'get around to it when I have a free day' probably has to be read in the context of the fact that they never have free days! Should we have a crystal ball and know exactly when the next crisis will happen, all BIA and contingency planning would no doubt be totally up to date and ready.

> *"Next week there cannot be any crisis. My schedule is already full." - Dr. Henry Kissinger (while US Secretary of State)*

Getting the urgency to complete a BIA often needs the task to be built into routine performance measurement tasks and timetables. This is an additional reason for ownership at the very top level of decision-making in the organisation. In these days of matrix management there is considerable value in having a main board member or equivalent with the responsibility for organisation-wide risk and continuity planning. Such a person's role is to take primary ownership and, where necessary, engineer the right level and urgency of activity across the organisation.

Defining the Objectives

A dozen people are quite likely to give at least fifteen different definitions on what risk is, and their reaction to risk. There is strategic risk, credit risk, health and safety risk, investment risk, and countless others. There are even risks about failure of the risk controls themselves! We remind the reader that the agenda of this book is restricted primarily to risk issues within the context of continuity planning. Even within this supposedly 'narrow' field there still can be differing views and agendas.

It is crucial to ensure that, when starting out on a BIA, the agreed objectives are defined. This is necessary to avoid project drift and, even worse, the players in the task becoming utterly lost in a project that takes off in different directions all at the same time, each then assuming a different life of its own. Any BIA within the context set for this book does need to focus itself on those risks which may stop the organisation from existing, or risks that are able, significantly, to divert the organisation from delivering its promised business model to its various and diverse stakeholders. This seems (at least on the surface) an easy statement, but it necessarily does entail that we must take a back-to-front view, i.e., we need to look at potential impact even before or at the same time that we begin to choose the risks themselves for our investigation. Of necessity, the objective encourages the BIA to deal with operational failure, but can also cut across many other risk arenas.

There is obviously great value in the organisation making a statement about its continuity policy before setting out on the task. Clearly the board must be clear as to what it wants, and the risk manager must be clear on the task ahead; but above all, any task that involves so many views and people must have a common denominator and clear framework.

This is one example of such a statement that could be used as one baseline for the work.

CONTINGENCY POLICY STATEMENT

The Company strategy is to identify, measure and control any factors that are perceived to be threatening business continuity and the ability to access essential information. The threat of serious harm comes from people or from natural causes and the impact is likely to be on financial, physical and intellectual assets, processes, suppliers, distribution chains or staff.

The strategy is to identify and evaluate these exposures in a structured way and, where realistic and cost-effective, to remove or at least reduce these risks. Where significant risks remain, the Company will put in place and quality-check a recovery plan that is designed to meet all urgent and critical organisational and stakeholder needs, accelerate recovery back to normal working levels and, by doing so, minimise the impact on Company operations and control.

An obvious challenge is this: How does one know that a risk is potentially destructive unless the risk itself is subject to a business impact analysis? We have already seen where apparently innocuous exposures can threaten the very survival of the organisation.

There is an additional dimension to the work of continuity risk and planning – time. A disruption or delay in a process can range from irrelevant to destructive. Whether the time delay is simply a hiccup or threatens the very existence of the business depends on a variety of factors. Obviously one is the length of the delay, but one organisation may find a period of delay insignificant, while another may find that the same amount of time lost would close them down. One business may have stock levels in a warehouse, or customers who can wait. Others may be delivering services live (e.g., a call centre, credit card authorisations, or e-commerce businesses) or it may be delivering into a just-in-time supply chain where the customer expects and demands an uninterrupted service.

We will now attempt to define the words we have been using; such as 'significant' and 'critical.'

Consistency In Definitions

One definition of **business-critical** can perhaps best be described as:

- "The information needed and the ability to undertake processes that will ensure that the business unit can:

- Meet the need to retain control of the business and the business portfolios.

- Retain all necessary compliance and regulatory approvals

- Retain its distribution base and place in the marketplace

- Meet essential and urgent customer needs

- Maintain financial control

- Retain and potentially continue to develop the brand value

- Meet any requirements in civil and criminal law

- And does not lose money – nor fails to meet targets – to the point that, in any stakeholder's opinion, a 'disaster' has occurred."

One challenge in defining impact is finding a common method whereby the BIA can measure both financial and non-financial losses in a consistent way. Another challenge is to be able to present the information evolving both concisely and clearly. Each risk and impact needs to be understood, prioritised between themselves, and cost/benefit decisions identified about retaining or otherwise moving that risk profile. The BIA processes should leave behind an audit trail of decisions made, and be able to set clearly the position at a moment in time against which any future changes in the business or its risks can be measured.

One useful presentation tool is to grade the severity of an impact as negligible, marginal, critical, and catastrophic, or "mission-critical." By defining these four words carefully we can embrace both financial and non-financial risk, and also the issue of "downtime". We can then begin to compare and rate the concerns that have emerged. We will have a consistent basis to apply those concerns against the organisation's appetite for taking risks.

Just one example of such a set of definitions may, in a group organisation, read as follows

LEVEL	DEFINITION
1	**NEGLIGIBLE** All problems can be resolved with no external impact whatsoever Financial losses: Capital: below $100,000 Revenue local impact only

2	MARGINAL
	
	It takes up to one day to reinstate customer-facing services
	
	Financial loss of: Capital below $1,000,000
	                       Revenue 10% local targets
	                                                3% of group targets
	Risk of share price falls by up to 5%

3	CRITICAL
	
	It takes up to three days to reinstate customer-facing services
	Fines by regulatory authorities
	Loss of confidence within the client base and other stakeholders
	Loss of confidence within the workforce
	Credit rating fall one half point or more
	
	Financial loss of: Capital below $10,000,000
	                       Revenue 50% local targets
	                                                  10% Group targets
	
	Unacceptable Health and Safety Risk;
	Health and Safety approvals for a building withdrawn
	Risk of share price falls by up to 10%

4	CATASTROPHIC It takes more than three days to reinstate customer-facing services Loss of regulatory or licence approval illegality within a business operational area Loss of confidence in the brand name by the general public Loss of confidence in the brand name by shareholders Financial loss of: Capital above $25,000,000 Revenue 25% group targets Credit rating fall one full level or more Risk of life Risk of share price falls by up to 25% or more

By using such a measure for the potential impact of each risk, financial and non-financial risks can be considered simultaneously. Clearly each organisation will wish to use its own measures and agree on them before commencing the exercise. Some businesses, for example, might accept a potential down-time of only 10 minutes into its critical or catastrophic category.

Pre-defining impact levels enables a consistency when measuring impact across the whole organisation. A major group will have profit centres and subsidiaries in one or multiple countries. A level of loss that could be critical financially to a subsidiary may be marginal to the group. If it is marginal to the group's ability to absorb risk it may therefore not justify the level of risk management energies that a self-standing unit would need to introduce. A business unit or subsidiary may, with formal Group approval, accept such a risk, knowing that it has the strengths of Group-wide resources to call upon. This may not work, however, in the case of some non-financial risk, such as brand damage or regulatory approvals. These and similar exposures could too easily and quickly spread to damage the whole Group.

We need at this stage to add a few more words of caution.

It is common in the insurance market to use the initials MPL This may mean either Maximum *Probable* Loss or they may alternately mean Maximum *Possible* Loss. This confusion in definition is of less importance to an insurer. There is usually reinsurance protection in place to protect the insurer itself against errors in estimating what is likely to be the maximum probable loss of an insured risk. It is however much more important for the organisation buying insurance or one that accepts risks for its own account to be absolutely clear of its own definitions. There is no protection for them against getting an incorrect estimate of *probable* loss wrong. A miscalculation that underestimates the maximum probable loss could cause a residual loss directly against the organisation's own balance sheets, revenue accounts and/or cash flows. That failure may be because the damage is in significantly in excess of expectations, a combination of causes have coincided to increase loss, or the cause has come from an entirely unexpected source.

Logically, therefore,, the Business Impact Analysis needs to define clearly whether it is dealing with the maximum *possible* loss or is a view as to what is the likely maximum *probable* loss. It may be reasonable to do the latter but the residual risk of any miscalculation needs to be explained within the BIA document and signed off by the Board.

Case Study: Maximum Probable Loss.

There are some nasty surprises about. The Rand Corporation, a non-profit research organisation estimated as of 2005 that more than 730,000 people have filed asbestos injury claims in the United States, costing businesses more than £70bn. Not all these exposures are insured, and thus the issue is a real business continuity threat.

The three-year study collated information from 60 lawyers and 300 defendants and showed that this sum had been paid so far. Stephen Carroll, the Rand senior economist said, "There is every indication tbat if we continue business as usual, we will have more claims in the future than we have today."

When accepting a level of impact the decision may implicitly be to accept such a hit from any one incident. A loss, however, may occur more than once in any one accounting period. During 2004 hurricanes across the Caribbean, Philippines and Florida were prime examples; in 2005, back-to-back Hurricanes Katrina and Rita caused massive losses in Louisiana and Mississippi. Decision-makers need to be clear precisely what their decision is; is it per incident or over a period of time when there may be multiple hits of the same nature?

Case Study

The World Trade Center in New York was insured on the assumption that there could be only a certain level of damage to two such separate and substantial buildings.

The terrorist attack in September 2001 not only caused an unimagined level of damage to each building, but damage to both buildings almost simultaneously. Some organisations had planned to use the second tower as a business recovery site. Another result was significant under-insurance. Additionally, litigation was needed between the insured and the insurers to establish what the policy wordings meant by one incident or two separate ones.

A further word of caution is warranted. The placing of a likely impact into one of the four impact measures is clearly a view that is taken by these authors and, however carefully this is done, this may be fallible. The failures may be in the definitions and criteria used; and also in the allocation of a scenario into one of the categories. As in the case study above the world of risk brings new scenarios regularly. Past experience may not be a full indication of what may happen in the future. The appalling situation unfolding after the earthquake near Sarawak in December 2004 is just such a desperately sad example. Who beforehand could have anticipated a scenario that an earthquake could create a tsunami so big that it could devastate a whole range of countries from Malaysia to Africa?

A Group organisation may be comfortable that financial losses in any one incident below, say, $1,000,000 anywhere across the group are considered marginal. A minority shareholder of a subsidiary, say with a 40% share, may be uncomfortable with a net exposure of $400,000. This would be especially so if the news came as a surprise after the event of the loss. Inner protection for that shareholder may be necessary using insurance or another risk transfer mechanism if that shareholder is not itself to be threatened by financially crippling losses..

A further word of caution is a reminder that there is not one simple approach that can be imported successfully into any organisation. Nor is there one catch-all approach that is successful. The approach, the project range, the words used and the processes applied need to relate quite specifically within the organisation itself, its pressure points and its cultures and marketplace. The Business Continuity Institute Good Practice Guidelines (2) for example states on page 26 that "... *A Business Impact Analysis should be completed in advance of a Risk assessment to identify the urgent functions upon which the risk assessment should be focused.*"

This statement makes assumptions about the BIAs and the RAs themselves and what they are trying to achieve. If the RA is all about assessing the physical and technological risks to a piece of technology that has been identified as critical, then this sequence has values. However, the much wider range of a risk manager's risk analysis goes beyond these physical aspects and takes on board much wider risk and consequence issues. There is an argument in this case that the RA should be done first not second so that the BCM and its detailed BIA work can be focused where there is the greatest strategic and consequence across the group. Neither is right nor wrong; the point is that the terminology must be clear and common to all participants in the objectives of business continuity.

Frequency Of Risk Incidents

When considering potential risk incidents, the risk manager routinely considers the likely frequency of damaging incidents. This is especially so when making cost/benefit decisions to reduce the cost of routine and fairly frequent risk incidents that will give an accumulated cost benefit over an accounting period.

A typical risk analysis matrix prepared by a risk manager would assess the likely event frequency and may produce a table on the lines of the following. This enables a projection of the total cost of a risk over the decided accountancy period; say, a financial reporting year. This in turn can then lead towards effective cost/benefit decisions on risk management spending and the projected return on that spending over a defined period of time.

It is valuable to look at the total cost of risk over a period when deciding whether to invest in risk management to reduce the cost of those losses. An example would be to spend on additional security to reduce shoplifting levels across a chain of shops. Such a period cost would be valuable in understanding the return period on such an investment, say on additional security and shelf design.

Risk managers routinely do this, but it has less value when dealing with potentially catastrophic risk. We explain this further below. A risk manager may use a frequency measure of, say:

1	Frequency lower than once in 10 years
2	Once in 10 years
3	Once in 5 years
4	Annually
5	More that 3 times a year

Risk Matrix

The risk manager will then take this frequency/expectation factor, together with the likely impact definitions into a matrix that brings them together.

By deciding the likely frequency and the likely impact of 10 numbered risks, for example, the risk manager can present a consolidated matrix as shown below. Shading is a useful way to illustrate the decisions made earlier about what is an acceptable level of risk the particular organisation feels it can handle comfortably. In this example, the organisation had decided that it would retain for its own account all marginal and negligible risks with an expected frequency of once or less than one occurrence a year; it also accepted critical risks that have a more than 10-year return time.

PROBABILITY		1 Negligible	2 Marginal	3 Critical	4 Catastrophic
5	> 3 times per year				2
4	Annually	1			
3	1 to 5 years		3		7, 8
2	5 to 10 years	9,10		4,5	
1	< Ten years		6		

SEVERITY

The Special Features of Potentially Catastrophic Risk

The business impact analysis that is targeted at continuity planning needs to focus on potential impacts that could close the organisation. In other words it is necessary to identify those risks that could stop the organisation from delivering its crucial responsibilities long enough to cause unrecoverable damage to itself or to its stakeholders. The 'timeout' factor is crucial, and can be all the difference between a hiccup and destruction. This timeout period will vary dramatically with types of business and stakeholders' expectations. The importance of speed in the immediate response to an incident is not only to meet the need to ensure taking control of the incident, but also to provide reassurances to a whole range of stakeholders that their needs are being met. The BIA definitions also need to ensure that thought is given, and resources pre-staged, to ensure that the damaged organisation can deliver survival-critical and urgent products and services fast enough to maintain contracts and also to maintain the wider credibility in the organisation and its brands. It is absolutely essential, therefore, that these response urgencies are built into the severity definitions.

We mentioned above that continuity planning is less concerned about potential frequencies and return probabilities of incidents. This is because the continuity manager – or the risk manager addressing potentially catastrophic risks - is likely to feel that **all** critical and catastrophic exposures need attention regardless of the frequency – or probability return period. It is of academic interest only to accept that a factory located in a hurricane zone is likely – based on 200 years of experience - to be hit by a hurricane every 25 years. A catastrophic business impact analysis may therefore exclude or demote the likely frequency dimension; just "could it happen; yes or no?"

> *The real message demanding a response is that such a hurricane could hit the area any time during the next hurricane season and the storm could not only damage buildings but, without effective business continuity management, could also destroy any ability to stay in business.*
>
> *It is much more crucial, however, to the risk of catastrophic loss that the incident may happen at all.*

The risk manager considering continuity exposures may still be asked to prioritise those risks that could threaten continuity. In such a case the same structure may be used, although the risk manager may wish to use *likelihood* rather than *frequency*. That would enable earlier attention to be given to the flood exposures of a factory in a known flood zone, for example, over perhaps the archetypal exposure of a plane falling out of the sky on to the same factory. It is again timely here to remind that risk managers considering catastrophic exposures are much more likely to be concentrating on impact to the business dependencies, rather than the precise cause of the damage.

The BIA Agenda

The agenda can now begin to take shape. The manager tasked to deliver a BIA can agree with the chief executives on the range and definitions of the risks which should be addressed; and needs to do so before starting the process of collecting information for the BIA. Should the BIA embrace just operational risk? Specific operational risks, or all risks? Should the analyst address wider risk concerns, including strategic and decision-making risk or potentially destructive financial losses? The approach can be determined from the wide range of risks named in the initial risk map.. Furthermore, impact definitions can be agreed upon that embrace both the organisation itself, and also its range of stakeholders and suppliers.

This can lead directly into an early agreement in principle of what the board considers are acceptable impact levels. These tolerance definitions can then be built directly into the definitions.

The risk manager now has an understanding, an agenda, and clearer objectives that he or she can explain and share with all the players that are about to take the stage. The agenda and definitions can remain constant right across the organisation and thus enable all risks to be measured not only in isolation but also against others competing for limited resources.

A clear picture of the relative priorities between risks is especially useful while responding to an actual live risk incident – and thus working with planning resources beforehand. The crisis teams, facing extensive damage to normal resource levels, will have to make hard decisions about prioritising the use of the very reduced level of resources, equipment, information and people that may be immediately available to them.

The BIA Process: A Suggested Project Outline Plan

1. Obtaining formal approval and "ownership" for the detailed project proposal at the very highest level in the organisation.

2. Ensure a consistency of approach across the organisation by agreeing beforehand on a range of definitions, formats along with precise objectives and deliverables. This would include a definition of negligible, marginal, critical and catastrophic risks (or whatever other classifications are chosen).

3. Decide and obtain approval for the methods to collect and verify information. This will no doubt entail the design of information collection forms and their explanations. The format will approach the information collection either from the point of view of the risks; or the point of view of the critical services and dependencies that need to be continued.

4. One approach is to get the service suppliers (internal facilities managers and also outsourced service suppliers as applicable) to define their current recovery plan scenarios right at the beginning. There is considerable value in obtaining a documented, signed, service level agreement that covers exceptional circumstances as well as 'normal business.' This will enable operational managers to consider the planned scenarios against their opinion of what they themselves need urgently in order to continue to meet their own department's responsibilities. Any shortfalls can then be identified for cost/benefit decisions on how best to ensure the recovery scenarios and the business needs coincide. (If the recoveries are too fast or more than needed, then savings could be made by bringing the responses down to the levels required).

5. Begin the process of obtaining inputs from operational managers and specialist managers across the organisation - hence the vital need for consistency of approach.

6. Obtain the formal acceptance and thus ownership from the contributing managers of the draft reports and the promised service levels and recommendations for their area of responsibility.

7. Present the risk BIA to the board for decision-making and final sign-off. The decision-making process could entail decisions to invest to avoid risk or impact, to accept risk, to transfer the risk, or to prepare continuity planning. The Board may wish also to establish its own ways of monitoring that the agreed recommendations and other action points have been completed satisfactorily and audited.

8. Establish a formal approved process of ensuring that the BIA is kept up to date at pre-agreed intervals.

9. Implement and monitor the updating process

Summary

This chapter set out to lead the reader into the world of the business impact analysis, its role, its values and some of the processes. It set out to bring together the needs and values of both risk and continuity planning. There is a vital need for BIAs to be credible and trusted by a wide range of participants and audiences. The consequence of getting the BIA right or wrong is no less than the very survival of the organisation, the jobs within it, the safety of the investments – money and otherwise – and the responsibilities to a whole range of investors and other stakeholders.

To be credible and measurable the BIA must have a consistent approach and consistent definitions throughout the whole organisation - from board level down to the shop floor. Furthermore, the information input needs to be trusted. That trust will come from input from a wide range of personnel and situations, and by verification of the sources by taking additional views and comparing them. The individual skills of the risk manager and other specialist contributors will add further credibility.

The deliverables are quality and continually up–to-date information upon which risk and business survival decisions will be made. Those decisions will be quality ones where the right level of authority takes on the responsibility and ownership of the need to make those decisions. Furthermore, the staff will recognise that some risks must remain and that the scenario-setting process can only be based on managers' current experiences and imaginations. The 20/20 vision of hindsight, beloved of courtroom lawyers, is not a luxury available to risk managers or their boards at the time of the BIA or the risk assessment.

The BIA has at least three clear purposes:

- *Provide clear, trusted, consistent, measured risk information to managers and the board against which they can make better quality decisions about accepting risk or otherwise managing the risks.*

- *Encourage facilities managers - computer, communications, factory and office managers, etc. - to have their own recovery plans that match precisely (no more, no less) what the operational managers need to continue vital and urgent services and protect critical information.*

- *Deliver critical and useful information into the process of continuity planning and planning documentation.*

(1) Speech by Sir John Bourn; Comptroller and Auditor General, National Audit Office, United Kingdom for the Institute of Risk Management in June 2001.

(2) The Business Continuity Institute: Good Practice Guidelines 2005. www.thebci.org

7

The Business Impact Analysis:
A Hitch-Hikers Guide

The objectives of this Chapter are to:

- Understand practical considerations when moving forward to deliver a BIA

- Identify the options to obtain information and gain a trust in the balanced picture being developed.

- Explain the importance of thorough investigations into cause and effect and thus aid credibility in the final document.

- Consider some options for tools to present risk concepts in a clear and concise way, ready for decision-making.

THE RESEARCH PROGRAMME

We have stated that the BIA has two challenges. One is to understand what risk incidents may occur and divert the organisation from its business model and plans. The second is to understand critically the very arteries of the organisation, including its relationships with a whole range of stakeholders. By bringing these two together the BIA can create real information around which decisions can be made and money and other resources invested. This information is equally about the dependencies of the organisation and just how quickly they need to be reinstated to ensure survival of the organisation. Furthermore, the principles apply whether the organisation is a profit-making company or a not-for-profit organisation. The stakeholders may be different but the pressures and headline responsibilities are the same. We have also stated in our objectives to this chapter that the BIA must be thorough and gain credibility over a whole range of both specialist and general managers. It can then go forward with confidence to the most senior body in the organisation for decisions, sign-off, and indeed to enable that body to meet the demands to report risk levels to regulators, investors and others.

INFORMATION SOURCES

Information is available from a whole range of sources; both internal and external to the organisation.

A. Internal Information Sources

We have stated that the day-by-day risk managers are the operational managers of each business unit; they are complemented by a range of specialist managers.

This information about understanding risks and impact can be farmed in variety of ways; an obvious starting point is amongst the published documents that are already available. These include published accounts and chairmen's statements, audit reports, board and management minutes, organisational charts, flow charts (internal and external supply chain), asset registers, project proposals, travel records, existing risk registers, insurance policies and claims, loss registers, accident logs and other routine management tools. Even a scan of internal job advertisements can give a clue as to how a business unit within the group-wide organisation is proposing to change. Any large organisation is already very likely to have a risk committee and an audit committee. Their output can be checked against the BIA agenda and definitions for a consistency of purpose and then, where of value, used.

The risk manager can then take the BIA format to the individual managers throughout the organisation whom he/she feels has something to add to the pool of information that is needed. This can be done in a variety of ways:

1. Checklists and Questionnaires

One of the best values in checklists or questionnaires is the use by risk management interviewers as a prompt to take them through an interview with an operational or specialist manager. They can be sent and explained by email or memo in advance, and thus give the managers time to consider the issues, and discuss them with their staff as necessary. They take the form of a detailed agenda for that meeting and in turn keep the meeting on track as it unfolds.

They are useful, too, but less so, if the risk manager needs to delegate information-gathering to others, for example, where the sources and the range of the area is so large that it would not be practical for the risk manager to do this personally. They can be useful in bringing information that may need to be gathered in different places back into a common format.

Great care must be taken in the preparation of the questionnaire to ensure that all the relevant and needed information is delivered. A disadvantage of giving a questionnaire to other people to complete is that they will be directed by the questions on the form itself. They may not appreciate the need to add any additional information that could, in that particular circumstance, turn out to be crucial. Another danger is that while the author knows clearly what is intended by the wording of a question – is it precisely clear to each of those who need to answer it? Could there be two interpretations?

> *I am told of early motor insurance proposal forms, searching for details of the engine of the car to be insured, that asked the proposer to respond in a box to the question; 'hp or cc?'. Perhaps not surprisingly the answer often came back as 'cash'. An interesting lesson for those designing risk management questionnaires.*

Checklists and questionnaires can still be an efficient way of getting basic information from a large number of different locations and people. The risk manager will recognise both the limitations as well as the value of this information. They can then add any further information gained from other sources, and can begin to take a view on priorities for further research or other attention; and how best that further information could be gained.

In summary, questionnaires and checklists have an important place in the risk manager's armoury, but care needs to be taken in their design and use. They can be a cheap and efficient way of collating large amounts of information, a way of updating information for current use and for monitoring trends against previous research and useful for putting diverse sources of information into a common format.

They may, however, be completed by someone who may not be skilled in the subject of the questionnaire, and/or be completed by someone who may not understand the objectives and ultimate use of the answers. They themselves carry the risk of being ambiguous to the reader, and at risk of being completed by someone who may have their own reasons for suppressing risk or someone in a hurry who considers simply that their own time is better spent elsewhere.

Table 1: Sample Risk Template

RISK: Ref (numeric or alpha)	
Description of the Risk:	

Risk Sponsor ....

Risk Leader ....

Risk Rating	
Impact (I) (example scale 1 = low impact and 3 = high impact)	
Probability (P) (example scale 1 = low impact and 3 = high impact)	
Significance (I x P divided by 2 or I x P)	
Approximate Numerical Estimate of Risk	
GB£ or US$	
Background to Risk	
Current Controls to manage risk	
Options to improve risk management	Responsibility & Timescale
Residual Risk (after the effect of the control/s has been assessed) rating	Red/Amber/Green

- Red: Target date has been missed or is likely to be missed

- Amber: Progress is currently behind target but plans are in place to complete the necessary action within a reasonable revised timescale

- Green: Action completed or progressing to completion in line with the target date.

DATE COMPLETED ....

COMPLETED BY ....

2. Physical Inspections

There are very few methods as useful as physically viewing the area being studied. This inspection not only allows a very clear and personal picture of the environment at risk, but it allows face-to-face conversations with people 'on the factory floor'. Time may not allow, however, for such visits to all of the business units. The weakness also is that risk managers may not personally possess every technical skill needed to fully evaluate what they see there. It is, nevertheless, an important part of the risk manager's job to visit sites as often as possible. Of crucial importance to the business continuity risk agenda is the urgency by which the service or product must to be reinstated. Important answers to these questions are not gained on the factory floor but in the compliance department, marketing department and elsewhere in the organisation. Furthermore, the view is but a "window of time" and the situation may change quickly.

3. Use Of Risk Surveyors

We have made the proposal earlier in this book that the risk agenda and the business continuity agenda are not separate issues to be considered in total isolation. The risk manager is concerned about reducing the potential for disaster and protecting or duplicating crucial dependencies. The business continuity professionals are equally concerned to ensure that the risk of survival threatening dependencies will not occur.

> *The best continuity management ensures as far as is possible that the damage does not happen in the first place; and if so it does not take away those things that are needed to keep the company alive and in its marketplace.*

There are specialist risk surveyors who can be brought in to carry out inspections and report back; adding their professional assessments to the report. They can be briefed to embrace the commercial concerns of both the risk manager and the continuity manager (for example, how long would it take to source, purchase, and install replacements to that particular production line). They may be employees of the risk manager, supplied by the insurer or by third parties under contract. They may otherwise be independently contracted by the risk manager who requires a specialist explanation of individual risks and consequences. Such knowledge may be around particular constriction exposures, for example, the likely impact on a building of measured windstorm, earthquake, or explosive damage. A professional view may be needed around the use of chemicals or other toxic materials. The range of specialties is as wide as the range of the organisation's different activities; and these specialist can be identified by insurers, their brokers, from with universities, or through their own professional bodies

Other organisations may send surveyors to visit the risk manager's organisation to satisfy agendas of their own. These visitors may include insurers, fire and rescue services, the United Kingdom Health and Safety Executive (or equivalent in another country) overseas representatives, and local authorities. These reports are very useful although they have been introduced for particular purposes and may not embrace all the questions that the host organisation needs answering. This is especially so where the surveyor is introduced by the insurance company or broker. It is likely that this surveyor will only be concerned with those risks that are insured – often a small part of the organisation's basket of worries.

This is not necessarily a bad thing, as long as these differing agendas are understood. In the event of business interruption insurance, there may be value in a sharing of views. Even then, however, the insurance risk surveyor will be concerned with the material damage impact and consequent losses of revenues that occur during the business interruption policy's precisely defined indemnity period of disruption after the loss. In the event of such a loss, there could very likely be a difference in view between the insurer and the insured where the latter wishes to make emergency and immediate expenditures to keep the business alive. The insured may be taking a much longer view than the insurer when considering whether an emergency expenditure is justifiable to keep the business alive. The return period for such an investment could easily be beyond the precise insurance policy indemnity period. This "additional cost" (unless specifically insured beforehand) will not be indemnified by the insurance policy..

Logically, the surveyor can only see those exposures that are present and visible on the day of the survey. It is, therefore, a snapshot in time and can reflect only the activity of the day. While questions can be asked, the survey cannot reflect fully the changes that are being planned and subsequently implemented. There is always the important question of whether the surveyor should surprise the local managers, or give warning of the visit. Giving a warning gives local management an opportunity to 'tidy up' and even hide anything that they suspect the surveyor will find unpalatable. A surprise survey can, conversely, damage an open relationship with the local team that is so important and one that can produce other benefits. There is no simple answer to this, and best practice will vary with the culture of the organisation, the objectives and the degree of concern.

A survey can raise confidence unrealistically. As said, a surveyor sent by another organisation, unless otherwise negotiated, will usually consider only the interests that the surveyor is charged to consider. If that surveyor is sent by the insurers, for example, the risk manager, and by definition the risk manager's board, will need to remember that many of the organisation's greatest continuity dependencies; brand, intellectual assets, staff retention, stakeholder support, ability to deliver on urgent contracts, and many others are uninsured and uninsurable.

Some of the organisation's greatest risks can be those where third party suppliers provide crucial and urgent products and services. The risk manager may have difficulty obtaining the authority to survey in detail these third party premises. This permission is, however, sometimes negotiated within the terms of the original contract of service and may also be a regulatory requirement.

It has been mentioned earlier that risk is the responsibility of each and every manager within the organisation. Regular visits by risk surveyors could, if not carefully managed, encourage the factory or office manager to believe that they can abdicate the responsibility for continuity risk to that surveyor.

4. Brainstorming

There is a clear logic to the fact that the person, who understands a particular risk and potential impact most thoroughly is the local manager of that operational unit. There is, therefore, a wealth of knowledge, experience and understanding among the organisation's own employees. This knowledge lies with both the business units' own operational managers and also with support from the range of experts and specialists we listed earlier.

The 'brainstorm' - or a series of brainstorms - is one way of bring together the risk managers' own skills and agendas and consistency of approach to the deep understanding of the business that lies right across its workforce. This brainstorming can be at any level; and the value of the process is that, with the local manager's support the level of the individuals involved can be chosen, not by 'rank,' but by their skills and understandings that match the precise need. The continuity agenda is much about critical dependencies and the urgencies needed in reinstating the service or product delivery. The wider risk agenda of the risk manager is also about the cost effective balancing or risk investment and risk return.

The risk/continuity manager will therefore set the required agenda, and use all the tools that will ensure consistency of objectives and measurements. Some risk managers prefer to chair such meetings and thus drive the discussion. Others prefer the meetings to be chaired by one of the business unit's own senior managers and to provide support and guidance only. The latter choice does reinforce the view about ownership of risk and continuity lying amongst these managers and avoids an implied suggestion that they can "delegate" the responsibility to the specialists..

The risk and continuity managers will bring the specialist risk management skills and knowledge to add to the thinking of the various other managers and will be able to inject their own thoughts, and those of other risk professionals we have identified, theformat
into the discussion. That input will be, as always, to bring a note of caution on glib "sound bite" answers that may be useful to move the discussion on but fail to get into the depths that may be needed. Harris Interactive undertook an interesting survey amongst hundreds of the world's leading corporate officers, risk managers and investment professionals. The survey, 2004 Protecting Value, (2) asked these managers for their views on what are the top threats to companies. There was a strong message in the differing views between investment professionals and the range of Chief Financial Officers, treasurers and risk managers.

Almost 70% of operational managers said collectively that property related hazards (fire, explosion, natural disaster, supply chain and disruption to the production lines) would cause most disruption to the revenue drivers of their organisation. Only 21% of investment managers agreed, considering that non-property-related incidents (pricing fluctuations, government and regulatory standards, management and employee malfeasance) represent the top threats. This is food for thought and also a reminder to ensure there is caution and "outside-the-box" vision during brainstorming discussions.

It is vital to document the thoughts and decisions formally. It is advisable for any agreed action points to be formally allocated to named individuals and given a time for completion. The person may, of course, be the risk manager or any one of the other participants.

5. Risk Committees

A risk committee is a group of people who meet regularly to share experiences, and concerns, about a particular risk environment. This may be at any level, 'group-wide' or at individual 'factory floor' levels. As above, the chair may not best be the 'risk manager.' If there are risk committees, ideally there should be one risk committee operating at board level.

A board-level risk committee has a delegated authority from the board and sets out to oversee the setting and implementation of the risks-related policies, tolerances and the oversight of risk-related performance. A workshop level team has a role more in the implementation, operational activity and reporting; albeit that this committee might receive its authority from the more senior team. At any level, its brief must be clear and accepted by all the participants. If the brief is to include continuity exposures then that should be stated clearly and the subject should be a standing item on agendas.

One of the most important roles of the audit committee is to understand risks and their potential impact. They will take a view on any risks that have been retained and also take a view on the effectiveness of any risk management controls. The audit committee has an important value in its position of independence from line management and with the inclusion of non-executive directors and external auditors.

These committees may also have a useful reporting line direct to the board and to stakeholders such as regulators. It can therefore be used by the risk manager as an additional communication line to the highest-level decision-makers in the organisation.

B. External Sources of Information

There is literally a world of information on risk and threats available to risk and continuity managers. These sources are both formal and informal. Newspapers and professional magazines, conferences and seminars are useful areas for experiences and ideas. Professional bodies such as the Institute of Risk Management, Business Continuity Institute, The Chartered Insurance Institute, The Disaster Recovery Institute International, Institute of Chartered Accountants, the Law Society, The International Emergency Management Society, American Society of Professional Emergency Managers, Canadian Centre for Emergency Preparedness and many others have quality articles and other information on a whole range of risk-related subjects. Some of these organisations bring quite focused information and skills, such as the Western States Seismic Policy Council and the American Chemistry Council. (There are less formal common interest groups that share experiences of which just one example is the Business Continuance Group in London and the Special Interest Groups of the risk associations of RIMS in the US and AIRMIC in the UK.

The web, of course is a primary tool and countless web sites offer risk and impact information. This can range from the websites of the emergency and other public service bodies to the websites of the organisations themselves that threaten, such as lobby groups that may use threats and violence. Many commercial organisations offer quality information through their websites directly. We include a selected list of these websites and other reading at the end of the book. The research and work done by insurers may also have value for organisations looking at their own risk profiles. The International Underwriters Association has developed a Hazard Atlas (3) in 27 volumes covering countries across Africa, The Middle East and South America. Insurers in the United Kingdom and America have developed flood risk maps where they have assessments of flood risk by postcode or by ZIP Code. Further assessments and maps on flood risk in the United Kingdom are available on the Environment agency's website www.environment-agency.gov.uk/floodmap. Many other useful sources are available, such as the terrorist map produced by the Risk Management Division of the insurers, AON on www.aon.com. Contact information is included in the list of websites at the end of this book.

There are also consultancy companies that specialise in delivering risk information, research and experience to their client organisations.

RISK MODELLING

We can at this point take a step aside and begin to consider the options available for the capturing of all this information and how it can best be presented for decision-making. There are many ways of doing this and there are both values and dangers in each to be considered.

The continuity risk manager needs to elicit, from the myriads of information available, which parts of the organisation deliver services or products that, if they failed, could threaten the survival of the whole. We have here the same dichotomy as mentioned before – how do we know which are potentially destructive unless we study them all? We cannot go on the departmental managers' own assessment of the unit's importance (!) and even more dangerous, we cannot make assumptions that some departments are unimportant.

Case Study

A clerk deep in an accounts department was asked by the continuity manager to explain what she did. The response came back that she produced some figures monthly to another department from a spreadsheet that she had developed and used on her computer. When asked, it became clear she did not know what eventually happened to the figures within the other department. She felt she needed to know more than what had specifically been asked of her and the importance of accuracy.

That other department was the compliance department, charged with producing figures regularly and to a very strict timetable to the regulator who had the power to close the firm down. These figures were a vital ingredient in the compliance department's own presentation.

The compliance department's BIA identified this exposure and above all the urgency by which this information process needs to be reinstated. It would be unreasonable to expect the supplier department to understand the criticality and report this in their own BIA.

Risk managers often begin to look at their wider risk landscape by developing a flow chart that maps the route by which critical deliveries are evolved. This can be a top-down approach where critical needs are mapped back through all the stages that are needed to make it happen. These needs, of course, can be within one business unit, come from another unit within the organisation, or indeed come from an external supplier. They may begin their journey overseas; indeed many are increasingly likely to do so. There are three issues to concern the risk manager:

- Is there confidence about future deliveries?

- Is there confidence about the timing and quality of those future deliveries?

- In the event of a damaging risk incident, can the organisation still continue to deliver urgent needs, fast enough to avoid maintain its brand values and avoid a critical or catastrophic loss?

It may be necessary, therefore, once a final product is identified as being sufficiently important to business continuity to trace those ingredients back through each stage. A risk model, for the purpose of this book's agenda of business continuity, can include the following information.

Risk description	The name, any allocated reference number and description of the risk. The potential cause and the consequences
	Which individual or department carries, and thus has responsibility, for the risk
Dependencies	The physical and financial assets that are at risk.
	Responsibilities that could be impacted by such a risk incident. The processes or dependencies that could be impacted
	The stakeholder expectations that could be impacted. Urgencies
Quantum and status of risk	Overall magnitude and rating of the risk using a pre-agreed measure of financial and non-financial impacts.
	Likely frequency of risk event (as applicable)
	Likelihood of a multiple and concurrent cause creating the damage and/or affecting the outcome.
	How can the damage from such a risk incident unfold throughout the organisation and its stakeholders
Risk Control	Risk control measures Risk measures in place
	Assessment of the practical effectiveness and the cost effectiveness of those risk measures.
	Costed recommendations for a change in risk control.
	The need for continuity planning
	Practical implications of any recommended risk management controls
Residual risk	Any remaining exposures after the recommendations have been completed
	Any new internal risk number or value allocation.
	Comments on future risk performance
	Recommendations for review frequency and updates.

Approvals and decisions required and	This section will raise awareness of risks carried.
	A Board may be asked to do one or more of the following:
	• Accept the risk and indicate that it has done so.
	• Understand risk and approve decision taken by individual business units and subsidiaries or approve that they have the authority to make those decisions.
	• Make changes in risk management or investment.
	• Ensure there is effective and trusted continuity planning in place
	• Confirm that it understands and accepts any remaining risks
Updating	The report will recommend the frequency by which this analysis should be reviewed. This period can reflect the pace of change within the organisation and set the procedures and responsibilities for the updating.
	That procedure is likely to set in place a procedure to ensure that any future decisions to change processes or markets which could affect the risk or continuity profile do not obtain approval without considering and reporting the view of risk managers.

For practical purposes a risk manager may wish to consider risks under various impact headings. These may be market risks, financial risks including liquidity and credit risk, operational risks, legal risks and reputational risks. Risk and impact, however, do not respect organisational boundaries and one incident can damage all these dependencies simultaneously.

A risk and dependency flow chart may graphically look something like the following:

Define Business Objective or Objectives			

Mission critical processes to deliver	1	2	3

Support and ingredients	1	2	3	4

Possible failures

Impact rating	Likelihood rating	Control possibilities

Impact level 1, 2, 3 or 4	

Assessment of balance between risk control, impact control and business continuity opportunities

Risk Reduction?	Recovery plans?

Sign off at each relevant level and spend approvals

Change management

This chart is adapted with permission from the book Enterprise Risk Assessment and Business Impact Analysis: Best Practices by Andew Hiles (2000, Rothstein Associates Inc.)

Particular Approaches

We now need to discuss the varying ways that we can reach the objective. We remind again that this book is directed particularly at one aspect of risk management; i.e., ensuring business continuity, and we must not lose this focus, nor at the same time we should not lose the vision of where business continuity fits within a wider risk agenda. Here we can also remind ourselves of the various objectives of the continuity BIA before we delve into the choices in design and approach.

The BIA needs

- Ownership and a clear place in the decision-making hierarchy of the organisation,

- Clear ownership separately of both the responsibilities and the tasks

- A clear agenda

- Ability to illustrate that the research is thorough and embraces all of the destructive exposures.

- Consistency in approach and measurement across all risks and across the whole organisation.

- To be up to date

- To report in a way that issues can be grasped quickly, and with real information that will enable effective decision-making.

We can approach this particular agenda in one of two quite distinct ways. We can draw up a list of risks which could impact the organisation (either singly or concurrently). We can alternatively come from the other direction and consider the crucial arteries and dependencies of an organisation and then ensure that they can be protected and continued. (See flow chart above) We may consider that a building that houses group-wide technology and communication infrastructures is a vital ingredient and may become damaged or inaccessible. There is an argument that, for the purposes of continuity management, there is less interest in what could be the cause of that damage and the focus is best on recognising its importance and simply ensuring its continuity of service – regardless of the initial cause of damage.

In the next chapter we will consider headline risks that may bring about a threat to continuity. The reader should detect a view that it is the impact of the loss – i.e., the dependency – not a wide-ranging list of risks - that is the focus of continuity planning and a primary driver for the authors of this book. Some of the BIA formats we use later against specific exposures will illustrate this approach.

This is not to say that the cause is unimportant. Knowing the likely cause of damage or loss can raise opportunities to reduce the risk of the incident happening at all. There are many examples, some of which could include firewalls against external viruses and hacking of computer systems. Another example might be sprinklers that would significantly contain fire damage. The best spend on these and other protections is when the potential impact of the loss to vital business arteries is understood clearly and prioritised.

To begin the approach with a huge list of risks will make focus very difficult to achieve and retain. One could also lose sight of the fact that, when a potentially destructive incident occurs, it will in reality be a potential impact to the organisation's survival sensitivities that will drive the board's concern.

There is a clear partnership between these two approaches. Looking at the crucial dependencies, then at what could take them away, enables us to ensure that they are then protected as much as possible against whatever may damage or remove them. Furthermore, an understanding that the potential impact of a small incident or tiny flaw in the value chain could be destructive, can be a powerful incentive to invest in risk diversion.

Case Study

A Business Impact Assessment discovered that a small room of only 10 meters square was a pivot in the intranet and voice communications structure of a large organisation. This room was on the third floor of a large office building. The original design and position of the room had been to service only the building in which it was contained. Furthermore, the building did not have sprinklers. As the years went by the organisation moved more and more staff to this location., and spread to other buildings in the town; one of which became the nationwide computer centre. It increasingly used technology for all processing and communication, including call centres and e-commerce, and thus replaced other means of communication and customer contact.

Changes to the technology and the use of that technology over the years had been introduced gradually. The data and voice communications now travelling through the equipment packed into this small room ranged among that computer centre, three call centres in different parts of the country and all the other operational units nationwide.. Had that small room become unusable (e.g., by fire or flood) the whole organisation would be unable to talk to each other, their supply chain and their customers. The lead time to replace the equipment was seven days although the rebuilding of a physical environment to re-house that equipment could have taken months.

As a result of the business impact analysis, a decision was made to spend substantially to ensure that there was an equipment and cable route around the building.

There is always a danger that any approach will only consider those risks and scale of damage that are within the experience of the managers involved. Examples of where this failed are the terrorist attacks in London in 1993 and in New York City in 2001, and Hurricanes Katrina and Rita in 2005. Indeed, all BIAs and risk management reporting need to carry a "health warning" on this limitation when considering future risk incidents.

Presentation of Risk Information

As information evolves the continuity objective, there will be a need to capture these messages in a format that can be digested so as to identify priorities and potentially destructive risks .

The format described below may be of value but we stress here that each risk manager will have reasons to design one that relates to their own needs. Software products are available which capture information in a format that will help to produce clear pictures of risk and impact. As always with software, the output is as good as the software designers can make it, and only as good as the software design corresponds with the user's specific and individual needs. One of the challenges of crisis management is that it deals with issues that too often divert from patterns and past experiences and come at the organisation from an entirely different direction and level of impact. An important consideration when looking to commercial risk management software is whether it support the ability to "think outside the box."

The format is a wide-risk format. If the agenda is specifically business continuity the column headed 'frequency' may be replaced by the need for urgency to reinstate.

RISK/IMPACT ANALYSIS FORMAT

Risk Reference Number: _____ Date: _____

Vulnerability Scenario

Caused By:	Triggers Single and multiple	Nature of impact and parties affected	Severity	Frequency	Opportunities to manage severity or likelihood	Other issues raised and actions needed. Combination of risk factors?

The Impact-Driven Business Impact Analysis

An impact-driven BIA format looks at anything which, in the view of managers, is a crucial and urgent element in delivering the organisation's own product or service. If we are looking at a building, for example, we can use the same format to consider the possibility of failure, not only due to loss by fire or flood but by destruction or inaccessibility due to a whole range of causes. That inaccessibility may be destruction to the building itself or the loss of power, water failure, telephony service, internal technology failure, disease, or even police cordon caused by an incident beyond the boundaries of the actual site.

Case Study
Nokia relied on a continuous and urgently needed supply of computer chips from a Philips Electronics factory in Albuquerque, New Mexico. Nokia had determined the critical importance and urgency of this source through its business impact analysis. Having established this clear risk and dependency, they had already decided what they had to do, immediately, should the supply fail.
In March, 2000 lightning caused a blaze at the supplier's factory. Within ten minutes of that strike the fire was out of control. Nokia immediately launched its business continuity plan; initiating urgent contracts with the alternate suppliers of this kind of chip. The supplies needed were so substantial that they had contracted with most of the alternate suppliers and as such denied their competitors – who had been sourcing from the same damaged factory – the ability to similarly gain alternate supplies they needed. The sheer speed of reaction; aided by a pre-event BIA and continuity plan not only kept their own business alive but, also disadvantaged competitors who were reeling from the same disaster.

In the next chapter we look at individual concerns and show examples of such BIA formats and how they can best be used.

BIA to Business Recovery Plan (BRP)

There are two fundamental considerations when preparing a business recovery plan. These are:

- What resources; information, people, services and equipment, are needed by the managers trying to retain control over the business, and to keep their business units alive until it is possible to get back fully to normal?

- How fast are these needed?

These decisions therefore are an important part of the business impact analysis. It is important to be clear that any delay periods agreed between risk managers and continuity operatives are timed not from the moment the incident happens, but from the time of the authorised decision to trigger the recovery plan. An example would be the service level agreement (SLA) whereby a technology manager would promise to deliver emergency computers within specified hours or days of damage.

In differing businesses and in differing circumstances these decision times can be crucial; not least when information about the extent of damage is unfolding slowly and there are difficult decisions in the early minutes or hours whether or not to trigger the recovery plan.

One particular deliverable here from a BIA is that the operational managers will formally consider the detail of that service level agreement and confirm – and document that decision – from one of three choices:

- That the technology recovery scenario service level agreement is accepted by them and confirms their view that the speed and quantum promised will enable them to remain in business,

- That they need to change their own department's procedures and controls, or

- That they have further requirements and suggestions of equipment and/or speed.

The technology and other service suppliers – whether internal or third party – can then cost those requirements for decisions that balance cost and effectiveness.

Case Study

A Corporate Affairs department of a large group is responsible for brand management, media affairs and communications with a range of stakeholders from investors to employees. The department management decides that it will need to have communications, tools and information within minutes of a disaster, long before these needs become critical for some other business units within the group. It is clearly not cost-effective to have contingency planning that will enable the whole group to recover fast enough to meet this department's particular needs for immediacy.

A commercially realistic decision was made that this department prepares their communication tools and downloads the information and software they need to an offsite desktop machine that is ready for immediate use. A process was established to ensure that this download is constantly kept up to date as changes are made to the primary computer database.

The BIA will supply other feeders into the recovery plan such as minimum critical needs in numbers of workstations, access to technology and information, communications, etc. It may for example indicate that only certain numbers of staff and workstations are needed within say 24 hours, then 5 days and then 14 days, making the facilities continuity manager's task more commercially realistic. The BIA will also drive what prompts, tools and information a business unit needs to include in its own plans to manage through a potentially disastrous situation. It will identify all those stakeholders who must be contacted proactively and ensure that contact information is protected. It may identify some manuals, critical papers and other things that need to be duplicated offsite. As said above, it will feed demands on facilities managers to deliver their infrastructures fast enough, in quality and quantity that will at least match the critical business need.

It will identify those staff whose skills are crucial – as part of the crisis teams but also to continue meeting stakeholder requirements into the future. It will then go on, as with all urgently needed stakeholders, to ensure contact information is agreed and recorded for instant access offsite.

Risk Reporting

The risk manager will be charged to advise clearly on the risks, risk management opportunities and the retained risks. This report should be delivered to the contributors and to a wider range of interested parties such as Compliance, Audit, risk committees, etc. They can then add their own thoughts. Ultimately of course the board should be in a position to understand the risks that are being carried and make effective decisions around those risks.

We began this chapter with a statement that the BIA needs to be owned and credible. The risk manager can achieve this by producing a draft BIA at each level of development and passing this draft back to the contributors for approval and ownership. This will give them the opportunity to reconsider their answers and also see where their exposures fit alongside others.

With that signoff and stated ownership the risk manager can then consolidate the more serious exposures at the next level in the organisation for the same ownership and acceptance. This will of course ultimately reach the board itself.

One of the ingredients of such a report will no doubt include a long list of action points accepted by the managers, to research further or take a specific action. These action points are best managed internally within those manager's own performance measurement and reporting lines that are already in place.

The risk manager may, however, be charged by the board, risk committee, audit committee or others to give a status report from time to time. This will necessitate going back for information on the progress and can be done specifically or at a later date when the BIA is generally being updated.

If a full new and updated BIA is not considered necessary the risk manager may choose to use a traffic light reporting mechanism to draw attention to individual exposures that may remain. The traffic light system will present all risks against all departments using red as, in the risk managers' view where a catastrophic exposure still remains, amber where a critical exposure remains and green where any such concerns have been removed.

A simplified example of such a report is as follows:

Summary

We set out in this chapter to introduce the reader to the role, shapes and the importance of the BIA. We set out to explain the crucial need for consistency, clear objectives and credibility across the organisation. We have encouraged the reader to think of the specific needs of the continuity business impact analysis within the wider framework of the risk manager's risk analyses.

We then set out to introduce definitions towards this purpose and show how the information needed can be gathered and used. In the next chapter we will present examples.

(1) International Convergence of Capital Measurement and Capital Standards: A Revised Framework; June 2004: Basel Committee on Banking Supervision

(2) 2004 Protecting Value: Harris Interactive/FM GLOBAL. www.protectingvalue.com

(3) Hazard Atlas: The International Underwriters Association. www.iua.co.uk

8

Application and Uses of BIA Information

Objectives Of This Chapter

- Illustrate the wider role and the practicalities of the BIA by reference to individual risks.
- Consider individual risks and impacts related to:
- Intellectual assets
- Physical damage to workstations and production lines
- Outsourcing and the value chain
- Illustrate the differing values of the BIA including the creation of tools and information that lead directly into business recovery plans.

Introduction

In this chapter we lead the reader though the uses and the application of BIA information once it is obtained. We propose to illustrate this by reference to risks that we believe are worthy of individual attention. In this way we hope to be able not only to bring out some special features of these risks, but also illustrate, by example, the wider message about how BIA information can best be used across the organisation. The risks we have chosen represent challenges to the risk manager in three different arenas;

1. Tangible physical risks;
2. Intangible risks such as those around critical information; and ,
3. Risks that emerge from crucial interdependencies within and beyond a fast–moving, contemporary business model.

We have already stated that a clear, consistent and measured understanding of risk and the potential consequences enables an organisation to make better quality decisions about risk and its continuity needs. Decision-making as always has to be commercially realistic and starts with whether the risks identified and measured are acceptable to the organisation. If so, there is a formal decision that the risk will be retained as part of the risk/reward balance of the company. Such a decision will hang on many factors, not least of which are the cultures, pressures, urgencies, strengths and weakness of the organisation; and indeed whether the risks are considered unacceptable to the organisation's stakeholders.

Once the acceptable risks have been recognised the process takes the risk manager through the task of formalising and documenting those decisions at the right level within the organisation. It is also necessary to set in place a process whereby those decisions are checked periodically against future changes in the organisation itself, its sensitivities and environment.

We can now begin to address the unacceptable risks. In this book we are concerned with those risks which are potentially destructive; i.e., will put at risk the very continuity of the organisation. The BIA sets out to identify these critical arteries, and therefore total dependencies and urgencies for the organisation. Once identified, the risk manager can then consider whether they are in themselves a single point of risk. By this we mean that if an identified "artery" was lost, something or someone else would not be available to them quickly enough to deliver that same dependency. In such circumstances the organisation would simply continue as before with perhaps negligible or marginal damage. If the artery does not have the good fortune of such a backup, then there is a business continuity risk needing management.

To clarify the focus, consider that there are many unacceptable risks that are not part of this subject. These could be described as frequent, relatively low-cost risks. They will encourage risk managers to consider risk management measures that would create a net reward over cost-benefit to their organisation over a defined period of time. For example, providing door security equipment and staff at factory entrances will no doubt reduce the cost of internal thefts, burglaries by third parties and distractions by nuisance callers. There may also be some investments in Health and Safety, for example, that provide important benefits at a level below the potential destruction of the whole organisation. These and many other risk management tasks are important but they are, again, to be clear, not subjects for this book.

There are, to be sure, lessons to be learned from frequent low-cost incidents; as well as in different events happening simultaneously and causing destructive consequences. The next one may have dramatic consequences indeed, but for this book we must retain our focus on catastrophic exposures.

We are concerned here with damage, howsoever caused, which could bring the organisation to a close; or at the very least reduce significantly its current position amongst its shareholders and in its marketplace.

We have identified already some of the main arteries of an organisation, which, conversely, are also dependencies that carry with them the exposure to such a total failure. They bear repeating as we enter further into the subject of this chapter. We also listed some, but probably not all, the arteries of the organisation itself. They are:

- Keep people safe;

- Remains legal and authorised by the relevant regulator;

- Protect vital physical and intellectual "assets" owned by the organisation and those assets belonging to others for which it carries important responsibilities;

- Retain confidence in the business and thus the value of the 'brand name;'

- Avoid of litigation costs; and

- Ensure the continuing ability to manage the organisation effectively and deliver on promises and contracts.

A cynical view has been expressed that 'An organisation's Board has three priorities: Strategy, Reputation and Lunch.' Recognising the admittedly often unjustified cynicism, this quotation does reinforce strongly the importance of reputation.

In an earlier chapter we identified a range of stakeholders and the ongoing need to meet their expectations. We listed also some of the different stakeholders and new stakeholder needs that can emerge powerfully even as a disaster is unfolding.

Decision-Making

Once risks and consequences are communicated to the right decision-making level within the organisation – ultimately of course the board or otherwise most senior decision-making body – a response and a commitment to action is essential. Knowledge of these exposures carries with it the clear responsibility to do something with that knowledge. This absolute responsibility to respond to knowledge and to make decisions comes from a demand for good business practice. It also comes specifically from regulatory and control requirements. Furthermore, many regulatory requirements demand not only that boards understand and respond to risk challenges, but go further and actually advise certain named stakeholders what those risk scenarios are, and what they are doing about them.

Knowledge of a risk is therefore not only a useful decision-making tool; it carries with that knowledge an unavoidable need to respond to that knowledge with, first, decisions about the acceptability of that risk, and if not, then what the board is going to do about it. That knowledge also carries another vital responsibility, and that is to advise justifiably interested stakeholders of that risk.

These choices are of course not for the risk or the continuity manager to make. It is ultimately the board that, in significant risks, will balance the whole range of factors we listed earlier before coming to a decision. The role of the risk manager at this point therefore is to consider and cost suggestions for decision making. We will illustrate this process later in this chapter by working with a choice of individual risks; but there are a few headlines that have general application at this point.

The choices – or tools – available to handle unacceptable risk come in four main headings:

- Remove or reduce the chance of the risk incident occurring at all

- Remove the likelihood that the risk incident could so damage the vital arteries of the organisation to the point that continuity is at risk

- Transfer the consequences of a risk to another organisation or person

- Deal with any residual risk by careful, trusted continuity planning that will allow the organisation to manage its way through an incident without unacceptable damage

Reduce or Remove the Chance of A Risk Incident Occurring At All

There are many steps that an organisation could take to reduce the chance of an incident happening which could damage one of the identified arteries. This is an agenda of value to both risk and continuity managers. An obvious example is to increase physical or electronic security around the people, the item or the process.

We need to beware of the difference between reducing the risk and removing it. People talk glibly about a "fireproof" safe. To our knowledge there is no such thing. There are indeed fire retardant safes that will delay the fire and heat damage to a defined specification. This is not the same thing and the professional risk manager must draw a clear difference between the two when considering business critical risks. Furthermore, the emergency services may deny staff access to a damaged building - and therefore the safes in there - for hours or days after an incident; especially if the site is deemed to be unsafe or a crime scene. Crucial tools and information, inaccessible to the recovery teams are as useful as having no survival information at all.

There are other situations which will certainly reduce the chance of a damaging incident but will not remove it; leaving the need still to manage the remaining exposure; often by continuity management

Whilst it may be good practice to work towards damage limitation – say by ensuring that certain processes are undertaken only in buildings with sprinklers – there could indeed be a residual risk of the sprinkler system failing, or even operating when it should not.. That residual risk needs evaluation as part of the whole process and quite difficult, realistic decisions need to be made about whether any risk of destruction still remains for the continuity manager and board's attention.

The organisation may consider that it has reduced the risk down to a potential chance, or frequency, that it now becomes an acceptable risk. That is a decision based on an opinion whether the new risk level, however reduced, is in itself an acceptable or an unacceptable risk. When dealing with catastrophic risk the decision needs to be clear whether the risk has been fully removed or just made less likely. This decision should be made with due caution; bearing in mind as ever we are dealing with concerns no less than the potential destruction of the organisation; not some lesser damage which could be handled internally.

One choice is that the organisation ceases activity altogether. It may decide to stop producing a particular product, or producing it in a particular way, or indeed moving out of a particular country or region. This obviously is a drastic and unfortunate choice to be considered only when no amount of cost-effective risk management or continuity management could return the risk/reward equation back into balance. The board, now understanding the risks, may decide that the profit or other benefits emerging from that particular activity do not warrant the risks being carried, i.e., that the "risk premium" is inadequate and cannot be raised enough to warrant the risk that would need to be carried.

Where an unmanageable risk is immovable and is potentially destructive to the whole organisation, then it is difficult to see where such a risk and reward balance could comfortably exist.

Risk management is not only about firefighting a threat. Risk management has a vital role in guiding the organisation in a much broader way towards reaching a comfortable balance between risk and reward. Decisions on a new venture, a major reorganisation, or even a new factory can gain tremendously from informed risk management at the design stage. A simple example would be for the risk manager to advise on flooding, earthquake, crime, hurricane, political risks and countless other situations when the board is at the stage of deciding between various countries or locations available to them. They would then be making more informed decisions and could indeed in this way avoid destructive hurricane or earthquake damage by choosing a location away from such risk areas. As such, the decision would not be simple, but the advice to go into a particular area may bring with it the cost of risk and continuity management that would be avoided if someplace else was chosen.

Remove the Likelihood That the Risk Incident Could Damage Vital Arteries

The important difference between risk removal and risk reduction applies again when considering the process of removing single points of dependency which could, if lost, bring the organisation to its knees. The board needs to be clear: is it removing the chance of a particular risk incident destroying vital arteries on which the organisation depends for its survival, or is it only reducing the chance? These are vitally different decisions; the latter leaving a smaller perhaps, but nevertheless residual, risk for understanding and managing.

The task here, if achievable, is to ensure the removal of the exposure to the loss of such an isolated dependency. A single computer system that feeds the whole organisation may be beloved by the accountant as cheaper than a dispersed system, but the additional costs and inefficiencies that would follow from separated systems may just become, once the BIA messages are understood, a justifiable risk management expenditure.

> *Certainly duplication – or the ability to gain access quickly enough to an alternate "artery" physically and electronically distinct from the primary dependency - is one solution that demands consideration. It is here, of course, where risk management and continuity management begin their marriage vows and the regular duplication of computer data and removal of the backup tapes far from the primary risk site are now routine data centre management actions. The frequency needed for those backups, and the speed by which new processing facilities become available to operational staff are of course matters that emerge from the BIA.*

Transfer the Consequences of A Risk To Another Organisation Or Person

Risk can be transferred to an insurer or to another party by contract. Insurance is indeed a common form of risk transfer but there are major limitations in what the insurance market can offer. Insurance companies are in effect finance brokers receiving money in some circumstances and returning money back in others. They may indeed be useful in replacing the financial cost of lost assets and even some revenues. They cannot, however, step in and ensure that the organisation's market, customers, credibility, brand values, legality and other essentials to survival remain in place as the work recovering the organisation and its stakeholders from the damage is underway. They may indeed be valuable to the organisation but perhaps only after, by luck or good management, the real essentials of the organisation can be kept alive and developing.

The organisation's lawyers may be able to transfer the potential cost of risk by contract to suppliers, distributors or other counterparties. There is no real value, however, in a risk incident destroying a just-in-time or critical supplier or distributor; that in turn, by its failure, damages or destroys the host organisation's ability to remain in business. The organisation's own customers will not wish to look beyond the immediate contracted supplier for causes and will expect that supplier to take all the consequences of the failure. Such outsourcing changes, but does not replace, the need for a BIA and resultant continuity planning.

Deal With Residual Risk by Careful, Consistent and Trusted Continuity Management And Planning

This of course brings us directly to the primary subject of this book, and positions continuity planning squarely as one of the tools in the risk manager's toolbox. The Board will wish to be assured that if recommendations are cost-effective, and have been approved, they will enable any remaining risk to be clear, quantified, and brought down to a level that is likely to be acceptable to all the stakeholders. This would also include the specific demands of regulators. The board will also want to be in a position where it feels that it can truthfully and clearly explain the level of any residual risks to those stakeholders.

In practice, the risk manager can hunt amongst all the three primary tools above in the toolbox to address a risk that is initially considered unacceptable. It may be a combination of those tools or, if there is real confidence in a continuity plan, then the recommendation may simply be to carry the risk alongside the investment made in producing and quality-checking a trusted continuity plan. Throughout, drivers towards the organisation's choice will be the costs of risk management; whether those costs are financial, the cost of disruptions to the primary business models, or lost opportunity cost. Risk management is not spared the routine cost/benefit business disciplines in all their various options and opportunities.

At this point there is the need for a word of real caution. If an incident could, while it is unfolding, totally destroy one of the arteries on which the organisation depends, then no amount of continuity planning will bring the organisation back to life. The plan will be no more than an expensive boot for kicking a dead donkey. An example would be if an organisation allowed itself to lose vital databases or other information around which the organisation conducts its business.

Effective, wide-picture risk management and continuity planning would plan to switch production to another site adequately and quickly enough so that, in the event of loss of one production line the impact on the organisation could be contained within the negligible or marginal descriptions of the previous chapter. This could be a good decision once all the "health warning" messages have been communicated and understood. Setting plans in place to quickly trigger such a switch could be an alternative to higher-level risk management hardware and processes in each of the factories.

We will now move on to consider some individual exposures and illustrate these principles in doing so.

Intellectual Assets

We have reminded the reader that many a modern organisation is no more than a brand, ownership or legal access to intellectual assets, entrepreneurial and control processes, and to a series of outsourced workforce and product suppliers and distributors. While this may be an extreme example it is by no means uncommon. The intellectual assets of the organisation are likely to be at the very core of its existence.

They come in many forms and of course the relative importance varies widely with the organisation's objectives and how it sets out to deliver those objectives. The wider definition of intellectual assets can include information in the organisation's own databases and paper files, as well as information held by others and third parties in the value chain on which the organisation depends. The wider value of this information of course assumes a physical – or legal – ability to mine that information in a way that enables the organisation to continue doing what it does.

We can extend the description of intellectual assets to include software, designs, patents, research output and research verifications, audit trails for auditors and accountants, recipes, and current work on software, products and other developments. Certain contracts can also be regarded as intellectual assets as indeed relationships and trust exist throughout the supplier and delivery chain to the wider list of stakeholders. The very reputation of the organisation can be described as an intellectual asset, with brand dependencies of reputation, goodwill, credit rating, stock market analyst support; and of course the avoidance of media attack. Last, but by no means least, is the culmination of experience and skills right across the workforce.

Computer Databases

Much of today's information banks are of course deep within the data files in computers. Modern computerisation allows massive amounts of information to be stored in spaces no bigger than some postage stamps. While this sounds like a dreadful concentration of risk, that same technology does provide opportunities to replicate those files wholesale and to have the duplicates well away physically and electronically from the original files.

There are some important decision drivers for arranging such backups. The impact analysis will, of course, dictate just how quickly that database needs to be restored after the original loss. As the use of computers has developed over the years we can now see that they have not only been an addition to the workplace but they have transformed it. A computer does or has done the following things:

- It has replaced large numbers of trained staff, and even some skills that simply do not exist any more;

- It supplies the baseline product and client information;

- It enables credibility in the audit standards and the audit trail.;

- It has the corporate formulae embedded within its software and it allows access by other authorised personnel;

- It communicates wholesale both internally and externally; and,

- It provides useable management information and it secures sensitive information.

Another need that will emerge from the BIA will be how often the backups need to be taken. Unless the BIA dictates the need to back up simultaneously online or in real-time, the backups will be taken periodically. This could be once an hour, once a day or even once a week. An information database in question is totally useless unless it is recovered at the same time as the hardware, software, communications and end-user equipment for that data to be read – or "mined" - and used for further processing. We will explore this in a later chapter.

The frequency of backup will emerge from what the BIA says about the extent of damage caused by the loss of the data that had been entered between the last backup and before the actual time of the loss. Murphy's laws dictate that if it can happen it will, it will happen at the worst possible moment, and therefore the loss will occur just before another backup is due to be taken!

The pressures that this will cause will include the challenge to find the information that had been entered after the last backup; and then apply time and people to re-enter it into the database. The needs to be done to the full satisfaction of auditors and regulators, and at a time when a backlog is growing rapidly. The backlogs will grow exponentially, as this job needs to be done just after there has been a gap in processing availability, and current work continues to flow in. All this will fall onto a unit that is most likely having to manage with reduced staff and workstations as the rebuild of the wider workplace is still underway.

There is rarely a more damaging statement in the Financial Statements than a "qualified" auditor's report saying that they cannot be totally confident of the credibility of the figures being reported. Many processes occur in real time with no paper trail to recapture entries made. A staff member may feel confident that he or she can remember what was done in the last 24 hours but will the auditors believe them?

The next issue is how fast end-user computer access can be restored. On-line, often 24 hours, seven days a week, real-time service providers such as banks, credit card authorisations, emergency services, e-commerce sales and others may decide that they need additional computers in waiting away from the primary site with the data and software already loaded. In the event of failure, key systems can be simultaneously and seamlessly recovered, as far as the stakeholder is concerned. This demands of course that the data backups are downloaded simultaneously to another site. This could be very expensive and will need to be supported by a business impact analysis to justify that considerable added expenditure.

Having computers configured, connected and ready with end user equipment for use in another location is crucial and is the subject of a separate chapter.

Paper Files

For most organizations, the paperless office remains a dream and much information is still kept on paper files that, if lost, could cause critical or catastrophic damage. Many organisations now scan incoming documents and this puts the information within the protection of the computer data files and backup files; as indeed most output is captured safely in "soft copy;" i.e., on computer databases. However, most of us are not yet at the stage where we can be confident that all-important information is scanned in immediately on arrival.

Some files are still needed in the original form, such as in a court of law where scanned or copied information may not be accepted. There may be large numbers of historical and archive files that would not have had a business-case justification to scan them all. The essence here is not the need to retain all the information, but rather to tease out what is potentially critical and catastrophic, and then capture and duplicate the information.

Case Study

A major life insurer was concerned about the loss of a warehouse containing over a million life assurance files. The long-term nature of the life assurance business meant that these files went back as far as 50 years and held massive amounts of information. Most of this information was simply routine adjustments and queries that had been satisfactorily dealt with over the years. To scan all these files would be a massive and costly job.

The business impact analysis report advised that current computer databases carried much of critical information such as payment records, names, addresses, policy covers and amounts, due dates, bonus allocations, and periods. The primary contractual details were intact.

There were, however, two issues demanding a management decision:

Σ The original files had the proposal forms that in turn held the original signatures of the policyholder.

Σ The files had information about mandates going back many years where policyholders had instructed the Assurer to pay named individuals on the life assured's death. The computer files recorded that there were mandates on individual old policies but did not record the precise instructions and the name and relationship of the payee.

As such, there were two issues calling for risk management decision-making.

The decision was that the Assurer felt it could and convince regulators and auditors that it could retain control over the portfolio and the subsequent claims without the policyholders'

---

signatures. Signatures do vary over such long periods of time and as an essential claims control they had a value; but not a crucial one. Managers could anticipate from experience how many claims there are likely to be where the presence of the actual policyholder is disputed. There were other ways identity could be legally established and the cost and resource demands of these occasional disputes could be anticipated and accepted. The decision was therefore to accept the risk of losing the policyholder's signature. This decision was checked with auditors and recorded in a board vote.

The Assurer could not, however, lose the names and details of a significant number of payees within its policy portfolios and continue to profess business control over future claims and maturities. The decision was therefore to create a project to go though the named files and capture this additional information from the old mandates onto computer databases.

When this project was finished the Assurer felt that it had put itself in a position that it could lose all these files in a fire, say, with only negligible or marginal impact. The costly alternative of fire resistant safes, sprinklers, etc. (with their own risk of failure) or other risk diversions was averted.

Appendix A to this chapter is a format used by organisations to guide their managers to think through what information they may be holding that is critical and at the same time unable to be retrieved from any alternate source. It will be seen within this format that identifying such information leads directly to action points that have become the responsibility of named people and have timelines when they need to be delivered. The format also enables managers to capture information that would be needed immediately, especially as a damaging situation is still unfolding. It may not be acceptable to wait for some information while databases and technology infrastructure are being rebuilt; for example, additional document copies on paper, CDs or on laptops may need to be stored separately; say in the recovery plan or offsite. An obvious example of this information would be staff phone numbers and next-of-kin information.

Crucial Information Held In Brains

Here there are various exposures. The organisation may lose access to human intelligence by death, injury or simply by resignation. If any information that is held or understood only by one person or one team, is crucial and urgent – for example, the workings of the technology around a single item of crucial communications linkage – then that risk should be identified and managed. The organisation needs to consider also that a person or a small team may be lost in the disaster itself. This is a subject for succession planning (and the training that goes around that process) and for developing and maintaining procedure manuals.

It is a mistake to consider that the importance of a person's knowledge to the organisation is a matter measured by current rank in that organisation. The issue here is a single point of knowledge about an artery on which rests a whole chain of other dependencies.

An important side issue here is the vital need to keep contact details up to date in the recovery plans. A brain is of no value whatsoever if the organisation cannot make contact with the body to whom it is attached!

Case Study

Following a major bombing incident the incident controller telephoned the house of a team leader he needed to urgently rebuild a LAN. It was a Saturday morning but the incident controller was still surprised by the lady's aggression when he asked to speak to her husband. She refused and after he had pressed her a couple times to do so, she told him, "My husband has been living with another women for six months now and I don't even care where he lives!" She then rang off.

Another exposure is around the confidentiality of that information. Once the BIA has identified the criticality of certain information, it is a relatively mechanical or electronic operation to build security around databases, around workplaces and also control access to buildings, parts of buildings, to individual reports and other papers. This not to say that these measures do not fail spectacularly sometimes! The detail of this kind of information and physical security is a subject in itself, but it is important to say here that such security is by no means the full answer to the problem.

It is much more difficult to stop loose tongues. It is of no value criticising staff for releasing information if no one had taken the trouble through a BIA to recognise a particular sensitivity and then go on to advise the staff of that sensitivity. There are staff who, by their lifestyles and perhaps financial difficulties, are more open that others to blackmail and coercion. These are day-to-day challenges for the risk manager in highly sensitive operations. Where the potential consequences are critical to business survival then they also are a matter for the continuity management of the organisation.

Case Study

A risk manager of a multinational had a phone call from a friend, a risk manager in another organisation. "Did you have a conference yesterday in Hotel X where you discussed future company strategy?" The answer was in the affirmative and the friend advised him that members of his own company had heard every word the speakers had said. They had had a conference of their own in a neighbouring hotel and their speakers had picked up the lapel microphones from the other conference.

Cheaper conference microphone systems have only three wavelengths. The more sophisticated – and thus more expensive ones – have many, dramatically reducing the chance of a neighbouring hotel using the same wavelength.

Whether or not to invest in the more sophisticated equipment is a risk management decision that evolves around the sensitivity of what is being discussed and how much damage the accidental release of the information would create.

The principle applies equally to whether identified individual staff handling very sensitive information should have – or have access to – encrypted telephones; or indeed additional background security checks.

Information Held Elsewhere Within the Supply Chain Or Delivery Chain

Risk and continuity managers need to be concerned about information that is crucial to their own organisation's survival, but is held elsewhere within the supply or delivery chain. We will cover this exposure separately below under the supply chain heading.

The Security of Information During A Crisis

We will develop this need in a later paragraph but there are a few information issues that should not be overlooked as the crisis is actually unfolding. The first deals with paper files. Papers left on desks may be considered by some to be safe in normal circumstances even though they may have sensitive and critical information. This is in itself a fallacy, as the information is left open to other staff, cleaners, contractors and anyone else who, during the night may be legally (or illegally) in the area. Furthermore, a significant and damaging incident to the building may remove security and or even destroy walls and doors; and thus may cause the information in those papers to be released.

Case Study

Bombs detonated by the Provisional Irish Republican Army (PIRA) in London and elsewhere destroyed windows, doors and in some buildings the very walls themselves. Papers were blown by the force of the bomb - and later by wind - out of the buildings and across streets. Papers from higher floors of multi-story buildings travelled many hundreds of yards.

Following the Bishopsgate bombing police took the decision to bring in shredders and shredded all paper that was found. These experiences reinforced the risk managers' demands for a "clear desk" policy at the end of each working day.

The damage here of course is not just around organisation-sensitive information that would cause damage if it were released. Many an organisation, of which banks are just one example – hold sensitive information relating to other people. The failure of the security around that information can bring at least a demand for damages, and additionally a loss of reputation to the whole organisation. There may also be prosecutions under such statutes as the United Kingdom's Data Protection Act.

Information during a crisis will be demanded by a whole range of stakeholders, not to speak of the particular agendas and demands of the media. These demands need to be fed by factual, up to date, and considered release of information. The two challenges, proactive release and the avoidance of uncontrolled release of rumours and guesswork, are addressed in the communications chapter that follows.

PHYSICAL DAMAGE TO WORKSTATIONS AND PRODUCTION LINES

An important exposure here is the loss of the workstation and the equipment within and around that workplace that enables employees to deliver their particular output which in turn is an ingredient in the organisation's final delivery. It may be a service delivered from an office environment or call centre; or a product emerging from a piece of machinery on a factory floor. As always the continuity manager is concerned with the urgency by which that product or service is needed; and therefore the likely "down time" until the equipment and workstation can be reinstated – i.e., normal business is resumed.

We will assume that the BIA has established that it is critical; and the urgency is such that the customer cannot wait until the entire workplace is rebuilt. Rebuild time should never be underestimated! Following major damage, an organisation may need to tread its way initially through damage assessment, then clearance or demolition of damaged area, and make decisions on how to rebuild. Before that rebuild is completed, however, negotiations may be necessary with employees, suppliers, insurers and planners. Then there is the detail design work, drawing of specifications, going for tendering, deciding which contractor to employ and then negotiating the details with that contractor. All this can take many months or even years before physical work is started. Then of course there is the time the contractors need to construct as agreed, equip, and effect the handover.

This lead-time can be extended even further as a board may wish to take time to consider and decide whether it wishes to take this new opportunity to re-engineer the processes by which the products had been manufactured or services ddelivered before the incident. They may wish to take the opportunity to take up new technology or machinery, move to a new location or to upsize or downsize to meet current market conditions and opportunities. An additional delay could be caused by the lead time for the delivery of individually designed, large units of machinery from a limited choice of manufacturers. This could take years rather than months.

Almost inevitably the risk manager will need to be able to offer temporary, but adequately equipped, alternate workspaces. It is not reasonable to expect that these can be easily found and sourced after the disaster in time to meet urgent needs. The risk manager must therefore prepare these options beforehand so they can be brought on stream when needed.

Commercial realism is likely to dictate that a smaller number of workspaces are created, at least initially; responding directly to the information in the BIA that has already established the critical and also most urgent services that are crucial to the organisation's survival.

These alternatives can come in differing formats.

They can be additional capacities in people and equipment elsewhere within the group so that they can immediately take on the additional burden from the damaged unit. By necessity the burden will be both on equipment and on trained staff. Both, of course, usually need to be available in the same place as well as in adequate numbers.

The organisation can arrange with existing or new service suppliers who are able to take up the strain at very short notice. An example would be where professional outsourced call centres can take the organisations software quickly and respond to calls from customers. In some cases, especially where there are reputational risks to the whole market, this support may even be supplied, by prior agreement, by competitors.

Case Study

A multinational financial services group had a range of subsidiaries providing banking, investment management, consultancy, insurance, life assurance and pensions services. The dealing room of one of the subsidiaries was destroyed by large terrorist bomb. The recovery plan stated that a smaller number of dealers would secure room in the dealing room of one of the fellow subsidiaries and thus be able to maintain market positions as required.

The regulator reminded them, however, that they must always maintain "Chinese walls" – i.e., total separation between the different, sometimes competing products sold by the different subsidiaries.

Dealing from the same dealing room would cause them to be in breach of the regulatory approvals. They were unable therefore to make use of this aspect of the plan.

There are contingency service contractors whose business is to supply replacement technology, communications and office workstations within a defined number of hours or days. These services are rarely available, however, for manufacturing industries due to the often-bespoke nature of the machinery in use.

Case Study

An international life insurer had a major office in the Isle of Man where they enjoyed relatively advantageous tax laws for themselves and their customers on the life assurance, pension and investment management products sold in many countries around the world.

They considered that one option to plan to continue service after damage would be for the UK parent company to produce their policies and deliver services from the large group computer suites and offices in mainland UK. They were advised however that, had they done so, the policies would be UK policies subject to UK regulations and taxation. The resultant tax charge on both the company and its policyholders would have removed all the values in the business model and the ability to compete with other international Life Assurers.Contingency workstations and technology had to be prepared within the same legal and taxation environment by contract with contingency technology and workstation suppliers within the Isle of Man.

SUPPLY CHAIN RISKS

Increasingly organisations are outsourcing crucial elements of the processes that lead in turn to the production of the final product or service to their own customer. Indeed there are organisations that will outsource the whole of the production; taking the role only of marketing and distribution.

In an earlier chapter we discussed the three risk challenges facing supply chain management:

- Even massive organisations often find from their BIA investigations that their whole organisation depends on the timely delivery of one supplier's ingredient, service or intellectual asset.

- A supplier, hearing of the customer reeling from serious damage, may not wish to continue supplying without renegotiating the terms of the contract. These renegotiations may include more expensive cost of credit, payments in advance or other guarantees of the continuing ability to pay.

- Some contracts have individual requirements fundamental to the very acceptance that the contract of supply has been satisfied. Contracts to deliver to a military client for example, may have special needs to ensure security around the product information. An incident that disables such security or other special needs can bring the whole contract to a close.

Case Study

Metro International is a Swedish publisher based in London. It publishes 34 local editions of its free newspaper and distributes them in sixteen countries. It is growing phenomenally even in the face of a weak market. The newspaper employs fewer reporters than most of its competitors as it buys most of its content from the news and picture agencies. It does not own any printing processes but outsources all its printing; as it does much of its distribution.

Kjell Nordstrum (1) describes the company model illustrated by Metro as a "hollow company." It is similar to other successful business models used by companies such as Dell, Lastminute.com, Google, and Ikea.

Successful as this model is, it does bring very special business continuity challenges for the risk manager in the area of outsourced supply chains.

The supply chain, indeed the delivery chain into which the risk manager's own organisation supplies, is a crucial single point of risk. Any breakage in that chain, however caused, could bring the whole business down with consequences to be faced along its length. That failure may equally be in a supplier failing to deliver a crucial ingredient, or to a failure further up the delivery chain causing customers to stop receiving goods from the risk manager's own organisation. Both can be equally destructive. Sobering thoughts emerged from a Gartner survey that said that the failure rate of outsourcing contracts is over 50%. Metrica Research, a UK research firm, suggested in its research that the greatest worries for risk managers involved outsourced processes. They were:

- Losing control over the process
- Losing control of customer relationships
- Potential loss of quality
- Threats to brand and reputation
- The operational and financial stability of the supplier

There is a further thought to take into decision-making. If the contract is to supply an urgently needed part or service essential to the organisation's own contracted promises and reputation, no amount of cleverly worded penalty clauses written into the contracts will be any value whatsoever to the very survival of the business that has been let down.

Some of these contracts are for huge service deliveries. For example, following a contract with BT and Ventura, over half of the 50 million telephoned rail enquiries in the United Kingdom will be handled by them from India. The sheer scale of such operations brings special challenges for risk managers if or when they fail.

The risk manager therefore will wish firstly, to be satisfied that the contracts to supply to, or receive from, his or her own organisation are in turn with organisations that are professional and of good reputation. Establishing comfort with that professionalism is increasingly taking the form of demanding assurances from the supplier about its own continuity planning

The reality is that however professional the supplier, it may experience a failure. If the failure involves the delivery of a part or ingredient that is essential and urgently needed to enable the organisation to complete to its own customer, then there is a critical or catastrophic risk that needs managing.

Continuity managers again have choices. They can start with the initial business model, and the best advice may be not to use one supplier but a number of different ones supplying the same part. This may not be initially as cost-effective and can diminish the bargaining strength with each supplier. However, the potential, possible greater cost could be seen to be an effective investment in continuity management where the exposure is felt to be so important. A similar risk management spend would be to incur the cost of a higher level of stocks kept in the incoming warehouse than would be thought necessary in a risk-free world.

The organisation may have outsourced a product or service delivery; e.g., has sold on or otherwise removed the ability to deliver a crucial part of the supply chain from internal resources. The assets and skills now belong to a third party. This of course increases the dependencies and reduces the options in the event of failure. This is at the sharp end of supplier management that always has a need to ensure timely delivery of quality supplies into any remaining production line.

When considering outsourcing to third parties the decision-makers need to be made aware by the continuity manager of the, often urgent and critical dependencies they are assuming. Of necessity the organisation will have less control over these dependencies. Furthermore, the supplier may be overseas, subject to different nature risks, environmental exposures and be working in different legal environments. The cities and countries where they operate may neither enjoy the same resilience in their public services nor the ability to respond efficiently to a major natural or man-made disaster. The transport and communication links add further risks.

It is crucial that the risks and consequences of outsourcing are clearly understood and documented decisions made about the acceptability of those risks and the risk/benefit balance as well as the cost/benefit balance.

> That decision needs to embrace the fact that, in an emergency, the supplier may not be able or willing to divert staff from other contracts to support the special needs of an organisation in distress. A damaged organisation will be able to make decisions to change its own priorities overnight and move its own staff around to fight for survival and to meet new and immediate needs. This may not be an option when the workforce is answerable to another party with its own agendas, priorities and responsibilities.

The supplier may have gained control over key elements of the product or service, without which the receiving organisation may never be able to step in and arrange an alternate supply. These are very likely to be in the realm of intellectual property and by way of example could include client databases, software codes, designs, manuals, patents and many other essentials. If the BIA indicates sufficient importance to this link in the chain, the receiving organisation will wish to establish both the physical access, and the legality of access, to these tools. It could simply be that the supply contract demands that this information be deposited into an escrow account, in the custody of a third party such as a solicitor. The solicitor will be empowered by contract between supplier and customer to release this information to the other party in defined failure circumstances. Laws such as the Data Protection Act in the UK may deny another organisation using a database of client information for its own needs and this constraint will need to be recognised in the negotiations and steps needed to protect from exposures.

In another chapter we will explore the ways of benchmarking and otherwise gaining credibility in continuity planning; and in doing so illustrate that this is not easy to achieve. This is not just because the risk manager is dealing only with circumstances that are within the past experience and current imagination of the planners. When trying to verify a third party's continuity risk and risk management the difficulty is much greater. Hence the need to ask –

- Are we satisfied they have managed the risk of failure as reasonable as we can expect?

- Does their continuity planning embrace the needs of the customers as well as their own urgencies and needs?

- What would happen to us if they fail us?

- What do we need to be able to continue to meet our own important responsibilities?

- How quickly do we need those things?

- What do we need to do beforehand to ensure we can meet those challenges quickly enough to retain credibility and stay in business?

The BIA as Feeder for the Recovery Plans

The primary purpose of the BIA is to discover whether the organisation has any single points of dependency or special urgencies that, if lost, could destroy any ability to recover. With those risks effectively managed, the recovery planning and the response teams have at least a chance of keeping the organisation alive.

An additional and important value of the BIA is to provide direct feeders into the recovery planning itself. We address recovery plans and their ingredients in a later chapter but it is valuable to highlight briefly here how the BIA can link directly into the recovery plans and can deliver specific ingredients into that planning and the planning documentation.

An effective BIA will bring out the sensitivities, the urgencies and the priorities for an organisation facing a potentially destructive crisis. This enables planners to embrace those needs quite specifically when putting their plans together.

The BIA will have engineered an agreement between facilities managers and business managers for the minimum service levels needed, post-incident, to meet immediate needs. The facilities managers will then have costed those needs, and then obtained approval for arranging, internally or by contract with others, for those facilities to be available **exactly** as required. This contingency level of technology, communications and other facilities will be stated in a service level agreement and will dictate levels needed at, for example, incident plus 24 hours, plus five days and plus 14 days. The schedule may look something like Appendix C at the end of this chapter.

The plans will have BIA-developed information on priorities, procedures, prompts and manuals either in the plans themselves or additionally in an offsite storage facility ready for immediate use. The BIA will also have identified crucial customers, emergency contractors, and other stakeholders whose names and contact information will similarly be made available immediately. The BIA may have identified people whose role is so crucial that they need to be part of the response teams and should be trained accordingly. If there are unhealthy dependencies on one person or team then the BIA will direct that information manuals, and information about the emergency succession planning in place, be made available immediately to the response teams.

Summary

We stated earlier that:

'In summary a BIA has a clear and practical focus to its objectives, and that is to enable more informed, and therefore better, decisions about continuity risk, its acceptance, and its

management. It is thus not an academic document but a working information tool that must be trusted, as complete as it is possible to be, and constantly kept up to date.'

Its value is to ensure that the organisation does not unwittingly carry a risk that is potentially destructive; and where such risks are discovered and measured that there is a suitable response to ensure that any unacceptable exposure or potential damage is managed down to an acceptable level. Where that response entails the use of a developed and trusted continuity plan, then the BIA will provide information and guidance in the development of that plan and will also direct ingredients into the finished product.

With this partnership of knowledge, decision-making and preparation, the organisation will be able to feel better prepared and will have a much better chance of survival through whatever disruptions may come their way.

Further Reading: Good Practice Guidelines 2005. The Business Continuity Institute. www.thebci.org

(1) Karioke Capitalism: Kjell Nordstrum and Jonas Ridderdale

Appendix A to Chapter 8
BUSINESS IMPACT ANALYSIS: CRITICAL PAPER-BASED INFORMATION

NOTES:

1   The attached has been designed to identify crucial business information which could be destroyed in a disaster; e.g. destruction of the building by fire or bomb. Please duplicate continuation pages.

2   We suggest that 'crucial business information' is that which is needed to meet the agreed definition of business critical or catastrophic. Please feel free to change that definition beforehand.

3   The intention is that this format is completed in a particular way. We ask that you first complete columns one and two only, i.e., identify all information that you have on paper that is crucial.

4   Only then do you go onto column three which is for you to decide whether you have enough of the information off-site to meet the above needs. This could be on a computer database, other premises, etc. Column four is for you to identify where. If you have indicated 'No' in column three then we ask you in this form to identify a responsible manager for that information.

5   If information is considered 'business-crucial or catastrophic' and deemed not replaceable, the identified responsible manager is charged with considering the potential business impact; then making a decision to accept the business risk or to protect or duplicate the information in a way he or she considers most effective. He or she will be asked to notify that decision.

6   The 'action point' list is therefore created from items marked 'No' in column 3 added to the risk analysis.

7   The 'same-day need' implies that special information will be needed to maintain service immediately after a disaster occurs and is therefore best identified in the separate recovery plan and stored in the off-site store or where it can be accessed immediately.

CRITICAL PAPER-BASED INFORMATION

Appendix A (2)

This form is best used in conjunction with the explanatory notes.

	Business unit / department	Critical information on paper	Is enough info available off-site to enable you to meet your key responsibilities?		If 'yes' where?	If 'no' who is identified to resolve this exposure or formally accept the risk?
			YES	NO		
1	2	3			4	5	6
Example: Client services			Yes			Same day need?
	Staff files			No	Information is available from computer databases	N/A
	Individual agency contacts			N/A	N/A	J Smith
						No

NOTE: Where NO is the response in Column 3 please establish an action point for the manager identified. "Off-site" can include computer database and sufficient information duplicated in an office more than half a mile away.

Appendix A (3)

1	2	3		4	5	6
Business unit / department	Critical information on paper	Is enough info available off-site to enable you to meet your key responsibilities?		If 'yes' where?	If 'no' who is identified to resolve this exposure or formally accept the risk?	Same day need?
		YES	NO			

NOTE: Where NO is the response in Column 3 please establish an action point for the manager identified. "Off-site" can include computer database and sufficient information duplicated in an office more than half a mile away.

Please note below any action points arising from this form. (All answers 'No' in Column 3 should be reflected as an action point.)

ACTION POINT	NAME	TARGET DATE
(Anything for offsite store immediate use?)		

Appendix B to Chapter 8
BUSINESS IMPACT AND RISK ANALYSIS

CRITICAL SUPPLIERS

Name	Internal?	External?	Product or service supplied	How could they fail you?	How could you fail them?	Urgency		
						24 hours	3 days	1 week

Appendix B (2) **CRITICAL SUPPLIERS**

Supplier	Internal?	External?	Product or service supplied	Alternatives needed				Urgency		
				Physical assets	Intellectual assets	Processes	Workforce	<24 hours	3 days	7 days

SOLUTIONS PROPOSED AND RISK MANAGEMENT IN PLACE

ACTION/DECISIONS NEEDED

ACTION	BY WHOM	URGENCY

Appendix C to Chapter 8

BUSINESS RECOVERY PLAN: MINIMUM RESOURCE REQUIREMENTS

DEPARTMENT/ LOCATION	PRIORITY	STAFF		PHONES	DESKTOP MACHINES	PRINTERS	FAX	OTHER
		Existing	Minimum Needed					Please schedule
1	A							
	B							
	C							
2	A							
	B							
	C							
3	A							
	B							
	C							
4	A							
	B							
	C							
TOTAL	A							
	B							
	C							

We would expect that some departments have A, B and C requirements. Please use separate lines

Priority

A   Implies essential within 24 hours.
B   Implies essential within 5 days.
C   Implies 2 weeks or can work from home/elsewhere.

9

Technology, Exposures and Continuity

The Objectives Of This Chapter Are To:

- Consider the special dependencies and the exposures around the technological services to an organisation.

- Embrace the dependencies and interdependencies of centralised computer services, distributed systems, communications and end user equipment, and, to embrace the exposures around laptops and other remote equipment.

- Encourage the risk manager to embrace the risks within both in-house as well as outsourced services and dependencies

- Bring together and match the opportunities available from the technology suppliers with critical and urgent operational needs.

- Consider the special expectations, exposures and dependencies of e-commerce

- Ensure the risk management and continuity of computerised systems embrace the mutual dependencies between technical services, the "old technologies" and people.

- Once the dependencies and opportunities are clear, encourage the organisation to develop technological continuity plans that will precisely meet those urgent crucial needs.

- Ensure as best possible a credibility in technology risk management and continuity planning

- Establish ground rules and checklists in creating technology continuity plans.

THE SPECIAL DEPENDENCIES AND THE EXPOSURES OF TECHNOLOGICAL SERVICES TO AN ORGANISATION

Who Best To Recognise These Dependencies?

Much of business continuity thinking still shows its roots in the technology arena. This was where the dependencies that emerged from the early computerisation of critical back-room services and information management were first recognised. As a result traditional business continuity guides began by addressing computer systems and other technology facilities. Next was the introduction of a "route map" addressing technical issues like the ability to back up information and the creation of emergency computerisation services to support a mainframe failure. The use and inevitably , therefore,- the dependencies on technology have moved on significantly in recent years from these "back-room" services, as has the art (or science?) of business continuity management.

This book is not written for the technician. As such, it has an important agenda: to ensure that operations managers and technical managers actually communicate clearly on matters of business need and priorities during a potential disaster. Sadly, experience does not always show a huge success in this aim, at best achieving near-misses in matching technology to needs. Bringing recovery levels and recovery times forward is very expensive. To plan to recover more and faster than is needed is a significant waste of money. To plan to recover too little too slow, by contrast, could be as destructive as having no planning at all.

Such mismatching is a critical, even survival, issue in a fast-moving, competitive business model or in an organisation that carries responsibilities to thousands or millions of service users. We should spare a thought of what would happen if such a mismatch occurred during a potentially disastrous incident such as the sudden destruction of the primary computer services that are the very backbone of an organisation. This failure may just as easily be technological in nature. It may be the failure of the building or other physical aspects such as access to buildings, air conditioning, power, or even water to staff toilets which will have the same ultimate result: disrupted services.

During a crisis that is potentially a life-or-death threat to the business or to its people, temperatures around the decision-makers rise rapidly, urgencies contract dramatically, the consequences of actions and decisions explode, and there is huge pressure on the (most likely diminished) resources that are available. A slight mismatch (or worse a failure to deliver) between the recovery scenarios planned by the technology managers and the needs of the operational managers can be totally destructive, rendering the recovery teams utterly impotent.

In any organisation the art is to get back the right balance of equipment and people and the right speed in doing so. It is not realistically achievable for an organisation to have a backed–up, fully serviced workstation available for every employee within minutes of a denial of access to the normal workstation. Commercially realistic and hard decisions need to be made about the minimums needed to ensure critical, urgent service levels and how fast they would be needed. It is quite normal to plan for a staged recovery with workstations increasingly becoming available minutes, hours and even days after the event. These workstations would need to be far enough away from the primary buildings without creating a separate risk.

A need for immediacy will typically entail the pre-positioning of fully serviced workstations with communications, software and data that has been simultaneously backed up to the contingency technology. Having these facilities available for immediate use is very expensive indeed and the longer they can be realistically delayed, gives more and more opportunity to defer the costs until after the event. Furthermore, post-event costs are insurable. Before–the-event preparation is just good management and not insurable.

As stated elsewhere in this book, the dependencies and criticalities do not differ one iota should those services be provided by an in-house team, a third party contracted to the organisation or, most often, a combination of the two. That disaster may be initiated within the service supplier organisation or separately in the customer organisation. The risks of failure can be very different, as can also the ability of these external service suppliers to react to a crisis. They may have additional resources to bring to a disaster suffered by one client; but on the other hand may not be able to re-prioritise their own resources sufficiently and fast enough from one client to another. Even the very links between the differing types of service suppliers, the understandings, the contracts, and the points of contact between them can be additional risks in themselves.

Remember the supplier is a stakeholder in itself and may become concerned about the creditworthiness of the client, just at the time when that client has an urgent need for exceptional service delivery to help them climb out of a critical disaster scenario.

> *Managing the ongoing exposures, whether in-house or external, and managing a live crisis therefore are vastly different challenges, but as we set out to consider technology continuity we need to remember throughout that the consequences of failure are the same. To consider just one part of the picture alone – the in-house technology team – which happens too often as a result of the business continuity function owned and run by in-house technology departments themselves, leaves major exposures. To criticise them for mentally staying within their own organisational boundaries is unfair. As said often in this book the responsibility for the helicopter view on risk and for engineering activity lies at the very head of the organisation.*

If the fundamentals of ownership and vision on business continuity are wrong, the roll-on effect of the dreaded 'tick box' of audit reports and regulatory questionnaires can raise expectations far beyond the reality of an organisation's true resilience.

Ownership

It is therefore vital that the ownership of risks to the continuity of technology is clearly and correctly placed and accepted by the nominated 'owners.' Business continuity management needs to make a distinct break away from its roots in facilities management and take its place clearly at board level. It must become an integral part of the operational decisions that are made about effective operational processing, change management, risk and the acceptance of risk.

Several features are necessary for such a sea change to be effective. It is too easy to dump the task on a facilities manager, hoping that by doing so the diversion will go away. The first threat lies around the skill base of the people nominated to do the work of continuity planning. An employee may be very skilled in the provision of technology infrastructures across the group. Can that person, however, command the respect of business and other operational managers when leading discussions on crucial operational risk issues? It is not always recognised that risk management demands, probably above all, a person who has well-developed people skills. This is because the work naturally demands gaining the attention and concentration of a wide range of different managers and employees from all walks of business life. Once that attention has been grabbed then there remains the task of keeping that attention and continuing to gain respect in the manager's own subject skill. There are many exceptions, of course, but people skills and computer skills are not natural bedfellows.

A facilities manager reading this may react that their values and inputs are being cheapened. This is exactly opposite to the message we are sharing. Placing the subject at the very top of the decision-making tree raises the profile of the task and the importance. The facilities manager clearly has a massive input into the decision-making process for technology continuity and is full of ideas as to how this can be done most effectively. It would be an arrogant and foolish risk manager who did not take those suggestions right into the centre of the decision-making process. We are talking about the need for responsibility for risk tolerance and risk management to begin right in the business itself, not in the technology. A carefully crafted, business-driven BIA will bring out concerns that will in fact empower a facilities manager struggling to gain recognition and budgets for business continuity. Conversely, it could bring out the fact that the business does not need the speed or quantum of recovery currently being planned. Thus savings could be made without endangering the organisation.

The statement from the technology department that could be the basis and starting point of this particular BIA data collection form is likely to embrace at least the following information. The statement will need to be individual to the range of hardware, software, communication tools and data used around the organisation.

• The period of delays before services can reasonably be expected to resume; measured from the time of the decision to trigger the technology recovery plan. The measurements could be in seconds, minutes, hours, days, weeks or more.

  • Specifically, the statement will include at least from where these services will be delivered and how they will interface and communicate with where staff is to be based

  • Delay periods before main software and databases will become available again

  • Delay periods before full desktop facilities and access will be available and numbers

  • Voice, data, web, intranet, email, call centre and other communication services delivery delay

  • The delivery of any special requirements

  • The number of workstations currently planned to be available and what the contingency workstations will contain

  • The worst-case scenario in lost data due to the backup frequencies currently used

Service Level Agreement

It is normal for the service delivery between technology departments and their users to be defined by a service level agreement (SLA). This is a legally contracted document where the services are supplied from an external contractor or another subsidiary company providing services across an organisation. It can also take the form of an internal statement of intent where the services are provided from the technical division within a company or group. Surprisingly what is less common, whether it be an internal or even an external resource supplier, is for that SLA to define precisely the service levels that can be expected in an otherwise damaging or disastrous situation. Informal 'promises' should be formalised in a documented and authorised service level agreement. Such an SLA would not only clarify ownerships of risk and delivery levels; it can clearly define the expectations against which managers look at their residual risks. It would also define the agreed delivery standard against which any future changes in technology provision or planning can be measured.

> **Case Study**
>
> A risk manager discovered there was a mismatch between the frequency of data backups and critical business needs. The central mainframe-based computer centre was then backing up current data weekly. One of the users of the technology services reported in their BIA that the maximum amount of data that could be lost before regulators would close down the business was just one day's entries. The regulators suggested that a loss of records of more transactions would mean in effect that the business had lost effective control over its business portfolios and finances.
>
> When this was reported back to the computer manager the response was one of joy. 'I have been trying to get a budget for daily backups for years but couldn't get the money to do it.' The BIA, taking an entirely different route to the board made it clear - right from the (business) horse's mouth - that weekly backups were a total waste of time. The company was exposed anyway to total destruction by loss of regulatory approval. If they did not back up more frequently they may as well save the money, not back up at all and carry the risk of destruction. The resources needed for daily (in fact more frequent) backups of data became unarguably an essential, not a luxury; and was agreed.

Best Endeavours

There is an important distinction to be made within service level agreements. This distinction is whether the technology contingency planner has already positioned, prepared and is maintaining the resources needed for recovery; or whether there is only confidence that these things could be resourced and installed after the disaster. The expression often used for the latter is that these can be installed and delivered on a 'best endeavours' basis. Clearly this is much cheaper contingency planning and an IT manager may feel, for example, that he or she could go into the 'high street' and purchase fifty end-user computers, software and configure and load them to provide this part of the wider recovery. Necessarily this entails a risk of failure; and if a commercially realistic risk decision is to be made then the risk of failure of doing this on time must be considered and be part of that wider decision-making.

The IT manager may be being optimistic or making assumptions about stability of supply even in major and widespread crises. There may also be over-optimism in the ability of the available human resources at that time while the whole of the computer infrastructure is being rebuilt. There may be unreal confidence that the current version of the software purchased is compatible with the file management of the database. A host of individual risks must be considered carefully, and above all they must be considered in the context of the urgencies demanded by the BIA to ensure the organisation's survival.

The Decision-Making Process

In summary, the risk of failure of their technology may, in some businesses, be an important one. It may even be number one in the rankings of risk concern. This does not, however, dilute the important picture that ownership of the risk remains firmly within the business and cannot be delegated to facilities managers to guess their way through. We repeat, getting it wrong by preparing for more than is needed is just a waste of money. Getting it wrong by under-preparing is waste of both money and time as the organisation may, in a damaging situation become dead anyway. It is useful to remember in this context that a business in such circumstances is not usually partially dead - it is more often fully dead.

We have here a classic situation where the important role of the risk manager is to bring together different people and cultures, bring to the discussion a consistent, group-wide agenda, and deliver very real value to the organisation.

The business manager can with guidance from the risk manager, set out a service level – quantum and speed - that is needed following a service failure. The needs would probably be defined by theneed for the recovered services to be sufficient and fast enough to avoid critical or catastrophic loss.

> *The operational manager, of course, is less interested in when the technology itself is reinstated. He or she has a single focus interest on when the entire infrastructure, including communications and end user tools, are available and alongside the people so that processing can actually begin again; and with the capacity to accept the anticipated work flows needed.*

In practice, and emerging from the way continuity planning has developed from computer service divisions over the last fifteen years or more, the technical managers probably already have a recovery plan that they have developed within the department. It can be time-efficient, therefore, for the business manager working on the BIA, to consider what is already in place and measure the offered services against the services deemed to be essential. In practice it is also helpful in this way for a business manager to begin to understand the practicalities and limitations of technical continuity and recovery. It is a rare manager who does not believe his or her function is not at the centre of the organisation and crucial for its survival. It would be too easy to throw out the cliché, 'I will need everything immediately.'

If a mismatch emerges between promises and needs then there are options to explore. If the planned delivery is too fast/too much, then there can be an informed business decision to reduce the level of continuity planning. The savings can therefore be invested elsewhere in the development of the business.

The mismatch may, however, be the other way; that is, the business manager considers the recovery to be too little/too slow. With the additional speeds/services/information now quantified the business manager and technical manager can work together to develop the optimum solution. There could be changes in the way individual, urgently needed processes are undertaken that will bring the needs down to current planned contingency levels. On the other hand the technology manager, armed with clear and precise needs can cost the provision of any additional needs.

The decision to spend or not to spend on the improvement of continuity planning can then be made at the right level of authority within the organisation. The options, now considered ones and perhaps commercially justified, could encourage a decision to make the expenditure. On the other hand the high cost to upgrade the planning may cause the business manager to look again at the urgencies, reconsider the unit's tolerance to risk, or make changes within the division itself to remove the criticality or urgency. Either way the process should lead to an informed and thus better quality decision, at the right level of authority within the organisation.

What Are These Dependencies?

We will look separately at the special urgencies and dependencies of e-commerce, but in this section we will look at the operational dependencies within other modern business models: dependencies that could be life-or-death to an organisation or indeed to the human beings involved.

The question to ask and consider laterally; is 'what has a computerised system done and what is it doing for the managers and teams who are delivering front-line services to customers and other stakeholders?' There is value at this stage to look back to the chapter on stakeholders and take in a reminder of the full range of stakeholders who have expectations, demands and the power to cause further damage when frustrated in those needs.

E-commerce apart, those broad service and dependency headlines can be summarised as follows:

- Computerisation has replaced a large number of trained and experienced staff who would be needed if the processes were to be done manually. Some of those skills have become extinct in the large numbers that would be needed. Just two examples in the insurance business would be motor car insurance and house insurance underwriters; a task almost all done by technological software products. Some of the 'old' motor engineering skills have become obsolete by the way that motor vehicle maintenance is technology driven and has now to respond to the technology designed into modern vehicles.

- Computerisation has enabled a simultaneous live-time relationship with a massive number of individual customers and in so doing has enabled organisations to remove layers of wholesalers and intermediaries from the supply chain. Had those intermediaries still existed they could, in a crisis, be vital communications and services resources between supplier and end customer.

- Databases that can be mined and differentiated from different angles, from different perspectives and for different needs to supply the baseline product and client information and targeted communications.

- An audit trail is retained for the satisfaction of financial recording, internal and external controls, compliance and other legal reasons.

- Management, quality control, marketing, product and other information can be trawled instantly from within the information databases held

- There is sufficient credibility in the completeness of its output to satisfy counterparties and regulators.

- The necessary formulae and any corporate process standards are built into the software.

- Access to an up-to-date, common database is provided to other interested departments and authorised third parties and partners.

- Sensitive information (whether corporate, client, employee, counterparty or third party) is secured.

There are two underlying issues with business continuity of technological frameworks:

- Are the intellectual assets of the infrastructure - the software and the data - safe whatever happens; and can they be accessed in a useable format in the short term and in the longer term? Backups are key here of course and there are important considerations when deciding the frequency of backups and ensuring trust in the processes and the readability.

- Can, after failure for whatever reason, this full range of urgently needed services be reinstated and useable by the front line staff fast enough to keep the organisation alive, under control, and in its marketplace? A director may respond that he or she could continue the business after an incident using paper while waiting for a computer system to be reinstated. The directors may feel that they could capture the work done and then enter the information later when the computerisation is reinstated. That indeed may be so but it is a decision that should only be made once all the dependencies listed above, and most probably others specific to the business too, have been fully considered.

We need therefore to consider not just the need for the information stored and the need to reinstate the service delivery, but just how fast that service delivery is needed if the organisation is to remain alive, keep its stakeholders on board and remain in its marketplace. In differing businesses that need for speed could be measured in seconds, minutes, hours, days or even weeks.

Protection of Information

Technology departments are vital warehouses of very large amounts of information. This information is so important that it, and the ability to access or mine it in different ways, is a foundation of the whole organisation. Lose it and you have lost the company; and in some fields you lose human lives, too (e.g., medical records needed for ongoing treatments and some engineering safety records).

Non-technical people may be concerned when they see such a huge and crucial dependency reduced to physically tiny computer media or when they are given a seemingly vague assurance that 'it's all OK, it has gone down a telephone line to another place.' Many would be happier if they could touch it and feel it, and at this level it needs a real statement of faith. At another level, however, it needs much more than that.

It is not enough to say that the file has a backup. Was that backup captured properly and is it readable in a way that makes the business needs achievable? Is the backup physically far enough away from the primary data that it really could not possibly be destroyed at the same time? Even then, this may not be adequate. Could a threat, say a virus, have damaged, or in the future damage, both backup and primary data at the same time? Physical distance in such circumstances would be irrelevant.

Case Study

A doctor's surgery maintained patient records on their computers; accessible by all doctors in the practice. The need was 'live' in that the doctors would log into the patient's file while the patient was in the surgery. Healthcare decisions would be made based on a combination of what the patient said in the discussion, and the knowledge of current and past medical history that emerged from the electronic file. The practice manager confirmed that the files were "backed up' onto a spare computer in the office once a day. This process retained the following exposures:

- A fire, explosion, theft of computers, or other physical damage to the building could destroy all data, backups and original at the same time.

- A situation elsewhere, say a nearby flood, riot, political upheaval, or scene of crime, could deny access to those records for sufficient time to cause death or further injury/illness to a patient.

- All the computers were linked into the same network creating a significant exposure to simultaneous damage by virus, hackers or other electronic cause.

- Whether a once a day backup on patient health records, potentially losing a whole day's input is an acceptable frequency or not is a medical decision. It is not a decision for the practice manager.

Terrorism and weather incidents keep moving the risk goal posts. This is not least in the geographical spread of impact and this demands further and further distances between the backup files and the original. Distances of hundreds of meters can no longer bring reassurance and modern risk managers are thinking countries apart for their backups.

The files need to be separated electronically with no chance of a technological problem spreading between the two. This is an issue for backups taken by downloading through telephone lines, broadband or intranet systems. It is also an issue to ensure that any virus, which may as yet not be identified but timed to trigger at later date, is not transported with the backup files. It is routine for organisations to have grandfather, father, and son backups (and more); i.e., retaining intact old backup files for an agreed period in case the later ones are contaminated and unreadable.

The backup files may be stored elsewhere within the organisation itself, downloaded electronically or sent by courier perhaps to third-party premises. There are increasingly a number of professional service providers who will contract to receive and retain data files in a way defined by the contract of service. These are stored in relatively secure conditions, including old coal mines where thought appropriate.

In large organisations, as it is with any task, it is vital the responsibility for taking the backups and also checking the readability is allocated, owned and accepted; with deputies or alternates for when that person is unavailable.

Case Study

A subsidiary of a company provided back-office services to the group's investment management business. This was a multi-billion pound group managing investment portfolios for businesses, pension funds and private clients. Furthermore this subsidiary earned additional income by also providing similar services defined by contract to other city institutions.

During the course of the BIA the consultant asked about backups to the AS/400 computers. This was confirmed and an introduction was arranged with a member of the computer department. Assurances were given that backups were taken daily and a discussion began about the decision-making that had led to backing up only once a day.

Further concerns were raised when the member of staff confirmed that he took the tapes home with him at the end of the working day. The warning lights were already on, and the colours deepened when he confirmed that he brought the tapes back in with him the following day. This in effect rendered both backup tapes and original tapes in the same building during the working day. This central city area had already suffered bomb damage.

It was after a long period of talking at cross purposes when it became clear that the member of staff had not been taking contingency backups at all. His backups were working backups that would help him if he had minor computer glitches to manage on a day–by-day basis. He was not aware that others believed that he was taking the main contingency backups and that he was the one thought to be taking on this wider responsibility. He saw no business-critical dependencies in what he was doing and thus stored and managed the tapes accordingly.

The point of this true-life story is that everybody else thought he was; and because of this misunderstanding, in effect nobody was taking contingency backups at all. It would be easy to cry stupidity but this is an organisational and communication failure, not one of personal inadequacy.

Information On Laptops And Free-Standing Desktop Computers

This book would be seriously incomplete if it did not mention – and stress most strongly – that information retained on laptops and freestanding desktops can be a significant continuity and security exposure.

In value terms the cost of losing the hardware is almost always peanuts compared to losing the data on these machines. The loss of the software can outweigh also the costs of the machines themselves.

It's a dangerous world for computers. They do crash, they get stolen, flooded, burnt, vandalised, poisoned by virus, dropped, left in trains and have a whole host of other threats to their safety.

Centrally managed systems are most likely to have a backing up regime in place together with people who are charged with ensuring that this regime is followed, audited and the backed-up data is checked for usability. Freestanding machines do not enjoy this discipline. The first question as ever is through the BIA and is 'is there any business-critical information retained solely on these machines?' If the answer is yes, then there is a risk issue to be managed and managed carefully.

Security of Information

We have already stated that information databases contain information that is sensitive to the organisation; perhaps price-sensitive or competitor-competitive or more. Clearly therefore the security envelope that sits around the primary data on computers also needs to be in place wherever there is backup data stored. This security envelope would need to be both physical and electronic. Laptops can be key security risks.

Another risk cameo is worth a mention at this point in the text. In spite of strong rumours and clichés to the contrary there is no such thing as a 'fireproof safe!' A fire retardant safe, maybe; but fireproof they are definitely not. Survival-critical information such as backup tapes kept in such an on-site safe, is still at risk, even though perhaps a lesser one. Also the issue of fireproofing does not cover such things as denial of access to the building.

IT security is of course a subject in itself and it is beyond the scope of this book to delve into detail on this subject. Suffice it to say that IT security and IT continuity are partners with at times, one objective.

Case Study

MasterCard reported that information on more than 40 million cards may have been stolen. This has affected about 13.9 million of their own branded cards, some 20 million Visa branded cards; and also other branded cards. 'In sheer numbers, this is probably one of the largest data security breaches' (James van Dyke, Principal Analyst of Javelin Strategy and Research in Pleasanton, California).

The allegation is that the security breach occurred at a third-party processor of payment data in Arizona where an intruder was able to use security vulnerabilities to infiltrate the networks.

MasterCard is not alone with these difficulties. In 2005 Citigroup wrote to 3.9 million of its customers apologising for losing their personal data that had been in tapes lost in transit. Furthermore the Japanese arm of the investment firm UBS apologised for losing a hard disk that contained confidential data on 15,500 customers.

Credibility In The Values of The Backup Data

We will begin this section with a case study:

Case Study

An organisation backed up its data from the AS/400 computers in daily use. They were stored elsewhere within the group on totally different computers many miles from the original. A flood occurred in the primary building causing the recovery plan to be triggered. There was a call for the backup data.

The backup data was unreadable. This was caused by a change in the file management system some months earlier that had not been transported to the contingency computer's software. The organisation did manage to survive but had many months and costs of additional work finding and then reinstating data that had been lost. This work could only be done by asking third-party intermediaries for help. There was significant reputational damage; reducing new business, and carrying a dramatically increased potential for fraud

---

The point is that the backup data should be checked to ensure that it could be read in a disaster environment. This is to ensure that it is not only readable but is able to be mined and used in a business-supporting way. When an IT contingency exercise is undertaken (see later in this book) it is not only important to read the data but to get operational staff to join the exercise and undertake routine processes using that data. There can be no substitute for this and inward-looking technological contingency exercises are missing a vital ingredient needed to gain credibility.

Availability of Software

Clearly the statements above regarding data apply no less to that other critical intellectual asset, the software products themselves that turn the digital data into accessible and useable information.

Off-The-Shelf Software

These products may have been purchased 'off the shelf' and thus are available again to buy. The software on the market at the time of damage however may be a later version and may not store files and access them in the same way. Even though the 'product' is still available on shop shelves, it may be useful to retain, with the data offsite, a copy of that same version of the software.

In-House Software

Some organisations develop their own software in house, using their own technical staff. This may be especially so for smaller programmes used for particular individual tasks. The issue of importance and survival here is not around the 'size' of that software package, nor the volume of the data that it manages. The survival issues are around what exactly it is that the software/data combination does and the effect it has on the ability to deliver the end product to the customer. The BIA will not necessarily worry much about its technical processing and/volumes of entries. It will more address what business processes it enables, and the importance and urgencies of that process, however small or large, in the delivery chain.

Should such operational transactions managed by such software be deemed to be business-critical, various risk issues need to be managed. Is there a full version totally 'offsite' (electronically and physically) and is there an unacceptable level of dependency on one person or team that can continue to maintain and develop the software? This 'team' of course may equally be a third-party software house that may have retained the computer codes needed for maintenance. Risk management may demand that a matching version is maintained and, most importantly, that whenever software products are maintained and developed that the project to do so embraces updating those backup copies too. It is too easy to forget them unless a structured project management plan demands that the project is not signed off before this contingency-related work is also done.

Case Study

A technology department learned a hard lesson about ensuring that change management should include changes in the continuity planning program as one seamless process. £10M was budgeted to upgrade a mainframe infrastructure. It was a major project and completed on time. The progression of the processing onto the new systems went smoothly. The Finance Director and Chairman were delighted to hear that the project had come in under budget and rejoiced in the saving of £800,000.

Heads were patted, promotions promised and they both took out the team to dinner. An article appeared in the staff magazine showing a range of smiling faces. The risk manager read the article with interest. He called the IT manager and congratulated him, adding quietly, 'How has all this affected your contracts with the continuity hardware suppliers?' The upshot was that the IT manager had to go back to the Chairman asking for most of the £800,000 back as this aspect had been missed. A lesson learned the hard way, but in fact there could have been an even harder way of learning of this omission.

The incident gave the risk manager an attentive audience to ensure all that, in the future, every change project proposal had risk paragraphs, and no change projects were ever signed off without his stated approval.

The risk management of the second exposure, a dependency on the knowledge of an individual or team, begins with ensuring that there is a manual prepared (not in the package itself!) that is adequate to take any computer-literate person through the technicalities and the access code words. We will refer back to this in the exercise section below.

Outsourced Software

Many large software products are designed and delivered by a software house who will spend months or years developing, trialling and delivering a bespoke or custom software for their client's needs. The comments above regarding in-house bespoke software apply no less and certainly more. We need further to risk-manage the issues of legality. Who owns the intellectual rights to that software? Would the future failure/closure of that software house mean that the software could not be maintained and developed further as needed? Would the failure of the designers mean that the access codes are 'sealed' inside the company and not be available for another IT skill to step in to maintain and continue to develop or enhance the softwares?

If the designers are bankrupt or are taken over the new owners – whether they are liquidators or new designers themselves – will see any proprietorship over a software package to be an asset to be retained and used for whatever value can be extracted. This extraction of value may not coincide with the interests of individual users.

An outsourcing contract to supply software demands clarity of copyright, detailed manuals and the storage of access codes where they can be accessed independently in defined circumstances.

A Mixture of Off-The-Shelf And Bespoke Development

This is a common way to move forward with software products. A 'package' is purchased and then further work is done, in-house, or by external consultants, to create a more precise match between the software delivery and the organisation's needs. All of the comments above therefore apply.

Software Licences

Licensing may be thought to be a side issue, but on no few occasions has been a critical one. When software is purchased, what are in effect purchased are not the software products themselves, but a licence to use them in defined circumstances and locations. There have been a number of occasions when an organisation in crisis and shifted suddenly and unexpectedly to another location finds that the software owner, far from being supportive, reminds the user that their licence does not extend to the new, emergency premises.

Spending time renegotiating licences is a delay, and a burden too far when all the pressures of handling a potential disaster are being thrown wholesale at the recovery teams. Waiting for administration staff to appear on a Monday morning before the designer's technical team can be authorised to assist is one problem the organisation could do without.

Continuity of Hardware

We will assume for the purposes of this section that hardware is delivering essential support to the service deliveries that are in turn considered, by the BIA, to be business-critical. We will assume also that that same BIA has established clearly the maximum amount of time the organisation can survive without reinstatement and usability of the services.

Speed Needed In Replacing Hardware

There is probably value in dealing with the time issue first. It is extremely unlikely that an IT department will have the time to set out, after a disaster and purchase new equipment. They would need to authorise the expenditure, find, purchase, and await delivery of computers, servers, software, switches, cabling and end-user desktop equipment.

They would then need to configure them, load software, install communications links and get the end user kit into the places where staff will be able to use them. Data would then be loaded, checked and stress-tested and approved as authentic. This is unlikely to be achievable in time even in the most slow-moving of organisations.

Preparation before the disaster is certainly vital. The level of preparation needed to meet the demand for speed established in the BIA will vary by that urgency agreed. In essence, the rule of thumb is that the quicker it is all needed, the more preparation and pre-positioning necessary and the greater the cost of doing so. A bank, for example, that provides information continually to and from cash machines; and authorises credit card payments 24 hours a day/7 days a week will have contingency computerisation in place continuously paralleling the original services. Another organisation needing such speed of recovery would be an air traffic control system. Yet a further example would be a call centre proving the only communications link between the customers and the organisation. Thus a prepared facility would enable services to be switched immediately to the other and without a noticeable break in service. This is of course the most expensive end of the technology continuity spectrum.

There will then be degrees of response by different organisations depending on the agreed need for speed. As stated this may be measured in seconds, minutes, hours, days, weeks or even longer.

A business decision could be that a recovery of services is needed, for example, in six hours from the disaster – or otherwise from the cessation of the primary technology delivery.

Any preparation by the technology departments to deliver after six hours does need to recognise, realistically, that the planning is for six hours – not from the disaster starting – but from the time that the decision is made to trigger the recovery plan. This is not necessarily six hours from the initial failure. The difference can, in some circumstances be significant; especially where the recognition is emerging slowly that circumstances have the potential of turning into a 'disaster' that could call for a triggering of the continuity plans.

The people authorised to make such important decisions may not be available immediately and they may wish to get more information about what is happening before making that important decision. It is an important decision because pouring resources into creating the contingency site diverts them from anything they can do to rebuild or access the old site's data, software, communications and desk top equipment. The decision 'do we or do we not have a disaster?' is not always simple nor obvious from the very first moment. .

Contingency Hardware

An organisation may have spare hardware; maybe obsolcte hardwarc available that can be stored elsewhere for emergency use. It is very likely, however, that this hardware is exactly that, obsolete, and of no real value in replacing primary kit at a minutes notice. Even if it is of a current specification at the time of storage, it is unlikely in these days of fast moving technological advances, to remain of use for long. It is however possible, if expensive, to have dedicated duplicate equipment in a contingency site in place, constantly updated, maintained and ready for use. This is a business decision balancing cost and benefit.

More likely an organisation that quickly needs replacement hardware will arrange with one of a range of specialist companies that will contract to have ready an agreed amount of the equipment needed and have this ready, configured, and software loaded within a period of time defined in the contract. The equipment to be supplied may be huge mainframe infrastructures, servers, desktop equipment, mid-range computerisation and communication links into public networks or intranets. Often the contract will also guarantee the provision of a number of workstations should staff be evacuated from their primary site.

There is a cost saving in sharing access to a site with other contracted customers of the contingency supplier but careful reassurances need to be obtained about the risk of multiple, simultaneous invocation meaning that the supplier cannot deliver as promised. The essence of the risks here is whether the supplier is accepting organisations as clients who could be damaged in the same incident; together with views of both parties about the spread of damage that could be caused by one incident. The better suppliers have their own linked second or third contingency sites that could be brought in to play should their nominated primary contingency site be overfull.

There are no guarantees with risk. Scenarios change with new experiences; not least in recent years the St. Mary Axe Bomb in London in 1993, the terrorist attack on the World Trade Centre in New York in 2001, the frequency of the Florida hurricanes in 2004 and the Asian Tsunami in December, 2004.

Nevertheless the use of such organisations can bring good value but the residual risk is one that needs to be understood, managed as best possible and communicated to the decision makers within the risk manager's organisation.

Specific Hardware Issues

Several aspects of replacing hardware are worthy of an individual mention.

1. Mainframe

The challenge here is the sheer size of the equipment in use, the volumes of data and the extent to which this equipment could need to communicate widely, often internationally. It is unlikely that an in-house contingent mainframe could be kept available cost effectively. Outsourcing the task of providing a replacement machine quickly is almost always unavoidable.

The further challenge is that the mainframe may provide a variety of computerisation services to different divisions or subsidiaries of the organisation. These different divisions are likely to need different speeds in the recovery of the services. There are very limited opportunities to deliver differing recovery times for different software packages and data from one mainframe. To recover the whole system fast enough to meet the needs of just one division is likely to be a very expensive option.

There are differing options for such a business; depending on what is operationally possible, the service demands and the cost/benefit analysis of each option. It may be just a part of the division's own service delivery that is so time-critical. If so, can that part be isolated out onto desktops, servers or elsewhere? It may just be information that they need urgently, rather than services to others.

Could therefore that information be transferred or better downloaded onto suitable, smaller computers that could be brought into use immediately to carry them through the period before the full mainframe service is reinstated? It could be that the entire computerisation of the division is removed from the mainframe and is handled separately by its own hardware that could be recovered fast enough.

Case Study

A London investment house, responsible for many billions of pounds of investment and pension funds, was asked to consider the recovery scenario of the IT department that serviced the entire multination financial services group. This organisation had one of the largest civilian mainframe computer centres in Europe. The recovery scenario - the best that the IT Manager could squeeze a budget for - entailed a potentially worst case of lost data of 24 hours (the data between the last backup and the worst-case disaster timing) and a three-day delay before reinstatement of end user services.

The response from the investment house was straightforward. 'If we lose that amount of recorded data, representing hundreds of millions of pounds worth of transactions, and be out of the market for that amount of time we would be closed down by the regulator. This would even be before news hit our stakeholders and we would lose all the credibility we need to stay in business.' In effect the answer came back very quickly, 'If that is the best you can do, don't waste your money on your existing plans as we are dead anyway!'

Needless to say this powerful message demanded an urgent and immediate response. The choice was to have the whole group recovery scenario improved, at great expense, to meet this business unit's needs, or to move the investment processing away from the mainframe onto a mid-range computer with its own recovery planning. The decision was to invest in the latter, bringing coincidentally additional local control and operating benefits to the investment house; all triggered initially by the BIA.

2. Special Needs

Some divisions of the organisation may have special needs that have been approved and are in place. These special needs may be 'nice to have' or they may be business-critical. In a disaster environment the 'nice to haves' are luxuries that are discarded. The business-critical special needs however do need to be identified and covered by the technology recovery planning. This is best illustrated by a case study.

Case Study

A claims department within an insurance company scans all documents on arrival. The information from these inputs fits into the computerised systems that record that the claims exist, allocate reference numbers, establish reserves, create an audit trail and provide screen-based information for the claims staff, loss adjusters, lawyers and others to progress the claim.

There is a substantial amount of information on-screen and the decision had been made some time ago that that department needed 21" screens as an essential, not as a luxury. There had been representations from the staff, the union and health and safety officials that it would not be reasonable to expect staff to use the software on smaller screens for any period of time. Those representations had been fully accepted and the screens were now in daily use.

The technology department, putting together their recovery plan had planned to supply 17" screens, not aware of the criticality of the larger screens. The BIA brought out this need and the recovery plans were changed.

Clearly also the large-scale scanning equipment is also now an essential, again not a luxury.

---

3. Outsourcing Of Technological Services

There is a section in the book on the additional continuity exposures when crucial and urgent dependencies are supplied by third parties under contract. Technology continuity is where the risks can be at their highest and are most important.

It is important, not only because the services supplied can be the most urgent and critical ones, but that extraordinary efforts may be needed from the work teams during the crisis itself. The crisis may not be caused in the supplier's environment but in the receiver's environment; nevertheless needing the supplier to shift resources urgently to meet the needs created by the catastrophe. Such exceptional services may not of course be covered in the contract terms. Certainly a supplier could be reluctant or unable to divert resources from other contracted clients – especially if those other clients are more substantial, and have, at the time, a better chance of being long term clients!

The continuity industry has suppliers that offer pre-prepared outsourced technology, communications, workspaces, and call centre handling equipment. This marketplace is, as ever, an opportunity for effective contingency services and at the same times also a risk. The former perhaps to be taken, and the latter, certainly to be managed. There are call centres offering a contingency service, not only in hardware but in providing staff trained in using the organisation's own software screens that would allow basic responses to calling customers.

This service has evolved from call centre companies that already have a business model that provides responses to callers to many different client organisations simultaneously. National boundaries are of course no longer operating barriers to the world of call centres with many services operating internationally.

E-Commerce

There are many definitions of e-commerce. One definition heard was the "The animal instinct of the entrepreneur fuelled by the ever more powerful computer and telecommunication tools." Another definition is "The exchange of perceived value between individuals or organisations by the use of open technology and communication networks."

The definition of e-commerce we will adopt for this book is:

"The buying and selling of goods and services over electronic networks, whether between businesses or between businesses and consumers." (1)

The first thing to say about e-commerce is that it is not a separate function within the organisation. It is integral to the very core product and service deliveries of the organisation's wider business model. It may indeed have its own risks, its own sensitivities and impacts, but it interfaces with many non-technical functions as well. Successful continuity is exposed, not only to technical failures, but to non-technical ones as well. All the risks and impacts discussed separately in this book apply no less to e-commerce; but sometimes more so because of raised expectations of speed and availability; and also dependencies on single points of total failure.

In this section we will consider only the additional threats and exposures to the continuity of using of e-commerce in delivering the business plan. We will discuss not only the fact that there are new risks that threaten the service, but that the business model's dependencies and expectations mean also that 'old' risks can have a dramatically increased impact on the chances of the organisation surviving problems.

E-commerce raises the temperature of risk in many ways, not least that client businesses and direct customers are promised on-line, live-time deliveries of information and products. Perceived failures to deliver are now measured in seconds – slow websites for example – rather than days or weeks. The temperature is raised also by the fact that the e-commerce product is often now the only portal available to the customer in contacting the organisation; all other portals of shop premises. Publicly accessible offices, branches and even call centres have probably been removed. Businesses have created their own business models with the dependency that their own e-commerce service suppliers will continue to deliver as promised. The dependency chain therefore becomes long and catastrophic delays can be measured in just seconds.

There are entirely new risks:

- Loss of domain name and domain squatting
- Legalisation of e-signatures
- New vandalism risks of website defacement, (including the alteration of prices/quotes and specifications), denial of service caused by swamping attacks and other viruses.
- New crime risks such as website spoofing or phishing, and other information security failures caused by hacking, sniffer programmes and Trojan horses.

- New legality and compliance concerns, especially as e-commerce crossing international boundaries with ease is both a major opportunity and also a risk.

- The single points of failure that could in one incident close down all effective services right across an organisation, however large and strong that organisation believes itself to be.

- New challenges in product failures emerging from the speed and scale at which new products go world-wide and the difficulties when product recalls are necessary or wise.

- Crime has new opportunities to be exploited. The opportunities to commit crimes wholesale, the remoteness of villain to victim, and cross-border opportunities can cause large losses and makes apprehension and recoveries much more difficult.

- E-commerce takes the organisation's brand under its wing in its flights around the world and a failure can destroy that brand and confidence not only across the e-commerce product but right across the organisation's other products and markets as well. There are special brand exposures around security of information in some businesses; for example banks and other financial institutions.

- E-Commerce often brings with it a much higher dependency on third party service suppliers than other business models. This as with all outsourcing brings a range of risks and sensitivities on good days, and additional challenges when an unexpected and potentially destructive incident needs managing through.

- Laws are evolving at a slower speed than the developments in the use of technology and when they do appear they do not cross country jurisdictions as easily. This leaves organisations unsure and exposed in their relationships with customers, third parties and Governments.

Case Study

The St. George Bank's online system in Australia had to be urgently reviewed after a customer informed the bank that she could access and transfer cash from other accounts. It was reported publicly, initially in an IT magazine that the employee of a Sydney-based venture capital company had been able to demonstrate to the bank that she could transfer money between her employer's account and her own via a personal account.

Cases Study

Virus attacks such as 'Melissa and 'I love you' are infamous. IT security managers believe that there are more then 50,000 computer virus existing at present and they are growing daily. Visa reports that 47% of all complaints received are Internet-related; even though only 1% of its European transactions are online ones.

Legalities

Legislation is increasingly being introduced giving some protections to e-commerce suppliers and customers. This legislation also raises challenges in that the organisations themselves must remain within these new laws. It is not easy for regulators, either. The Australian

Prudential Regulation Authority (APRA) stated that 'the increasingly common practice of outsourcing electronic commerce to third parties makes regulation difficult.' It went on to say 'the increased role of outsourcing in electronic commerce is a potential source of concern to the APRA, especially where there are systemic implications resulting from a third party providing services to a large number of institutions.'

It is beyond the scope of this book to delve into detail on specific legislation but the following are cameos of the laws around the world and the interested reader may wish to research further.

* Financial Services Authority (United Kingdom)
  The steps being taken by the British Financial Services Authority to monitor that firms and markets have adequate IT systems and controls to address the risks in their business (including of course e- risks). An FSA discussion paper stated that "it is vital that the regulatory framework helps firms and consumers take maximum advantage of the opportunities presented by e- channels such as the Internet, digital television and mobile telephone."

* The Electronic Signatures in Global National Commerce Act
  This is a USA Federal law known as E-sign. It gives, *within its jurisdiction*, the same legal standing to e-signatures as is now available to hand-written ones. There is a parallel law in the United Kingdom, the Electronic Communications Act 2000.

* BS (British Standards) 7799
  This deals with information security. There are sections dealing with the security of electronically stored and transmitted information.

There are numerous other legislative controls that are minefields for the risk and continuity manager. Some are designed directly for e-commerce, some have implications which cannot be ignored. Further examples in the United Kingdom alone include the Privacy and Electronic Communications Regulations 2003, Electronic Commerce Regulations 2002, Regulations of Investigatory Powers Act 2000, Consumer Protection (Distance selling) Regulations 2000, and the Data Protection Act 1998.

Continuity Of E-Commerce Business Models

One thing is for certain: A business going down the e-commerce route is usually taking a one-way street. It may be a new start-up business or it may be making major changes to an existing business. Whether it is the former or the latter there will not be many of the pre-e-commerce infrastructures in place – or remaining – if it is to extract full value from this business model. The economics are too significant; whether it is the opportunities or the costs that are being counted. The Zurich Life Insurance Company reported that in three years it had sold, over the Internet, the same number of policies that it had sold over the last 70 years. A survey in the USA of banks reported an average cost to the bank per customer transaction within a branch of $1.07. Getting customers to complete transactions over the Internet reduced the cost per transaction to $0.01.

> Should the e-commerce infrastructure fail, therefore, there can be no falling back on an old business model and its resources to continue in business. The skills and other resources are just not there, and the expectations raised by e-commerce trading cannot be supplied in any other model.

Business continuity managers must therefore look only to the Internet to continue in business. Fortunately while the risks are high, there are opportunities to manage them. With preparation the technology risks within the organisation can be spread and if still lost can be switched elsewhere to other websites, backup technology, and even to hosted websites, call centres and other contingency service providers.

It gets difficult in areas where technology makes contact with the real world. Orders or instructions taken over the Internet must still at some point interface with the 'old' world; whether that be staff working in warehouses, banks, delivery systems, lorry fleets, call centres, airlines, post rooms and in countless places elsewhere. We begin therefore to move back into the 'old' world of risks but with the additional task of ensuring that the wholesale communications that are necessary remain sound between the e-commerce and technological infrastructures and the physical world that it is driving. Furthermore, where staff are needed to take any step in the process, that the contingency computer technology and live people can still, wholesale, communicate with one another.

As ever, but more so in the worlds of e-commerce, both the technological services and the physical services are likely to be outsourced, bringing all of the special risk issues that arise with outsourced value chains. These dependencies may be much more than web hosting, manufacturing, warehousing and deliveries: there will be massive dependencies on international communications links, power and water systems. These may be old risks but the impact on e-commerce systems feeding large numbers of customers out of physically small and concentrated computer centres can be massive, dramatic and worldwide in scope.

Case Study

At 3.20pm the 20th November 2000 a 39,000 km SEA-ME WE3 cable was cut. This was then the world's longest telecommunications system and it was damaged on the sea floor about 100km from Singapore. Telstra was then Australia's largest Internet Service Provider with more than 650,000 subscribers. Telstra relied on the cable for 60% of its traffic. A Telstra Bigpond spokesman told the media that internet traffic was 'in a massive logjam and was probably the biggest ever seen. Telstra was of course just one of its users.

E-Commerce And Insurance

In a later chapter we discuss the relationships between continuity management and insurance. Businesses operating in the world of e-commerce are no less exposed to normally insurable risks. These can include such as legal liabilities to others, physical damage and repair costs, loss of information and other intellectual values, loss of revenues and the extra expenditures that are necessary to ensure places are preserved in market places while rebuilding is under way.

The essence of e-commerce, however, is that this damage can now be caused in entirely new ways – misuse of electronic signatures, cyber squatting and webpage phishing perhaps – that the exposures create new horizons for insurance underwriters. The damage that can be caused also can be instant and dramatic worldwide raising issues about the adequacy of sums insured; and thus the cost of insuring against sums insureds that would meet even part of the potential losses. If that is not enough there are some losses, to which e-commerce businesses are particularly vulnerable such as the instant, wholesale, and international destruction of credibility and the brand name.

All this makes the transfer of risk into the conventional insurance market very difficult, very expensive and sometimes not commercially achievable. Indeed any insurance contracts exclude the greatest exposures to the business; for example to commercial value of computer data banks.

Summary

In this chapter we set out to discuss the special implications of ensuring commercially realistic continuity of technological support services and businesses. We identified the need to risk-manage the special urgencies, dependencies and the exposures around the technological services to an organisation. The package of concerns embraces centralised computer services, distributed systems, communications and end-user interfaces; not least the exposures around laptops and other remote equipment. That package of worries also embraces the communication structures and inter-dependencies between them as additional risks; not least of which are where computerised systems and the "old technologies" meet and share mutual interdependencies.

The risk and continuity manager needs, as much as in any area of risk and probably more, to understand, measure and manage equally the risks within both in-house and also outsourced services and dependencies. At this high temperature end of business continuity lies the immediacy expectations that have been raised amongst e-commerce customers and e-commerce business-to-business relationships.
A significant driver for technological recoveries is the speed by which these business-critical dependencies must be reinstated; and any prioritisation between the services that are needed by operational managers. These decisions, however, are importantly ones for the board and operational managers to decide; not for technological managers to guess. Working as a team these two divisions have the best chance of developing cost-effective and real, business resilience.

Some tasks within technological risk and continuity management are common to other areas, even though individual challenges are different. We will in later chapters discuss the building of continuity plans, checklists and the gaining of credibility in them..

Service Level Agreement: Between Technology Suppliers and Users

The usual service level agreement between technology and other infrastructure suppliers and users can gain in value by having a section that deals with exceptional circumstances. The agreement will ensure clarity of responsibilities between supplier and user during a disaster and will establish the ownership of source codes and other intellectual properties. This may need to include for example the legal ownership of the data itself.

The service delivery promised during a failure of 'normal service delivery' will in effect set out the expectations of the continuity planning but will turn these expectations into a legally binding agreement. Setting them out in this format will also ensure that there is great care in making promises and attention given, by both sides to the residual risk of failure to deliver as promised.

The service delivery promises will include at least and in each case be clear as to whether this is already in place and guaranteed or simply 'best endeavours.' As said the difference is crucial:

- The frequency of data backup: in effect the maximum amount of time possible between the last backup and the point of time of the loss of current data.

- The amount of time needed between the (a) decision to trigger the recovery plan and (b) the ability of operational staff to access and actually use processing and communications tools. This may be 100% of all services reinstated consecutively or there may be an agreement to bring services on line in an order established by the business need.

- The full range of end-user equipment that will be available and by when. This may need to include, scanners, cheque writing machines, manufacturing machinery, specialist call centre call handling equipment, specialist printers and many other tools that were deemed by the BIA process to be business-critical and urgent.

- The numbers of working end-user equipment available and the power and range of services available. (If contingency communications and processing facilities will initially be less powerful and slower than normally expected this needs to be explained).

- The speed and numbers of the wider facilities needed such as desks, telephones, other workstations, equipment, and other staff support systems. This again may be an agreement to deliver all current services within one timeline; or more often a progressive reinstatement that clarifies what and how many by when.

- From where these facilities will be delivered and how the facilities and the staff can be effectively brought together.

- The expectations of the user in communicating with, and gaining support from supplier staff during the crisis.

Any additional services that may be needed during a crisis and needing pre-agreement and contract. This may, for example, include a separate agreement to divert incoming phone calls instantly to a contingency switchboard or a call-answering device.

The service level agreement will need to embrace; not only a technological failure (i.e., services can be delivered from a remote site to the normal working environment) but also denial of access to the normal working environment that demands a movement of staff as well.

(1) *E-Commerce: How trading online can work for you. Department of Trade and Industry (United Kingdom)*

10

Dependency Management:
Supplier Management, Outsourcing
and Business Support

Objectives Of This Chapter Are To:

- Provide definitional language for supplier management, outsourcing and in-sourcing

- Explore the implications of supplier management and lead times for replacement following loss or disruption

- Examine the issues involved and the planning required in managing the exit from an outsourcing agreement

- Examine with the use of case studies the implications of single-source and critical components in production and supply-chain processes

- Investigate the issues associated with production-line management techniques including just-in- time

- Consider the services provided to support business continuity management and the issues of dependency associated with these

- Offer an approach for dovetailing business continuity with supplier and outsourcing management

Transferring Risk, Not Responsibility

Using suppliers or outsourcing providers is one way of transferring risk away from an organisation, but it is not a way of eliminating risk or transferring responsibility for managing risk to others. Further, while services or processes can be passed on, there are risks associated with finding an appropriate partner, in managing that partner relationship and in ensuring effective and efficient ongoing retention of contracted goods or services with appropriate control and governance.

The Rising Tide of Dependency On Suppliers And Outsourcing Providers

Outsourcing remains the star turn in the IT services and solutions sector. But as economic pressures to compete escalate, and organisations search for ways to shed cost, many organisations are focused on reducing the overheads associated with running their operations and are looking to:

- Reduce process costs by improving process efficiency
- Reduce overheads by taking out people and facility costs
- Avoid capital expenditure.

The outsourcing of other business processes is close on the heels of IT.

At Risk - The Business Value Chain

Every organisation has direct, indirect and quality assurance value activities. Direct activities are those that create value for the buyer, such as assembly. Indirect activities make it possible to perform direct activities, such as maintenance. Quality assurance ensures the quality of the other activities, such as monitoring and inspecting.

These activities are important components of an organisation's value chain and understanding these concepts is consequently key for appreciating the construction of an organisation. Poor analysis of the value chain may translate into components being inadequately addressed as part of any business process, including business continuity arrangements, and consequently contribute to organisational failure in the event of disruption to business as usual.

But analysis does not stop at the doorstep of the organisation. These activities must also be analysed for any supplier or outsource provider that forms a link in an organisation's value chain. "Defining relevant value activities requires the activities with discrete technologies and economics be isolated. The linkages between suppliers' value chains and a firm's value chain provide opportunities for the firm to enhance its competitive advantage" (1). Dependencies between an organisation and its suppliers and outsource providers may be complex and deeply entwined. In the event of an incident which leads to the failure of a supplier or outsource provider's value chain, a resulting "domino effect" may have serious consequences for all parties in the relationship.

Supplier Management

Supplier Management - A Definition (2)

The effective management of a supplier relationship and the associated activities from both a contractual and performance perspective, and from a strategic perspective, to ensure the appropriate relationship management model is applied to the given supplier(s).

Supplier management differs from "contract management" in that it covers the more holistic approach of ensuring the supplier's surrounding operations and strategy are aligned to those of an organisation, as opposed to the tactical management of an individual contract.

The risks associated with supplier management are fundamentally the same as the risks associated with any third-party relationship.

However, the absence of effective performance monitoring of contract management will present risks in relation to service delivery (in the short, medium or long term) and the total cost of the associated service. It is therefore essential that an effective framework is built to manage such risks prior to the outset of any major supplier relationship.

The principles of effective supplier management include, but are not limited to:

- Effective management of the contract(s) related to the supplier;
- Effective performance management of the supplier;
- Effective alignment of the supplier strategy to internal strategy; and
- Effective approach to, and management of, the end-to-end relationship with the supplier.

Supply chain risk management solutions include:

- Dual sourcing of materials where interruption of supply would rapidly halt production;
- Holding inventories off-site at another site or at the supplier's site;
- Significant penalty clauses on supply contracts (though this will not protect against bankruptcy or the consequences of failure to deliver urgent ingredients that are critical to the next link in the supply chain); and
- Inspection and assurance of supplier's business continuity plans and the dovetailing of these with the organisation's own arrangements

Supplier Management Under The Microscope - The Process

Most organisations would be surprised if they analysed their supplier network in terms of how many supplier relationships they have.

Few organisations however, go on to evaluate what types of supplier relationships exist. For example, relationships can be assessed against a variety of criteria:

- High dependency - high availability: utilities, generic components
- High dependency - low availability: highly specialised product components
- Mid dependency - high availability: generic IT equipment - monitors
- Mid dependency - low availability: specialised IT equipment - scanners
- Low dependency - high availability: consumables - paper
- Low dependency - low availability: redundant design furniture

By undertaking this analysis an organisation can develop a hierarchy of suppliers. This hierarchy in turn can be used to help an organisation focus on those suppliers which are critical in terms of business dependency and supply availability, and which should as such be positioned at the top of the supplier 'pyramid.' Consequent business continuity solutions should be focussed on strategically significant supplier dependencies enhanced through risk assessment and business impact analysis (BIA).

For strategically critical suppliers, appropriate contract and service level agreements must be in place and the dependency of the business on them clearly mapped.

Where multiple dependencies exist these should be traced through the end-to-end business process. The resultant supplier 'road map' will provide an organisation with a picture of where the critical suppliers interface with the business processes and provide an opportunity to build business continuity management solutions that are fit for purpose.

Organisations, and especially those with high–dependency, low-availability suppliers, may demand risk and recovery standards embedded within the supplier contract to mitigate the risk profile. If an organisation operates in a regulated environment with associated regulatory rules and guidelines, business continuity performance capabilities for such suppliers may be a minimum requirement to achieve compliance.

Given the punitive nature of contractual or regulatory compliance failure, an organisation may be driven to seek recovery support through risk mitigation solutions such as those provided by specialist third party business continuity suppliers (which in itself could become a further link in the supplier chain).

An illustration of this type of dependency might be a single-site call centre supplying specialist services to a customer. A customer buying unique services may demand that the supplier guarantees recovery capability to a level only achievable through a 'hot' recovery site - either owned by the provider and left dormant or procured from a specialist 'work area' provider.

Michigan State University - May 2004 (3)

A Michigan State University (MSU) study has found that companies are courting disaster if their business continuity plans fail to ensure supply chain continuity. The findings suggest that supply chains have become increasingly fragile. When something does go wrong, the event and the resulting supply chain disruption can have a significant if not catastrophic impact on the buying firm. Consequently, managers working within 'best practice' companies have developed an awareness of these potential risks and, more importantly, they have introduced systems and procedures aimed at proactively managing the risk. The result is not only better performance, but the emergence of a potentially important competitive advantage.

Two issues appear to be at the heart of a company's supply chain management problems:

• Reduced visibility (often the visibility into the supply chain ends at the first tier supplier), and

• Reduced control (the ability to influence and shape the actions of suppliers, especially at the second and third tier levels).

These problems are compounded by the application of 'lean' practices, which reduce supply chain buffers in the form of inventory, lead time and capacity. Consequently, many managers are unaware of what their suppliers are doing to ensure business continuity. With so many companies depending on a reduced set of suppliers for key components, the potential for problems is real and increasing.

If a key supplier is unable to perform, the impact on the firm – as measured financially, strategically, and in terms of market share – can be sizable, even catastrophic.

The study identifies four major factors of a good supply chain business continuity plan:

1. Awareness that the supply chain is susceptible to potentially crippling disruption;

2. Prevention through risk identification, risk assessment, risk treatment and risk monitoring;

3. Remediation plans for recovery from a disruption; and,

4. Knowledge management calls for a shareable, post-event audit of supply chain disruptions throughout the organisation and supply chain.

Outsourcing

> ### Outsourcing - A Definition (4)
>
> *The transfer of a business function or functions to an external or internal service provider over a set period of time, during which the service provider performs a defined service within agreed limits of discretion for a price.*

Outsourcing differs from supplier management in that its characteristics might include:

- The transfer of people and/or assets (for example property or systems)
- The transfer of service responsibility
- Agreed service scope and service levels
- Long-term pricing (usually with incentives and penalties)

The options for the types of outsourcing include:

- Sole supplier
- Multiple supplier
- Prime arrangements
- Sub-contractor arrangements
- Framework or "call-off" arrangements
- On-shore in the country of business origin
- Off-Shore in a country which is not the country of business origin

The following offers a categorisation for outsourcing risk:

- Core Activities: Some activities may be considered as core and may not be outsourced. These may vary from time to time but such capabilities might include Internal Audit, Product Pricing, Risk Management, Strategy Development and Compliance.
- Key Risk: Other activities may attract a higher risk profile because of the nature of what is being outsourced, how the activity is being outsourced or to where. These will vary over time to time but such capabilities could include the following types of contracts:
  - Outsourcing capabilities offshore from the country of origin
  - Outsourcing confidential client data management
  - Outsourcing a customer-facing activity
  - Where the tender has been offered to only one service provider
  - Where there is a material risk of adverse publicity (e.g., contracts involving significant redundancies)
  - Where there is a need for a special-purpose vehicle to be established (e.g., a joint venture with a third party)

There are inherent risks in finding the right outsourcing partner, managing the relationship effectively and the impact on the risk profile of an organisation. Outsourcing may affect the way a board perceives and manages risk. From various standards, regulatory guidelines and the response *of individual organisations, it would seem that outsourcing can lower an organisation's appetite for risk.*

Standards required of outsourcing providers can often exceed those of the ceding organisation. While it is probable that an outsource provider can provide as good if not better service standards than those of relevant industry and organisation-specific technical and performance standards, there can be a sense in the ceding organisation that management control has been lost.

Successful outsourcing demands:
- A high degree of trust in the provider
- A detailed assessment of risk and the design and implementation of an appropriate control environment (including business continuity plans)
- Clear and unambiguous service standards that are proactively managed and monitored
- Clear ownership of intellectual property rights regarding client and corporate data and the ability to 'mine' it

Outsourcing Under The Microscope - Outsourcing Phases

The risk profile will vary throughout the life cycle of an outsourcing arrangement and consequently an organisation should ensure that risks are assessed at each significant phase of the process.

An organisation should consider:
- Its organisation and reporting structure - including the adequacy of oversight as part of the overall governance and risk framework
- The extent to which outsourcing supports the business strategy
- Whether a firm's contracts, service level agreements and relationship management framework allow it to monitor and control risks which arise from the outsourcing of people, processes and systems.

Source: The Financial Services Authority; FSA Handbook (5)

There are seven key phases to the outsourcing life-cycle. The phases are identified below with a brief description of what is included in each phase and a summary of the primary outputs from each phase.

1. Strategy Development

An outsourcing strategy based on an organisation's overall strategies, policies and risk appetite, should evaluate, assess and document all options available and the outsourcer's capabilities to support them

2. Preparation

This is the first major stage of an outsourcing project. Detailed consideration must be given to the specific scope, strategy/policy fit, processes to be outsourced, and outsourcers' capabilities, etc. All processes to be outsourced should be documented, a risk analysis undertaken and cost/benefits modelled.

3. Selection of Service Provider

Potential providers will be short listed and agreed, a request for information and/or request for proposal issued, selection criteria developed, and the service provider selected.

4. Contract Negotiation

All teams and work streams should be in place. Suitable third party advisers will have been appointed. Standard contracts/terms and conditions will have been accessed either from precedents which exist within the organisation or using third-party assistance. At the conclusion of this phase a contract management team will have been formed and a Retained Transition Organisation (RTO) governance structure established with roles and responsibilities documented and approved - including those for business continuity management.

5. Transition

Transfer of staff, assets and service will commence. The RTO will be in place, monitoring of service established and transition signed off and the new service operating smoothly.

6. Relationship Management and Monitoring

An agreed framework will be followed which will include: schedules for regular service level reviews, problem reporting, a process for escalation and dispute resolution, and organisation/provider meetings to discuss improvements and change. At the end of this phase regular reports and meetings will have been established between the RTO and Outsource Supplier (OS), benchmarking carried out and findings implemented.

7. Termination and Renewal

The outsourced arrangements will be reviewed in the light of an organisation's strategy/policy, provider performance, and other factors that might lead to contract changes or termination. Where required, an organisation's plans for transition of the capability back to the organisation will be formulated and exit plans may be invoked. At the end of this phase a decision to renew or terminate the contract will have been made. Where appropriate, monitoring processes will have been reviewed and updated and exit plans will have been reviewed, updated and tested.

Intra-Group Outsourcing

An assumption should not be made that outsourcing always involves an external third party. In many larger organisations it is common to find central units providing goods and services to other internal organisation functions. This is more commonly found where a single, specialised unit exists to feed units that otherwise could justify dedicated, specialised solutions of its own.

This might comprise components of a high technical specification or a financial service such as an investment capability. While some of the principles applied in the phased development of an outsourced relationship do not apply here, nevertheless there remains a dependency of an organisation on these areas in a way that mirrors the issues associated with an external provider. When issues regarding business continuity are addressed below, these internal suppliers should be included in any risk and BIA analysis and appropriate solutions to sustain the continuity of the organisation identified and embedded.

Off-shoring

Regarded by some as a controversial trend, off-shoring involves outsourcing away from the domestic country of manufacture, production line or service provision. This is a relatively new development for the services industry but nothing new to manufacturing. During the 1960s and 1970s many industries in the mature economic world moved production line capability to more cost-effective, high quality environments. Today there are two main drivers for off-shoring receiving 'prime time' interest:

- The impact of the Social Responsibility agenda - especially in global and multi-national organisations (e.g., as in clothing manufacturers and the extraction of oil and minerals) that now see this as an established component of their governance framework

- The increase in the off-shoring of service capabilities to (e.g., as in financial services to call centres in the Far East).

As with outsourcing generally, off-shoring can lead to a feeling at board level that complete command has been lost. Consequently this may lead to raising the governance bar in terms of the board's perception of risk profile, resilience and recovery performance expectations. The challenge with off-shoring is "choosing a reliable partner…choosing a partner who will deliver the service that they promised, is critical. Once a business has been outsourced it is remarkably complicated to take it back. In our experience processes carried out offshore are no more prone to risk arising from error or fraud than processes performed onshore" **(6)**.

The risk analysis should be divided into five parts:

1. The decision to outsource;
2. Where to move the process;
3. The drive for operational efficiency;
4. The challenges for corporate governance and ongoing risk management; and,
5. Common to supplier management, outsourcing and off-shoring, consideration at all project stages, processes for business continuity - including contract exit protocols and procedures

But this attitude is likely to be short-lived if outsourcing involves an off-shore location that in turn involves a country considered an 'over-achiever' in the governance stakes. Confidence in the governance environment will lessen any negative impact and allow an organisation to manage their business off-shore with confidence and realise the undoubted benefits that are available.

Case Study

The Rain Falls in India - July 2005

Massive rainfall in July 2005 resulted in major business continuity problems for companies based in Mumbai and other parts of the western India region. India Daily reported that many people were killed and 48,000 evacuated from the area.

995mm of rain fell in 24 hours, causing flash floods, landslides and physical damage to buildings and critical infrastructure. Telephone services and power supplies were cut, roads were blocked, and rail and air transport were disrupted. India Daily reported that a one-day emergency public holiday was declared in the affected areas of Mumbai, Thane and Raigadh. Although aimed at allowing people a chance to start personal disaster recovery activities, the measure further complicated company attempts to restore business continuity.

Banking services came to a standstill in Mumbai and were almost crippled in other cities as well, as online service choked because most banks have their central switch for Automated Teller Machines (ATMs) and core banking solutions in Mumbai. The disaster also had a knock-on impact on Western companies, many of which have outsourced call centre and other activities to Mumbai-based providers.

The Regulator's Reaction - August 2005

Close on the heels of the Mumbai deluge, shock waves were sent out across the financial services industry in India. Banks are now moving to set up their respective disaster recovery centres. The Indian Banks Association (IBA) has set up a working group to review the disaster recovery systems in banks and to prepare a model business continuity plan for them. The roadmap for business continuity had been documented in 2000, but most banks have failed to put the systems in place, although the level of preparedness for disaster does vary from bank to bank. "Banks, which are based in Mumbai and have their centralised computer system here, should take extra precaution, to see that services in other part of the country are not affected, in case any natural disaster of this kind hits the country's financial capital," said D Krishnamurthy, general manager (IT), Bank of India. "At BoI we have set up a high availability 'hot-site' disaster recovery centre at Bangalore. This helps us to restore our services through all delivery channels within 15 minutes," he said.

ICICI Bank executive director Chanda Kochhar viewed that there was a case for banks to set up efficient disaster recovery systems. "In any case, it is easier to replicate and run a parallel IT system than run a parallel system using manpower. I am sure all banks are looking at their business continuity plan seriously," Ms Kochhar said. She added that ICICI Bank has a robust parallel system in place already. "We managed to bring normalcy in banking service on Wednesday in pretty quick time," she claimed.

There is a case for a business continuity plan in all banks. "In a Basel 2 environment, this is a necessity. Banks need to take care of such operational risks. Otherwise, the capital assigned to such risk is bound to rise and would have an impact on banks' capital adequacy ratio," said Mr Chandrasekhar, general manager (IT) of Bank of Baroda.

Case Study

Local police have identified India's software and services outsourcing industry as a likely target for a terrorist group operating in the country.

Documents seized from three members of the Lashkar-e-Toiba (LeT) terrorist group killed in an encounter with the police revealed that they planned to carry out suicide attacks on software companies in Bangalore, Karnal Singh. LeT is demanding independence for the Indian states of Jammu and Kashmir. The Indian government has claimed that LeT and other separatist groups are aided and abetted by neighbouring Pakistan, which also occupies a part of the disputed territory of Kashmir.

"The terrorists planned to hit these companies in an effort to hinder the economic development of the country," said Singh. Bangalore has a large concentration of Indian software outsourcing companies, and a number of multinational companies have software development and chip design facilities in the city. Two of India's largest software and IT services outsourcing companies have their headquarters and large facilities in Bangalore. Bangalore also has some of India's key defence research and development organisations.

Most of the technology companies in the city have already set up disaster recovery plans and special disaster recovery sites that could be used in the event of a terrorist attack, according to Kiran Karnik, president of the National Association of Software and Service Companies in Delhi. For example, one has a disaster recovery site in Mauritius. Besides tight checks on physical entry into their facilities, Indian software companies have business continuity and disaster recovery plans in place to ensure that a terrorist attack does not disrupt their operations, Karnik said. Terrorism is a global problem and the threat in India is not greater than that in other countries, he said.

Source: John Ribeiro IDG News Service - July 2005

In-Sourcing

There is a degree of confusion about the meaning of in-sourcing. There are at least two definitions:

a) "The bringing back of a business function or functions following the failure or termination of an outsourcing contract."

As with outsourcing, in-sourcing attracts the usual generic business and operational risks as well as its own specific risks. The specific risks associated with in-sourcing emanate from two sources - the impact of bringing in-house the perceived benefits of outsourcing and the potential difficulty or inability to do so in the absence of relevant assets - physical and people - to do the work at a competitive price. In-sourcing risks generally result in losses or liabilities arising from:

- Inadequate or failed internal processes

- Inadequate or failed systems

- People issues

- External events

It is therefore essential that each of the above risks areas is considered and suitable mitigating actions are put in place throughout the pre- and post-contracting phases.

b) "The provision of operational services without the core product or service.".

In this situation, the provider of the services will have the same expectations of them that they might otherwise expect from others in an outsourcing relationship. An example of this situation might be an insurance company providing claims management-related services but not risk transfer.

This situation might also exist within the boundaries of an organisation and only involve intra-organisation relationships. However as with any business relationship, similar business principles should apply and in some industries, the regulator may impose standards which are comparable to those of external situations.

Outsourcing Under The Microscope - Risk Management

Any new outsourcing arrangement will involve significant or material change - material in this respect meaning change that may affect an organisation's risk profile. Expected changes to an organisation can be a major source of risk and an organisation should plan to design mitigating actions to reduce the likelihood of the negative effects and to minimise their impact. A risk assessment should be conducted when there is a planned change that might threaten the achievement of an organisation's strategic and/or operational objectives. Assessments relating to planned change such as an outsourcing arrangement should consequently be conducted at the outset of the process, and then periodically throughout the lifetime of the process, and post implementation.

Material change is defined as an internal transaction, project or event that by its nature causes the risk exposure of an organisation to increase. It may include projects or initiatives such as:
- Restructuring including the implementation, modification or termination of key outsourcing or supplier arrangements;

- Significant changes in regulatory or legal requirements

- All mergers, acquisitions or divestments

- Business re-engineering projects that involve significant modification to, or implementing of new practice, process or systems

- Any other change initiative or project that incurs total cost which exceeds an organisation's appetite or tolerance for risk, and

- Retrospective review following any unforeseen event when the impact to an organisation exceeds the level of risk tolerance

Earlier outsourcing arrangements have generally been low on the 'value chain,' such as back-office functions and information technology. There are signs, however, that outsourcing and off-shoring are moving up the value chain to include functions such as finance and marketing.

> *"While outsourcing can bring cost and other benefits, it may increase the risk profile of an institution due to, for example, strategic, reputation, compliance and operational risks arising from failure of a service provider in providing the service, breaches in security, or inability to comply with legal and regulatory requirements by the institution. An institution can also be exposed to country risk when a service provider is located overseas and concentration risk when there is lack of control by a group of institutions over a common service provider. It is therefore important that an institution adopts a sound and responsive risk management framework in outsourcing."* **(7)**

"Although outsourcing is a long-term trend being driven by labour costs and economies of scale, it could accelerate if business conditions deteriorate as a way of driving growth in profits through cost reduction" **(8)**. This could pose a risk if insufficient care is taken in conducting due diligence and risk-related processes of potential outsourcing providers or contracts are unclear about all material aspects of the arrangement. These trends underpin the importance of effective risk management at all phases of the outsourcing process.

Outsourcing Under The Microscope - Business Continuity Management

It is key that throughout the term of the outsourced arrangement, that an outsource provider implements and sustains an effective approach to business continuity management in a manner that is appropriate to and commensurate with, the nature, scale, geography and complexity of the services provided.

The plans implemented should form an integral part of the retained organisation's business continuity management plans with integrated communication, notification, escalation, invocation and reporting processes. Furthermore, plans should meet the industry, regulatory and internal business continuity standards otherwise adopted by an organisation both at the time of the outsourced arrangement inception and as needs and standards change over time.

> *The principles and practices outlined elsewhere in this book should be applied as if the service or solution outsourced remained in-house.*

A business continuity management plan for an outsourced arrangement must:
- Have the support of the outsource provider and the retained organisation's senior management, appropriate budgetary funding and adequate internal and external resources to effect an acceptable recovery

- Have appropriate integration and linkage to the business continuity management approach taken by the retained organisation and the relevant plans and teams within the organisation

- Have lines of communication including those for notification, escalation and management of incidents as defined

- Be based upon documented risk assessments and Business Impact Analyses (BIA), with recovery time objectives and recovery point objectives agreed by both parties

- Document the strategies, resources, information, processes and actions that will be taken in the event of an incident resulting in the retained organisation or the site operated by the outsourced provider being rendered unusable (e.g., due to fire, flood, building collapse, explosion), supply failure (e.g., gas, electricity, water) or technology failure (e.g., hardware, software, data and voice communications), or in the event of a rapid withdrawal by a key supplier to the outsourced provider, or in a situation that necessitates that the retained organisation exits the relationship

- Have relevant skilled and competent people within both sides of the arrangement with clear roles and responsibilities documented should the need arise

- Be understood by the people of both sides of the relationship

- Address all phases of the arrangement, and

- Be regularly reviewed and tested, together with the people, technology and other resources that underpin it

The plan should include:

- Introduction and overview of the outsourcing arrangement
- The retained organisation's approach to business continuity management
- Business continuity plan, aim, scope and ownership
- Key roles and responsibilities
- Summary of key strategies, and
- Notification, escalation and invocation processes

The following are key components for both sides of the arrangement:

- Emergency response
- Business recovery from one or more alternate sites including the relevant production, warehousing, desktop, server and communications recoveries
- Recovery of the relevant information technology and communications infrastructure – in a secure environment, and
- An 'exit' Plan

Business Continuity management requirements for the arrangement should be covered in a specific schedule within the outsourcing contract and tailored from relevant legal precedents to suit the nature of the contract and parties to the contract. Such a schedule might include:

- Definitions
- General business continuity management requirements: including governance, reporting, right to challenge and audit
- Service levels and supporting management information
- Business continuity management approach during and after transition
- Roles, responsibilities and organisation
- Risk assessment, BIA and alternative strategies
- Interdependency mapping
- The business continuity management plan headlines
- The approach to business continuity management for specific plan components, e.g., information, information technology, telecommunications and networks
- Suppliers used by the outsource provider and the retained organisation, and
- Plans for third-party support services such as those provided by commercial suppliers for alternative site locations

Plan Review, Update And Testing

A section on business continuity management for supplier and outsourced relationships should be included in any internal manuals or guidelines provided by the business continuity manager to an organisation. This should define the organisation's specific continuity requirements for the approach to planning, review, update and testing in detail.

Exit Management

Despite the recent serious downturn in the technology sector, the market for IT outsourcing services is growing in North America, Europe and Asia. It is estimated that the European market will grow from $16 billion in 2000 to around $26 billion by year-end 2005. **(9)**

Notwithstanding this growth, it is a sad reality that a significant number of outsourcing relationships fail in their first two years. In Dun & Bradstreet's report on global outsourcing, (10) the conclusion was that relationships failed not because outsourcing was the wrong approach, but because important details had been overlooked.

Consequently, outsourcing contracts are terminated and while it is difficult to transfer a contract to an alternative supplier it is even more complex to recover the outsourced arrangement back into the retained organisation. A well thought through and documented exit plan is therefore a key phase in the development of an outsourced arrangement. Typically the exit plan will form a specific schedule in an outsourced arrangement contract.

The primary objective of this schedule and plan is to ensure that there is a comprehensive plan in place designed to provide for business continuity for the organisation and, as applicable, its customers; upon expiry or termination of the outsourced agreement (or any constituent service) through the smooth transfer from the outsource supplier to the organisation or to a replacement supplier. It should document relevant responsibilities, services, employees, assets and any other items or information as provided for in the schedule. These items are those that are reasonably necessary to enable the organisation or a replacement supplier to operate and to receive the replacement services with effect from the date of expiry or termination of the outsourcing agreement (or constituent part of the agreement).

The Exit Schedule should state:

- The supplier's responsibilities
- Interim services for short notice of termination
- Knowledge transfer
- Technical advice
- Records and data
- Third party agreements during the exit period
- Facilitation of supplier change
- Avoidance of unnecessary costs and charges
- Removal of supplier property and vacation of customer premises
- Security, and
- The Exit Plan

The exit schedule should establish the minimum contents to be included in an exit plan including an outline of any regulatory rules, guidelines or industry standards to be adopted, and the process for plan development, review, update and testing.

Exit Plan - Objectives and Content

The objectives of an exit plan will be set out in the outsourcing agreement schedule which will include the format and subject headings under which detailed information should be provided. The plan approach must recognise that information will be varied from time to time to reflect the status of the agreement and the services or goods provided.

As with any business continuity plan, respective roles and responsibilities should be clearly articulated and the process for notification, escalation and invocation documented.

In the event that a plan is invoked, exit plan activities should be managed and implemented through a set of sub-projects, which will cover all the required subject areas. The following is a list of activities that might be included although these are likely to vary from time to time and between agreements:

Human Resources Sub-Project

This sub-project manages the resource plan activities required to effect a smooth transfer of staff back to an organisation or to a replacement supplier. The activities are designed to provide the information and access required in order that the assuming organisation is able to effect the transfer of the relevant outsource supplier personnel. The type of activities to be considered should include the following:

- Workforce interviewing and information gathering
- Skills assessments (key skills confirmation)
- Contracts/HR policies and practices communicated
- New contracts of employment for all staff
- Payroll personnel information updated
- Staff communications
- Employee handbooks and other information created as appropriate
- Management and employee induction education consideration

Communications Sub-Project

The communications sub-project identifies the key stakeholders requiring communication during the exit period and develops, agrees and executes a communication exercise that will fully brief these stakeholders on Exit Plan progress and content as deemed appropriate by both parties. The list of activities to be considered within this sub-project might include the following:

- The organisation's internal publications
- The supplier's internal publications
- Communications plan for the transferring employees
- Press releases
- Milestones to be included at first and subsequent Exit Plan reviews

Service/ Knowledge Transfer Sub-Project

This sub-project provides information about the scope and operation of the services to enable the transfer of operational responsibility for the services to the organisation or replacement supplier. It includes appropriate briefings to the organisation or the replacement supplier on the details of the current delivery of the services to allow the organisation or replacement supplier to provide continuity of service. It will also cover the arrangements for support to any agreed due diligence process. The list of activities to be considered within this sub-project might include the following:

- High-level description of the services
- Description of the scope of services and service levels
- Base documentation and as applicable a Procedures Manual
- Service management information
- Status of in-progress projects
- Milestones to be included at first and subsequent Exit Plan reviews

Logistics and Property Sub-Project

This sub-project is responsible for the vacating or transferring any building space, facilities and services, and defines the necessary activities to support the transfer into the replacement office or production infrastructure environment. The list of activities to be considered within this sub-project might include the following:

- Health, safety and security
- Communications
- Technology and systems access needs
- Access to facilities, processes, services and people
- Access to supplies and suppliers

Supplier Management Sub-Project

This sub-project is responsible for the transfer arrangements of third-party contracts from the supplier to the organisation or the replacement supplier.

Technical Environment Sub-Project

This sub-project will provide the organisation or replacement supplier with technical platforms required in support of the services and transfer of data in accordance with the contract. This activity will remove the supplier intellectual property from the systems environment supporting the services, in accordance with the contract. This sub-project would also cover the transfer of equipment, software and hardware according to the conditions set out in the contract:

Management System

The aim of this sub-project is where required, to provide information to allow the organisation or the replacement supplier to provide continuity of management of the services and to implement its own management processes. The type of information might include:

- Documentation (including procedures, meeting minutes, records)
- Meeting structures
- Existing action lists
- Existing issue lists and risk logs
- Current projects details

Security Sub-Project

This might include the following:

- Review of existing security requirements in the Agreement
- Review of existing security issues
- Development and delivery of an implementation plan for the transfer of security arrangements

Hand-over Sub-Project

The hand-over sub-project will formally manage the transfer of all items between supplier and the organisation or the replacement supplier. This will identify those items to be transferred, log them, build a plan to achieve the transfer, execute the transfer and maintain a formal log confirming that the transfer took place using the signatures of both Parties as the approval method.

Sub-Project/Area	Considerations
Human Resources	Numbers involved in each location Names for system ids Names of leavers, transfers Names of those with special needs (disabled etc.) Welcome communications Pension, sickness and overtime files
Data Security	Procedures required for each location in respect of: • Physical requirements • System security changes

Sub-Project/Area	Considerations
Logistics	Secure stationery and other secure assets
	Keys (offices and bank etc.) and data lock numbers
	Authorising signatures
	Secure waste and spoilt instruments/waste
	Badges for transfers / removal for leavers
	Removal of items off-site
	Office and property assets
	Stationery
	Systems, tokens
	Catering
	Parking, shared and at specific locations
	Signs / publications
Handover Service Plan	Procedures of individual areas
	Problem management procedures
	IT assets
	Storage of media
	Procedures manuals and documentation
Management System	Procedures
	Meetings lists and descriptions
	Meeting minutes

Throughout the process, a risk register for exit activities in respect of the exit project and each sub-project should be established, updated and the control environment agreed, developed and maintained.

Exit Plan - Approval and Version Control

Each updated version of the exit plan must be signed below by both parties before the exit plan is deemed to be agreed.

The primary issue throughout this process is the similarity with the process to be adopted for effective business continuity management and it might be argued that the business continuity manager is either the driver or a key player in this activity.

There are a number of generic strategies to mitigate the impact of a disruption or reduce the probability of a threat event. Each strategy has parameters of speed of resumption, reliability of availability and cost which will be appropriate to different parts of the business so an organisation may require several elements to form an appropriate solution, depending upon the individual business functions.

UK Financial Services Authority (FSA) Report into Off-shore Outsourcers' Business Continuity Arrangements - May 2005 (11)

Planning points from the report include:

- All of the operations visited had contingency plans in the event of a serious problem. The size of operation examined influenced the business continuity planning and disaster recovery planning arrangements. Companies with larger operations have already been able to spread to multiple locations.

- Some suppliers have a policy not to employ more than 3,500-4,000 in any one city. Some firms already have offices located in more than one city (either as captives or via their suppliers) and others are considering this. This enables them to attract different skill sets as the nature of the work undertaken in India broadens, but also gives them some local business continuity opportunities. This minimises risk through multiple delivery locations.

- Others are experiencing significant problems organising local business continuity options. There is no external market for warm sites as the cost of buildings is prohibitively high in comparison to the cost of labour. (Conversely, in the UK, labour cost is higher so companies want full utilisation of staff, which is one of the reasons for having a warm site.) Propositions to resolve this include having a joint site with other companies. Others are considering developing their own warm site once their operations get to a critical size.

- In most cases building evacuations are tested regularly. Most test their business continuity plan at least annually and business continuity forms part of the initial migration project planning. As ramp-ups occur, business continuity requirements generally change in line with the business needs. The priority of most processes is defined along with their time criticality. Of those suppliers and subsidiaries that have a warm site option, at least one felt that the warm site is the last resort as resource is flexed between India and UK first, where appropriate.

- Most companies still have the capacity in other parts of the world to pick up critical workloads from India should the need arise. The fact that the data storage and main systems are outside India, with data only passed there as necessary for processing, makes this easier. However, firms do have to ensure that staff remain suitably familiar with the processes to be able to fill in. At least one firm has a deliberate bi-polar business continuity strategy. As several other firms do, they conduct tests at least annually to ensure that the UK can undertake work on behalf of India and vice versa (i.e., the UK also tests its BCP in reverse with India taking the calls, etc.). This highlights an added benefit from off-shoring, which is to maximise business continuity between the UK and India.

- Exit strategies:

  - Most companies still have the capacity in the UK to repatriate if need be, which is particularly important for smaller operations.

  - Some companies had multiple strands to their exit strategy depending on whether the requirement to exit was due to the operation or supplier failing and therefore another option offshore needing to be pursued. Exit requirements (e.g., transition support and penalties) are generally built into the contracts with third party suppliers. The speed with which processes can be transferred to another supplier or repatriated back will depend on the type of process and amount of work offshore.

Production Line Techniques

Say the words "production line" and one probably conjures up a view of what production lines looked like a decade ago or more. Today's modern production technology and supporting management techniques combine to form sophisticated production line control systems far removed from distant cousins of labour-intensive and grimy worksites. Of course the distant cousins still exist and this should be born in mind when managing suppliers and selecting outsource providers. An organisation should consider whether the environment of these key players in their production process should perform to standards and in an environment very different to those of their own.

Say the words "production line" and one probably also conjures up only a view of a factory shop floor. However, many organisations using production line techniques do so in an office environment.

And whether one thinks factory or office, grimy workshop or modern environment, the role of technology has moved to centre stage in the dependency stakes for production line management

Production Line - Tools and Techniques - Just In Time

Just In Time (JIT) manufacturing and distribution is to provide:
- What the customer wants

- When the customer wants it

- In the quantity they want it

Just In Time

The principles behind JIT are to ensure a smooth and seamless workplace, under an umbrella of systems that moves to an agreed pace to meet customer demand with the ability to start and stop the process to ensure that the correct sequence of production is constantly achieved. The goal is to reduce the manufacturing lead time from supplier to customer with minimal requirements for carrying expensive overheads of stock.

Within JIT management, there is a further "tool kit," some components of which are outlined below:

Gemba Kanri: This is a Japanese expression and means "workshop management." This process encourages team leaders and operations management to work closely together and is the process for designing and implementing operational standard management. It addresses how to initiate and maintain standards for the management of people, parts, plans and process - with an objective of continuous improvement.

5S: This is an improvement process which can be applied in a factory, service or office environment. Again derived from a Japanese concept, this has been translated into English as the 5S and 5Cs.

5S	5C
Sort	Clear out
Store	Configure
Shine and service	Clean and check
Standardise	Conform
Sustain	Custom and practice

This is an approach that impacts on the work place, making it clean and safe ensuring that the right equipment in working order is available and that employees work in a pleasant and efficient environment.

CAPDo: This tool centres on ensuring that non-compliance with agreed standards is identified and eliminated. The goal is to ensure that every manager when faced with a similar set of circumstances will take the same action.

All businesses must decide what strategy they want to adopt for delivery - from inventory to order. The decision will depend on a number of factors, including the location, quantity and mix of finished and work in progress throughout the supply chain and the conditions for successful distribution. While upholding the principles of JIT, organisations are complex and as with a business, BIAs and the recovery plans must appreciate that changes in demand and seasonality, for example, will impact on the success of processes. While not explored in detail here, for the interested reader it is recommended that they go onto to explore the concepts as 'flow,' 'takt' and 'pull' as these are the guiding principles that help an organisation to meet effective demand in times of normality - and in times of change, including disruption.

It is an established management principle that manufacturing, service and back-office processes should be designed using JIT techniques. Consequently, the risk assessment and BIA should be conducted with these principles in mind and business continuity plans designed to reflect appropriate recovery. Failure to recognise these principles may result in a disjointed recovery with loss of the correct production sequence, along with disappointed customers coupled with an increase in production costs. This is a plan for failure, not recovery.

In Support Of Business Continuity - Asset Protection - A Supplier Issue

Various options exist for alternative work space in the event of a business continuity plan invocation. Initial risk assessments and BIAs will identify key risks and potential impacts to the business. Alternative work space requirements should consider options for denial of access, partial loss of a site, loss of a whole site, loss of an area with several sites (or 'campus'), country and regional situations. While thinking the unthinkable must be the principal approach; in reality, the majority of incidents and invocations do not involve total loss of a site or long-term denial of site access. The majority of incidents affect partial space loss.

Whatever the approach, alternative arrangements must reflect the risk assessment. If the assessment assumes a worst-case scenario of large–scale, territorial denial then alternatives outside city boundaries must be considered. Following the events of September 11, 2001, some of the most successful recoveries involved relocation well outside the boundaries of Manhattan, avoiding congestion, lack of space and the daily distress suffered by those who had been closely touched by the events and continued to work in dust-filled environments reminding them through taste and touch of what had taken place. Whatever the location, it must be able to support a recovery. Vacant space awaiting sale, while attractive, may suddenly become unavailable when disposed of, may have the original cabling removed, or may have cabling which is out of date and unable to cope with the demands for capacity, speed and security of modern technology.

Considerations of distance from the recovery site also include:
• Denial of access if an exclusion zone is established. Think of exclusion recommendations of five years ago and treble these;
• Denial of access if transportation systems are closed down ; and,
• Transporting people to use remote sites away from homes and their families. Are there employees that are not flexible in their working arrangements both in terms of time and distance?

Options for Support

The list of challenges is considerable. Whatever the options, the strategy taken must be maintainable, testable and executable at all times.

- **Do nothing**: This strategy may be acceptable for certain non-urgent functions identified in the BIA. In the event that alternative facilities are required an organisation may accept the fact that purchasing, leasing or renting alternative buildings and installing utilities may take several months

- **Commercial work area facility**: There are several contract options for space invocation and allocation. These include syndicated space offered on a first–invoked, first-served basis, 'budge-up' where the provider will attempt to accommodate as many invocations as possible, reducing space allocation per organisation as invocation numbers increase, or dedicated space where only the organisation under contract may use the space which is kept at a ready state at all times. Contracts are usually taken out for periods ranging from three to ten years and typically around five years. Contracts can have negotiable flexibility to increase or reduce space but as this is a long-term business for the supplier, contracts with easy flexibility to change space requirements should be carefully challenged.

Whatever the space, it is usually configured to recover on a 'cold,' 'warm' or 'hot' basis - the temperature indicating the degree of preparedness for access and occupation - and cost.

The state and speed of site readiness will be influenced by the level of IT and other equipment provided, the degree of systems customisation to customer specification, response times and of course price. Typically contracts will be priced on the number of seats required, the number of locations in which they are required, the level of IT support and the ease of access through whatever network capability is in place.

Purchased on a 'syndicated' basis, higher level costs cut in once invocation has taken place and a customer is on site. Typically made available for between eight and twelve weeks, these are excellent stop-gap solutions but not for the long term. Some regulators have expressed concerns about this type of facility in that access cannot be guaranteed, and the only effective way to have dedicated space is to pay for it in total. For key systems and processes identified in the BIA or for customers where potentially punitive penalties exist in service level agreements for service failure, dedicated space may well be the most appropriate option.

The buyer of this service should check out the syndication policy of the supplier in terms of exclusion zones and how many times each site may be 'sold.' These considerations should still be made if an 'enterprise' deal is struck, meaning that an organisation may recover any named site into any named recovery location - in isolation or in aggregation. Some contracts will allow for a simultaneous multiple site invocation if an incident is severe

- **Budge-up**: this expression is used in connection with commercial and in-house recovery solutions. It can make use of existing in-company accommodation such as a training facility, canteen or warehouse to provide recovery space or increasing the office density. Locations used as potential backup may not have been designed for the purpose of the business that might use them as a backup. For example, a training facility may have limited power, transport and even toilet capability. If temporary buildings would be used at such a site to supplement recovery, will the ground support the foundations of these buildings and will access allow such accommodation to be moved on-site? This solution while feasible will require careful planning and technical preparation. It will also prove challenging to test. Commercially, this expression can relate to recovery sites sold on a syndicated basis where contracts state that space initially allocated to those organisations which invoke may be reduced to accommodate additional clients which invoke subsequently. This solution, when sold commercially, can offer limited assurance in that space may not be available to planned expectations - however slick the invocation subsequently turns out to be.

- **Displacement**: This concerns displacing staff performing less urgent business processes with staff performing higher priority activities. It may involve moving employees and their work to a similar facility, combining two operations and displacing those function and employees that are considered non-critical in the BIA, until an alternative facility is available. The risk with this solution is that one incident affects two operations. The location to which the interrupted operation is moved may also start to perform at sub optimal levels, thereby reducing the effectiveness of two, not one, operation. Further, budge-up plans agreed on paper in times of normal operation can prove difficult to invoke if the receiving location is particularly busy and needs all the accommodation and capability that it has. However, if this option is considered appropriate, even if in-house, there is a need for formalising these arrangements between departments; with the risk or business continuity manager taking ownership for oversight.

- **Remote Working**: This includes the concept of working from home or working from other locations which do not form part of the usual business operation, such as hotels. Working from home can be a very effective solution but care must be taken to ensure health and safety issues are addressed and sufficient dial-up or other appropriate connectivity and capacity is available. Used more frequently in the US than the UK and Continental Europe, this solution can be effective for wide-area disruption and denial of access to usual in-city locations. There is a human factor here that should also be considered. Locating people at home may remove the opportunity for networking with colleagues, for which there may be an acute need following an incident. The desire to bring employees together for briefings and networking should consequently form part of the recovery considerations should this option be invoked. Consideration should also be made to the nature of the work in question. Some work simply may not be suited to this environment - for example, interactive design where team capability and specialist equipment are called for.

- **Reciprocal agreements**: This can work in some selected services and industries with similar recovery needs but care must be taken when establishing this type of agreement. Procedures must be in place to ensure that periodic checks are performed to ensure that the required arrangements have not changed. Reciprocal agreements must consider other planning principles such as suitable exclusion zone criteria and have written agreements, a clause in the contract to ensure that expectations will be realised and that testing is permitted.

- **Commercial or dedicated mobile facilities**: These can be in use rapidly but provide limited space and may require service connections. Resembling caravans or trailers, this type of recovery facility is suited to small 'high street' recovery needs. Ideal for the loss of a retail or banking outlet, a suitable site will need to established and surveyed, and zoning and building permits obtained. A further use might be for an organisation to use these facilities as temporary outlets from which it can support its customers - for example by an insurance company to establish a temporary claims centre from which to service claims in the event of a major natural disaster such a tropical storm or flood.

- **Commercial or dedicated prefabricated**: These units take a minimum of four days to build (the average is eight) depending on the site and weather conditions. Temporary buildings with relevant equipment can be either purchased and held in store or purchased on a syndicated basis as with commercial work area solutions discussed above. Specialist recovery needs such as data centres, often plan for this type of facility. There is a range of commercial services including fixed, mobile and prefabricated sites, and typical locations are car parks or other areas with adequate foundations. This solution will require preparation including site surveys to ensure that the potential location is suitable for the purpose.

- **Commercial 'Ship in' Contracts**: These include generators, IT equipment such as PCs, servers and printers and specialist hardware and equipment such as telephony systems. This may be an appropriate strategy if an unprepared building is to be equipped to provide an appropriate working environment. Most ship-in contracts permit the delivery location to be nominated at invocation, allowing a more flexible response to a specific incident compared to a fixed site recovery capability.

- **Resilient Operations**: These include dual site operations and continuous availability solutions. In the event of an interruption at one site the business function is transferred to one or more alternate locations at which staff and facilities are already prepared to handle it. These options are normally amongst the more expensive to implement but provide the appropriate solution where quick resumption is necessary. To be a viable recovery strategy this configuration should have no single points of failure and an appropriate geographical separation and diversity of the two or more sites.

Infocomm Development Authority of Singapore (IDA)

Industry-led Business Continuity and Disaster Recovery Service Providers Standards

The Infocomm Development Authority of Singapore (IDA) has announced that Singapore's industry-led Business Continuity / Disaster Recovery Working Group of the Information Technology Standards Committee (ITSC), has developed the world's first industry standard for business continuity and disaster recovery service providers. The industry standard specifies stringent requirements that business continuity and disaster recovery service providers must possess so that they can provide a trusted operating environment and help companies secure and recover critical data in crisis. These requirements include stipulations for operating, monitoring, maintaining and 'up-keeping' business continuity and disaster recovery services offered to clients. The standard will serve to differentiate between service providers and help provide guidance for end-user companies in choosing the most suitable providers.

- *December 2004* **(12)**

In Support Of Business Continuity - Systems Protection - A Supplier Issue

The increasing use and sophistication of technology in most industries is helping those industries to lower costs and to provide new and improved products and services to their customers at more competitive prices and with greater reliability.

This scenario does, however, have its downside in that complexity in technology and dependency on technology can have a profound effect on the risk profile of an organisation. Complex technology can open up new routes for criminal activity. Greater technology complexity makes for greater risk complexity, and a potential concurrent increase in the risk of business interruption due to systems failures and the consequential effect of this.

As with office or manufacturing site recovery, recovery of most technology capabilities addressed in Chapter Nine can be supported by third-party suppliers.

> *"Some things are best left to chance - a card game or roll of the dice. Other things need to be planned, carefully planned and tested."*
>
> *- Network Disaster Recovery (NDR) 2005*

Information technology third-party business continuity management supplier options include:

Hardware and software. Desktop, server, mid-range, mainframe, hand-held and 'e' units and the software that these require can all be provided by a number of specialised technology providers.

Network. Local area network (LAN) and wide area network (WAN) capability may be required to connect either an in-house alternative site options or that of a third-party supplier. These may be supplied through third-party contracts and the capability should be closely integrated at all stages of the recovery design process with those of the hardware and software options.

Power. For those situations where site and employees are unaffected but discontinuity is due to loss of power supplies, third-party supplier contracts can be arranged to provide temporary generator capability - assuming that there is sufficient space and fuel storage capability adjacent to the site in question. Contracts can be on a variety of bases from assured to 'best efforts' - the degree of certainty of supply and supply time-scale operating as determinants of the contract price.

Case Study 1

Power failure in New Zealand - February 1998

Mercury Energy knew two years before the power failure that the power cables supplying Auckland's central business district (CBD) were "unreliable," had a "history of leakage" and were likely to fail. But nothing in board reports at the time indicated that the power supply was at risk and that the matter was urgent. "It was a matter that had to be addressed at the right time."

All four of the main power cables into the CBD failed over a period of four weeks. During February 1998, for several weeks the business district had to survive on around 30% of capacity; this came from generators and a low-capacity line fed in from outside. Within a week of the power failures some small business had already been forced to close for good.

Businesses thought laterally and moved their back offices to the front rooms of houses of company officials. One ingenious firm of accountants set up business on an Auckland Harbour ferry which starved of daily commuters provided backup complete with its own power, catering and toilet facilities.

Those businesses which did manage to function in situ did so with the help of generator power. Where contingent arrangements were in place disruption was the most minimal - fortunes were made by others who purchased kit flown in from Australia.

Case Study 2

Power failure on the US East Coast - August 2003

At 4:15pm on Thursday August 14, 2003, a power outage occurred which affected parts of the Northeast from Canada to Detroit, Michigan. The reports of the outage were dramatic as pictures from space showed a coast in darkness.

However, all business were largely back on line over the weekend and open for business on Monday August 18, 2003. But many took this as a warning shot there was talk of weaknesses in the overall grid during times of peak demand (extreme heat and cold). Those with generator capability stayed on line; others thought it time to power up with suitable support contracts.

Telephony. Commercial options exist for temporary and pre-configured switchboard capability provided in mobile trailers or installed in temporary fixed locations. These can include intelligent call routing of individual Direct Dial In numbers (DDIs) to any remote location, minutes after disaster strikes. This is essential for today's call centre facility with the need for highly time-sensitive recovery delivered through instantaneous and seamless re-routing of incoming calls via a telecommunications system on an individual DDI basis to an alternative location of choice.

Data backup and restoration. A number of suppliers provide solutions for data storage and recovery. The concept of data warehousing has taken off in the last decade, although a number of suppliers have been financially stressed through over-investing in warehousing capability resulting in supply over-capacity. As with any supplier, financial robustness is a key requirement of supplier credentials.

As discussed in Chapter Nine, the cost of technology recovery services will be a function of a number of factors, the primary ones of which are the robustness and speed of recovery capability. Generally, the faster and more robust the recovery the more expensive is the solution. High availability services which mirror a production environment will be available in a ready state - but this comes at a price.

Technical support. While the focus has been on the recovery need and the technology options, the greatest value-add from a supplier contract can be the ability to call down expertise from the supplier in support of the technology product. Skilled in the product or service supplied, but more importantly its use in times of disruption and stress, the support they can offer may be the difference between survival and failure - especially when an organisation's own personnel may have been casualties in an incident and may be unavailable or not operating at optimal levels. This institution was evident following the events of 9/11 when a number of organisations lost not only their business capability, but also IT, IT backup capability, and those skilled in its operation.

Mobile technology infrastructure. As discussed above, work site recovery, mobile and temporary units can provide (in addition to space, equipment, and voice and data communications lines), complete contact centre voice recovery, with call recording and customer support functions. These temporary locations can be of such high specification that if required they can also provide a longer term information technology recovery location should that form the optimum recovery solution in terms of price and location.

Quick Ship solutions. Complementary to work site and other technology solutions, contracts can be positioned for the rapid supply of PCs, servers, telephony and LAN equipment. This type of contract is particularly relevant if an organisation has non standard or otherwise redundant equipment which in times of stress may be difficult to obtain to the right specification, quickly.

Summary

Organisations now face increased reliance on their IT infrastructures as business process automation continues apace. At the same time the extension of the business and IT supply chain from internal users to end customers add additional complexity to the challenge.

"As part of its own strategy for maintaining business continuity an organisation should know precisely how their suppliers and outsource providers would react in the event of an incident. What priority will your organisation have as part of their plans? When can they expect their critical business processes to be restored?" **(13)**. If your organisation's recovery plan is contingent on the behaviour and performance of outside sources, it will only be as strong and reliable as they are.

Single points of failure have brought many organisations to their knees. Suppliers and outsource providers provide goods and services as part of the overall business process model and if they fail, they can provide a single point of failure. Consequently, their position within the complex business must be understood and appropriate resilience and continuity arrangements designed and embedded as if they were part of the business. The argument was made at the start of this Chapter that services or production capability can be outsourced and goods and services in the supply chain can be provided by third parties - but responsibility including that for the continuity of an organisation cannot be transferred to a third party.

This concept extends to the supply and outsourcing of services that support the process of business continuity management. The principles that apply to supplier and outsource management should be applied - and one might argue that given the dependence of an organisation on these partners where management control is at a distance, then even higher levels of performance might be understood and expected. Some regulators have expressed concerns over the reliance of organisations on business continuity management suppliers that provide facilities and services on a syndicated basis. In this regard an organisation should take great care to ensure as far as possible that such support will be available when needed, through effective contract management, robust and challenged service level agreements with regular testing of the services and facilities in question.

Bibliography

1. Competitive Advantage - Michael Porter - 1985

2. The UK Financial Services Authority - Handbook – www.fsa.gov.uk - 2004

3. Michigan State University Study - www.bus.msu.edu/msc/documents - 2004

4. The UK Financial Services Authority - Handbook – www.fsa.gov.uk - 2004

5. The UK Financial Services Authority - Handbook – www.fsa.gov.uk - 2004

6. Alan Jebson - Chief Operating Officer HSBC - extract from Growth and governance - KPMG - 2004

7. Guidelines on Outsourcing Monetary Authority of Singapore - 2004

8. Financial Risk Outlook - the UK Financial Services Authority - 2005

9. Internet Week.com - 2005

10. Dun and Bradstreet - 2004

11. www.ida.gov.sg - 2005

12. www.fsa.gov.uk

13. Operational Resilience the Art of Risk Management - IBM - Financial World Publishing - 2002

11

Opportunities and Other Applications for Business Continuity Tools and Principles

Objectives Of This Chapter:

The objectives are to consider the work done and the tools that have been created in the business continuity field and:

- Recognise where those principles and tools can be used elsewhere in the organisation

- Make as much additional use as possible of the Business Continuity tools, information and resources that have been created

- By maximising all such values, improve the business case further for the resources and time applied; and any monetary investment made in business continuity management, and

- Illustrate these additional values by considering individual exposures

The Principles and Tools To Be Applied

We will begin this chapter with a reminder of the principles we believe are at the very core of business continuity risks and continuity planning. They are relatively straightforward and common sense in nature, but it is important that, as we delve into detail from time to time, we do not lose sight of the overall objectives. We have stated that they are:

- To understand the risks

- To understand critically the potential impact on the organisation and its stakeholders

- To make better informed decisions about the commercial acceptability of those risks
  - To manage the unacceptable exposures so that the risk or the impact is reduced to acceptable levels by best use amongst the choices of (or a combination of):

  - Risk-manage the potential cause of damage

  - Risk-manage and duplicate as necessary where the impact could be destructive

  - Transfer risk to another party if this can be done without destructive exposures still remaining

  - Prepare with contingency planning to manage through the remaining risks without unacceptable damage to the core dependencies of the organisation.

In this section of the book we will consider these principles against risks other than 'continuity risks' and explore where these needs and values are common and where the value of work done can be maximised in the risk arena. We do not drift here at all from the basic principles of risk management that are explained throughout the book and are summarised by one of the risk management standards:

> *'The focus of good management is the identification and treatment of these risks. The objective is to add maximum sustainable value to all of the activities of the organisation. It marshals the understanding of the potential upside and downside of all those factors that can affect the organisation. It increases the probability of success, and reduces both the probability of failure and the uncertainty of achieving the organisation's overall objectives.'* **(1)**

Reaction Plan

There is also value in recapping the objectives of a recovery plan, or perhaps better described for this chapter, a reaction plan. The needs that are met by such a plan are to ensure a rapid and best-possible-resourced response to any situation that may disrupt operations or control of the organisation. This need is for the unit directly involved and also to ensure a coordinated response together with support teams that may be drawn from other Group divisions. These other Group departments may have a vital support role to play at the time of a disaster and will have their own plans to react quickly and fulfil that role. The best recovery is a co-ordinated one making rapid use of all these services.

The specific objectives could be summarised as follows:

Objective 1: Speed of reaction to ensure:

1.1: Damage assessment

1.2: Retain control of the business

1.3: Damage limitation and news management

1.4: Continuance of security standards

Objective 2: Formation of suitable and authorised teams to:

2.1: Set short term and long term objectives

2.2: Set priorities

2.3: Enable central control and coordination

2.4: Enhance channels of communication

2.5: Achieve the set objectives

2.6: Monitor the recovery process.

Objective 3: Anticipate resources and information likely to be needed and accelerate access.

3.1: Information

3.2: People

3.3: Equipment

We will now move forward and explore how these values and tools can be of use elsewhere to manage risk in the organisation.

FRAUD

Fraud risk is a subject large enough for a book of its own and we set out here to draw some parallels between fraud risk management and continuity management.

Clearly the risk management process chain we describe above is relevant. The exposure to fraud is best managed when time and energy have been invested to understand the risk weaknesses and where damage could occur. Clearly the most energy is applied to where the opportunities for theft best lie and where the greatest values are exposed to loss. Clearly those fraud exposures also come from within the organisation, from counterparties and from third parties. Some company boards find it difficult to recognise that the greatest opportunities for fraud lie within the organisation itself, due to the very knowledge of systems and procedures amongst staff members.

One report (2) estimates that fraud is costing United Kingdom businesses £40 billion pounds a year. Some larger companies report fraud as much as five percent of their turnover; with identity fraud increasing dramatically. The authors of that report admit that these are just guesses and could be 'the tip of the iceberg.' The very nature of fraud is that the organisation only knows it had been defrauded when the fraud is uncovered!

Organisations are also extremely shy about sharing actual fraud losses and near-misses although a number of industry-based groups do exist through which data is shared. Fraud is primarily an issue for the control environment within an organisation, but one fraud could be so significant that it can put at risk the other dependencies; not least financial stability and reputation/brand values amongst the many stakeholders.

One relevant aspect of fraud risk to the business continuity process is where the fraud is large enough to be in the public arena and threaten the confidence that fellow employees, other stakeholders or the public may have in the organisation. The fraud may be in information rather than money. It may be in an employee working beyond authority levels to take risks and thereby raise the chance of increased bonus payments or status; accepting such a risk profile for his or her employer may well be way beyond the organisation's own preferred risk tolerance. Leeson is a high-profile example and by no means the only example of this kind of corporate or individual rogue trading. Regulators in 1991 seized about seventy-five percent of the $17 billion assets of Bank of Credit and Commerce International (BCCI) following a fraud; Sumitomo Corporation incurred losses of almost £3 billion through excessive trading of copper over a decade.

Such frauds could bring other serious legal, compliance, business control, competition, share price, insider trading and confidence consequences.

We will assume, for the purpose of avoiding straying too far from the agenda of this book, that the fraud risk is recognised and realistic controls (with a humility and due diligence to recognize that controls can fail) are in place. In headline form only therefore, the fraud security controls can be electronic, physical access controls, financial controls and processes, delegated authority procedures, secure 'whistle-blower' opportunities, staff vetting procedures, other procedures and controls delivering security around information and assets, and finally, project risk control.

We are still left with the need to handle that point in time when a major fraud is just suspected. This is the most difficult stage of all. In the event that there is suspicion of a significant fraud, the worst thing often that an organisation can do is to tramp in with accusations without preparing the ground carefully beforehand. That 'trampling' on the scene could destroy criminal evidence, can reduce opportunities to recover stolen assets and money and could alert the fraudster early enough so that he or she can destroy evidence.

Case Study

Sadly, a too common experience is for the fraudster, alerted of suspicions, destroying records to avoid recriminations. That destruction may be by way of destroying computer records (with a knowledge of where backups are kept) and even the use of fire or explosives to destroy paper records.

There was one case where an employee, accused of fraud, admitted the crime but stated that he had also copied and hidden company books and papers. The accusation was countered with a threat that, if the organisation pursued him in either criminal or civil law, he would disclose to the authorities certain corporate activities that had taken place that were not legal. The fact that the Group Head office had not been aware of these local illegal and tax evasion activities was not the issue.

What begins as a fraud with a worst-case loss being to lose tolerable amounts of money, then can turn, if not handled quickly and efficiently, into a major crisis threatening the very survival of the organisation.

Furthermore, making accusations of fraud without being sure of your ground beforehand could actually be found subsequently in error; and bring legal charges by the accused; perhaps with morale damage amongst employees and others.

While we are concerned here with the reaction to suspected fraud, it is worth mentioning that fraud management can help a suspecting person to pass information forwards in a non-threatening way. 'Whistle Blowing' contact numbers are now embedded in most large organisations as a form of 'incident notification and escalation.' Anti-money laundering responses, for example, often demand availability of such a service to employees. All this leads us to the fact that, even having risk-managed the exposure as best possible, the organisation still needs a contingency plan that will provide guidance right from the beginning of the time when there is a need to respond to suspicions. The person in the front line of that response may neither be the group security manager nor the chief auditor. He or she may be a local factory or office manager who has been alerted that 'something is amiss'. The next step is all-important, and could if handled clumsily create damage of much greater scale than the original fraud (if indeed it is a fraud – or a fraud by the person under suspicion).

This response shares many of the same objectives and needs as the response plan described above. Clearly there is need for damage assessment, to retain control, ensure damage limitation (including as necessary news management) and also retention of security standards (objective 1). Study of objectives 2 and 3 above again bring out common themes.

Should a board need further convincing, there are examples of frauds that have, in themselves, threatened the existence of an organisation – even before senior managers stumbled in without deep thought into such a sensitive situation.

Case Study 1

Leeson and Barings Bank: A dealer took his employer into risk profiles for personal reasons way beyond his authority level and effected losses that destroyed the very organisation that employed him.

Case Study 2

Enron: Senior executives hid the true financial position from regulators, employees and shareholders; again causing destruction of one of the largest organisations in America. This fraud also brought down the advisors, Andersen, from their ability to continue trading in the way they had previously enjoyed.

A fraud reaction plan would need to have in place the same requirements of any contingency plan. It would need to inform and train the potential players who may have to face real-life situations; guide them; advise them of company policy; and, resource them by letting them know how to gain immediate access to information, specialist support and tools.

The company objectives are likely to include

- Identifying all those responsible (not just the individual in the spotlights);
- Closing future leaks; including media management and other releases of information;
- Recovery of assets;
- Prevention of the use or value of unauthorised information by competitors or others;
- Protection of brand and confidences amongst stakeholders;
- Maintaining morale; and,
- Protecting critical or catastrophic exposures (such as regulatory approvals or wider legality).

The plan will also address difficult questions such as whether it is company policy to inform the Police; or at least ensure that such a decision is made at the right level within the organisation. Informing the Police is in the wider public interest, and may increase the chance of recovery of assets and could lead to a criminal prosecution. The downside risks of involving the Police are the loss of control as events unfold; challenges created by the bureaucracy of public service; the shifting of the agenda to one being driven by public prosecution rather than asset recovery; and, loss of control over announcements to the media. The Police will have its own agenda, and may be constrained by limited resources that it could apply to the individual incident. The Police may also not see this particular fraud as a criminal priority for them. Once reported, it is also impossible to stop procedures unfolding should the organisation feel later that it would prefer to do so.

There are jurisdictions where it is an offence not to involve the Police following some types of fraud and others where the Police may be associated with the fraud and/or those who perpetrated it.

The plan could ensure, for example, that skills, information and other resources that the plan may quickly bring alongside and guide the local manager (24 hours a day/7 days a week if necessary). These skills could come from internal audit, external auditors, specialists in the group risk department, specialist technology auditors, the security manager, human resources (employment law and procedures), the legal department, and private consultants and investigators.

The skills and resources of these departments and experts may be valuable in all manner of ways; to assess the situation, protect sensitivities and to ensure the corporate objectives as above are secured before a move is taken in the open against the suspected fraudster.

The initial, secret, investigation may establish that there is indeed a high likelihood of major fraud. Just one strategy that may be chosen by the team may be to prepare and stage a 'dawn raid' on the suspected fraudster's workspace and, if duly authorised, home. Such a raid would seal electronic and paper evidence, take and secure film from CCTV cameras, telephone records, computer access logs, other audit trails, fingerprints, and DNA. It would set out to take and seal any information in a way that could later be used for further investigations, or for establishing proof in a way that would be admissible in either a civil or criminal court.

All of these steps my be needed extremely quickly and the preparation of people, information, communication and other tools, by way of a reaction plan, may be the only possible way they could all be brought together in time.

KIDNAP AND EXTORTION

Once again there is the need initially to manage the risk. In the case of the kidnap and extortion risk; once a risk is identified the risk management can then unfold. Such risk management work is designed to remove or reduce the opportunities or the interest of a kidnapper in the target. Risk management also ensures, again, that the vitally important first response to a kidnapper's demands, the very subject of a contingency plan, is best likely to keep the victim alive and to preserve assets.

Risk management – emerging from the information developed in a risk analysis - will be all about recognising where the risks around the organisation lie. Higher risk areas can be as a result of the nature of the employer's business, a particular employee's responsibilities within the business, or because of the countries and areas where their job takes them. Risk management will identify those risk levels and those areas where kidnapping is at higher risk and will inform the employees accordingly. It is most clear that the kidnap victims are not necessarily the most senior personnel.

The employees identified to be at risk are likely to receive a package of advice, a measured level of security, contact numbers and other tools and resources. All employees may be banned from certain high-risk countries without an individually negotiated reason to go; and then with a security 'envelope' pre-arranged locally for the visit. Specific information about such areas is available from consultancies such as Control Risks and Kroll Associates; and a broader assessment is available from the websites of such agencies as the CIA or State Department in the United States and the Foreign and Commonwealth Office in the United Kingdom. Their websites and others are in the list at the end of this book. Kidnappings in such 'hot spots' as Colombia and Mexico can average, over a period of time, as many as four a day. The objectives anywhere can equally be political, financial, or both, where funding is needed to finance a political or terrorist campaign. As with all issues of this nature the number of kidnappings made public is only the tip of the iceberg in terms of the true total.

> *Kidnap risk management may not only be in ensuring close security for the individual during the visit or ongoing in some situations, it will also prepare the organisation should it ever need suddenly to respond to a threat from terrorists or other kidnappers.*

A fundamental decision is whether to respond to the kidnappers' demand. There are conflicting public interest pressures and also an understandable desire to save the life of the victim. The planning will establish the corporate view in principle. The primary objective of any response that is made to kidnappers is to preserve the life of the victim. The two first drivers in any negotiations towards the safe return of the victim must therefore be

1. Prove that those negotiating are actually the ones holding the victim; and

2. Confirm that the hostage is still alive.

It is a powerful aid to the preservation of life if the organisation's representatives demand that they will only talk, each time there is contact, if new and current proof of life is given. Basic risk management precautions prior to the visit to a known kidnapping environment may therefore be to take the fingerprints of the traveller, recent photographs, medication needed, a voice recording, and ask them also to place in a sealed envelope personal information that only they and their family could know. DNA kits are used more and more. Once again, just as in fraud above, the reaction plan, that follows the principles and ingredients of a continuity plan (see above) can add tremendous value. Such a plan would enable the person receiving first contact to marshal immediately the information and specialist skills that would ensure that the very first response would be professional and would further the aim of life preservation. Once again the plan clearly sets the company policy; including such difficult questions as whether it is the organisation's policy to pay ransoms to criminals. The other key issue here is that if there is a written plan it can improve the response. If the local and central teams know the strategy and plan content this improves communication, and each knows what the other will be doing. Also if there is a strategy, employees can be advised that this exists and this can reduce the chance of a victim trying to negotiate their own release, cause confusion and lead to their harm.

Advisers and potentially professional negotiators will be identified beforehand and will be named in the plan together with their anytime contact numbers. In some countries the view may be taken that the local Police would not be advised; as they themselves may be corrupt, incompetent or even likely to be involved in the actual kidnapping. The plan would address how the organisation would respond to any media interest that emerged, and as best possible, try to avoid this interest threatening the safe return of the victim. It would also address the important aspect of ensuring support is available for the family as the situation – often extending over a period of months or years – unfolds.

Needless to say, continuity plans, as indeed all contingency plans, will be strictly confidential. Widespread knowledge of such a plan beyond those (and their families) that should be advised because they are considered high risk, could actually encourage a kidnap from a fellow employee or someone else who may have learned of the policy.

Clearly the full plan is a 'secret' document restricted to those who need to know. The information disseminated company-wide would simply advise where any concerned person can make contact with support at all hours.

Product Contamination and Product Recall

This is another area where the organisation may need to respond, at any time of the day or night to a call to any employee or to a switchboard, that may be the start of organisation threatening developments. The call may be a one-off advice that a product has failed someone or injured someone. It may be a criminal threat of product contamination that in turn may be a hoax, may be a bluff to extort funds, or alternatively may the beginning of a situation that could begin to threaten the very credibility and survival of the whole organisation. Deciding which, at the time of the call, is very difficult and a wrong decision can itself damage brand survival.

Such a situation is again likely to happen without warning, and to someone whose work experience has not trained them to deal with it. They may also panic and deepen the damage. As in dealing with kidnapping , that very first reaction could be the pivot on which the professional managers later have any real chance at all of handling the situation without damage to the organisation.

Case Study

The tampering, or threat of tampering designed to get someone else to take particular actions, may not just be money driven. While the risk manager's product may be the target, the demand may not be directly on the manufacturer of that product. Anti-apartheid extremists in Canada and Europe have threatened South African fruit; Tamil separatists in Sri Lanka have threatened to contaminate tea, Sri Lanka's primary export; and there have been threats against Israel's leading export, citrus fruit. Animal rights activists have also contaminated products of companies involved in animal testing; including cosmetics and turkeys.

The targeted organisation, therefore, may not be able, even if it wanted to, to respond by meeting the demands raised at the time.

Dr. Deborah Lowe examined 45 Fortune 500 Companies in the food and pharmaceutical industries. All had experienced product tampering threats or incidents. All of these threats took place over one twelve-month period and all involved named brand, packaged consumer products. **(3)**

Faulty and dangerous products are also a frequent reason to trigger an urgent recall. The main cause for recalling faulty products is potential electrical faults (46%), followed by those that could cause a choking risk in children. 59% result from design failures and 32% from manufacturing processing problems. **(4)**

As is all these areas, work begins with understanding the risk and identifying where the higher levels of opportunities and vulnerabilities lie. Clearly some retail industries – food, drink, tobacco, cosmetics and others – are more susceptible than others. The work starts with consistent product quality standards in the original service delivery or product manufacture; transport security and in the design of packaging whereby contamination is not possible without visible evidence that the package has been opened. All these areas and others are routine risk management issues that fall in the same skill bases and often tools as the continuity BIA and risk management in its wider sense.

A further clear parallel is the need to have a contingency plan that will trigger, empower, and resource crisis managers. That objective is also to provide fast and clear communications between the risk event, the crisis managers and wherever additional skills and resources can be brought to play. Important and difficult decisions will be whether the threat is real or imagined, and if real, whether to go public or recall products from the marketplace. Such a decision will be similar in form, if not in content, with crucial early decisions about threats of any kind and will need the empowerment, skill to assess the information then at hand, and knowledge of the impact assessment. Once more therefore a contingency plan is needed and will again follow many of the headlines and content of the wider continuity plan we discuss elsewhere in this book.

It is crucial that people are prepared beforehand and are at the ready, also that equipment, resources and information are in place to deploy very quickly indeed should the decision be to go for a product recall. There is just no time to sort these things out after the decision to do so.

The plan may therefore position these resources, ensure instant communications as needed, and address, or prompt, the issues that will need to be considered if the decision is made to recall a product. These plan prompts may include the following as well as those that are specific to the actual product or industry.

Recall Or Not?	• Someone suitably skilled, informed and authorised needs to make the vital decision – "Do we recall or not?" • Safety will be factor of such a decision; as will be any legal considerations. • Is the perceived information and threat credible? • Should there be further enquiry before a decision is made? • Is there time to do so, or must the decision be made on the information known so far?
Who Needs To Be Reached By The Recall?	• Distributors alone or customers who may have already purchased to product? • Is the media in this circumstance a resource or a threat? • Can customer information be used for the recall without contravening the Data Protection Act (United Kingdom) or other relevant legislation? Is the customer information available in anyevent?
The Message	• Clarity of message is crucial, including: • The precise products affected, • What is wrong, • What customers need to do or not to do, and • Need for clear understanding of legal and safety aspects
How Best Is The Recall Message Delivered?	• The answer to this will depend on a whole range of variables and indeed what is possible. • If the media is involved a further range of challenges will need to be faced. The issues here are identical to those confronting contingency planners in any potentially catastrophic scenario. • Is it necessary to staff and brief a call centre to handle the inevitable flow of enquiries that will emerge? • There are special challenges and opportunities for those retailing internationally and by the use of e-commerce.
Monitoring The Recall	• Progress will need to be monitored throughout the recall. • Decisions may change in the light of the unfolding situation. • Prompts to ensure an assessment is made throughout of the success or otherwise of the recall
The Debrief	• Two main lessons to be learned and certainly not to be missed: • How can the organisation prevent it from happening again? • How can the process of recalls be better managed in the future?

Bomb Threat

There is yet another situation where members of staff may, unexpectedly and suddenly, find themselves having to react to a life- or business-threatening, situation. The wrong instant response may be all the difference between life and death or the destruction of the organisation. That person may be at the most junior level or at the top of the organisation but it is likely they will face making a response in a situation that is extremely unfamiliar and personally threatening.

Once again we are in the realm of a crucial need for contingency planning; and planning that again follows the overall standards that we address in this book. As in all the subjects of this chapter, it is beyond the agenda of this book to provide full and detailed guidelines on each of these risks; but we believe it is of value to highlight the need for contingency planning in these circumstances. We set out here to draw parallels with the continuity management work and illustrate how the widest values of contingency planning can be exploited.

The work starts once more with an understanding of the risk and impact and designing out the threat as much as it is achievable to do so. A bomb threat, whether it is to the organisation's own switchboard or to elsewhere naming the organisation, needs once more the difficult decision-making we describe above. Is it credible? Is it real? Is it a hoax? It needs therefore the advice, communications, skills and authorisations that are essentials for a best possible decision to be made.

> *The framework and the objectives of the bomb threat plan have common ingredients with all contingency planning and will go further on to address the particular issues that arise from such a threat.*

Such preparedness must begin with prompts and training of the likely receivers of such calls to follow guidelines as to what to say that may elicit information to help the incident managers. Telephonists, for example, may be routinely supplied with a bomb threat response guide and questions to ask. Reminders may be issued when the organisation feels that risk levels are raised. This risk level could be as a result of the particular business of the organisation; or as a result of the wider 'risk state' for their buildings or their city or wider environment.

The threat may be that the bomb is a vehicle device in the street, that it is inside the building, or indeed, this information may not at this moment in time be known. Police, who will be taking control of safety issues, may demand that employees stay inside the building. This imposes a responsibility to protect staff as is best possible and safer bomb 'invacuation' areas may be chosen and prepared beforehand. Emergency communications to staff and visitors throughout will be agreed and in place beforehand and there will be a range of prompts, communication tools and other resources available to pre-agreed incident controllers.

Case Study

A hold-all was left on the windowsill of an Army recruiting office. Police considered this to be a credible bomb threat, closed the road and called bomb disposal experts. They stopped all pedestrian and vehicular traffic and thus contained people inside their offices, homes and shops.

Staff in many of these locations were caught up in the excitement of the scene, and pressed against the windows watching the police movements, army arrivals and the controlled explosion.

Fortunately the bag did not contain a large impact bomb but the 'swag' following a burglary. The thief had panicked and dumped the bag in an unfortunate location.

There are two more particular difficulties. The building may need to be searched. The Police may advise that that search needs to be done by the organisation's own staff; not themselves. This is a very real human challenge for the incident controller to manage. There is another difficulty in that, if no bomb explodes, at what elapsed time is it safe to return to work? Again, for sake of length, this book does not set out to address each of these issues in detail but to bring out comparisons and similarities with other contingency plans, why preparation for these issues is so crucial and why they are so much better done beforehand.

Such a plan could also be critical in the event or the fear or reality of substances sent in envelopes or packages to the organisation or to individual employees.

A further threat where the immediate response is critical to safety is when there are threats against individuals; such as those extended by animal rights activists in the United Kingdom to firms even remotely involved in using animals for drug testing. That immediate reaction to the threat or the actual package can be all the difference between safety of individuals and longer-term continuity of the use of the buildings.

The Supply Chain

We have addressed the special challenges of the supply chain throughout this book where there is an aspect of risk that is being addressed that has implications for supply chain management. The risk 'temperature' as always is at its highest where the item being supplied – whether it is a service, information, skill or product – is both crucial and is needed urgently to enable the receiving organisation meet important delivery promises of its own.

Case Study

"Deep sighs of relief all round at the vehicle manufacturers Land Rover's Solihull factory in the United Kingdom (and many neighbouring suppliers too, no doubt) when it was announced that the company had reached an agreement with administrative receivers to end the deadlock over Discovery chassis supplies. Land Rover has agreed to buy the chassis makers UPF Thompson for a reported £16 million.

"Had the parties failed to reach an agreement following UPF Thompson's financial collapse, Land Rover's Chief Executive, Bob Dover, had threatened to close Discovery production until a new chassis supplier could be found. The resulting job losses can only be estimated, but many thousands would have suffered." (6)

The risk of failure can be managed to some extent by care in the choice of quality, more resilient suppliers and by checking, as best possible, on their own contingency arrangements. The receiving organisation will often demand to have information about the suppliers' own contingency plans, the alternatives open to them, and their exercising regime. It may have a detailed questionnaire to enable it to assess as best as it can that resilience planning. It needs also to ensure that the supplier's own continuity management does not just protect the interests of the supplier alone. They need to be reassured that it goes on to recognise the dependency of the receiving organisation and builds this dependencies into its priority decisions. Taking and trusting such a view on a third party's contingency plan is notoriously difficult; and of course, as always, it only illustrates the position at that one point in time.

Such supply chain risk management, however well done, cannot provide guarantees and huge risk is likely to remain where the BIA identifies high survival dependencies on that supplier.

Furthermore no amount of financial penalty clauses in the contract nor any other financial assurances will be able to keep the receiving organisation alive and well if its very foundations stones are destroyed and consequently its own stakeholders walk away.

Case Studies

The terrorist attacks in America in September 2001 caused many risk and continuity managers to reconsider their scenario setting. This was not least around the risks carried through from their just–in–time, outsourced, supply chains.

Businessman Ross Perot is quoted as saying: "Lean only works in a free and open society. In the world of terrorism, just in time doesn't work. Companies are going to have much fatter supply chains."

"We're probably looking at everything in terms of how do we run the business in a mode of crisis," said Dan Flores, a spokesman for General Motors in Detroit. Laurie Harbour-Felax is a Vice President of Harbour Consulting in Troy, Michigan and which tracks the motor industry. She added, "Instead of relying on GM plants in Mexico to supply a particular vehicle, the auto maker may increase the production volume at a stateside plant that manufactures the same model'."

The additional outlay on less cost-efficient, but more resilient systems of sourcing and storage were described succinctly by Jorge Gonzalez, Chairman of the Economics Department of Trinity University, San Antonio, as a "terrorist tax."

A supply chain failure may 'creep up' on the company rather than be announced by one large, dramatic event such as a terrorist attack or tsunami. This makes early decision-making even more difficult.

The contingency plans will, once more, trigger an instant, authorised response to an emerging disaster and inform and resource those incident managers, as is best possible. It should, if at all possible, go on to give them quick access to some pre-prepared options. The BIA will have clarified precisely the urgent needs, whether they are legal or physical access to information and skills; soft or hard assets; or; the wider ability to source the ingredient from elsewhere fast enough to retain confidence, the wider brand value and to meet urgent deliveries. These alternatives are likely to come at a cost; even if it is the higher ingredient cost where the receiving organisation is not able to offer exclusivity to one supplier, nor offer them the economies of scale that would bring down the individual item cost. These additional costs are investments in risk management that can best be evaluated and decided upon once the BIA has provided real risk and impact information.

As explained elsewhere in this book, there are opportunities to go into the specialist contingency market that can offer, at cost, prepared call centre, communications and other technology services to address these issues.

Media and Brand Attack

The media may take it into its head to attack the organisation. The attack may be justified or unjustified; but the impact can be the same. At risk is one of the greatest dependencies of any organisation, its credibility and its brand values. The loss of such credibility amongst the public and whole range of stakeholders is obviously life-threatening to a commercial organisation with competitors ever willing to take advantage of the weakness. It is less obvious, but no less real, that such a loss is also extremely damaging to a not-for profit organisation or a public service. The issue here is how their own stakeholders may react to such a loss. That wholesale reaction could bring dramatic additional demands on its services. A run on a bank is not pretty nor is it easy to manage, but neither is wholesale panic about delayed passports for tens of thousands of people needing them for imminent business and holiday trips.

Yet again the shoulder to lean on is provided by a well thought through BIA and contingency plan. This is crucial to managing the attack quickly and limiting damage. Once more those ingredient headlines of continuity management find value, both in assessing the risk and developing plans to authorise and resource incident managers.

The best approach is developed in calmer circumstances, and is a considered and careful assessment of what the risk is, from where it can come, and where the impact is going to be most damaging. Information emerging from a BIA may even encourage the board to quickly address a particular area, activity or supply chain that would open them to greater risk of media attack. The risk/profit equation of that activity may no longer balance as comfortably when the decision-makers are a better informed on the risks.

'News is something that someone does not want to see in print. All the rest is advertising'
William Hearst

There are some unique features of a media attack though that will need to be built into the media risk BIA and plans. Worthy of mention in this brief coverage are:

The Sheer Scale Of The Attack	The massive number of radio companies, television media companies and increasingly internet news groups and blogs create a scrum and weight of attack that can be very difficult to manage. This is especially so if the interest is an international one. There are now numerous 24-hour news channels that have an apparently insatiable and constant hunger for information; and with a focus only on their own agendas that they are bringing to the incident. There were 600 members of the press in the Shetlands just three hours after the Braer disaster; and 15,500 descended on Paris
Speed Of Attack	The speed by which the media responds – all in competition with each other to be the first with the news - can be astonishing. The pack can descend even before the organisation itself is aware of what is unfolding.
Infotainment	This is word used by Kate Aidie to describe the commercialism of media coverage. It capably describes the way that modern media producers feel that it is their primary role to attract and retain viewers by feeding those viewers with what they think will keep them listening or watching. Clearly there is an agenda to personalise the news and to look for villains and victims; even better when this is a 'David against Goliath' situation. It is just too easy to find that you have become the 'villain Goliath' role model.
Multiple Messaging	A special challenge is that – through one wide reaching media – there is a need to feed different messages to different stakeholders. There are real dangers, as a ferry company found to its great cost, to send out media-transmitted messages to the city that the share price will not fall at a time when by far the majority of listeners were worrying about some 900 lives at risk.
Reaction To The Media Interest	Once the media is interested and in full flood, there is a need also to respond to the reaction that is triggered by members of the public. The organisation may find itself, not only coping with the media scrum itself, but with thousands or millions of individuals calling for more individual attention as a result of the media coverage.

Once the BIA h as established the likelihood of a media attack, risk management can be focussed where there is best value. The media, for example, is unlikely to be satisfied for long by the company's professional spokespersons and will wish to speak to the chief executive or others that are in direct management responsibility. The damage they can do in a few minutes - doing what they perhaps are not best skilled to do - in front of a camera can outweigh the incident itself many times.

Risk management therefore may suggest the need for awareness training by media professionals. The other side of the risk coin is for any one member of staff responding to reporters' questions with their own uninformed and personal views on what is happening. Risk management's role would be to ensure that staff is advised that, in the best interests of the organisation, media enquiries should be directed only to the centre of information and media handling skills. Those contact points are best distributed immediately once there is a perceived interest by the media in any unfolding situation.

The media and communications plan should provide for 24-hour contact with those best able to manage and deliver the responses. It can add further values by:

- Positioning resources in place to ensure there are continuous and up-to-date flows of information from the crisis scene into the media centre and its spokespersons.

- Ensuring that the media is never reduced to guessing or speculating.

- Listing the 'do's and don'ts' prompts and guide all involved.

- Establishing a media centre that is known; suitably positioned; with enough telephones and other communication tools; and, of sufficient physical size to handle a scrum of such proportions. Advise of that centre and how to make contact.

- Reminding all staff that media enquiries are not to be handled other than by the media centre.

- Drawing attention to the importance of recognising the different audiences and their needs. Staff, trade unions, media, relatives, the city, customers, suppliers, market groupings, the regulators and countless other groupings will need to have their own way of asking for and receiving information.

> 'The vacuum caused by failure to communicate is soon filled with rumour, misrepresentation, drivel and poison'. – C. Northcote Parkinson

EMPLOYEE OUT OF OFFICE EVENTS

Earlier in this book we brought out the employer's responsibility to keep employees and visitors as safe as possible wherever they are while in a work-related environment. This is a given, reinforced by legislation in most countries, and the reasons do not need to be explained further.

There is an additional dimension that fits more directly within the agenda of this book. This is the issue of intellectual assets on which the organisation depends; and of course the threats to brand and confidence when things go significantly wrong. Safety and security while staff are within the workplace itself is almost certainly to be the subject of 'Health and Safety' procedures and the detail of those procedures is best left for the myriad of books and courses on that particular subject.

The risks of the loss of knowledge and skills dependencies gets less straightforward when a staff member is away from the workplace itself; and even more so when they are with a whole group of colleagues attending an out of office event. Clearly we have a concentration of risk in one conveyance, hotel or conference venue, and there are special risks around activity events that are sometimes used as staff development or reward tools. Risk managers quite rightly concern themselves with such events and wish to be reassured that a risk assessment has taken place, not only covering health and safety matters, but also the risk of losing any skill or knowledge on which the organisation depends for its survival.

The first BIA matter to be addressed therefore is not so much what their title or rank is, but whether any of the skills that anybody carries are crucial, and also are exclusive to the individual or to the group. For the purpose of this section we are going to assume that any skills and knowledge that are exclusive to one person alone have already been picked up by the intellectual assets section of a BIA. We need to assume also that if there are, that risk has already been managed by preparing manuals, and emergency succession planning that ensures that the identified successor is already trained. We will therefore focus here on the subject of group out-of-office events. When a diverse group of people are brought together for an 'out of office event' the issues of dependencies and collective intellectual assets may need to be reconsidered.

We delve again therefore into the mechanics of continuity management and planning. The cycle remains exactly as before: understand the risk, understand the impact, and then take commercial decisions about the acceptability or otherwise of those risks. Having discerned the unacceptable risks then do something about them to ensure that any residual risk then falls into the acceptable level. The BIA therefore is about both the nature of the event, where it is, and the risks that lie around that nature and place. The BIA is also about the collection, exclusivity of, and dependencies on, those skills, experiences and knowledge.

In addition to the tragic loss when anybody is killed, there can also be a huge ethics and reputation threat if even one person is injured or killed during an organisation-sponsored event.

Case Study

A life assurance company decided, for the annual reward and motivation trip of its best new business producers, to transport them and their wives to Jamaica for a mixture of developmental work and as reward for the last year's achievements. Key members of the board were in attendance and were there also as speakers at the event.

Violence is not unusual in Jamaica for many political, drug trade and historical reasons and at the time of the visit there was considerable unrest that in effect closed the road from the conference hotel to the airport. In effect the best new business producers; producing between them some 25% of the total new business of the company were trapped, at serious risk, together with the major decision-makers from the board of directors. Fortunately the group were able to leave later and without injury or loss of life.

The individual delegates and their wives had trusted the company in its choice of location; and the company had placed at risk enough of the decision makers and producers that, had they been lost, the impact on continuity and confidence could easily have destroyed the company.

While this is an extreme risk and grouping case, there is a range of situations where staff risk is unavoidable and needs to be managed. It may be vital, for example for an individual or a small team to make a visit to a high-risk country such as Iraq to protect crucial corporate assets or liabilities.

As stated elsewhere in this book advice on the current political, environmental and security levels in individual countries and cities is readily available from consultancies and governmental agencies. It is also possible to review the security and other safety issues around a proposed location. The extent of this investigation is undoubtedly related to the perceived damage that may be caused by the loss of those people. Clearly of course there is again much by way of common agenda here with the Health and Safety team and there are good values in cooperating with them.

Once again the risk manager's task is twofold. There is of course the risk recognition, evaluation and risk management. This would demand justification for people entering unusually difficult areas and if so justified, identify as best possible the events there that could cause them injury or death. One measure often implemented is to ensure that the whole group does not travel on one plane.

There is also, once again, the contingency planning so that resources, communications, and facilities are in place to respond fast enough and locally to meet the three objective groupings for response plans that were outlined at the beginning of this chapter.

The plan will have features that will be generic to all such exposures such as ways to communicate to get help and support as necessary. As always access to vital initial contact information will help trigger the plan. The level of planning for further responses and the positioning of more extensive resources will depend of course on the perceived risk and exposures to that risk. It may prepare the ground locally for fast emergency evacuation of the staff members and it may ensure that 'first world' medical facilities and medical evacuation services are on alert to move in. Local security companies may be employed to ensure that security is as best possible in the circumstances. If there are worries for example about local blood transfusions and Aids, for example, a medical pack may be supplied to each traveller.

Chemical and Biological Threats

Situations where people and buildings are threatened with injury or inaccessibility due to chemical agents or diseases need managers to respond instantly to even the likelihood that the threat may exist. Once again they are suddenly taken into a world beyond their usual experience and expertise and need to respond immediately and communicate to all concerned and ensure a large and diverse group of people respond as needed to preserve safety as much as possible. In other words all the needs and core ingredients of a recovery plan are needed at that time. The need would be the same, regardless of whether the chemicals are part of a terrorist attack or accidental by way of a nearby lorry of train crash. The cause may even be something like Legionnaire's Disease disseminated by a building air conditioning system.

The detail of the plan (or plan sector) in this case would add vital advice concerning the nature of different chemicals and the best physical and medical responses that would be needed. Furthermore, the plan would ensure quick links with the medical authorities and from where the best advice can be obtained.

Summary

We set out in this chapter to consider where business continuity management tools, resources and principles can be used to good value elsewhere in the organisation. The objective is to gain as many additional benefits as possible. In doing so we can maximise all values, and by doing so strengthen the business case for investment in resources and time applied; and any monetary investment needed.

We were able to illustrate that the principles that underlie business continuity management have a real value wherever there is a risk to be identified and managed, and where a sudden unexpected incident can demand an instant, coordinated, authorised and adequately resourced response.

For the purpose of this chapter those underlying principles were

- To understand the risks
  - To understand critically the potential impact on the organisational and its stakeholders
  - To take, thus, better informed decisions about the commercial acceptability of those risks
  - Manage the unacceptable exposures so that the risk or the impact is reduced to acceptable levels   by best use amongst the choices of (or a combination of):
  - Risk manage the potential cause of damage
  - Risk manage and duplicate as necessary where the impact could be destructive
  - Transfer risk to another party if this can be done without destructive exposures still remaining
  - Prepare with contingency planning to manage through the remaining risks without unacceptable damage to the core dependencies of the organisation.

We illustrated the application of these values by considering the individual exposures of fraud, kidnapping and ransom, product contamination threats, bomb threats, failures in the supply chain, media attacks, employee 'out of office events' and chemical and biological threats.

Bibliography

(1) A Risk Management Standard. AIRMIC, ALARM, IRM 2002

(2) Fraud report by RSM Robson Rhodes, Chartered Accountants. 2004

(3) The Development of Corporate Management Responses to Incidents of Consumer product tampering Dr. Deborah Lowe.

(4) Product Recall Research. Department of Trade and Industry; United Kingdom. 2000

(5) Guidelines on Outsourcing. Monetary Authority of Singapore. October 2004

(6) Land Rover Monthly April 2002

12

The People Factor

Objectives of this Chapter are to:

- Gain an appreciation of the issues associated with people and business continuity management

- Gain an understanding of why some people excel following an incident while others falter - and what makes the difference

- Examine the dynamics of team performance, the team players and issues associated with plan invocation and recovery

- Consider the people success factors of an invocation

- Examine post-trauma considerations and management

- Consider supply chain, outsourcing and off-shoring people-related issues

- Consider business continuity management training and education needs and the options for delivery

The People Factor - An Introduction

Scientific research has discovered that frogs cannot perceive an increase in surrounding water temperature if the water is heated gently so that the increase is slow and steady. Eventually the frog dies, still unaware of the threat it faced.

A panel of experts at the World Economic Forum's meeting in 2005 warned that "international corporations suffer from boiling frog syndrome and are in denial about the daunting array of risks they face, including terrorism, disease pandemics, climate change and a potential Chinese economic slowdown."

"Corporations ... all-too-often plan only for the risks they already know about," panellists were reported as saying: "Unfortunately, there is a widespread tendency among many businesses to be well prepared only for the last event that has occurred - not the next one coming around the corner," the panel wrote in its report to the World Economic Forum. "Denial is an all-too-common strategy, and there is a natural tendency not to react until the catastrophe is unavoidable." **(1)**

Panel members called on businesses and political leaders to think innovatively about how to face down the growing array of risks and warned that without new approaches, the dangers would grow.

Risks associated with people are of course not new, but it is an area in which risk management is often unfocussed and which can be assigned to a number of management silos.

There are two angles to people issues:

• Those associated with how people are managed; and,

• Those associated with the competence and capability to perform the role assigned within an organisation or that are adopted external to an organisation.

"One of the areas that is often left out of the planning process is the management of disasters that may have an impact on the health and well-being of people - including employees, customers and the public." **(2)**

The impact of an incident will often be dependent on which angle the incident is viewed from, that of the individual or that of the organisation. The perspective depends on where people and the organisation sit within the hierarchy. For example, the loss of a small shop may be considered a trivial event to a community as a whole - but if you are the shop owner or an elderly or infirm customer who cannot travel easily to an alternative shop it could be a disaster.

The Executive Perspective

Executives should be inquisitive about risk, its sources and causal and control factors. Responsibility to manage risk cannot be delegated. However, to ensure effective delegation of risk management, clear ownership with appropriate and documented lines of authority must be in place throughout an organisation. Further, if good risk management is to be aligned with organisational goals, then an organisation's incentive packages should reflect this.

Better risk information will lead to better informed risk-related decisions and a balancing of the risk-reward return. Risk measurement in isolation of risk management is, however, ineffective. "In isolation the measurement process does not have much value until the numbers are integrated back into management, for instance, and used in a performance management or behaviour modification sense." **(3)**

Responsibilities and Performance

The responsibilities and skills set for risk or business continuity management are quite specific and as with any role within an organisation should be described in a job profile following an organisation's approach for any other position.

There is considerable debate as to whether risk and business continuity management should be closely aligned and form part of the same departmental function. There is no right answer to this question.

The Business Continuity Institute Certification Standards

The ten subject areas listed below cover the competencies required by a professional practitioner in order to deliver effective Business Continuity Management. They are not presented in any particular order of importance or sequence.

1. Initiation and Management

2. Business Impact Analysis

3. Risk Evaluation and Control

4. Developing Business Continuity Management Strategies

5. Emergency Response and Operations

6. Developing and Implementing Business Continuity and Crisis Management Plans

7. Awareness and Training Programmes

8. Maintaining and Exercising Business Continuity and Crisis Management Plans

9. Crisis Communications

10. Coordination with External Agencies

These standards are published in co-operation with the Disaster Recovery Institute International (DRII) of the USA and are used by both bodies in their certification programmes.

www.thebci.org

www.drii.org

Whether these roles should sit together is a matter for each organisation to consider and will be dependent upon the framework and approach taken for managing risk. In larger organisations a range of dedicated risk and business continuity roles may exist which could be positioned in a range of departments. For example, those charged with leading the development and implementation of IT-related business continuity may best sit within the IT function, while others charged with non-IT-related responsibilities may sit more appropriately elsewhere.

Caution should be extended in creating roles and teams which are positioned in a way that inhibits their integration with the business and promotes isolation from the skills and resource they require from others to effectively deliver their responsibilities.

Whatever the approach, the success factor will be the production and adherence to clear and unambiguous job profiles. Job profiles will be driven by an organisation's approach to profile design, the objectives and scope of roles and responsibilities, the source and level of authority and the skills and experience required to deliver the role effectively.

The concept of performance measures is not new and has been part of generally accepted good management practice for nearly fifty years. The best organisations have successfully used performance measures and as the best risk managed organisations have merged, they too have harnessed the power of the performance culture.

However it is only when an organisation moves from risk measuring to risk integration that measures become part of managing risk. As high reliability organisations such as utilities and the military have successfully embedded 'concern for safety' as a core competence then perhaps so too could 'concern for risk management' be considered in a similar fashion.

This has the added value of demonstrating greater management attention focussed on risk and a commitment to recognising and rewarding good performance.

"With a core competency evaluation of concern for risk can be dealt with from the outset and as part of normal course of a business, rather than being major shifts in how it operates." (4)

Objectives of a Business Continuity Manager

- Define the business continuity strategy and policy for the organisation

- Design the framework and standards to support the implementation of agreed policy

- Ensure that business continuity costs are controlled within a dedicated budget

- Develop processes to maintain the currency of continuity capabilities and the plan documents in accordance with the organisation's strategic direction, industry, legal, regulatory and insurance requirements

- Educate the organisation in business continuity management

- Provide each location with connectivity and user systems to be available in alternate locations

- Ensure that suppliers and outsource providers have appropriate business continuity plans

- Ensure that the organisation is able to respond to internal and external audits and challenges

- Become an expert practitioner in business continuity management

---

Fit For the Job

The primary role of risk mitigation is to reduce the impact of risk. To achieve the maximum improvement will require recognition by people of the role they have to play in building resilience, potential modifications to their role required following an incident and how these modifications are exercised if an incident occurs. An organisation that provides clearly defined roles and responsibilities with effective performance management will have a firm foundation for extending core management practices and behaviours into those associated with business continuity management.

If management of an organisation in times of stability is more effective with these components in place, then in times of disruption and instability people management skills and capability will be in even greater demand. When adrenalin is pumping in the veins, the heart is racing and the mind has little time to take reasoned decisions, if people understand their duties and role in an organisation this can mean the difference between survival and failure - between life and death.

Therefore, generally accepted management principles apply equally to good business continuity management practice. As with the processes of strategic and operational management, setting the vision and values for business continuity is the starting point for people management issues. The principles adopted when recruiting and training people should be upheld when approaching business continuity management. People who are fit for their role and are trained to standards consistent across an organisation are more likely to achieve a successful response and recovery.

But people may have a number of business continuity-specific roles. These extend from ensuring that all are aware of an organisation's approach to business continuity management, both in terms of building resilience within an organisation, through to the response to take when things do not go as planned.

In Chapter Four we addressed the importance of the performance management system and the setting of goals as a mechanism for the embedding and underpinning of business continuity management within overall management processes either as part of building resilience or acting in response. People must be competent and available where needed to perform their role. If goal setting can be a risk mitigation tool then compensation can be the motivational factor. Financial incentives for desirable performance will underwrite focussed behaviour, although some of the best incentives are by no means always financial ones.

" Key principle of value creation in a firm is to create or modify the compensation system such that people at all levels of the firm are motivated to contribute. That should include risk reduction and optimisation. Conversely a firm might punish individuals responsible for deleterious actions concerning operational risk and loss." **(5)** This is a tough call demanding competent managers capable of taking fair and balanced decisions based on factual evidence and will be counterproductive if open to challenges of subjectivity.

Inappropriate management of an organisation's employees may affect the organisation's and its customer's susceptibility to some types of incidents and losses. "A firm should ensure that all employees are aware of their responsibility and role .... and are suitable and capable of performing these responsibilities." **(6)** Organisations should pay particular attention to those employees in key roles and especially those involved in functions identified as critical by the Business Impact Analysis (BIA) or those in positions of authority or controls identified by the business continuity plan.

People - Building Resilience

Resilience as a term is used to indicate that something can suffer a failure and yet still continue operations. However it is often used as if it were an absolute (e.g., 'this computer is resilient') - but the term resilience is relative and needs to be qualified.

There are a number of generic strategies to mitigate the impact of a disruption or reduce the probability of a threat event. Each strategy has parameters of speed of resumption, reliability of availability and cost which will be appropriate to different parts of the business so an organisation may require several elements to form an appropriate solution, depending upon the individual business functions.

For example:

- Machine resilience may relate to hard-disc failures but do nothing to protect against loss of that machine in a fire

- Site resilience may improve vulnerability to power interruptions but a site can still become unusable if flooded

- Organisational resilience may improve as the geographical dispersion and diversity of an organisation and its locations increases, but there may still be sites that alone could bring an organisation down if they are the source of critical goods and services

All people in an organisation have a role to play in building resilience. But as with designing the approach to business continuity, the options for building resilience will be dependent on the critical areas of the organisation being identified and matching these with the relevant solutions from the options available.

Business Impact Analysis (BIA) is the foundation from which the business continuity strategy and plan are built. It identifies, quantifies and qualifies the business impacts of a loss, interruption or disruption of business processes of an organisation and provides the data from which appropriate continuity strategies can be determined.

People As A Risk

While gaining in recognition, the majority of organisations do not systematically assess the risks associated with people and therefore do not consider the controls that might be needed to manage these risks. More typically, people issues are managed in a number of organisational silos including human resources, health and safety, security, operations, business units, information security and risk management.

It is essential that these silos are broken down and people viewed from the angles of their profile, the nature of risks, the risks to people and the risks arising from people. For example:

Inside the organisation people profiles include:

- The Chairman
- The CEO
- Key employees
- All employees
- Contractors
- Visitors
- Customers

…. And all of the other stakeholders we addressed in Chapter Two

Risks concerning employees include:

- Death
  - Illness
  - Walkout
  - Catastrophe

    Other absence
  - Morale/motivational decline

Risks to people include:

- Ineffective segregation of duties
- Non-aligned work environment
- Inappropriate management behaviours
- Ineffective planning

- Inadequate training and education

Risk from people include:

- Inappropriate behaviour
- Misunderstanding of roles and responsibilities
- Class action against real or perceived discrimination
- Unavailability to work
- Criminal behaviour
- Deliberate exceeding of authorities

There is a wide variety of sources in any organisation about the risks associated with people. Internally, inspection of accident books, absence records, incident and security reports all deliver a wealth of data. While this information is available in most organisations (albeit often managed and held in different teams), far fewer organisations will have data about the incidents that nearly happened or the near misses. This type of information can be the most valuable as it is the significant near miss that could have resulted in the most damaging incident had events travelled a slightly different path.

Externally, industry benchmarks, insurance statistics and government data are accessible and available without charge in the public domain. Research, surveys, leagues tables, professional bodies and the web offer a wealth of comparable data.

Internal and external data can be harnessed to provide background for realistic models to be developed and to supplement what might be a paucity of actual experience to produce realistic 'what if' scenarios for evaluation. The time of course to undertake such assessments is during periods of stability and the team to engage in this activity should be designed to reflect the type of people who might be affected, as well as internal and external environmental factors.

Just as with any other risk assessment, a people risk assessment should identify those risks associated with people that might threaten achievement of the business objectives at risk.

Implementing A Business Continuity Culture

We will not revisit the ground covered in Chapter Four but it is worth taking a moment to reflect. There are two potential extremes to the approach for embedding culture and associated change: slowly by evolution or quickly by a 'big bang.' Evolution is generally considered to be the more sustainable of the two, but if change is rapid and the potential impact severe then evolution may be an unaffordable luxury.

Business continuity or risk culture can be regarded as a function of "the workforce's combined perceptions and behaviours in the face of the company's actual risk profile." **(7)**

Every culture will be unique, reflecting the people, circumstances and history of the organisation. So it makes good sense for any initiative to take this carefully into account if changes made in the name of business continuity are to 'stick' and become a part of the corporate culture.

A relatively small number of large organisations have achieved this with great success, permeating their workforce with the knowledge, awareness and authority to manage risk and continuity effectively. Many more have dipped a toe in the water and achieved partial or temporary success.

However successful an organisation is at developing and growing a strong culture, sub-cultures will emerge. An organisation is a blend of attitudes and approaches to risk taking. In a risk-averse industry such as pharmaceuticals the governing culture will most likely be one of zero risk tolerance, whereas in a young and emerging industry such as that trading in e-commerce the business environment is more likely to engender a risk-taking culture

But despite leading cultural influences, the marketing department in the pharmaceutical business is likely to be less risk averse than the IT department in a dot-com business. The risk assessments from each department will provide an insight into these differences and business continuity strategies and responses must take account and balance these mindsets and the behaviours that are likely to stem from them.

Achieving cultural consistency requires an understanding and careful management of these differences. Business continuity is as much about people as it is technology or asset management and IT often (and quite reasonably) doesn't have the right skills on hand to do the job. At one end of the scale, responsibility may be handed to an evangelist who beats an irritating drum in the face of every executive as a business-critical 'must-have;' at the other end a junior member of the team may find themselves ill-equipped to interview senior executives with authority.

In the face of this, business people frequently find it hard to digest the value of business continuity and fail to take the 'whole business welfare' stance. Consequently, they sideline or reject it and urgent business continuity matters sink to the bottom of the in-tray.

Cutting Out The Jargon

IT speaks its own language, using acronyms and jargon to describe what it does. This has the effect of causing some business people to simply switch off. For them, once business continuity is aligned with IT, it becomes an IT-only issue and frequently they use this as an excuse to abdicate responsibility. Business continuity also has its own jargon which needs explaining in terms people understand. However, if you don't speak these languages, you cannot deliver business continuity effectively.

Time is a scarce resource, yet business continuity is a long-term, full-time job, especially in large or fast-moving organisations, so making it the part-time responsibility of an IT (or Facilities) staff member reduces its profile and its chances of success. New employees do not know the business; more experienced employees do not know business continuity.

Business continuity projects typically have a profile characterised by a high-intensity start followed by a long maintenance cycle, which requires a particular blend of skills. The chance of releasing or finding the right people with the right skills to perform both effectively is remote and one reason why many organisations often employ consultants to complement in-house skills at various stages of programme development.

Engaging The People

There is little incentive for people to become involved in business continuity, but as we explained above, to change a culture you must engage the workforce. Yet business continuity is invisible to most people since they are not involved in drafting plans, conducting exercises or taking part in rehearsals making it hard for them to see the value.

Further, most organisations conduct their business without regular discontinuity - or at least without evidence of this to the average employee.

This implies a need for wider education, training and communication so that employees are equipped to understand what is being asked of them

It takes time to achieve lasting change (and while not to infer that plans only require updating infrequently), the beneficial effects of a six-month project will last perhaps two to five years. Beyond that people change; they forget; the profile of the subject drops; continuity measures lose their value, and incidents and the experiences from these are sporadic.

Strategy Based On Disasters - Only As Effective As The Last Memory

Many organisations only achieve a profile for business continuity when something goes wrong and the impetus for action is a response rather than part of established management practice. Selling business continuity on the basis of the most recent failure is an acceptable strategy but not a sustainable one in isolation. Memories quickly fade, and with these recollections access to a dedicated budget can be challenged. "Unfortunately, sticking-plaster reactive continuity measures have a greater chance of rejection than designed-in measures, yet these are the most likely to be applied following such a failure." (8)

People and the Business Impact Analysis

While we address BIA elsewhere in this book, it is mentioned here to serve as a reminder that it is essential to obtain the full support of the Executive or most Senior Managers in an organisation before a BIA is attempted. It is unlikely that managers will be prepared to dedicate time to this exercise unless this top-tier support is demonstrated; appointment of a project sponsor and champion from within the Executive or Senior Management Group is essential

Planning and Response - Success Factors

While the last fifteen years has seen considerable development in the approach to recovery of business operations following an incident, there is less research dedicated to the issues involving the recovery of people in similar circumstances. Risk assessment and response for people is a somewhat neglected area.

Business continuity plans are a set of instructions and procedures in hard or soft copy for the teams named in the plans to follow. These are fine until it comes time to use them.

If faced with the choice of a state-of-the-art plan and a mediocre team in terms of suitability and preparedness, or a mediocre plan and a team of individuals skilled and rehearsed in response and recovery management, which would you choose? Experience dictates that the latter is the best option every time.

It seems some people, faced with disaster, can take on very different characteristics to those in times of stability. People who are usually the leaders faced with an incident can retreat into the background, confused and unable to adopt their leadership position. Others who quietly work away in the back office environment faced with an incident may come forward as natural leaders. Whatever the business continuity plan states the old saying that "leaders are born and not made" can often be most vividly experienced when disaster strikes.

Responding To the Plan

The word 'plan' conjures up the concept of tasks, schedules and Gantt charts. Expectations are set that events will follow the route of the plan and it comes as a surprise to some that real life does not necessarily follow the scenario that was envisaged when plans were drawn up.

Buildings become unstable at the most inappropriate time, authorities impose their requirements and timescales which may not match those in the plan, 'after-shocks' from the initial incident may occur, recovery sites may not be accessible or available. The list is extensive.

The business continuity manager must step back from the planning process and consider the people factor. When might the plans be used, how, and by whom? If the culture of an organisation in times of stability dictates certain behaviours as the 'norm' serious consideration should be given to adopting familiar procedures in business continuity plans. When faced with a disaster and the potential for confusion and shock which follows, this is the last time that people in response and recovery teams need to face management processes which are alien to those adopted when business is as usual.

When disaster strikes, the distribution of power and how that power is used may change; priorities can shift urgently and dramatically; and, the boundaries between established organisational silos eroded or removed. However one thing that will not change for the majority is the expectation that leadership will be forthcoming. Employees, contractors and customers will look to the usual focal point within an organisation for instructions - unless they are directed to do otherwise.

Clear lines of command and control are essential in times of disaster but people must be informed and educated as to what these are, otherwise they will use and act upon their own initiative with potentially unfortunate consequences.

Lines of command must be considered during normal operating hours, and also when the organisation is closed for business or operating at sub-optimum levels - for example during weekends, holiday periods or on night shift.

Plans - Communication and Accessibility

The author of plans should ask themselves challenging questions about the plans. Are they easily accessible, clear and simple to follow? In times of duress people picking up and using these plans will not find it helpful if they have to read the first twenty or more pages before they find out what they should do.

With demands for instructions coming in fast, the command of an organisation's reaction and recovery approach and leadership moves into the management spotlight. This is essential to keep an organisation and its people on track and in control.

People may be working in unfamiliar surroundings, experiencing pressures and difficulties outside their experience and almost certainly will be under great pressure.

"Because of the nature of the situation in which they will be used, any plans should be easy to read and easy to understand; and they should not be cluttered with any unnecessary information – business impact reports, risk matrices, inter-departmental memos, etc." **(9)**

The business continuity management policy and framework should establish the ground rules for an organisation's approach to planning and the 'DNA' of its plans. Depending on the needs, culture and industry, it must be agreed up front what plans will contain and how they will be used.

Clarity and consistency in this regard is important. In the event that more than one location, system, supplier, group of people or combination of these is affected by an incident, it is essential that those in control have a clear idea of what their plans contain, how they will be used and how these might need to relate to other plans within the overall organisation.

Plans might be designed to provide step-by-step instructions to be followed at the time of the disaster, a source of comprehensive reference material or serve to provide a specification of what is planned to happen and not for use at the actual time of an incident. But in a disaster situation the most important component of any plan is a set of actions and procedures for people to follow with clear instructions.

Up To the Task

Training and exercising sessions based on a simulated disaster will focus the minds of the team. By starting with the crisis, they are immediately faced with deciding what they need to have in place to deal with it. This includes not only the procedures, information and alternative arrangements, but also making sure that the right people are in the right place at the right time. Teams may need to act simultaneously rather than in sequence: salvage teams may need to be on site reacting in parallel to the CEO meeting the needs of press and media attention.

Research into the more successfully managed incidents demonstrates that effective people management can lead to business recovery with added value. "Surely, therefore, it makes sense to 'put people first' on your list of business continuity priorities?" **(10)**

People Under Fire - The New Rules of Response

Professionals in the world of mental health recognise the altered state phenomenon "any victim or emergency responder after a disaster will be in an altered state of consciousness. The degree of that alteration is the variable." **(11)** This means that brains are processing information 'under the influence' of the incident.

The brain releases hormones into the blood when people are under duress and the effect of these can be 'fight or flight.' Given that every situation following an incident is likely to be different the response team in an organisation is potentially faced with the challenge of unfamiliar circumstances and unpredictable people.

What would you do if you found out that some people in your community had become sick with smallpox after having been exposed to the virus in a terrorist attack at a major airport? What if terrorists exploded a dirty bomb a mile away, when you were at work and your children were at school?

According to a study **(12)** released by the Centre for the Advancement of Collaborative Strategies in Health at The New York Academy of Medicine, in these crisis situations, many Americans would not be safeguarded because existing terrorism response plans do not account for how people would behave. The investigators found that current plans had been created in a top-down style, telling people what to do in the event of an attack without considering all of the risks and concerns that drive people's actions.

The study revealed that only two-fifths of the American people would follow instructions to go to a public vaccination site in a smallpox outbreak and only three-fifths would stay inside an undamaged building other than their home after a dirty bomb explosion. "It's not that the rest of the people want to be uncooperative," said lead investigator Roz Lasker, M.D., director of the Centre and of the Academy's Division of Public Health. "The problem is that current plans unwittingly put them in extremely difficult decision-making predicaments. So even if first responders work out all of the challenging logistics, far fewer people would be protected than planners want or the public deserves."

The study gave the American people their first opportunity to describe how they would react to two kinds of terrorist attacks: a smallpox outbreak and a dirty bomb explosion. In the event of a dirty bomb explosion, the study showed that people need to be protected from more than dust and radiation. They also need to know that they and their loved ones would be safe and cared for in whatever building they happen to be in at the time of an explosion.

Three-quarters of the people who said they would not fully cooperate with instructions to stay inside the building after a dirty bomb explosion would do so if:

- *They could communicate with people they care about, and*

- If they were sure that they and their loved ones were in places that had prepared in advance to take good care of them in this kind of situation.

Study by the Centre for the Advancement of Collaborative Strategies in Health at The New York Academy of Medicine

---

The study's proposed smallpox plans included specific strategies that protected both the people who are at risk of contracting smallpox and the many people who are at risk of developing serious complications from the vaccine. The study's dirty bomb response called for the development of safe-haven plans in the broad array of places where people are likely to be when an attack occurs, such as work sites, shops, malls, schools, day care centres, and entertainment facilities. That means preparing to keep the people inside fed and safe during the crisis.

And these issues do not just relate to the terror of the fallout from a 'dirty bomb.'
During the ice storms experienced by Montreal, Canada in 1999, organisations quickly learned that they could not expect their employees to help recover business operations until they were confident that their own families and friends were safe and cared for.

Case Study

The Canadian Ice Storms of 1999

It isn't unusual for parts of North America to experience ice storms which comprise rain falling as ice. The difference on this occasion was the level of precipitation, the degree of coldness and the length of the storm and duration of its consequences.

Organisations affected by the severe ice storms in 1999 quickly learned to appreciate that unless their employees were confident that the needs of their families had been dealt with, business recovery and restoration of customer services could not begin to commence effectively. It was unreasonable to expect employees to focus on their regular jobs in extreme circumstances (and the additional pressures this brings), if they were worrying about the welfare of their partners and/or children. Without power supplies, limited fresh food and transportation for their loved ones - how could employees think about the welfare of others? Communications were also badly hit as telephone lines were brought down by the weight of the build-up of ice. Consequently checking back with home was also a difficult task.

Centres were established in community and sports halls, hotels and other large facilities where people could be accommodated in safe and warm surroundings. A number of organisations arranged their own sponsored facilities. Some even arranged for families to be relocated away from the area most affected, but as transport was often impossible to source and as many families did not want to leave the area this was not always a realistic option.

Once arrangements to the satisfaction of workers had been made only then could employees reasonably be expected to focus on the needs of others.

Case Study

Viruses have always been with us, finding ways to reproduce and spread. Mankind has always been under the threat of new, more dangerous viruses emerging and causing massive epidemics. Our modern transportation systems, however, make it easier for such viruses to spread quickly throughout the world. Man's exploration and encroachment in previously inaccessible parts of the world make it ever more likely that something nasty may emerge.

SARS: 2002/3

Severe acute respiratory syndrome (SARS) is a serious respiratory virus, which killed nearly 800 people worldwide in the months following its emergence in November, 2002. The World Health Organization announced that the outbreak had been contained in the following July. However, experts predict the virus will continue to pose a threat - and warn that health authorities need to be ever vigilant for its return.

In the summer of 2003 as the first global SARS epidemic stuttered to a close, the Royal Society in the UK organised a meeting to take stock of the year's events and to ask what could be learned. The meeting also addressed Horizon Scanning - which is aimed at questioning "what is coming next?"

The first step was to describe where SARS came from. Research concluded that it came from wild animals being sold for meat in markets in China.

As SARS spread the only control option to emerge was to quarantine exposed people and to introduce methods of care that minimised transmission. Discussion included the rights and wrongs of individual freedoms in a society that can be controlled only be quarantine.

The meeting at the Royal Society concluded that SARS was an infection relatively easily identified by existing laboratory networks and successfully controlled by with quarantine methods and infection control in hospitals. The meeting concluded that the next time may well be quite different.

www.pubs.royalsoc.ac.uk

Bird Flu: 2005

Britain is planning to buy almost 15 million doses of a powerful antiviral drug to protect the country against a pandemic of the deadly bird flu that could claim tens of thousands of lives. The UK Government has developed an Influenza Pandemic Contingency Plan which sets out the steps being taken to prepare for a flu epidemic. The drug purchase, which will cost almost £200 million, will be enough to treat one in four of the UK population, the level recommended by the World Health Organisation.

Forty-six people have died in southeast Asia since an outbreak of bird flu in late 2003 and public health experts fear that the virus could soon mutate, opening up rapid transmission from human to human.

Around 12,000 people die in the UK every winter from 'seasonal flu,' but experts say that a global flu pandemic, involving a new strain of the disease, is overdue. If a pandemic broke out there would be a delay until an effective vaccine could be developed - during which time the anti-viral drug could be used to control the illness and alleviate its effects.

The effects of a global pandemic would depend on the virulence of the flu strain that eventually emerges, but the Department of Health says an outbreak could claim 50,000 lives in the UK or more.

"It might never happen, but what is clear is that the experts tell us the risk of if happening is high enough to make it necessary to plan for it and spend some serious money on antiviral drugs - it's not inevitable, but for planning purposes we're assuming it's inevitable." stated a Department of Health spokesman.

The official contingency plan includes quarantine measures and arrangements for the emergency services. Concerts and football matches could both be banned and travel restricted in the event of an outbreak to stop the virus spreading.

Measures set out in the plan include:

Improving surveillance of avian or 'bird' flu in Southeast Asia - seen by experts as the most likely source of a pandemic strain of flu transmitted by people. The UK Government recently gave the World Health Organization £500,000 to boost avian flu monitoring in the region and improve the chances of an early warning of a pandemic.

Ensuring robust surveillance of possible cases in the UK, using the existing procedures of the Health Protection Agency and Royal College of General Practitioners to monitor flu-like cases seen by physicians.

Informing the public about the likely risks of a pandemic and what they should do in the event of pandemic flu.

Being prepared to take steps to reduce the risk of spread of the disease, such as advising against certain travel, possibly closing schools and cancelling events where large crowds gather such as football matches or pop concerts.

www.timesonline.co.uk/article/0,,2-1506055,00

Team Dynamics - Building A Successful Team - Purpose and Direction

"If an organisation is unprepared for the intensity of an incident and the attention that this may draw to an organisation or if a communication vacuum is allowed to develop, then an impression can be created that an organisation does not know how to respond - or worse still, doesn't care." (13)

In their research Knight and Pretty (14) identified four key determinants governing the shareholder response to catastrophes:

- Initial shareholder loss can be massive
- The potential impact on cash flow is enormous
- If fatalities occur
- If management are judged to be at least partially responsible for the incident

However their research concluded that the ability of organisations to recover lost shareholder value and the longevity of the effect following catastrophe varied significantly. What is the reason for this?

While most organisations will suffer an economic loss following an incident, the determinant between a successful and unsuccessful response in the longer term is one of managerial ability and specifically leadership. "Management is placed in the spotlight and has an opportunity to demonstrate its skill or otherwise in an extreme situation." (15)

Characteristics noted by Knight and Pretty are those typically identified in most research and good practice for effective leadership:

- Leaders balance appropriate direction with support and openness

- Leaders discuss key issues with the team

- Leaders delegate responsibility to individuals who are fit for the job

---

Team DNA

Any team should:

- Fit the nature, scale and complexity of the event
- Collect the facts
- Analyse the facts
- Assign tasks
- Communicate• Assume control
- Escalate and invoke other plans and teams

If good leadership is all about setting direction and management through trust then effective management is all about understanding what is required and identifying and equipping teams to deliver their respective responsibilities.

A key goal is for members to understand their own strengths and those of each member of the team. It is the role of management to ensure that the right teams are available, properly resourced, and that meetings have only the relevant team members present, with an agenda and documented actions.

We have already addressed the fact that the people most effective at managing in times of normality may not be the same as those most suited to managing in times of abnormality and stress.

The Dynamics of a Successful Crisis Management Plan include:

- Integrated and organisation wide
- Easily accessible and quick to implement
- Able to deal with multi-events and to address interdependencies
- Equips team members with clear roles and responsibilities and relevant experts
- Identifies key actions with timescales
- Includes a communications infrastructure: internal and external
- Flexible to change and circumstance
- Rehearsed against scenarios

The Dynamics of a Successful Crisis Management Team include:

- Strong organisational leader
- Competence and skills mix suitable for a crisis
- Right membership for the level of materiality of a crisis
- Optimum size between four and ten
- Empowered
- Strong team alternates
- Rehearsed against scenarios
- Rehearsed with other planning teams

Whatever the dynamics of a crisis, business recovery or support team, the team must have a clear mission and purpose and be made aware of this together with their position within the team. Those outside the team should also know who formed and authorised the team to avoid conflict and confusion in times of response.

The organisation's expectations of the team should be delivered through a vision with a set of key success factors just as with any other team.

Success factors can subsequently form a benchmark against which team performance can be judged; generally in times of rehearsal and test and as necessary as part of the "lessons learned" evaluation following incident notification, escalation and plan invocation.

If roles and responsibilities of any team member are unclear or difficult to articulate then an organisation should challenge the need for that team member. Regardless of the position of the team in the planning process, the characteristics of the team members must suit the responsibilities delegated; regardless of the rank or relative importance of individuals in 'normal' circumstances.

Functional profiles of these teams are quite different and the profiles of the respective team members are likely to follow the nature of the responsibilities in the planning hierarchy. But few teams will operate in isolation and it is essential that all teams appreciate the plan "big picture" and how their team may need to react with other teams - internally (laterally and vertically) and externally (for example with suppliers, outsource providers and the relevant authorities).

Members of any team in a business continuity programme, all employees, consultants and others identified should be qualified to fulfil their role. In addition to alternates, a long-running incident may demand additional back-up team members to avoid burn out - and these individuals should receive the same level of information, training and support as any other response and recovery "player."

And depending on the timing of an incident and the area affected, otherwise available team members may be out of touch or inaccessible due to personal circumstances including family commitments, or denied access to response and recovery locations.

Faced with a crisis, people may react differently. People who normally would be sound team players can become insecure, aggressive and unhelpful. They may even abandon the team. Good leadership will help the situation by setting ground rules and protocols for behaviour. Expectations should be clearly defined and it will help if a team is educated in the type of behaviour they may experience or encounter in others when faced with pressure.

Testing Times

To ensure that rehearsals or exercises of business continuity plans are effective, it is essential that the principle of defining clear roles and responsibilities of respective teams is extended to these activities as with any other in the process.

Using the set of roles described in Figure 1, while the Facilitator and a number of the Simulators might come from outside an organisation, bringing into the process experience from other organisations and scenarios, other roles should be delivered by members of an organisation's own teams. However, external roles can only be delivered effectively if all concerned have been adequately briefed concerning the organisation, its approach to business continuity and the plans to be applied.

Figure 1 - Exercise Roles (16)

Facilitator (Lead Controller)	• Possesses overall knowledge of the scenario. • Supervises the exercise Monitors sequence of events, adjusts pace, and controls timeline. • Introduces action messages. • Provides exercise oversight.
Controller	• Introduces artificial stimuli at the direction of the facilitator. • Acts as an extension of the facilitator. • Makes decisions in the event of unanticipated actions or resource requirements. • Helps eliminate safety and property damage issues by maintaining order as well as tracking and aiding actions of participants. Simulator
Simulator	• Adds realism to the scenario - portrays private citizens, companies,agencies, and organizations as they would normally interact with participants. • Acts as victim, adversary, media member and any other extra role that needs to be filled. • Uses groups such as local college students, community theatre troupes, and volunteer organizations.
Observer	• Strategically positioned to observe and document performance. • Should be knowledgeable about the subject matter or function being evaluated. • Evaluates the actions of participants and the effectiveness of the Business Continuity Plan.
Participant	• Assume crisis roles and perform actual or simulated activities commensurate with the type of exercise and scenario being used.

Exercise Type	Facilitator	Participant	Simulator	Controller	Observer
Orientation	X	X			
Drill	X	X			X
Tabletop	X	X			
Functional	X	X	X	X	
Full-scale	X	X	X	X	X

People And Business Continuity Management

We have addressed the issues concerning those who form a team in response to a crisis but we should also focus here on those parallel management issues involving people.

All employees should be aware of an organisation's response to business continuity management. Employees can be informed via a simple document or intranet message underpinned by briefings and rehearsals.

Consideration should be given to installing pre-arranged emergency contact numbers for employees, families, friends and customers to access for advice and guidance. A wide variety of recorded messages or switchboard operator-assisted services are available from commercial suppliers. These services can very quickly become overwhelmed and adequate capability should be installed. Whatever options are chosen details of the numbers to use should be made widely available (for employees these can be printed on security access passes or stickers on lap tops or "BlackBerrys" or family, friends or customers via news updates or newspaper advertisements).

All employee records should be kept up to date with details of next of kin. Where stored off site, storage should be secure and maintained in a manner that does not contravene local data protection or confidentiality requirements.

Human Resources departments should have their own business continuity plans which set out how they would respond in support of an incident and how they would recover their own capability. (This dual approach of recovery for others and recovery for in-team capability of course applies to all "support" functions). Out of hours contact information for teams must be retained and where specific means for communication are supplied - such as pagers and mobile phones - should be maintained and kept switched on. But remember in times of crisis, mobile telephone networks may become overloaded or even denied if emergency services exercise rights of priority access.
In a number of jurisdictions priority rights to mobile telephone networks is given to regulatory and governing bodies. Limited lines of access to these services may be granted to key organisations to ensure that contact can be maintained and commercial and financial infrastructures sustained. Details of these facilities and how to access them should be clearly documented in the plans.

Following the events of September 11, 2001 the most desired technology was email. Email and web sites can provide excellent means of communication with remote maintenance and support.

Dealing With Death and Injury

We will consider issues associated with post trauma management later in this Chapter. However we need to consider here a number of issues that may relate to the responsibilities of an organisation in the event of death or injury.

An organisation will have responsibilities to anyone in their care and control. Whether an employee, contractor or customer is injured it is probable that statutory as well ethical considerations will operate. Failure to report to statutory requirements could constitute an offence with serious punitive consequences including legal liabilities.

In some jurisdictions the police will adopt a responsibility for informing relatives of a death, in others an organisation may be asked to adopt this role by the authorities. Whoever does accept this duty must be equipped and willing to do so.

Appropriate professional counselling may be required for the families and friends of those touched by a death - and for those involved in managing the response and recovery by the organisation.

In some organisations plans do exist to deal with issues of injury and death "however, few plans adequately deal with the psychological needs of the employees most closely affected." **(17)**

Relocating People And Teams

In the event of an incident a number or support locations may be invoked:

- **The Command Centre:** Located at sufficient distance from the potential scene of an incident this will provide a location for crisis and as defined other response and recovery teams. This could be a room in a neighbouring business, hotel or third party supplier. Equipment to facilitate the responsibilities of the team should be on site - in a battle bag or box.

- **The Holding Centre:** If evacuation from a site takes place but it is uncertain as to whether a recovery plan will be invoked, a short-term holding location for those evacuated may be required - especially if weather is poor. Holding those evacuated in one location will improve the ability to communicate with those involved and help to ensure that safety and welfare issues can be addressed as necessary.

- **The Recovery Location:** In the event that a backup site is invoked as part of a planning response a whole raft of other considerations come into play. The logistics of relocating significant numbers of people a distance from their usual and familiar place of work may involve transport, catering, temporary overnight accommodation, child care provision and other support needs and services. All of these requirements should be identified as part of the planning process, pre-arranged where possible with suppliers and contact details noted in the plan.

For many organisations, the best solution is to have a business recovery centre on hand, to where people can relocate and business critical systems can 'fail over.' In essence, this helps the business stay available to suppliers, customers and partners. And, more critically, it helps to minimise the damage to revenue and brand value.

Today though, getting the most out of people in a disruptive situation is becoming a science in itself. Business recovery centres are designed to help the business stay up and running and can be organised in such a way that people can work just as if at their own desks.

This can go some way to help acclimate employees into their new environment. However, unfamiliar surroundings and the background of disruption will mean that not all employees will work at their optimum all of the time. Many will be unsettled, distracted and disoriented.

In analysing what can help, psychologists have found that the ambience of the facility is of far greater importance than previously thought.

Organisations pay a great deal of attention to the working environment, making it safe, clean, equipped for the purpose and conducive to good performance. Areas frequented by customers will adopt similar standards and on occasion, higher "showcase" appearance and facilities.

In the event that a workspace must be relocated due to the unavailability of the regular facility, much less attention is generally paid to the working environment that a temporary site might offer. The word temporary when used in the context of recovery facilities has generally translated to mean clean, functional and "vanilla." Yet these facilities can be in commission for a considerable length of time.

Today it is more widely recognised that environment has an enormous impact on the psychological well-being of people, and that living and working spaces should reflect this. The business continuity manager should not only consider backup capability that offers the functional needs of the organisation and a safe, comfortable environment but also one where (often still traumatised and or confused) employees feel at ease and can be productive.

"Although colour and surroundings will not solve emotional imbalance as a consequence of wide scale disasters it can help to offer employers a facility that sets a tone for well being in unfamiliar surroundings during a relatively routine invocation. That in itself can have remarkable effects on maintaining levels of company performance and help keep the business available." **(17)**

International Issues

If an organisation operates in an international or global environment then additional considerations may apply: managing time differences, language barriers, cultural differences and dealing with death and bereavement with poor or limited support are all issues that may apply.

Communication - Crisis, What Crisis?

One of the most critical issues following an incident is communication.

Communicating 'immediate actions' and relevant information may be the factor that determines the ultimate effectiveness of a recovery and should not be left to chance. As with all other aspects of business continuity management, communication should be subject to pre-planning and rehearsal.

And as with team dynamics the dynamics of communication in times of crisis will vary to those of a steady-state environment. An incident will create a thirst for information from all stakeholders. Messages must be clear, consistent and honest yet may need to be issued in circumstances where reliable information is in limited supply.

Most organisations conduct initial communication with large numbers of people by "cascade," where a message is relayed in sequence from person to person. This sounds straightforward but rehearsal is essential on a regular basis and these will almost inevitably reveal points of failure. People change departments, telephone numbers and locations, new joiners arrive and others leave. Nothing can be considered as static.

The majority of organisations facilitate cascades by using a manual process. These can be quite slow to achieve. People will be away from the workplace, during down time out socialising, may switch off or not respond to pagers and telephones or be away on holiday. Most organisations underestimate the time needed to make contact and any process could take hours or even days, certainly not minutes.

Even if an organisation has pre-agreed approaches to cascade messages or the preparation of these, messages can be unclear, become distorted and by the time they arrive, out of date.

"Like ripples on the surface of a pond, once a manual cascade utilising multiple levels is started, the ripples can only go outwards. If the message needs to be changed, updated or stopped, it simply cannot be done effectively with this method." **(18)** And for those in control what checks are in place to ensure that the message has arrived correctly and been assimilated?

Case Study

The Manchester Bombing - June 1996

(A) It was a warm and sunny Saturday morning in Manchester when the Provisional IRA bomb went off in the central retail district. An organisation affected by the impact of the bomb had a cascade process in place to contact the site incident management team but this was initially ineffective.

Members of the team were variously out on the golf course, shopping with their families, or watching a European soccer match.

Mobile phones were not commonly in use in those days and as television did not cover the details of the bombing until quite late in the day, information and initiation of the cascade resulted from news heard over local radio channels. Unsurprisingly the cascade took some while and did not reach all team players.

(B) A number of employees were injured by the bomb blast and the debris resulting from this. Chaos followed the bombing and it was unclear for some days who had been injured, how badly and where they were located. Three days after the bombing the organisation was ready to bring back employees to recover business operations. Managers were asked to implement a manual cascade and contact those employees required and where they would be based from the following day. An employee contacted had thought that her manager was calling to ask how she was. The employee in question had significant injuries and was scheduled to have stitches removed from wounds later that week. The employees' response took the manager by surprise - he was unaware of her injuries and had just used a standard message calling people back to work.

(C) An employee who decided there was no point in going into work following the bombing decided, without telling anybody, to visit relatives in another part of the country rendering himself as "a missing person" for the period in question. This just serves to illustrate the problems associated with tracking down all those affected following a major incident.

Manual cascades cannot effectively deliver answers to questions. Control over information flow is almost impossible. People want to know what is going on and to help. Informal networks and in effect cascades will take place. This can decrease the effectiveness of "official" cascades.

Since the events of Manchester, technology has played an increasingly important role in the formation and delivery of cascades.

If technology is deployed in this way then its use should be considered as part of risk assessment and Business Impact Analysis processes. Resilience may be critical and the questions that may be posed might include:

- Location and access of the kit and software: whether it is remote or local and easy to use
- Dependencies: on other technology and facilities
- Quality assurance, including maintenance
- Response times
- Backup: capabilities and support
- Security: especially where personnel-related data is concerned and to avoid unauthorised use
- Currency of data, linked if possible to other relevant data bases such as employee systems
- Exercising on a stand-alone basis and integrated with other processes and solutions

Measuring The Success Of Invocation

As with business continuity management generally, plan performance measures should be aligned to the scale, nature and complexity of an organisation and the incident. Measures can be quantitative or qualitative.

Quantitative measures might include:

- The value of physical assets damaged and reinstated
- The level of downtime and associated loss of revenue
- Consequential loss and increased costs of working for organisations with listed shares - the impact on shareholder value

Qualitative measures might include:

- Perceived harm to the brand
- Perceived harm to reputation

While measures of plan success or failure might include the extent of death (when most organisations would adopt a zero tolerance measure) and injury, measures of success for the most important asset – people - are difficult to establish. While the physical effects of a disaster are hard to avoid, the emotional and psychological effects can be difficult to identify or manage.

Response And Recovery - The People Factor

Business continuity management demands that different approaches are taken for different scenarios. From technology failures to petrol blockades, from flood and fire to denial of access and the impact of disease, every business continuity manager must assess each scenario and ensure that plans are in place to address the most significant and probable.

The mass movement of people is never an easy task, but when there is the potential for panic, chaos can ensue. Rehearsal, is therefore, absolutely critical to minimise the bedlam. Making sure people vacate premises via designated routes and know the fundamental dos and don'ts for quick and safe evacuation will help to minimise the risk of this occurring.

However, getting people to react in such a way that they switch to 'auto-pilot,' react sensibly and follow instructions to the letter in an evacuation is not easy. It takes time and a real appreciation by employees of both the risks and the need to pay full attention to drill practice and communications and to the business continuity and safety teams.

As with any rehearsal, the urgency of the 'real thing' is rarely present. So business continuity planners must take into consideration what actually happens to staff when they make it to the designated evacuation point in the event of a true invocation.

All In The Mind - Post Trauma

The World Health Organisation offers a category of definition for stress within classification of diseases and within this offers three diagnoses:

- **Acute stress reaction**: this appears without any other mental disorder. Symptoms usually appear in minutes and disappear within hours following traumatic exposure

- **Adjustment disorder**: this usually relates to a significant life change or stressful event. Symptoms usually appear with a month of an incident and disappear within six months

- **Post-traumatic stress disorder (PTSD)**: this usually arises within six months following exposure to trauma. In addition to evidence of trauma there must be a repetitive, intrusive recollection or re-enactment of the event in memories, daytime imagery or dreams

Following the classification of PTSD as a psychiatric disorder in 1980, this remains a developing area of clinical knowledge and further research and debate will continue to emerge. What research has already revealed is that of all the people exposed to traumatic experiences only a small percentage go on to suffer from PTSD and has considered consequently what other factors might lead to its onset.

It is generally considered that an employee's reactions to trauma fall into three main phases each of which has its own characteristics:

- Immediate reactions at the time of the trauma

- Acute reactions in the month following the trauma

- Chronic or long-term reactions

Research **(19)** has shown that the magnitude and duration of trauma responses is determined by a number of factors, the main ones being:

- The intensity and nature of the traumatic event

- The employee's perception of the trauma

- The employee's level of training

- Their preparedness to meet the demands of the trauma

- The availability of appropriate support

Current thinking is that counselling imposed, however well meaning, by third party authorities can be harmful and may damage the often more beneficial support mechanisms of families and colleagues.

Just as with most other aspects of business continuity management the business continuity manager can work with partners within an organisation to build resilience and response. Research has indicated that effective training and education can prepare the workforce for trauma and provide a barrier of protection or first line of defence.

Employees are able to deal with traumatic situations providing that they can balance their perception of the magnitude and nature of the trauma with their perceived ability to deal with it.

However, if following exposure to trauma an employee breaches this barrier then a second line of defence can be installed through effective organisational and peer support, debriefing and counselling.

There is no textbook for building resilience and response. People will introduce their own experience and values into any situation and post trauma issues in this respect are no different. The culture of an organisation will lead to the embedding of certain expectations of behaviour.

For example "the introduction of trauma care can be problematical when despite the organisation's best intentions, the employees form negative views of their motives. An organisation that is otherwise highly expense conscious and/or ambivalent towards employee welfare issues will attract scepticism in the event that cash is thrown at post-event treatment." **(20)**

An organisation cannot be forced to care but it is the organisation that offers leadership post-event consistent with leadership during business as usual and an environment where normal behaviours do not need to be suppressed that is likely to succeed in this area. "Where the expression of normal reactions to trauma is suppressed, secondary problems such as depression, alcoholism, relationship difficulties and suicidal tendencies may develop." **(21)**

Undertaking regular risk assessments will assist an organisation in identifying issues that may place people at risk. These assessments must be undertaken as part of business-as-usual risk and business continuity management but revisited and actions refreshed during and following a traumatic event. These assessments will also indicate potential changes in the business that could have an impact on the company's ability to respond in a disaster.

In a number of countries, authorities may see the provision of post-event "treatment" as one of their responsibilities. Organisations should make themselves aware of how authorities may respond, consider this and adopt a stance as part of their approach to planning.

Do's And Don'ts Post-Event Include:

- Do plan – don't react unprepared. Research indicates that those counselled have a more effective recovery than those that are not

- Do be cautious about following a textbook approach when managing people but don't throw away the text book The experience of others may indicate appropriate response times for debrief and counselling but individual needs will vary.

- If people are physically injured it may be some while until they feel able to deal with other "scars"

- Do encourage employees to take comfort from one another. Others who went through the same experience and had been there and knew how it felt may offer support

- Do facilitate closure. If an affected site is rebuilt consider a planned visit

- Don't put your own feelings first. Consider employee needs on a case by case basis

- Don't wrap people in cotton wool. Some employees may wish to recover in their own way

- Don't overlook the needs of the teams leading and effecting recovery. Their needs may be no different from others involved

- Don't assume that this is a short-term issue. Those affected may continue to suffer post-traumatic stress, high levels of anxiety and depression more than two years after an event. Assign a manager responsible for ongoing management and continue to review until professional advice indicates this is no longer necessary

---

Where should you go for advice and support? Seek out those individuals with appropriate credentials and experience. Support services may comprise a number of solutions including:

- Help lines manned by skilled operatives. Contracts should be negotiated during times of business as usual and made available to employees and their families as required. Sometimes purchased as part of an Employee Assistance Programme (EAP), access numbers should be widely communicated and embedded within plans. Invocation can be immediate.

- Face-to-face debrief and counselling services can be purchased as an automatic extension of help line services. Organisations should however assure themselves that providers have the capability to effectively deliver the service offered - specialist and suitably qualified assistance may be required as a supplementary service.

Supplier, Outsourcing And Off-Shoring - People Issues

The issues here in one respect are relatively straightforward and in another quite complex. As was observed in Chapter Ten, while an organisation might use suppliers and outsource providers to transfer the provision of services and functional capability, it cannot transfer overall responsibility - that remains firmly within the governance structure and responsibilities of an organisation, the Board or its equivalent.

The key word is responsibility. It is the responsibility of the ceding organisation to ensure that those organisations they use for supplier and outsourcing arrangements perform to levels acceptable to the ceding organisation - including those relevant to people management. In most respects any template used by an organisation for people-related risk and continuity management issues should be the basis on which suppliers and outsource providers are assessed. This is a relatively easy statement to make but gaining assurance that the situation is as expected can be much more complex. A ceding organisation will not have the daily access to people in other organisational structures or to records concerning employees that are strictly off-limits to external eyes.

A suite of key indicators regarding people issues should be established as part of the contract negotiation. These indicators may well be based on those used in the ceding organisation although other routes to assurance could be to adopt relevant external standards - for example do the suppliers or outsource provider attain any accreditations such as in the UK Investors in People, or in Information Security International Standard ISO 17799 and in business continuity management the British Standard PAS 56? If organisations operate in a regulated environment what standards does the regulator demand and are they compliant?

All of these provide opportunities to create benchmarks against which an assessment of performance may be judged.

Focussing on business continuity management, a ceding organisation should be within its rights to request details of the business continuity programme and outcome of the exercises and rehearsals. To ensure that the right level of detail is supplied indicators setting out expectations of data are essential. The often seen question in a tender document of "do you have business continuity plans YES/NO" is totally inadequate but without providing clarity of expectations may be all that a ceding organisation will receive by way of assurance.

Turning briefly to off-shoring, the question of ethics may well raise its head. Some of the most damaging impact on the reputation of organisations has been the exposure to perceived exploitation of people in developing economies by those in the Western world.

The call centre capability in countries such as India, China, Indonesia and Russia involves sophisticated operations using high calibre (often graduate level) employees working to standards acceptable in any country. Often involving relationships with financial services organisations and overseen by world-class providers, the standards achieved in terms of resilience, output and treatment of employees is as good and in some cases even higher than those experienced within the ceding organisation. Regulators notably in this sector will demand nothing less in their respective rule books. However care should be taken to ensure that environmental considerations specific to the location are considered as part of the supporting risk assessment, including those relating to climate, political stability and security.

In some other sectors experience has been different. We have all heard stories of exploitation through the use of children and the payment of low wages to people working in a number of industries including textiles, footwear and heavy industry. The balance between ethical considerations and those of local individual and government economic need is complex.

The issues in these cases are more ones of assessing the conditions of supplier production against an organisation's ethical policy and standards and ensuring that these are assessed and not breached.

But whatever the situation, the fundamental point is consistent: organisations must consider what is supplied and outsourced within their business continuity framework as if provisioning remained in-house.

Investment In People - Training And Education

If people are the most critical resource at the time of a disaster, why do so few organisations pay proper attention to the training and education of people in issues associated with business continuity management?

"Experience has shown that, in disaster situations, organisations that have invested in business continuity training programmes effect a smoother recovery than those that have not made a similar investment." (22). Additional benefits may arise as training can reveal ways of improving business performance in business as usual circumstances especially in building resilience.

Investment In People - Developing A Programme

The design of a training and education programme should follow the business continuity management process and be tailored for the varying stakeholders and their positions within the process. Everyone within an organisation should be provided with a consistent and minimum level of awareness of the subject, the response that an organisation will take and each individual's position within this.

The most effective training and education is achieved through engagement.

An organisation can design the process of steering and delivery of business continuity management through a number of teams structured at different levels and functionality - as a management matrix.

This approach allows for the maximum numbers to be involved for the minimum level of time - yet achieves participation and ownership. This concept applies from the Board through to a team in a factory engaged in making a single component.

Beyond this a programme might include:

- Briefings for senior management, covering the organisation's approach to business continuity, recovery plans and their responsibilities
- Briefings for those identified in the BIA as key to the organisation and its recovery, setting out the process the organisation has followed and what is expected of them and their employees during planning, response and recovery
- Workshops for response and recovery teams addressing any areas of specialisation
- Brochures, intranet sites and perhaps an occasional newsletter
- The use of scenarios and role plays will be of value at all levels of training. These will encourage interactive discussion and almost inevitably lead to modifications to the plans.

SUMMARY

Every organisation should consider the risks associated with people. Organisations need to develop risk assessments and BIAs which include people-specific risks and business continuity plans that bring together the needs of both an organisation and its people within a single framework and plan. The plan should deal with issues that might only affect people as opposed to physical and information assets - for example injury or death away from a site during a business sponsored activity or wide-area disease such as with SARS in 2003 or Avian Flu in 2005.

Whether it is the failure of a business leader to exercise good leadership at the time of a disaster or a shop floor employee who turns the wrong way leaving a building at a time of crisis, the results can have similar consequences. A disaster affecting an organisation involves its people and the families of those people.

Managing people requires specific professional competence as with any other managerial discipline. It would be unusual for a head of personnel to be inexperienced in managing people. Consequently when faced with extraordinary circumstances an organisation should consider the use of relevant experts. Dealing with the fallout of trauma and the effects of this on people should be left to the professional.

Organisations and their managers have a (usually legal) responsibility for the health, safety and well-being of the people in their care. The gravity of these responsibilities should be reflected in the treatment of people as part of the organisation's business continuity framework, policy, strategy and plans.

Bibliography

1. World Economic Forum - 2005

2. Workplace Trauma - Noreen Tehrani - 2004

3. Managing Operational Risk - Douglas G Hoffman - 2002

4. Concern for Risk - INFORM - David Herratt - January 2005

5. Managing Operational Risk - Douglas G Hoffman - 2002

6. The Financial Services Authority - Operational Risk Systems and Controls

7. John Robinson - Continuity Central - www.continuitycentral.com

8. John Robinson - Continuity Central - www.continuitycentral.com

9. Keith Pursall - Continuity Central - www.continuitycentral.com

10. Keith Pursall - Continuity Central - www.continuitycentral.com

11. Emotional Terrors in the Workplace - Vali Hawkins Mitchell - 2004

12. Called 'Redefining readiness: terrorism planning through the eyes of the public' and funded by the W. K. Kellogg Foundation

13. Linda Lewis - Lewis News Media - November 2004

14. Knight and Pretty - The Impact of Catastrophes on Shareholder Value - 1994

15. Knight and Pretty - The Impact of Catastrophes on Shareholder Value - 1994

16. Generally Accepted Practices for Business Continuity Practitioners drafted by Disaster Recovery Institute International (DRII)/Disaster Recovery Journal (DRJ) - Draft published for review and consultation - Part Vll Appendices - b) training and awareness - July 2005

17. Tomkinson - Human Resources for Disaster Recovery - Risk and Continuity - 1999

18. Dennis Thomas - Synstar

13

The Value of Insurance When Facing Potentially Catastrophic Risk

Objectives Of This Chapter Are:

- To consider insurance products from the viewpoint of the critical or catastrophic risks carried by an organisation

- To understand whether and where insurers' products and the insured's need for continuity interface effectively with each other.

- To assess the value of conventional insurance products to organisations facing potentially catastrophic damage

- To identify in particular where these insurance products do not provide protection for the continuity needs of an organisation.

Assessing Insurance Needs

It is a major disappointment, when looking at many an organisation's insurance programme, to see just how much the design of the protection package is driven by the 'off the shelf' insurers' products rather then by the risks of the organisation itself.

Where there are large numbers of small value and smaller premium risks – say households, shopkeepers, hoteliers, smaller manufacturers etc. - there is a real value in accepting 'off the shelf' products. The smaller commercial insured can see that there is value in accepting the 'package' even if it provides protections that it does not need, because negotiating individual changes would cost more than the premiums that have been built in for the risk protections that are not needed. The very real danger here however is when the package does not provide protections that are needed. We will revert to this issue in this chapter.

> *The larger organisation has no excuses for not looking carefully for and identifying its own, unacceptable risks. Once those risks are understood, and a risk tolerance level established, only then is there real value in setting out to consider insurance as one of the options of managing the unacceptable risks. To do otherwise must increase the risk of buying insurance protections that are not needed, or alternately, not having insurance protections to cover potentially critical exposures. The former is a total waste of money, the latter potentially destructive; however much premium is spent on other protections.*

Risk management sadly still shows its roots in the role of 'risk manager' to be one who is tasked only with buying the insurance programme. The other side of the same coin is the risk manager, who probably evolved from and is certainly steeped in the insurance industry, not having the vision or skills to see beyond that inner horizon. Some of the larger brokers are now paying more than lip service to risk management as an alternative to insurance. They are however organisationally and culturally too often hemmed in by the fundamental product that drives their own business; that of selling insurance products. Too often, they constrain themselves to the comfort boundaries of risk-managing only insurable risks.

The visionary risk manager has been kicking against those traces for some years now and the successful ones have encouraged their boards to grasp the much wider values of risk management. In some cases the Boards have been the first to see the opportunities; and they have needed to replace their 'risk manager' jobholder with new skills.

Another driving force has been the ever-increasing interest by regulators and stock markets in the risks being carried by organisations they police or, in turn, in which they have investments. While publicly quoted companies and some others have, for decades, had sophisticated financial risk models in place, these regulators have increasingly been driving organisations to manage and give information regarding non-financial risks. These are much more amorphous challenges, where boards are much less experienced and feel much less comfortable.

Organisations are seeing more and more that both the tasks and the opportunities of risk management are much wider than auditing the flows of money and other assets. The sometimes surprise bonus that has emerged from this trend is for organisations to recognise and grasp the business opportunities that lie in understanding and managing risk; and thus seeing measured risks not only as a threat, but also as an opportunity for effective business development.

In too many instances however that dull partnership of the erstwhile, so-called, risk manager's horizons is still seen within organisations and indeed even within the insurance industry itself. We explore this background in the next few paragraphs to set the scene for now moving on to consider the values or weaknesses in the insurance industry in offering support to a modern organisation facing potentially catastrophic risks. We now set out to examine where the insurance product can, and currently cannot, interface those needs successfully and aid continuity; the risk subject of this book

What Is A Catastrophic Risk?

In the earlier chapter on Business Impact Analysis we considered some template definitions of the potential impact of risk incidents. Those definitions are designed to be starters for conversations about an individual organisation's own risks and impacts. They gave a very basic description of what could be regarded as negligible, marginal, critical and catastrophic risks for a hypothetical organisation. For the purposes of this chapter we are addressing critical and catastrophic risk only; i.e., those risks that could significantly damage or even destroy the organisation. The template descriptions of these two risk levels were:

CRITICAL IMPACT

- It takes up to three days to reinstate customer-facing services

- Fines by regulatory authorities

- Loss of confidence within the workforce

- Delayed access to business critical information or other intellectual asset.

- Credit rating fall one half point or more

- Financial loss of:

Capital	below $10,000,000	
Revenue	50% local targets	
10% Group targets		

- Unacceptable Health and Safety Risk;

- Health and Safety approvals for a building withdrawn

- Risk of share price falls by up to 10%

CATASTROPHIC IMPACT

- It takes more than three days to reinstate customer-facing services

- Loss of regulatory or licence approval

- Illegality within a business operational area

- Loss of confidence in the brand name by the general public

- Loss of dependent information or other intellectual asset.

- Loss of confidence in the brand name by shareholders

- Financial loss of:

Capital	above $25,000,000
Revenue	25% group targets

- Credit rating fall one full level or more

- Unacceptable risk of life

- Risk of share price falls by up to 25% or more

We then went on to bring out two very important dimensions that sit around these definitions. One was the role of frequency modelling in critical or catastrophic risk. We made the point that, where an impact is potentially critical or catastrophic, it is of less interest to the organisation how often that incident can happen. The focus will be on the fact that it can happen at all; and of course the fact that boards do not know when. It could happen the very afternoon of the discussions taking place. Potential frequency does of course have its relevance; especially where risks around a new venture are being assessed. It is important also when considering how best to finance the consequences of risk incidents.

Potential frequency is also a factor when considering any cost/benefit balances in any risk management investments against relatively frequent, relatively lower-cost, risks. It is not, however, a primary driver when the first incident could in effect destroy the organisation altogether or remove it from its marketplace and stakeholder responsibilities.

> *Critical or catastrophic risks expose the very survival of the organisation from the very first time that the risk incident occurs; and they will therefore bring quite specific and additional challenges to both planners and responders.*

The other dimension we brought out in the earlier discussion was the issue of 'time out.' An organisation's ability, to step out of its marketplace for a period of time while it handles crises, will vary dramatically. It will vary between each organisation, its business models, its regulatory environment, its market place, the ability of competitors to react quickly, and the demands of its own, specific range of stakeholders. The first and often the most damaging thing to be lost is the value of the brand. This could happen in minutes in some industries or after days or weeks in others. This feature of business impact is embraced in our definitions above but it is worthy of mention again at this point as we move on to explore further the role and values of the insurance industry to an organisation in crisis.

These factors, both as dependencies and also therefore as risks, are headlines only. By way of a case study we list the risk concerns of one individual company, the multinational pharmaceutical company AstraZeneca; as listed in its annual report.

**Case Study
AstraZeneca**

- Loss of or expiry of patents, marketing exclusivity or trade marks
- Impact of fluctuations of exchange rates
- Failure of Research and Development to yield commercially successful new products
- Competition, price controls and price fluctuation
- Taxation
- Substantial product liability claims
- Reliance on third parties for material and services
- Delay to new product launches
- Difficulties obtaining regulatory approvals on new products
- Failure to observe regulatory oversight
- Performance of new products
- Environmental liabilities
- Forward looking statements **(1)**

The Organisation's Dependencies

When considering the pressures on an organisation facing catastrophic damage, it is a valuable thought process to stand back from the day-to-day aspects of the business and think through the individual foundation stones of that organisation. Only then can we see the real post-damage pressures, and the needs the directors may face when struggling to keep the business or organisation alive.

In recent years, there have been important changes in the way businesses deliver and market their own products, changes in their relationships with their stakeholders, and even in the risks themselves. These changes are influencing how potential damage can hit the very cornerstones of the organisation, not only by 'new' risks but also a new level of damage caused by 'old' risks. Often the real consequences of damage, moving right up and through the organisation, are unrecognisable from the consequences of a similar incident some years ago.

To explain, clear to all business watchers are the dramatic changes in the way that businesses have reorganised themselves as they take up the opportunities now available to them. These opportunities have emerged from new technologies which have enabled faster and direct business-to-customer (B2C) and business-to- business (B2B) communications. The sheer scale of merged companies, encouraged by more open markets across the developed world and the Internet, has enabled them to be increasingly multinational. Spin-offs have the ability to squeeze new values out of supply chains and distribution chains, often outsourced. These new alternatives to volume labour are now enabling a shift of the power base from the workforces towards company management.

During a potentially catastrophic disaster in a modern multinational, the board's attention is on the survival of the business. It is too easy to consider only the insurer's view and belief that the most important concern is the replacing of buildings and contents (or defending against litigation). That is the easy bit. The massive organisations of today have, however, built into their procedures some new and dangerous points of exposure that, if and when the risk incident occurs, could remove crucial dependencies on which the whole organisation depends. In other words, a sudden death or removal from their marketplace is now increasingly, not less, likely.

It is valuable for the continuity risk manager to consider the organisation through the perspective of its stakeholders' expectations, and through whether the failure to meet any one of them can be a single point of potentially catastrophic failure. The reader will certainly gain at this moment from looking again at the various stakeholders, their roles and their needs as explained in Chapter Two.

Changing Risks Within the Ingredients of the Delivery Process

The delivery chain - sometimes called the "value chain" - is often unrecognisable from the cosy, locally controlled, in-house delivery chain of yore. A failure, deep within a third-party, just–in–time, supply chain can have catastrophic and immediate consequences on the final production line. A manufacturer of new motor cars is unlikely to succeed if it delivered its cars with a note that that the door handles will follow later. It is certainly cheaper to build and staff a call centre in Bombay, Calcutta or Manila, but will the infrastructure, and the emergency responses of those cities, be at a level at which stakeholders have become accustomed?

The better-managed organisations try to understand the resilience of their suppliers' deliveries; i.e., to quantify their suppliers' soundness and continuity planning. The question though is how to do that that with real confidence; embracing the critical suppliers to the suppliers, and that supplier's suppliers down the line. Those jobholders who immerse themselves in continuity risk have a healthy respect for whether the in-house continuity management will or will not work in circumstances that can only be guessed at. Moving on into assuming confidence about a third-party organisation's planning increases the difficulty and exposure exponentially!

The dependence on technology brings its own risks and not just the obvious e-commerce exposures. Failures will not only cause wholesale disruptions in manufacture, other processing and communications. A technological failure can often be the single point of failure that could bring a multi-national to a halt right across its entire organisation. That failure may not just be electronic, it may be in the areas of security of information, communications, software or even the hardware infrastructure within which the electronics reside.

Modern organisations have dependencies on intellectual assets that cannot possibly be overemphasised. Many a 21st Century organisation is no more than the sum total of owned (or rented) intellectual assets, a contracted out delivery and marketing process, and a group of key stakeholders can move away as fast as they moved within. The intellectual assets are much more than data on computer databases. These assets lie further in licences, paper and even in employee brains. The organisation's resilience depends not only in the safety from harm of this information but also in the ability to regain access. Access from elsewhere needs to be possible, not only physically, but also legally or contractually. The Data Protection Act in the United Kingdom defines quite clearly who can use what personal information and for what purpose; as also may the contracts right through the various layers of the supply chain. Other statutes demand similar and additional controls in other countries.

The brand or credibility amongst the range of stakeholders is a single, organisation-wide value on which the entire organisation depends for its survival; or at the very least for the current market position that it enjoys. Without this there may be no company left; as has been found out the hard way by many organisations.

We have touched upon the new relationships between employer and employee and perhaps there is the need now only to reinforce the concerns as a new risk. As stated, the relationships with workforces are very different than in the past. Any organisation that gives the impression that its workforce is as disposable as an old piece of office furniture or left-over food from the table is naïve to believe that, in a crisis, that same workforce will continue the loyalty and deference of years ago. More and more 'employees' have been 'outsourced' to an entirely different organisation which of course has its own stakeholders and its own business models, priorities and preferences. A crisis almost always demands a sudden switch of urgencies and massively increased pressures on one part of the organisation. This may be to meet new, urgent communication needs to a whole new range of different people, or to set about the urgent task of rebuilding a critical aspect of the working environment, or heal the break in the supply or delivery chain.

An employer can move internal resources around if the employees are supportive and confident of the ultimate survival of the organisation. A third-party labour supplier may not wish – nor be able – to dramatically and urgently move labour or infrastructure resources around so quickly.

The modern organisation enjoys a speed from concept to delivery that an organisation of the 20th century could only dream about. This speed is not only in computer aided design work but right through to the delivery of the product through business-to-business, and business-to-customer, e-commerce delivery. It is said, for example that if a banking product does not go from concept to critical mass in its marketplace within three months it is a failure; and a massively expensive one at that. Speed brings all sorts of new risk into the equation.

The risk that could totally remove an organisation the quickest is a failure to continue to meet the requirements of a regulator or the wider law of the country. If a regulator decides that the controls needed to remain within the regulatory envelope have failed then the organisation is stone cold dead. The regulator will close them down if the organisation has lost the ability to continue to meet the regulator's statutory requirements. Only too often this is in the area of information on which the organisation depends to deliver secure and effective control of the products sold. That information may lie in an audit trail of previous activities or in ongoing information that is needed to retain business control to the satisfaction of the regulator. Even a fine could lead straight through to a weakness in the brand value; leading in turn to marketing damage and other costs far greater than the fine itself.

The Evolution of Impact

The risks themselves have therefore not only changed, but also the potential for damage to the organisation from these new risks is totally different. Furthermore, the potential for damage that can occur from old, perhaps insurable, risks can also be unrecognisable from the extent of damage we could envisage in the past.

In older business models the organisation was dispersed around the host country to be situated next to their customers. Had such a unit been destroyed the Board would no doubt have expressed an interest; but the bottom line assets or revenues of the organisation may not have been affected to any significance. Now the product delivery is often from one or two key and technological "factories" that, if inaccessible, could close down the whole organisation. Furthermore, these factories themselves often depend on information technology and communication technology components that can fit onto a postage stamp.

Consequently the skills of an individual or small team can be skills on which the entire delivery of a multinational depends. We have the potential and reality of much deeper impact from the same incident that would have been a blip not many years ago.

We explored in an earlier chapter how computerisation is an important example of where there is a potential new impact of damage or a failure. It is not the loss of the hardware that is the real concern, it is the process for which they are used, the data it stores; and what its introduction has done to the wider production process. To recap, it has replaced large numbers of trained staff who simply do not exist any more. It supplies the baseline product and client information. It enables credibility in the audit standards and the audit trail. It has the corporate formulae embedded within its software and it allows access by other authorised personnel. It communicates internally and externally. It provides useable management information and it secures sensitive information.

These are examples only. The Risk Manager needs to bring together these new exposures to both new and old practices within organisations, the newly identified stakeholders and their needs, the new risks themselves; and assess how they can seriously damage or totally destroy even multi-billion pound multinationals. It is only from these assessments that well-informed business decisions can be made about risk acceptance and, where unacceptable, risk management in all its various forms and tools and, above all business continuity

Crisis Brings Crises

We discussed in an earlier chapter how stakeholders may react to a disaster; extending the damage and demand further. Even if the best employees don't just walk away they may see the weakness of the employer as simply a new environment within which negotiations can begin afresh. Headhunters read newspapers too!

Just as dangerous are those employees, often with the best of intentions, all setting off at a rapid pace doing what they individually perceive to be the next most important thing. A large workforce of headless chickens, devoid of its usual communication tools and controls, is a frightening reality. They can do so much more damage than the original incident. There are those doing what they genuinely believe is best from within the perspective of their own responsibility and job horizons, and there are the "Rambos" who feel the need to be seen doing something dramatic and career building. These activities can be seriously damaging and could divert limited resources from real, board-driven, priorities and urgencies.

Earlier we mentioned stakeholders whose importance only really becomes clear after the disaster. They bring unexpected and further problems – as if there weren't enough already! Just one example is the media. Should the operational risk incident only damage and not destroy, there is a more than even chance that the media will finish off any brand values that may remain and thus finish off the organisation. The rat pack in full flow looking for fools, villains and victims on whom to create stories is not a pretty sight and needs managing very carefully indeed.

We have mentioned already the competitor as a post-incident stakeholder. The very speed by which a modern organisation can now create a product and get it to market becomes a significant threat in itself. When a competitor recognises a weakened company it therefore has these same opportunities to quickly 'upsize' and get new choices in front of the damaged organisation's erstwhile customers.

> *If you can keep your head when all about you are losing theirs – it's just possible you have not fully grasped the situation.* - Jean Kerr

Business Survival

We need to meet the agenda of this particular chapter to see how insurance can aid the management of these risks, and the management of the evolving crisis, to aid the very continuity of the organisation. Its values could lie in any one of the process stepping-stones and we recap these again as follows:

- A process of identifying and managing unacceptable risks that begins with a structured search for potentially destructive risks and the potential consequences. Once identified and both risks and impacts measured; there is the activity possible only then, to put the organisation in a position that, whatever happens, the very foundation on which it depends for survival could never be lost or destroyed.

- An emergency response structure that limits damage, puts the heads back on the chickens, can communicate urgently wherever there is a need, and has prepared at least minimum resources for the authorised and clear new urgencies and priorities.

These legs on which an organisation depends will include at least the:

- Skills of the workforce,
- The ability to communicate
- The brand value and other credibilities
- Legal and physical access to the information and other intellectual assets on which the organisation depends
- Alternate means of delivering urgent goods and services into the marketplace fast enough to remain a credible player in that chosen marketplace – and to keep out the competitors.
- The demands that enable the organisation to remain legal, credible, secure, and with the approval of regulators.
- Tools and information needed to remain in financial and operational control.
- Ability to respond fast enough to keep the organisation alive. Quite literally, the response needs to be available over 24 hours/365 days; especially to take control, limit damage, communicate as necessary, and to get back into the urgent demands of the marketplace. These are rightly the subjects of the business continuity plan.

THE ROLE OF INSURANCE

The Insurance Industry

The need for the product called insurance emerged from the fact that entrepreneurs wished to take risks. In the early days these risks were encountered when sending their sailing ships off on hazardous sea journeys to trade with far countries. The entrepreneurs were nervous of the fact that a failure of one venture could cause losses that would destroy them financially. The need for insurance evolved further when these entrepreneurs needed to obtain financing for their ventures. The financiers had an even smaller appetite to take on the risk of one large failure fully on their own account and they demanded some protection against loss.

The principle of the day - the higher the risk, the higher the cost of investment capital - still remains a business ethos to this day, and methods evolved that began to share the cost of any individual failure larger than one entrepreneur could realistically carry. The method of spreading losses across many different traders by way of mutual funds - and then insurance contracts - emerged as an instrument whereby the cost of failure could be reduced to a pre-agreed, reasonably fixed and manageable cost.

As said above, modern corporations, their structures, their risks and the consequence of damage have however moved on significantly since the 18th Century. They have greater strengths, but greater sensitivities too and can be totally destroyed just as quickly. The modern organisations, however large and strong, still have a need to protect large amounts of assets from simultaneous, sudden loss, and also to stabilise over time their revenues and profits. They and their stakeholders as well do not wish to take on the risk of a significant level of loss of their assets nor damage to their financial stability.

The roots of the insurance business therefore lie in spreading financial losses across many people so that the impact on one is bearable. It is in effect a money brokering business; and it receives in an amount of money that the risk underwriter considers to represent monetarily the risk the insured activity will bring to the overall fund and when. The insurer will then accept the call back from their own capital from one insured when a loss has occurred that falls within the predetermined definitions of the policy contract. Generally speaking, the payment will be measured to precisely reimburse, or 'indemnify' the policyholder for the losses that were incurred in the risk incident.

> *It is important to retain this financial perspective as we delve deeper into the relationships between insurance and the losses that are potentially business-destructive ones. Where we go on later in this chapter to illustrate that insurance does not have any value whatsoever to some insureds facing catastrophic loss, it would be unfair to see this necessarily as a failure of the industry. It is unfair, after all, to criticise someone for not achieving what they do not set out to do. The question is more about a matching and mismatching of products and needs; and the responsibility to ensure a precise match must lie, not with the insurer, nor with the broker, but with the organisation that is carrying the risk. These clear, precise and unarguable responsibilities need to remain 'on the table' as we proceed further.*

On the other hand, whether insurers fail to meet the implications that they build in to their product marketing, is a deep subject in itself, and one that is way beyond the realms of this book. As is the question of whether they should be now taking a hard, lateral look at their product and service offerings in this modern world.

Operational risk is historically the natural world of casualty insurance providers. Indeed the very brand values of a commercial property insurer are built around the fact that the insurance provider will be there to "see you OK" in the event of damage. The branding even includes a product named "all risks insurance." We should stop a second and ask whether this product in particular is seriously misnamed when taken into the very real world of an organisation in distress. Having said all this, the responsibility for ensuring a match between risks carried and the insurance programme remains as defined in the paragraph immediately above and is clear and loud.

> We appear to have two fundamental mismatches between the product and the particular potentially catastrophic needs of the insured.
>
> - The first mismatch is that the insurer is contained by the need to reduce all loss into monetary terms; whereas continuity managers see their greatest exposures not to be monetary; but exposures to continuity of the operational delivery processes, to intellectual assets and other ongoing stakeholder support.
>
> - The second mismatch is that the insurer, to be able to assess and cost the risks that are to be assumed, needs to have the cause of the loss as the primary driver in the covers and negotiations. The insured, considering potentially critical or catastrophic loss, sees the impact, not causes as the primary concern.
>
> These mismatches need to be managed in themselves if the parties are to deliver effective insurance protections that meet the business need.

There is a further aspect that needs to be said. Organisations need to ensure that their cost of risk is evened out over a period of time and they will be considering a period of some years; maybe even a decade or more. In other words, they are not able to maintain stakeholders support if their stability varies dramatically year by year. Insurers have a history of withdrawing the availability of cover just at a time when it is most needed. This may entail an outright refusal of cover in some trades or a significantly reduced market capacity that has the effect of dramatically increasing premiums. Examples include the cover against terrorism and also some liability covers when claims patterns show increased claims frequency.

"More than four out of ten organisations feel that the insurance market is not meeting their business needs nor providing the amount of cover that they require. This is the highest level of dissatisfaction in ten years since we first asked these questions." (2).

No doubt that some of the increased dissatisfaction results from changing needs and insurers' inability to respond to those changes.

We will now move on to consider the product range of the insurance industry, then come back to these needs and explore where, if at all, they join in with each other.

Insurance Products: The Headlines

The headlines are that the primary level and conventional insurance products usually come in two forms:

- The 'material damage' policies that protect against physical damage or loss of assets; occasionally extended to include some resultant loss of revenues

- The liability policies that will reimburse monies should the policyholder be successfully sued – or indeed incur costs being unsuccessfully sued - by another person or legal body.

Material Damage Policies

These are aptly described and are concerned with the loss of physical assets. Those assets may be ships, factories, machinery, money, a motor fleet of cars or lorries, or a host of other things identified by their physicality.

The perils insured against do vary with the type of policy. Marine covers are very wide and can even cover war risks. Other policies however are restricted in that the primary cause of the damage – known as the proximate cause – must be one of those perils that are mentioned in the policy. Putting the motor fleet on one side, traditionally these perils have been fire, some crime risks and natural catastrophe risks such as weather-related damage. If the cause of the damage is not one of the stated perils, then simply the indemnities are not available for the damaged policyholder. Some perils are quite specifically excluded to avoid any confusion in the wordings. These include nuclear damage, emerging damage such as pollution, war risks, (increasingly) terrorism, and other risks. The fact that these perils are not insured or insurable does not mean that they will go away; they remain a concern for the risk and continuity manager.

It is important to bear in mind that conventional insurance protection may not concern itself with what the damaged things do for the insured organisation; nor the values of and dependencies on the insured items. The policy may not concern itself either with the question whether a precise fit of a replacement item is or is not available immediately. As stated above, the need for recovery speed varies dramatically across different organisations. The contract between insured and insurer only converts that contributing asset into figure of money, i.e., its potential replacement cost; and pays that monetary value to the policyholder. When that commodity can be delivered is not an issue for the contract nor especially the insurer. It is a vital issue for the continuity manager.

"Increased cost of working" or "business interruption" covers are available from the insurance market. They set out to replace revenues, maintain those ongoing fixed costs that do not reduce directly as sales reduce following damage. The policy can also, if purchased, replace the profits, that fall below expectations following a period of insured business interruption. The policy can cover also any increase in operational costs of working to meet deliveries while the main delivery faculty is being rebuilt.

Two common elements of the cover – and thus the right to indemnity – are worthy of mention at this point. The first is that the interruption must be as a result of an incident that is simultaneously covered by a material damage policy. Thus the constraints on the indemnities as described above follow precisely that material damage policy.

The second element of interest to the continuity manager is that the replacement of lost revenues and extra costs is over a period of time that is defined in the policy. This is called the indemnity period. At the end of that period, typically ranging from six months to a period of some years, cover ceases and the insured organisation is on its own. The cover that indemnifies the 'increased cost of working' is valuable to an insured that needs to spend additional sums to ensure that it stays credible within its marketplace and to its stakeholders. Such expenditure may, for example include marketing costs to keep the brand value alive, and the costs of outsourcing supplies that were previously built in-house. Clearly care needs to be taken to assess what is needed by way of adequate sum insured and that the chosen 'period of indemnity' is adequate to cover sufficient time needed to get back to normal. There is an important, additional constraint related to this period of indemnity. Any such increased expenditure must, to be recovered from the insurer, be 'economic' to the insurer. In other words that expenditure would need to bring about a reduction in the insurance claim of at least equal to the amount spent. Needless to say, the claim amount is constrained by both what is insured, and also the contracted period of the indemnity.

Boards, fighting to keep customers, and for their long-term foothold in their markets, often need to consider much longer timescales than the named indemnity period. The view therefore as to what is an economic spend may be entirely different between insured and insurer. Any investment in the future of the organisation that goes beyond the base policy protection - i.e., with a vision that goes beyond the policy's period of indemnity - must be at the insured's own cost. This is just at a time when revenues, assets, cash flows and even credit ratings are already under great strain.

Liability Covers

These policies will be structured to protect against the liabilities the insured may acquire to their employees and to third parties. They may arise following an accident or other injury in and around a wide definition of the 'workplace' and also liabilities to third parties following injuries, product failure, and the failure to satisfy professional standards in the services and advice given. The cover may be extended to the legal entity of the organisation itself, or to people while fulfilling the role of employees and also to the directors and officers of the company themselves.

This book is not the place for a detailed summary of aspects of liability insurances but there are a couple of important aspects for the risk manager when considering business survival exposures.

The first aspect to stress is the importance of the adequacy of the liability covers; both in the range of cover and in the adequacy of the limit of indemnity. Liability awards can be so large that they can be many times the net asset value of the organisation. In other words a successful claim combined with a failure of the insurance protection can destroy the very financial stability and lead to closure of the entire company. That insurance failure may not only be in the inadequacy of the limit of indemnity. Policies will have exclusion clauses. One exclusion, for example, may be claims brought in the jurisdiction of American or Canadian courts; another may exclude any products or services sold to the aviation industry.

Policies may also have warranties that will demand certain activities or controls must be maintained for the cover to remain in force. The task of the risk manager, and indeed it is a business survival issue, is to stay in touch with the detailed activities around the organisation and ensure that those activities remain within the insurance policy understandings. There is yet another cause for failure of the insurance; and that is when the insurer feels that the insured has not provided full information on the risk to be carried; either at inception of the policy or at each and every renewal date. This is another reason the risk manager needs to stay in touch with the minutiae of the organisation and ensure that all material changes in the risks and (insured and uninsured) loss experiences are fully disclosed.

Finally, in this flying visit to liability insurance we need to remember that insurance will never protect against a deliberate act. Fines by a regulator or the criminal justice system are not insurable. We made the point that the amount of any legal liability incurred will have no bearing on the free asset value of the organisation and may indeed be destructive of any financial ability to continue. This clearly places the adequacy of liability insurance as a business continuity risk issue. The first case study below illustrates some of the sums involved and is by no means the largest.

Case Study 1

Caledonia North Sea Ltd v (1) London Bridge Engineering Ltd; (2) Pickup No. 7 Ltd; (3) British Telecommunications PLC: (4) Wood Group Engineering Contractors Ltd. (5) Norton No. 2 Ltd (in liquidation) (6) Kelvin International services Ltd; (7) Coflexip Stena Offshore Ltd.

In July 1998 there was a fire and subsequent explosion on the oil platform, Piper Alpha, in the North Sea off Scotland. There was extensive damage and many employees were killed. Under the terms of contracts between the defendants and Caledonia, the operator of the oil platform, the defendants were liable to indemnify the latter in respect of damages paid to the contractor's employees. This was notwithstanding that (a) the contractors were not themselves negligent; (b) the operator had already been indemnified by their insurers, and (c) the damages that had been paid had exceeded the normal level of damages anticipated under Scots law. The insurers of Caledonia, having paid the claims exercised their rights under the subrogation condition that enabled them to recover any indemnities that their insured had been entitled to under contract law or in tort. The awards had been significantly enhanced because of the serious risk that further actions may be raised under Texan litigation. The insurers succeeded and the amount of the claim was £82,011,254.48.

The second case illustrates that it is not just the finite sum that catches the breath of an organisation but the relationship between that sum and the ability to pay and still be able to continue in business.

Case Study 2

(1) The Gleaner Company Ltd, and (2) Dudley Stokes V Eric Anthony Abrahams

Eric Abrahams, the Jamaican Minister of Tourism at the time, alleged that the Gleaner had, in 1987, published libellous articles about him. The Gleaner's defence of justification and qualified privilege failed and an award of J$80.7million (£1.2m) was made against them. This was reduced on appeal in 2003 to J$35m (£533,000) but this was significant and damaging when measured against the size of the company.

The Matches and Mismatches Between Insurance And Catastrophic Loss

To fully appreciate the value of insurance protections in catastrophic loss situations we need first to remind ourselves of the dependencies on the back of which an organisation continues to survive. These are the issues, rather than the cost of replacing buildings and machinery, that will drive the board's concentration during these difficult times. They are the issues which, if lost, will lead to the damage falling into the critical or catastrophic losses we describe above.

We have listed some dependencies that if lost could mean that the resultant damage could fall within our headline definitions of potentially critical or catastrophic loss. We return now to each of these 'features' of those definitions in turn and look for the place in this world of concerns for the conventional insurance market.

Time Out of Marketplaces While Workplaces Are Reinstated

Material damage insurance covers can provide the funds that will enable the rebuilding process to begin. The physical work of rebuilding has to go through many stages however before the factory of office is back in business 'as normal.' The site needs to be cleared. Decisions then have to be made on exactly how the new facility is to look; and planning approvals are very likely to be needed. Only then can the tender document be prepared, estimates obtained and negotiated, and decisions made again. There follows the wait until the builders or the machinery manufacturers can begin work and a further wait until the facilities are completed and delivered. Material damage insurance does not offer any assistance in meeting delivery problems during this wait; other than the infrequent use of business interruption policies; and the weaknesses of those policies are outlined above.

We have not included in the above the time needed when the board or managers may wish to take this opportunity now to investigate re-engineering the business and set out to consider moving, upsizing, downsizing, off-shoring, web enabling and other opportunities that they may feel have emerged directly as a result of the damage to existing infrastructures.

The 'time out' however may be caused by a failure that is not related to the loss of physical property. The supply chain, whether it is external or internal, can fail for a variety of reasons. They may include financial failure of a supplier, transport blockages such as the petrol strike in the United Kingdom, non-renewal of supply contracts and a failure of raw material supply. None of these exposures is insurable and therefore the organisation is facing these issues on its own

Fines By Regulatory Authorities or Worse,
The Loss Of Regulatory or Licence Approval

Fines and penalties are not insurable; neither is the often-greater resultant damage to confidence and brand values

Loss of Confidence In the Organisation Amongst the Client Base, Shareholders, Workforce and Other Stakeholders and In the Brand Name By the General Public

These exposures are not insurable as such. If the cause of the loss of confidence is, say a major fire, that fire itself will be insurable but the policy indemnities are usually restricted to the replacement of the physical things that were damaged by the fire itself. Policies do not go on to protect against the losses, many times more costly, when a consequence is that customers and other stakeholders lose confidence and walk away

Illegality Within A Business Operational Area

It is not normally possible to insure against becoming illegal; however unwittingly. This cause can bring about the fastest way that an organisation can come to a complete closure.

Delayed Access or Unrecoverable Loss Of Critical Information Or Other Intellectual Asset

We have made the point that information, whether it be corporate, customer, or other information, is the very lifeblood of a modern organisation; as is the ability to 'mine' that information in particular ways for marketing, management information, regulatory needs or otherwise business control. Intellectual assets are however not just data. We can extend the description to include computer software, designs, patents, research output and research verifications, audit trails for auditors and accountants, recipes, and current work on software, product and other developments. Certain contracts can be regarded also as an intellectual asset as indeed relationships and trust from the supply and delivery chain through to the wider list of stakeholders. The very reputation of the organisation can be described as an intellectual asset, with the brand dependencies of reputation, goodwill, credit rating, stock market analyst support, and, of course, the avoidance of media attack. Last but by no means least is the culmination of experience and skills right across the workforce.

These are crucial, business-threatening dependencies - yet insurance against the full cost of their loss is not generally available in the insurance market. Some insurance policies even set out to avoid indemnifying intellectual asset exposures by specific exclusions.

A common exclusion relates to lost data and can read as follows:

> *(excludes) 'loss from magnetic or electrical injury or disturbance to data processing media or erasure or disturbance of electronic records or distortion or corruption of information on computer systems or other records, programs or software.'*

The very thing that could cause the most destructive damage to a policyholder is therefore and by this clause excluded.

Significant Fall In Credit Rating

This may result from an 'insured loss' or a whole range of factors that would cause investment or credit analysts to downgrade the company. Again this loss, once more one that is significant enough to destroy business models, does not feature in the indemnities paid by insurers; even if the 'proximate cause' of the falling credit rating was a peril insured by one of the stable of insurance policies.

Financial Loss Sufficient To Threaten the Financial Stability Of the Organisation

In financial losses we are in the traditional realm of the insurer and one where it feels more comfortable. Financial losses can have many different causes however and the insurer needs to be assured that the cause of the loss falls within the cover provided by one of the policies in force. That policy may be a liability policy or a policy that covers stated material damage to physical property. If that initial cause is not one of the causes listed in the policy, the 'insured' is unprotected however large and destructive that loss.

Unacceptable Health and Safety Risk; Health And Safety Approvals For A Building Withdrawn

The insurer traditionally is concerned with the consequences of a risk incident. In other words if a person is injured, protections are available to cover any damages that may subsequently be needed to be paid.

The insurer does not however concern itself with situations arising before a death or injury; although it does expect and demand that the insured manages the health and safety risks with all seriousness.

Denial of access to a workplace due to health and safety management failures is not an insured peril. Again, the 'insured' is alone.

Significant Share Price Falls Changing the Financial Business Models.

The issue here, and the insurer's involvement, parallels the comments above regarding credit ratings.

Summary

In summary, the insurance market is undoubtedly useful for rebuilding balance sheets and revenues from losses caused by some damage and by some litigation. This use is for organisations looking to protect themselves against measures of financial loss that they cannot comfortably bear internally.

The real concern, however, is that such an insurance claim is useful to rebuild balance sheets only if the insured organisation is lucky enough - or well managed enough - to keep its dependencies going and thus actually survive a major loss. Should the organisation be neither lucky nor well-managed, the real value of the insurance claim is insignificant in the scheme of things that then unfold.

It is clear that the greatest damage that a major, modern, multinational can face is too often not monetary - it is operational and intellectual. It is clear that insurers, constitutionally are driven by the need to identify individual causes of damage whereas the continuity/risk managers are concerned primarily with the potential for destructive damage to one of the crucial cornerstones of the organisation's survival. This is a cause-versus-impact debate; and they are entirely different approaches.

To reinforce the point we list below the top 10 concerns that emerged from a 2005 survey by AON amongst the UK's top 2000 companies. (3) They are listed in order of importance, as perceived by the businesses themselves. It is sobering to those who believe insurance is the answer to all risk problems to consider to what extent, if any, these exposures can be able to be protected by insurance products.

1; Loss of reputation

2: Business interruption

3: Failure to change

4: Product liability/tamper

5: Impact of regulation/legislation

6: Physical damage

7: Employee accidents

8 Terrorism

9. Corporate Governance

10. Professional indemnity

Unless the underlying conflicts can be brought effectively together, insurance may continue to have very little real value in the survival stakes of the modern organisation.

It has not been possible within the constraints of one chapter in a book on business continuity to delve into the deeper theories and practices of the insurance industry. We have not attempted to explore the, as yet, relatively little–used, alternative risk transfer markets where money markets rather than insurance markets are used to transfer wholesale risk. This is a very specialized arena used mainly by insurers to transfer and swap insurance portfolio risks and also by only the very largest of multinationals that wish to even out financial results over longer periods of time.

We have set out, though to encourage the reader towards a realistic assessment of the values of a conventional insurance programme to a modern company and, above all, to be quite clear where insurance is not able to extend assistance to an organisation facing potentially catastrophic damage.

Food for thought is a quotation by Augustine who is reported to have said:

"There is no magical number that you can call to extricate yourself from such a predicament. You are in a fix and you get yourself out of that fix. It is that simple. There is no way to run a sausage machine backwards to get pigs out of the other end. After all if it were that simple it would not be a crisis."

The responsibilities for understanding and managing risk lie still and irrevocably within the organisation carrying those risks and sadly there are no easy options for passing those risks on to others. Too often, directors have been heard to say, "We do not need risk management as we have insurance." Food for more thought perhaps?

<u>Bibliography</u>

(1) Lee Coppack: Strategic Risk. October 2004

(2) Biennial Risk Management and Risk Management Survey. AON. 2003

(3) Biennial Risk Management and Risk Management Survey. AON. 2005

14

Communications

Objectives Of This Chapter Are To:

- Examine the role of communication
- Consider aspects of reputation
- Consider communication by stakeholder and the options available
- Gain an appreciation that building resilience applies to communication too
- Consider communication as part of the planning process
- Consider communication as part of the notification, invocation and recovery processes
- Evaluate the opportunities and threats associated specifically with the media
- Review the communications issues associated with team training, rehearsal and exercising

Communication And The Organisation

The ability to communicate is ranked the number one key to an organisation's success by leaders in business, government and the professions. "It can sell a point of view, gain media attention, win over an audience, make a sale or enhance one's career." **(1)**

In this Chapter we will examine internal communication and that external to an organisation as part of the planning process and post-incident.

All phases of the planning process require consistent and effective communication and yet in many of today's organisations cultural, management and organizational structure can all work against the effective achievement of this objective. Today many organisations have been intentionally engineered into highly diverse, decentralised and autonomous operating entities.

This can complicate a number of the fundamental principles of business continuity management. Business entities within an organisation can focus on their own strategies and objectives mindful of their own performance rather than that of the greater "corporation." This can render aggregate, cross-business criticalities that are notoriously difficult to identify and assess.

Communication - As Part Of The Business Continuity Planning Process

Typically many organisations operate vertical business and communication structures. In such structures, directions originate from the top and cascade down with information, decisions and resources flowing vertically from business units to top management. Units sit in between to oversee the vertical process and reduce the need for direct control by top management. Organisation-wide strategic planning and incentive systems reinforce the vertical nature of decision-making and control.

Impediments exist to achieving interrelationships within an organisation. (2)

The extent of impediments varies widely as a result of:

- Histories
- Mix of business
- Organisational structures
- Policies

The greatest difficulties seem to occur in the following conditions:

- Highly decentralised firms with many small business units
- Firms with a strong tradition of autonomy
- Firms that have made little or no effort to create a corporate identity
- Firms with conflicting cultures
- Firms with little or no history of interrelationships or who have had a bad experience in attempting to pursue an interrelationship

---

Horizontal organisations, on the other hand, overlay the business structure and facilitate collaboration amongst the business entities. Grouping mechanisms in such a structure might cluster certain business units, committees, policies and practices. This horizontal structure is not intended to undermine the decentralised approach but to supplement and exploit opportunities which come from converting aggregated opportunities.

One of the ways that a business continuity manager can overcome the barriers decentralised organisations can present is to use horizontal management structures to overcome barriers to communication. The business continuity planning "executive" or "steering group" can be created using existing patterns already embedded within the horizontal management framework. The purpose of lingering on this structural concept is to serve to reinforce how important it is for the business continuity manager to understand the strategy and structure of their organisation before venturing into the detail of their approach.

Traditionally business continuity management has been for many organisations a reactive process. Effective and efficient communications can transform this reactive position into one of proactivity and business continuity management as an integrated part of good management practice. It would be unusual for any organisation not to have some form of communications programme regarding business objectives. Given that business continuity management is focussed on supporting delivery of these objectives, the same scenario should apply.

Communication - Delivering The Message

The Dilbert Principle

"Any business school professor will tell you that the objective of business communication is the clear transfer of information. That's why professors rarely succeed in business."

Scott Adams (3)

While the quotation above was included to raise a smile, there is of course a serious message and a nugget of truth in that effective communication is indeed about clear transfer of information.

It is however rather more than this.

Effective communication is about *getting the right message to the right audience at the right time, in the most effective and efficient manner*. And to achieve effective communication it must overlay the structure for business continuity management within an organisation and form an issue for consideration at each stage of the planning process.

The Business Continuity Management Programme

The design of the overall programme should consider how the programme and its component parts will be communicated. A Board will be unreceptive to documentation and an implementation plan that offers no synergy with established policy and practices elsewhere within the organisation. Ask yourself:

- Are policies high-level or detailed?
- Are policies optional or compulsory?
- What degree of territorial or business division should be considered?
- Does the organisation encourage working through committees?

The answers to these questions will affect the approach that should be taken to programme design. While it might seem trivial, the business continuity manager should be aware of any organisation-wide or entity variation to communication style. This might include the use of type font and size, and the application of organisation identities - global, local, and by subsidiary. Small details perhaps, but nevertheless these can be important especially in larger organisations that take a keen interest in presentation "house style."

Consideration of which identity will appear on materials, including Board presentations, should be agreed by day one of the programme. The appearance of a third party name is not always a negative situation. It might be advantageous to encourage the use of an advisor identity - or shared identity - on presentation material and documentation, especially of the advisor is known to and respected by the Board.

Whatever tactic is pursued, the business continuity manager must avoid devolution of programme authority and ensure that a process of transfer of programme leadership and knowledge to the host organisation from the third party is agreed and delivered as part of the programme deliverables. Any reputable third party advisor will seek this transfer too.

At this stage of the process, development and communication of relevant case studies may help to sell buy-in to the programme at Board level, especially if case studies concern organisations that

Board members relate to, respect and admire. Communication should be focussed, relevant and where possible visually stimulating. Business continuity management will neither be their core discipline, nor possibly that high in their in-tray of priorities. Beside that, time on the agenda may be limited.

Understanding Your Business

Identification and cooperation from a wide variety of individuals and teams will be required to achieve the required level understanding of the business - from the Executive, through to Regional or Functional Coordinators and those who support the organisation such as Human Resources, Facilities and Information Technology.

Often viewed as "just another job I'm not paid to do," communication will need to focus on ensuring business continuity management is not viewed as a burden. Communications must be tailored to meet the needs of each of the players in the business continuity management planning infrastructure.

When a programme is established it will be helpful to have a position statement which demonstrates how the mission, vision and approach to business continuity management engages with the more general but similar statements within the organisation.

Communication with the Executive or Steering Group should be of a workshop style and delivered if possible via an interpersonal style rather than via remote means - however well executed. This team is critical to the success or failure of the programme's success and establishing the team should be viewed as an investment. Consequently, time spent in an interpersonal manner is time well invested.

Engagement of management layers beneath the Executive (business and support) will be most effective through business division and functional sponsors or champions who may also be best engaged, at least at the programme initiation stage in an interpersonal fashion.

As one travels down the vertical hierarchy of an organisation, communications can be more generic, while appreciating the need to explain and engage people in terms of their own role and responsibilities.

Communication at this level can be through newsletters, email, desk drops, etc., and must be sympathetic with the communication culture of the organisation. This may serve as an opportunity to provide background as preparation before workshops take place or questionnaires are issued to complete fact-finding for Business Impact Analyses. The path can have been paved to explain what business continuity management is, why information is required and what the role of each individual and team is within the overall planning process.

Business Continuity Strategies

There are a number of generic strategies to mitigate the impact of a disruption or reduce the probability of a threat event. Each strategy has parameters of speed of resumption, reliability of availability and cost. These will be appropriate to different parts of the business. Consequently, an organisation may require several elements to form an appropriate solution, depending upon the individual business functions.

The communications required in an organisation should be tailored to meet the needs of the strategies chosen, but the principles of communication at this stage of the planning process remain the same. It is during and after this stage of planning that most organisations focus their efforts on the design of their approach to communication.

Communication - The Board

The relevant role of the Board is to agree what should be protected and to accept or reject proposals in this respect. "If a crisis arises, the board and senior management should be able to show the public a company that is conscientious, caring and in control of the situation." **(4)**

Some members of the Board will have a role to play post-incident and they must be informed of what these roles might be to obtain their buy-in and agreement. In most organisations it will be the role of the Chairman to continue to steer an organisation post-incident. The role of the Chief Executive will be to offer operational leadership to employees and other key stakeholders including customers, shareholders, financial markets and as relevant, the media.

These roles must be explicit. If in the event of an incident there is ambiguity, confusion may arise which may impede the speed and success of response and recovery. The identification of alternates also applies to this level of an organisation. The Board should nominate a Board member who might be required to step into the Chief Executive's shoes, who is the most appropriate in terms of knowledge of the organisation and interpersonal skills.

The Board must be trained to perform the roles they are allocated, especially if this involves direct contact with the media. The ability of the leader of the organisation to communicate effectively could be the difference between the life and death of an organisation.

The factors that might influence an organisation's ability to recover have been the subject of considerable research and it is evident from this that the "management factor" including the quality of communication, has an influence on the effectiveness of response and recovery. "Management is placed in the spotlight and has an opportunity to demonstrate its skill or otherwise in an extreme situation." **(5)**

Whatever roles and responsibilities might be agreed in advance of an incident, an organisation must accept the fact that if an incident involves the death or injury of employees, or is of such magnitude that it might affect the future viability of the organisation, the Chief Executive is likely to want to take command of the situation immediately post notification and response. This is a natural reaction on their part and rather than resist an immovable force, this potential response must be factored into planning and communication strategies.

Commitment to business continuity management and the communication of this must come from the top. Communication to employees must bear the name of the relevant Board member, which in most organisations will be the Chief Executive or equivalent. Without this support it is unlikely that the hearts and minds of employees will be captured and they may fail to see and grasp the importance of the subject.

The rising tide of regulation and interest of key customers is likely to add an impetus to the Chief Executive's desire to understand this business continuity and his organisation's response. This interest has in many organisations put business continuity management in the spotlight and assisted, where necessary, in making the Chief Executive own the subject at the most senior level. While there is a benefit in the added energy this brings to the business continuity programme, this interest can place additional pressures on the business continuity manager, and where evidence of compliance with regulatory guidelines is required, an additional burden.

The knock-on effect is that the skills of the business continuity manager must be up to the job!

The style of communication at this level will depend on the state of maturity of business continuity within an organisation.

At the start of a programme a "kick-off" communication might include a "letter from the desk of the Chief Executive" or a prominent article in a regular newsletter. Where business continuity is at a stage of maturity, reference may be made in established internal and external publications, such as the annual report and accounts as part of the section on corporate governance and risk management.

Whatever the state of maturity and style of organisational management structure is deployed, (vertical, horizontal or a combination), messages should be consistent and set out the scope of the organisation to which the message applies. Messages from the top of an organisation should also demonstrate the devolution of authority from the Chief Executive to the business continuity manager to perform their role and deliver their responsibilities. Consequently, getting these messages right is time well spent.

Finally, the Board should ensure that communication is two-way. The Board should demand that progress reports are made on a regular basis to the Board against business continuity programme deliverables, measures of plan fitness and performance, including invocations of a defined nature and scale and relevant "near misses."

Communication - The Business Continuity Steering Group/Executive

The role at this level of planning is to ask the business stream in an organisation what they do and why they do it. Further they will consider the costs associated with protection and make provision for what is agreed in terms of resilience and recovery capability. Finally this group has a responsibility to check that what has been agreed is in place and working.

This is the level at which it is most likely that the overall business continuity communication strategy for an organisation will be agreed.

Business continuity strategy is usually driven by a Steering Group or Committee. The composition of this group will be driven by the scale, complexity, nature and geographical coverage of an organisation.

In the larger corporations this might comprise vertical, regional, business, and technical representatives together with horizontal functional heads such as human resources, information technology, facilities, finance, risk and communications. Leadership and facilitation will be provided by the business continuity manager.

The group should communicate its existence to the organisation. This can be achieved through a letter, newsletter or email depending on the organisation's approach to communication.

Consideration should be given to posting details of the group on the organisation's corporate intranet web site and if this exists, the web site dedicated to risk or business continuity management, together with the group's terms of reference, individual "CVs" and photographs.

Communication - Stakeholders - Internal

A communication strategy should set out the Mission and Vision of business continuity management, which should be sympathetic in style and content to those more generally of the organisation, its approach to governance and risk management, and how these interrelate.

The business continuity management approach must not be counter-culture to the organisation as this will potentially dilute the programme's success. Those receiving communication must be able to identify the approach with "business as usual." In times of uncertainty and disruption, a response that has a degree of familiarity will have a greater chance of success than an approach however innovative, which is unfamiliar.

"The same people who are accountable for normal business operations are accountable for business continuity planning. The existing organisation should be leveraged using everyday systems to build and maintain plans. Existing corporate resources should be leveraged including the intranet, communications vehicles, databases and directories. All of this will help business continuity planning to be 'baked into' normal business operations." **(6)**

Part of the responsibility at this level of planning is the commission and sponsorship of whatever is adopted by way of business continuity standards - including a glossary of terms. There is a mixed reaction professionally as to whether the adoption of a glossary constitutes good practice. Various external Institute and Standards-sponsored glossaries exist.

As a mechanism for ensuring clarity across vertical organisations, especially with diverse businesses and geographic considerations, a glossary can provide the foundation for a common level of understanding and language. To ensure effectiveness, a glossary might adopt an element of "industry" language coupled with that specific to the organisation - for example team naming conventions may vary.

Business continuity managers have an array of communication medium options available to them including:

- Written
- Electronic
- Verbal
- Visual
- Auditory

An organisation's communications suite might include:

Static Communications

- A letter from the CEO
- Articles in newsletters or employee magazines
- Videos and CDs
- Posters (especially during Business Continuity Awareness Week)
- Desk drops
- Mouse pads and desk accessories
- Notes for contractors and visitors
- Letters or newsletters to customers and intermediaries
- Information printed on security passes
- Information on organisation-wide, territorial and dedicated web sites
- Features on knowledge management exchanges

- Press releases
- Web-based messages: internal
- Web-based messages: external

Interactive Communications

- Key messages implanted in the Performance Management System
- Key messages implanted in Strategic and Operational planning
- Presentations to key influencers
- Discussions and focus group meetings with key managers
- Business games
- Training packs including work books
- Workshops
- Rehearsals and exercises

Communications cover a range of options which can be used individually or collectively, but the option should match the need.

Communications from the CEO to all employees should usually be simple, perhaps in the form of a letter that confirms their support and ultimate responsibility. This might also set out the organisation's position and confirm formally how authority for the subject is devolved.

A document setting out an organisation's overview to planning and how each major territory or business unit fits might work best as a newsletter or brochure.

A message on security passes that confirms numbers that might be required by every employee (and contractor) in the event of an incident and the invocation of plans might comprise just one line and a contact number. Similar messages can be produced on stickers for PCs, lap tops, telephones (home and at work) and "Blackberries."

The policy for business continuity management adopted by an organisation should be accessible to all. Intranet sites and notice boards probably form the most often used mechanism for communication. The overall risk and business continuity framework will most likely comprise a series of subordinate policies, internal standards, tools, techniques and a suite of management information reports. These more technical documents might also be located on an intranet site or embedded within any software package that an organisation might deploy for business continuity planning, or simply in a hard copy manual which is distributed with relevant document distribution and control. Where possible, this type of document should be protected to avoid uncontrolled amendment and modification. The business continuity programme might adopt a theme or "strap line," thereby building up recognition of the programme. For example:

- Bad things can happen to good companies
- Keeping the continuity in business
- Planning for success

Communication Is A Two-Way Process

Organisations should seek feedback on how well business continuity management is performing in both qualitative and quantitative means.
Quality assurance will receive more in-depth attention in a later Chapter, but the value of these mechanisms should not be overlooked in terms of the communication process.

Communications to the CEO should include success stories, failures, near misses, rehearsals and tests as well as examples of incidents that have touched other relevant organisations and external authorities such as Government and Regulators. This information, supplementary to any agreed score cards or metrics will keep the subject alive and on the Board table, and contribute towards the rationale for management and budgetary support.

Feedback should be encouraged from the Executive or steering group on the documentation that supports the organisation's approach to planning including how each major territory or business unit fits in. This group will provide the information to the Board and they should be encouraged to respond to the results they feed in and the format in which these are presented. This will ensure that documentation and reporting remain fresh and relevant.

Line managers should be encouraged to consider issues associated with continuity as part of the strategic and operational planning and performance management mechanisms of the organisation. Output from these processes will provide insight to the business continuity manager regarding potential impacts to the business.

Feedback from employees should be encouraged, especially following rehearsals, exercises and incidents. This type of feedback might be fed back to all employees via articles in newsletters and facilitated discussion as part of departmental and team meetings.

Communication - Stakeholder - External

Communication is not only an inward-looking process. Before we leave pre-incident communication we will take a brief look at what external communications an organisation should be aware of.

We addressed the subject of stakeholders in Chapter Two. The reader will recall that an organisation has a range of different stakeholders who are like lifeblood and are the real beneficiaries of the work to be done in risk assessments, the business impact analyses and recovery planning. While all may have a stake, their needs and interests will vary.

As reputational risk arises from a mismatch between what a company does and the reasonable expectations of its stakeholders, there should be an effort made to ensure that the company's plans and those expectations are aligned as far as is practical, or at the least not incompatible.

An organisation must understand current and emerging needs of stakeholders' expectations. "Many cases of reputational damage are incremental, the result of the neglect of a particular stakeholder relationship, or perhaps a number of small incidents building up and gradually undermining the external perception of the company." **(7)**

The Management Principle

"The art of management consists of issuing orders based on inaccurate, incomplete and archaic data, to meet a challenge which is dimly understood and which will frequently be misinterpreted; to accomplish a purpose about which many of the personnel are not enthusiastic."

General William Reader

It is not the role of the business continuity manager to manage all the relationships with stakeholder groups in an organisation, but it is their responsibility to understand the "map" of current and emerging stakeholder interests for an organisation and to ensure that lines of communication exist between those "owners" and business continuity management.

Managers in the horizontal structures of an organisation are often best positioned to form part of the business continuity management Executive or steering group - as they have a wide-angle view of the organisation.

This will ensure that business continuity management retains a focus and that plans are "coordinated with Corporate Communications and HR – don't let your message get lost in the noise." **(8)**

On occasion, the business continuity manager will have an interest in specific issues arising from stakeholders.

For example, customers may set specific requirements of business continuity performance as part of their contract with an organisation. Shareholders may require a report of business continuity performance levels as part of the governance framework and external annual reporting process.

Regulators, while not in the business of setting standards for business continuity, will certainly have an interest in the subject which may be at an intense level if the organisation is perceived to be of high level interest (defined by the Financial Services Authority (FSA) in the UK as a "Core" or "Significant" firm). The business continuity manager must be aware of these specific needs and ensure that processes are in place to deliver communication to agreed levels and standards.

The resilience of organisations that support national or industry resilience is a valuable source of information for the business continuity manager.

The press releases and business plans of these entities provide direction and expectations that should be considered and built into the business continuity plans of those organisations touched by these entities.

Case Study

Euroclear* is to launch a state-of-the-art business continuity programme

Brussels 13 October 2003

"Euroclear is pleased to announce that it will implement a new, state-of-the-art business continuity programme over the coming years that will strengthen safeguards for the financial markets against operational failure due to physical or other disaster. This programme, which will represent an investment of over EUR 100 million, is based on new standards that Euroclear has defined in the aftermath of September 11.

These key standards include the use of three data centres to store and process transactions for clients ... of the Euroclear group, and the spread of critical business expertise across several distant locations.

These new arrangements will enable each of the Euroclear entities to resume their technical operations within one hour of a local disaster or within three hours of a major regional disaster that disables both of the primary data centres ......

...... In addition, Euroclear intends to spread the business expertise of critical functions across several office locations situated at a sufficient distance from each other to avoid the risk that they could all be impacted by a single local disaster ... "

* Euroclear is the marketing name for the Euroclear System, Euroclear plc, Euroclear Bank and their affiliates. Euroclear is the world's largest settlement system for domestic and international securities transactions, covering both bonds and equities. Market owned and market governed, Euroclear provides securities services to major financial institutions located in more than 80 countries.

Each year the Financial Services Authority (FSA) in the UK issues a Financial Risk Outlook and associated business plan. This provides insight into the context and key priorities of the FSA and is essential reading for any business continuity manager - within or outside of financial services. Full of useful information on social, legal and regulatory trends, most organisations will have interest in the financial sector's continuity and resilience.

Important to the health of the UK economy, financial services have been designated as one of the five "essential services" by the Government. Following an incident, people and businesses will need to draw cash, make and receive payments, borrow and lend, settle deals and raise capital.

The UK financial Sector authorities publish a variety of documents that set out their respective roles and responsibilities and the collective and individual business plans targeted to achieve delivery of these.

Financial sector dependencies documented by the FSA, Bank of England and the Treasury include:

- Physical infrastructure
- International
- Telecommunications
- Public authorities and emergency services

The business continuity manager must be aware of how authorities' plans would respond following a major disruption and where they fit into these.

The UK financial Sector authorities publish a variety of documents that set out their respective roles and responsibilities and the collective and individual business plans targeted to achieve delivery of these.

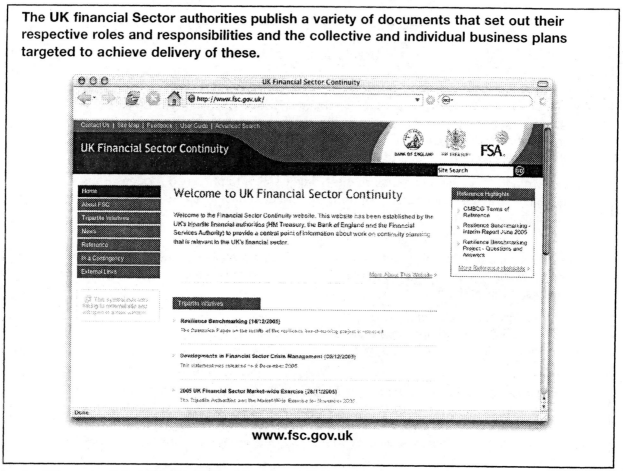

www.fsc.gov.uk

In the US, on April 7, 2003, the Federal Reserve, Office of the Controller of the Currency (OCC) and Securities and Exchange Commission (SEC) issued the "Interagency Paper on Sound Practices to Strengthen the Resilience of the U.S. Financial System." **(9)** The paper identified three new business continuity objectives for all financial institutions with special importance in the post-9/11 risk environment. It also identified four sound practices to ensure the resilience of the U.S. financial system.

These practices focus on minimizing the immediate systemic effects of a wide-scale disruption on critical financial markets.

The three business continuity objectives are:

- Rapid recovery and timely resumption of critical operations following a wide-scale disruption;

- Rapid recovery and timely resumption of critical operations following the loss or inaccessibility of staff in at least one major operation location; and

- A high level of confidence, through ongoing use or robust testing, that critical internal and external continuity arrangements are effective and compatible.

As a minimum each plan must address:

- Data backup and recovery;

- All mission-critical systems;
- Financial and operational systems;
- Alternate communications between customers and the member;
- Alternate communications between the member and its employees;
- Business constituent, bank and counter-party impact;
- Regulatory impact; and,
- Communication with regulators.

Of the eight requirements, three are specifically communications-focussed.

Communication - As Part Of The Notification, Invocation And Recovery Processes

On paper the response to an incident looks quite straightforward:

- Receive notification of problem
- Assess the situation and either respond through plans or invoke crisis management team

If a response is required are you in a fit position to manage it, is support from others required, and is it necessary to communicate the matter upwards?

There should, however, be no assumption made that those responsible for drafting the plans are the most qualified to lead an invocation.

The characteristics of successful crisis management include:

- The demonstration of decisive remedial action
- Access to the right information
- A consistent corporate message
- A full appreciation of the needs of all stakeholders
- The ability to admit to mistakes
- High speed in response
- High speed in communications
  - Synstar **(10)**

At the end of 2004, one of the most severe disasters in terms of loss of life struck the world - the South Asia Tsunami.

Had effective early warning and response mechanisms been in place, one must speculate the impact this might have had in terms of lives lost.

Case Study

Grand Cayman is a small island but an important global financial centre. During the development of Category 5 hurricane Ivan in September, 2004 winds in excess of 200 miles an hour were recorded. As the hurricane hit, these winds joined with a tidal surge causing a devastating effect to the island.

Modern tracking systems such as the web-based TSR **(11)** meant that there was sufficient warning of the storm and its likely path for response plans to be invoked and escalated. Property was secured and hurricane shutters erected - although there was still considerable damage.

In advance of the storm hitting the island many financial institutions relocated their vital functions to other centres such as the Channel Islands off the coast of the UK. Professional staff members on leave outside the island were called in to operate the functions at these other centres, given that leaving the island proved difficult.

Saturation of documents and restrictions in the ability to move documents "off-shore" caused considerable problems. Where documents could be removed these were taken variously to Canada and Switzerland - especially where the US was "out of bounds." IT recovery was less problematic for most and the use of generators to provide backup power capability meant restoration for many within a day of the storm.

"Few Cayman firms appear to have had formal business continuity plans in place. The recovery of most appears to have been due more to the rapid response of senior management and a tremendous effort by staff, but with a considerable degree of improvisation. Some of the many challenges here can teach valuable lessons in business continuity planning." **(12)**

In the Pacific, where extraordinary weather-related incidents are experienced on a reasonably regular basis, there are some early warning and response mechanisms in place that have been deployed on a regular basis.

The concept of early warning and response mechanisms is, however, not confined to natural disasters.

Organisations must acknowledge that as with natural disasters, managing the response to a major incident begins much sooner than the incident itself. There are a number of actions an organisation can take as part of their communications preparedness:

- Be prepared before an indent happens.
- Conduct a risk assessment to consider what key risks might exist - and those which might emerge.
- Perform rehearsals and exercises with mock scenarios, spokespersons and stakeholders - including a realistic worst-case scenario.
- Decide who your spokesperson is - prepare that person with practice by aiming hard questions at them.

Questions from stakeholders are usually predictable - and while it is not possible (or indeed advisable) to second-guess all questions, being prepared will help if and when the worst occurs. Lessons learned from scenarios and exercises should be reviewed and as appropriate absorbed within the planning, notification and response processes.

Research **(13)** suggests that businesses are endangering their reputations through a muddled approach to communications during a crisis.

- Under half of the UK businesses surveyed involve communications professionals in the management of crisis communications.

- Half rely on the already over-burdened services of a business continuity manager or another senior business manager to resolve critical situations and communicate with both internal and external audiences.

- 58 percent would only nominate someone who is media trained to deal with everyday press enquiries. (One might expect this to be 100%)

- One-third of spokespersons are selected according to their area of crisis expertise rather than seniority. (This can be good or bad: experts may lack authority and senior management may lack relevant knowledge).

- 14 percent would wait until it would influence their share price or their investor relations if nothing was said. (Research indicates that this position could lead to corporate melt-down!).

- 39 percent would only release a statement when they had 'something to say,' by way of an update on how the crisis was being resolved.

- Just under half of senior IT business and business continuity managers would issue a statement to the media at a point when the crisis would affect their employee, supplier or customer relationships if they did not.

"The essence of crisis communications is keeping all those involved updated so that they are able to make informed and educated decisions regarding the respective incident. A business continuity manager can be doing everything to contain a situation but leaked information to employees, suppliers or the press can quickly undo this hard work." **(14)**

Communicating Immediate Actions - Key Internal Stakeholders

- **Employees:**

In the immediate aftermath of a business threatening event, an organisation needs to invoke its business continuity plans and organise the recovery.

Communicating 'immediate actions' and important information is vital to the overall success of the process. This stage is a critical factor as part of a successful recovery and an organisation should carry out a specific pre-incident assessment on its ability to effectively communicate on a large scale in a short time frame.

There are a number of methods and systems that can be deployed to address this critical issue, each with specific risks. The traditional method of communicating rapidly with large numbers of people is the so-called 'cascade,' where a message is relayed in sequence from person to person. For example, one person may call three; that three then call six; and so on.

Manual Cascades Are Slow

People often underestimate the amount of time needed to make contact. Even if people are available the time taken to contact even small numbers of people is usually measured in hours, not minutes.

Manual cascades, whatever modern communication technology is used, are subject to distortion, misinterpretation and confusion. Stress and language differences often colour a person's perception of a message and the context in which it is delivered.

Survival Of The Fastest - (15)

The growth of cyber-crime brings with it a huge challenge for e-business. Threats change daily while technology changes yearly. And increasingly it is not teenagers who are hacking into systems, but organised crime. The stability of risk is not something you can even consider as part of the planning process.

Despite the serious level of risk many companies are finding their IT departments have neither the expertise nor the time to provide adequate security. And sporadic checks may not be enough. For security to work you have to be scanning the infrastructure almost all the time. Having multiple levels of defence in place is the only solution.

Most experts concur that outsourcing of security services will grow rapidly as companies stop trying to run their own. All of these issues emphasise the importance of rapid detection and response. Traditional techniques of notification, escalation and response need to be challenged to meet the pace required for response to such issues. Communication needs to step up to the task.

There is also a significant risk of a message being out of date by the time it is delivered. Crises are dynamic events, and effective command and control relies on rapid communication. The lack of dynamism in manual cascades is a significant constraining factor.

"Like ripples on the surface of a pond, once a manual cascade utilising multiple levels is started, the ripples can only go outwards. If the message needs to be changed, updated or stopped, it simply cannot be done effectively with this method." (16) And has the message got through, and is it being acted upon? Feedback loops are difficult in manual cascades, and critical information on which to base reactions and further response can be unreliable, or unavailable.

Business continuity managers have realised that they can deploy technology to address the shortcomings of manual cascades, but these systems should be carefully assessed. If technology is being relied upon to deliver a critical element of an organisation's recovery capability, resilience is a key requirement. Equipment must be effectively maintained, suitably located, and easy to use, with robust telecommunications and accessible 24/7. Furthermore, staff need to able to remember it is there and how to access it.

Automated systems must be protected against accidental and malicious use. Security should include access to the equipment and the data held on it with access restricted to competent and authorised personnel.

The power of the web should not be underestimated. This is an additional communication channel, accessible by many from work or home - messages can be placed with great agility and an organisation has the confidence of knowing that messages are effectively controlled, consistent and timely.

Most large organisations will have some form of telephone line that employees (and their families) can call to ascertain the status of an incident, whether their organisation is involved and what they should do. Messages can be updated quickly, but as with the web, this is not be an interactive communications vehicle and therefore messages must typically be generic.

A number of suppliers do provide a more interactive, call-centre-styled response service, but even here the telephonists will be working from a script. That said, following an incident people may find it more reassuring speaking to another person rather than listening to a recorded message.

As part of the response process, if an organisation offers support to employees and family through an Employee Assistance Programme (EAP), communication of this can be via a card and pre-arranged telephone number, providing immediate access to qualified assistance on a range of services, including counselling.

Communicating Immediate Actions - Key External Stakeholders

- **Shareholders:**

Shareholders will want an assessment of any impact on the ability of the organisation to deliver shareholder value, business objectives and targets of performance. They will be tuning into the communications delivered to the general public concerning the overall event. Specific communications might include a letter from the Chairman, or if sufficiently important an extraordinary general meeting.

The annual report provides an opportunity for comment and reflection and as applicable, an assessment of the impact on the shareholder value and profit earnings of the organisation.

- **Markets:**

Markets and analysts, as well as rating agencies, may demand specific briefings - especially if an organisation is already on watch or on the threshold of a particular rating level. Analysts will have responsibilities to their investors and their needs must be sympathetically addressed.

Generally the longer an organisation takes to deliver a message to this group of stakeholders, the more detailed and reliable these stakeholders will expect the message to be. They will be forgiving of high-level impact assessments in early days but less so as time progresses.

These stakeholders might usefully be segmented and communications tailored according to the nature of their interest and relevance to the organisation: key stakeholders may benefit from a face-to-face briefing delivered by a suitable senior person, such as the Chief Executive, Finance Director, Head of Corporate Communications or Investor Relations.

- **Regulators:**

Regulators will vary in the degree of sophistication of response and need for knowledge. In markets such as those of the US, UK, Singapore and Japan, the regulators may establish lines of communication in anticipation of delivering their role in wider plans for national response. Organisations that are considered significant may be required to communicate their recovery status.

Tripartite Action in the UK

- In the event of major operational disruption to the financial system, the authorities' main objectives would be to keep financial markets open and functioning except where this is physically impossible or where by so doing there would be a material threat to financial stability, and would facilitate an early return to trading, for example by seeking to ensure the availability of reliable information

- The main role of the Financial Services Authority (FSA) would be to monitor the health of individual institutions which fall within its regulatory remit and ensure continuing regulatory compliance:

- In the first instance individual financial institutions should communicate with the authorities via their normal business or supervisory contacts.

- In the event of an incident the authorities would aim to use the fsa.gov.uk website as a vehicle for communicating key messages

    - Tripartite Standing Committee on Financial Stability

    - Progress Report, October, 2004

- **Suppliers:**

Business continuity planning for suppliers and outsource providers was considered in Chapter Ten. Lines of communication may concern those from the organisation to their supplier seeking extended credit terms if in distress, cessation of supplies if manufacturing/assembly has been disrupted, or to request additional supplies if stock items or work in progress have been destroyed.

Communication may also, however, involve the supplier advising an organisation that they have suffered an incident and are unable to honour supplies or services for which they have been contracted. Whatever the message, clear lines of communication are the key issue. Focal points available 24/7 with suitable telecommunications equipment and backup by alternates should exist within each entity. These should act as the conduit through which standby warnings of an impending disruption or notification, escalation and invocation of plans should be made.

Depending on the nature of the incident, timing and close cooperation between entities could be critical - for example in the event of a product defect and subsequent recall. In such circumstances the entities must work in harmony to ensure consistent messages and the timing of release of these. It may be the high profile organisation's reputation that is at stake through the failure of the more anonymous supplier.

- **Customers:**

The majority of customers will see events that affect organisations they do business with emerging in real time on satellite or terrestrial television following an incident. But there may be situations where the customer is unaware that their supplier is affected - where an incident affects a large area or where the incident is sufficiently detached from the customer. For example, organisations that use off-shore outsource providers may be impacted by a natural disaster and the customer is unaware of the connectivity. Organisations must communicate with customers thoughtfully:

A manufacturer's or retailer's product recall demands swift and accurate communication where customers are most likely to see it - for example, newspapers of appropriate demographic distribution, radio or television.

A retailer that suffers a fire may decide to undertake door drops with leaflets in the immediate catchment area of the store indicating when service might be resumed, and where in the interim customers can find an alternative outlet.

A financial services organisation must take care not to create a drama out of its crisis. Customers who deal with a remote call centre may be unaware of the organisation's disruption - especially if telephone calls are answered by the organisation seamlessly switching calls to an alternative location.

An outlet of a chain of retailers, bank or other service provider may direct customers via letter, email, telephone and local advertisements to the outlet in the next town or to a temporary location established in a mobile facility.

There is no single answer to customer communications but there are a number of principles and communications should:

- Be simple and unambiguous.
- Use the most appropriate medium.
- Be timely and repeated as necessary to reinforce the message.
- Be careful to avoid creation of problems where they otherwise do not exist.
- Consider incentives for customers to continue to do business.
- Create the impression of a planned response with control and confidence.
- Be prepared and "print ready."
- Announce recovery as appropriate, for example, a return to the usual trading location.

Case Study

Product recall: Sudan dyes are red dyes used for colouring solvents, oils, waxes, petrol, and shoe and floor polishes. They have been found in some chilli powder imported from India. They have also been found in a number of food products containing this chilli powder. Sudan dyes are not allowed to be added to food in the UK and the rest of the European Union.

One of the largest product recalls in the history of the UK was triggered by the discovery that the harmless-sounding "Sudan 1" food dye, a potential carcinogenic, was present in a 2002 batch of chilli powder used as an ingredient to make Worcester Sauce.

Four hundred and forty seven products had been recalled as of 24 February 2005 and several major retailers were affected.

At issue was the speed and effectiveness of the crisis management plans that retailers have. An example of this is the way that the supermarket chain Tesco was able to minimise the effects through forward planning and allocating an electronic "emergency product withdrawal" flag on its systems.

When an alert was raised by product buyers a report was automatically sent over their network which was then printed off in stores as a high-priority job, alerting staff to remove goods from shelves and warehouses. If in the meantime, a customer was trying to purchase a related product, a warning came up on the check-out operators' screens saying that the product could not be sold and that it should be removed from the customer's purchases.

The UK Government Foods Standards Agency (FSA), however, was criticised for being slow in issuing a public statement – it took nearly two weeks.

The following statement appears on the Food Standards Agency website 3 July 2003 (17) - an early warning signal?

"Food Standards Agency Scotland has alerted stakeholders to a European Commission decision relating to the dye Sudan I in hot chilli products. The dye is not a permitted food colour in the European Union, and is a suspected genotoxic carcinogen."

Managing the Media

Ari Fleischer, a former White House press secretary, has a unique view of crisis communications. During his time at the White House, he worked through the September 11th attacks, two wars, and economic turbulence. What was his most challenging media briefing? "No question about it, and this surprises most people, the anthrax briefings. The reason for this is because I didn't know the answers to the questions. Even on 9/11 and when we went to war with Iraq, I knew what I was going to say. For anthrax, we didn't know what was going on, and that's the hardest briefing to handle…one where you don't know the answers."

And his best piece of advice? "Dig in deep, learn the facts, find out what the truth is, and share everything you possibly can." **(18)**

A number of practical pointers should be deployed:

- Take good care of the press' logistics and needs - it's important to make the press' life trouble-free and that you recognise their deadlines and technological needs

- Recognise that the press has a hard job to do - the more people that can help with all the detail, the better

- Reporters are human - they need a good work environment just like anybody else

- Consider establishing a pre-arranged, dedicated press room

- Response teams should work towards an objective of regaining the confidence of the outside world that they are in control

Managing the Media

It is likely in major incidents that the media will approach staff. It is vital to contact all staff at once and remind them that all enquiries should be directed immediately to officials who have been trained specifically. Below are some "do's and don'ts" when dealing with the press.

No one should communicate with the media unless they have authorisation. Authorised persons will always ensure that they have the latest correct information. It is often vital to give an immediate reminder to all staff together with the contact numbers of the authorised spokespersons. In the face of either a formal or informal enquiry they should be advised simply to inform anyone of these contact numbers.

- Do move fast. Time is critical. Collect all the available facts of the crisis in order before formulating your response to the nominated Press Officer

- Do alert the nominated Press Officer immediately

- Do take guidance from a trained person who can work closely with you to manage the crisis. Unless you are an authorised spokesman already, or have been given temporary authorisation to speak to the media, all press contact should be handled by such nominated person(s)

- Do alert your switchboard and tighten up lines of communication in your location or business unit. Centralise the flow of communications and establish lines of communication with the PR team and, if authorised, the media

- Do establish your crisis team and formulate a strategy and options for handling the crisis

- Do ensure that, if you or one of your team is authorised to be a media spokesman, he or she is available 24 hours with contact numbers for the media

- Do keep your eye on the ball; try to concentrate on the main problem and how to solve it

- Do avoid paranoia. Be reasonable, calm and cooperative. If you are authorised to speak to the media, keep cool; never lie, speculate or be bounced into an unwise statement. Remember the media have a job to do and they will get angry and frustrated if you ignore or do not respect their deadlines

- Do not try to manage the crisis on your own in the early stages, thinking that you can handle it. The 'snowball' effect in crisis management can be dramatic and fast

- Do not ignore media calls - they will not go away! Always log them and inform the spokesperson who will be acting as 'Air Traffic Control.' Never feel obliged to talk to a journalist. Tell the journalist that an authorised spokesperson will get back to them as soon as possible

- Do not give press interviews, even if you are ambushed in the street, the pub, outside your office or at home, unless you are authorised to do so and have the relevant facts to hand. Beware of idle gossip to friends, family or colleagues about the crisis. Journalists pick up more leads through this route more than any other

Keep your messages short and simple.

An organisation should take time out to identify, authorise and ensure availability of those who may act as spokespersons for an organisation and then ensure that they are properly trained.

This type of training, while important, can be fun and a good opportunity for team building across the crisis management team.

Apart from press conferences, contact with the press can be achieved through timely and informative press releases. Information that is factual and professionally delivered will be more positively received.

Case Study

Fire at Deloitte Office Tower in Madrid, February 14, 2005.

A building fire in Madrid destroyed the local Deloitte office. In response, Deloitte Spain issued the following communication:

"Deloitte greatly appreciates the work of the fire, police and emergency departments for ensuring the safety of all its professionals and building residents. There have been no casualties reported as a result of this fire.

Currently, our Madrid office is working to recover its IT and information systems. We have activated contingency plans, which include the help and support of Deloitte Touche Tohmatsu, our global office.

Except for the local phone lines and other communication sources in Madrid, all other Deloitte offices in Spain have not been affected. Communications from our Madrid office are being redirected to other firm locations, as part of the contingency plans.

Most Deloitte professionals in Madrid will resume work on Monday. Client service operations will not be impacted by this event. All 19 Deloitte offices outside Madrid will continue with their normal operations.

Deloitte has started researching several options for the new location of its Madrid office. The Firm expects to resolve this situation in a few days.

Deloitte thanks the unconditional support and collaboration from its clients, suppliers and professionals, which is helping the Firm to normalize its activity.

Deloitte will make further official communications through www.deloitte.com or its online Spanish press room, accessible via http://deloitte.acceso.com."

Communicating with the media is one area where consideration should be seriously given to using external expertise. Most organisations are confident in dealing with the familiar such as core business issues. However, following an incident an organisation will be faced with the unfamiliar. Having the opportunity to call on the experience of those who are familiar with facing the media will not remove the need for representatives of the organisation to act as spokespersons, but they may do so with greater confidence and reassurance.

Experts used for media management purposes should be validated as part of the planning process against the reason for their use in terms of competence (technical, security, safety, financial, scientific) and independence.

And in this electronic age organisations should not underestimate the value that may be harnessed by using their web site. With an ability to match the speed of an incident emerging, web sites can provide an additional and often under-used source for communication, "allowing you to talk directly to your stakeholders and the public at large without having to run the gauntlet of journalists firing questions." **(19)**

Web-based technology can offer an organisation the ability to tell their story and get across key messages in a visible, accountable way, without the risk of editing. And suppliers exist that can offer "E-emergency services" with advice on how-to-do-it, how-to-say-it and how-to-manage-it using the web.

Team Training, Rehearsal and Exercising

Most training is delivered through a combination of remote learning and presentations. The nature of the training and the medium used should match the need of the audience and be relevant to the position of those being trained in the business continuity management "food chain." If training is not positioned in this way, the audience may consider that the issues covered are too remote and consequently so unlikely as to be irrelevant, and the message will be lost.

There is a role for external consultants in these processes and their experience may prove valuable in the design of training, rehearsals and exercises. A consultant will also potentially prove helpful in training the trainer, although an organisation should always retain responsibility for delivering such events and their facilitation.

Interaction is the most effective way of ensuring that learning sticks and there are a number of options that an organisation can take. Classroom-style sessions can work but there are some interesting software packages available **(20)** that can not only support the classroom but may be used in times of invocation to guide and offer support.

Whatever solution is selected, a range of questions should be identified that allow a team to prepare strategy, appearance and responses - with suitable exercises designed to test these out and the fitness of those who might be called into the spotlight.

Summary

There is a clear difference between crisis management and crisis communication: the story in the headlines should be about the response, not the crisis.

Catastrophe leads to a unique opportunity for an organisation to be revalued due to the excess of unusual information. Experience indicates that well-made, early judgements lead to strong recoveries. There is value in responding quickly and effectively with honesty and compassion. The Chief Executive cannot devolve their responsibility although a whole raft of communications will exist beneath that level. Whatever is communicated it must be transparent, timely and relevant.

Regardless of the physical reality of a situation, people will respond according to what they perceive.

Bibliography

1.   "The American Experience" - Risk and Business Continuity Expo - 2005

2.   Competitive Advantage - Michael Porter - The Free Press - 1985

3.   The Dilbert Principle - Scott Adams; Harper Business - 1995

4.   Chris Latjha - Consultant - Presentation - Risk and Business Continuity Expo - 2005

5.   Pretty and Knight - Oxford Metrica - www.OxfordMetrica.com

6.   Patrick Alesi, Lehman Brother, Resilience 2004, London

7.   Atkins and Bates - Reputational Management - Caxton - 2005

8.   Brotzen Mayne - http://www.brotzen-mayne.co.uk/home.htm

9.   www.nasd.com

10.   Synstar - 2004

11.   TSR.com (Tropical Storm Risk website supported by University College London, the UK Met Office, Benfield, Crawford, Hazard Research Centre and Royal & SunAlliance)

12.   Recovery in Paradise - CIR January 2005

13.   George Williams - Synstar - 2004

14.   Harvey Fawcett - 247i Limited - Continuity Central - 2004

15.   Paul Wood (Messagelabs) and Richard Miller (ISS) - CIR January 2005

16.   Ari Fleischer - Recovery Chronicles - Strohl Newsletter - 2004

17.   http://www.food.gov.uk/safereating/sudani, www.premierfoods.co.uk/news/press, http://www.tesco.com/corporateinfo/

18.   Ari Fleischer - Recovery Chronicles - Strohl Newsletter - 2004

19.   Linda Lewis - Lewis Media - 2004

20.   Damocles – "Media Tennis" - 2005

15

Emergency and Governmental Services

Objectives Of This Chapter Are:

- To consider the role that emergency services and other governmental departments play in business continuity

- To consider the role that emergency services and other governmental departments play in crisis management

- To explore the value in understanding those roles and in cooperation when undertaking a process of continuity management.

- To recognise the opportunities and challenges brought by public authorities throughout the management of a business-threatening incident.

Introduction

The Business Continuity Institute advocates as one of its ten certification standards for business continuity practitioners, that they establish "...applicable procedures and policies for coordinating crisis, continuity and restoration activities with external agencies (local, state, regional, national, emergency responders, defence, etc.) while ensuring compliance with applicable statutes or regulations." **(1)**.

We will explore the reasons for this important recommendation and go a little further as we explain the values of cooperation, both in crisis risk management beforehand; in addition to the needs and benefits in cooperating during the crisis itself. This chapter does not set out to explain regulatory requirements as these are dealt with separately in a different chapter of this book. Instead, it deals with the practical uses that can be made of Government agency resources; and conversely where an organisation in distress must, as part of its process of recovery, understand and take on board the wider issues that are the responsibility of these departments.

Risk managers, setting out to address potentially destructive risks – and indeed any risks – gorge themselves on information. Satiated as best possible, they then will begin to filter, cross check and quantify that information to produce, as best possible, a measured view of the risk being carried and the likely consequences to the organisation, to its people and to its other stakeholders. Much of that information,, of course, needs to come from within the organisation itself; but importantly it also needs to come from beyond. That wider information also has to present trusted pictures of threat, source of threat and potential consequence.

As to risk and likelihood, many public authorities are addressing the same issues and need, not only to consider threats to themselves, but also threats to the wider environment within which, their own organisation fits and can be threatened. Public authorities – and not just emergency services - have further crucial and wide-ranging roles and responsibilities during a crisis. These public service bodies need to encourage and guide the community to respond to a crisis in a way that fits their model of how that wider macro community needs best to react and prioritise their own responses.

The safety of human life is an irremovable priority. Public authorities are likely, also in a widespread power or telecommunication outage to demand that priority be given to reinstating infrastructure services in those areas where the emergency services, hospitals and similar are situated. No amount of pleading from another type of organisation facing commercial distress will divert them from this. It is left to that organisation to handle the loss as best as it can until its turn comes for reinstatement of service

Public Service Bodies As An Information Resource

These public service bodies have access to information that is usually not available to other organisations but they do usefully share a measured amount of that information to the general public. They will also occasionally share more detailed information with those organisations that are seen to be directly in the firing line of specific risks. We illustrate some of these organisations later in this chapter.

The first step in accessing this information is by looking at the websites of the country-wide security organisations such as the Federal Bureau of Investigation (FBI), CIA, Department of Homeland Security in the United States; the MI5, Foreign and Commonwealth Office (FCO), Home Office, Health and Safety Executive (HSE) National Criminal Intelligence Service (NCIS) and others in the United Kingdom. Each country will have its own agencies from which useful information can be gleaned.

Advice From Public Service Bodies

Within the emergency services there are organisations providing advice on risk-related issues. One such example in the United Kingdom is the National Counter Terrorism Security Office (NaCTSO). NaCTSO is a Police unit working to the Association of Chief Police Officers, and provides a coordinating role for the Police service in regard to counterterrorism and protective security.
There are many more geographically focused organisations such as London Resilience and the Security and Contingency Planning Group of the Corporation of London (2). This latter authority has responsibilities within the square mile of the City of London and is one of 33 local authorities within Greater London. They bring encouragement, information and guides to other organisations within their area of operation, and, as we will explore in later paragraphs, encourage valuable coordination and communication across private and public organisations during a crisis.

London Resilience is a partnership whose aim is to improve London's resilience to disruptive challenge

> *"... through working with partners on anticipation, preparation, prevention and resolution of such events and to make sure that the emergency plans and procedures on London Organisations vital to keeping the Capital running, fit together effectively and can stand up to different scales and types of threat."* **(3)**

The <u>Emergency Plan For London</u> has been produced and any risk manager considering risk for a London-based division needs to understand how that would unfold and the likely impact of that planning on their own recovery.

There are industry-wide bodies that bring organisations together; and public service bodies are no exception. These bodies are a useful further source of information and advice. In the United Kingdom alone they include the Emergency Planning Society, Association of Local Authority Risk Managers (ALARM), and the Building Research Establishment. Others include the International Emergency Services Society and the Securities and Exchange Commission (USA). We include the access websites of these societies and others at the end of this book. There are also pan-country organisations such as the United Nations, the Red Cross, the Red Crescent, and the Organisation of Economic Development (OECD) which provide useful information for international services and business.

While we are not discussing regulators' requirements in this chapter we must not overlook the value of regulators as providers of useful guides and information. Most countries have their own of which the Financial Services Authority (FSA) in the United Kingdom, the Australian Prudential Regulation Authority (APRA), the Monetary Authority of Singapore, the U.S. Securities and Exchange Commission, are just four of many such resources worldwide.

The information that emerges from public service organisations is not only useful in trying to understand current perceived risk levels of terrorism or environmental disasters. They will also set out to explain how they themselves have prepared to manage such a crisis. To understand whether a response is being prepared, the quality of that planning and the consequences on the community are vital clues as to how such a crisis will unfold for each individual organisation in the hours and days after the incident. That understanding will also enable an organisation, setting out to establish its own resilience in the face of a wide area crisis, to see how it will need to fit into that wider planning picture. It will see how it can gain value wherever possible and understand how a wider community need could in some circumstances constrain their own in-house recovery. The FSA, for example, has a communication capability in place for certain regulated organisations. This includes access to emergency mobile networks and videoconference facilities.

A further real value of public service information is that organizations are likely to advise and set current risk levels based on intelligence feedback from all their various intelligence agencies. They may describe the current threat level by number, name or colour code. These definitions will be explained and recommendations given for organisational response levels in each case.

Addressing Non-Public-Body Issues

Where information comes second hand, the risk manager will need, as always, to be satisfied that the source is a credible one and that the supplier's own agenda in producing the information is not clouding what would otherwise be a clearer picture. In essence, and as in any court of law, the decision maker will wish to check the credibility by taking views from as many sources as possible. A scientist making holocaust claims may just be putting a slant on the information as a part of a campaign for research funds. Information offered by a government agency on the risk levels within another country may be compromised by a wider political agenda. Single-focus pressure groups can claim disproportionate publicity on the back of the most recent newsworthy incident. It is up to the risk manager to see through these agendas and discern hard facts from the rhetoric.

Very rare, catastrophic events are very difficult to quantify for risk decision-making. Following the Asian tsunami in 2004 there were quite rightly many questions to be asked to search out the lessons that can be learned. A report by the Geological Society in 2005 on 'super eruptions' was addressed to the Natural Hazards Working Group. This group was created after the tsunami and is composed of scientists who have the objective of advising the British Cabinet on predicting global disasters. The report points out that super eruptions may occur only once every 100,000 years, but of course that they can result in the death of millions. This time span has to be relevant to decision making.

There are certainly questions now, with hindsight, about the drama that developed around the millennium Y2K computer concerns as well as concerns raised in the 1990s by scientists warning of meteor strikes. There is controversy still about concerns raised in 1999 that a landslide in the Canary Islands will devastate the American eastern seaboard. The claim was made by a team at the Benfield Hazard Research Centre at University College London. It sparked criticisms from other experts who accused the team of focussing on worst-case scenarios. There were criticisms in particular that the team is sponsored by the Benfield Group, a leading reinsurer. It is not within the ability, nor a role of this book to suggest that there is conflict of interest in this case or in other individual cases. Many insurers and reinsurers produce very high quality work. The suggestion simply is that the aware risk manager will always look beyond the current headlines and ensure that decisions are made based on real, quality, tested information that is cross-checked wherever possible and is much more than the current day's headlines.

An extreme view:

"Almost all communities are playing the disaster game. Behind it all lurk the vested interests of researchers, campaign groups, politicians, charities, businesses and the news media."

- Dr. Benny Peiser, a social anthropologist at John Moores University. Liverpool.

The sources that are available to a risk manager are as wide as the views offered, and later in this book we will provide some of those sources and their web pages.

Agencies that provide useful risk understanding are used as brief case studies below.

Case Study

London Emergency Services Liaison Panel

"'The group meets once every three months under the chair of the Metropolitan Police. Its purpose is to ensure a partnership approach between all the relevant agencies in the planning for, and the response to, a major incident of whatever kind. This could be anything from a terrorist attack to a natural disaster such as a severe flood, which may occur within the Greater London area.

"This web site aims to give an overview of London's emergency services' joint response to major incidents within the capital. The links page will provide access to these organisations' individual websites.

"The site is based on the **Leslp Manual,** a full version of which is available to download from this site. The Leslp manual has been drafted in accordance with the latest agreed procedures of the Association of Chief Police Officers (ACPO), the Chief and Assistant Chief Fire Officers' Association (CACFOA), The Ambulance Service Association (ASA), London Boroughs and the Home Office. Extensive consultation has also been undertaken with the military, voluntary services and emergency services of surrounding county areas." **(4)**

The manual has the following amongst its objectives:

"This Manual has been prepared for the information and guidance of the emergency services and local authorities but may be used by any other responsible organisation which may have to respond to a major incident. It must be remembered that the procedures within this Manual are generally related to activities at, or ancillary to, the scene of the incident, that have a bearing on a number of the agencies involved. Detailed descriptions of single service functions are not included. The Manual includes references to roles and responsibilities of some non-emergency service organisations. The list of organisations included is not exhaustive and it is recognized that a wide range of organisations are likely to be involved in supporting the response of the emergency services." **(5)**

Case Study 2
UK Resilience

This is a product of the Civil Contingencies Secretariat in the UK Government Cabinet Office. This public service provides links to both governmental and non-governmental sources on a wide variety of emergencies and crises that can affect the United Kingdom; plus emergency planning guidance and government information. Their own particular 'cut' **(6)** of wide ranging civil contingencies is an interesting one and is listed under the following headings:

Aviation

Chemical, Biological, Radiological or Nuclear

Chemical Accident

Civil Contingencies and Emergency planning

Energy and Power Supply

Epidemics and Health issues

Fire Safety

Flooding

Food Alerts

Fuel Situation

Nuclear Accident

Severe Weather

Terrorism

Train Crash

Water Shortage

Web and Internet Alerts

This organisation publishes a range of plans and other publications that are accessible by the general public. The business issues they address include:

- Promoting business continuity
- Providing advice and resources to business
- Fast Time communications to business
- Address concerns and issues raised by business and tourism
- Representative in briefing, planning and response
- Links into other work areas in London and nationally

Case Study 3
The New York City Office of Emergency Management

The New York City Office of Emergency Management (OEM) sets out to achieve interagency coordination before, during and after disasters or emergencies, whether a small water main break or an event as catastrophic as the September 11, 2001 tragedy. To accomplish this, the OEM maintains a corps of emergency management personnel — including responders, planners, watch commanders, and administrative and support staff — to identify and respond to various hazards. The OEM assists Federal, State and City officials and their respective constituents with disaster response and mitigation. The Agency also provides information for the Mayor concerning hazard identification and mitigation procedures. Through its public information arm, OEM provides the public and media organisations with information regarding emergency management planning, response and hazard mitigation in New York City.

In 2000, the OEM launched the Public-Private Emergency Planning Initiative (PEPI) — a program designed to strengthen private-sector relationships and increase the City's preparedness level. Through this program, private businesses receive help developing business continuity plans, and participate in exercises and basic emergency management training. The PEPI has also established information-sharing and participation programs to keep businesses in tune with local news and events.

Legislation

The bodies we mention above are usually empowered, and often have objectives that are set out in legislation. Further, there is far-reaching legislation in some countries that sets out the roles of certain governmental bodies in a wider context, not only what is expected of them but also what they in turn are empowered to demand of the wider community. Those demands may be on the risk manager's own organisations and colleagues and may apply before or during an incident. They are relevant to this chapter in the way that they offer added challenges while a risk incident is still unfolding. Clearly the organisation in a crisis is no less expected to continue to meet the regulatory requirements and furthermore will be expected to be able to offer reassurances even as they are otherwise setting about to face the challenges created by the incident and work to stay in business.

The events of 9/11 and a series of well-documented corporate scandals in the US, Europe and the UK have resulted in the introduction of stricter regulatory environments for global business.

In the UK, The Combined Code on Corporate Governance imposes a positive responsibility on executive and non-executive directors to ensure that effective risk management controls are in place. There is an increasing tendency in the United States (Sarbanes Oxley) and the EU (Transparency Directive) to fix Directors with personal liability for non-fraudulent negligent mistakes. There are clear signs that the UK may follow suit in the not-too-distant future, not least in the form of the government's proposed 'corporate killing' legislation, which is currently at draft stage.

The following are examples of legislation that is relevant to this section of the book as well as the separate covering of legislative requirements in another chapter.

Civil Contingencies Act 2004 (United Kingdom)

The purpose of Part 1 of the Act is to establish a new statutory framework for civil protection at the local level. This, together with accompanying guidance and regulations, sets out the expectations and responsibilities for front line responders at the local level to ensure that they are prepared to deal effectively with the full range of emergencies. It divides local responders into two categories.

Those to be identified as Category One responders are all principal Local Authorities, Government agencies such as the Environment Agencies, the Emergency Services, and the various National Health Service Bodies and the Maritime and Coastguard Agency. Those Category One responders have duties placed upon them to:

- Assess local risks and use this to provide information for emergency planning;

- Put in place emergency plans;

- Put in place Business Continuity Management arrangements;

- Put in place arrangements to make information available to the public about civil protection matters and maintain arrangements to warn, inform and advise the public

- In the event of an emergency;

- Share information with other local responders to enhance co-ordination;

- Co-operate with other local responders to enhance co-ordination and efficiency.

The Act has redefined an 'emergency' to include an event that threatens to cause an emergency as well as an event that actually creates an emergency. An organisation may therefore find itself embroiled in a disruption that is stopping them working which is a result of a perceived threat; not just as a result of a situation that has actually happened. That 'perceived emergency' may now be a region or a city alone. It does not need to be a national one.

These changes could be an important distinction in wording of insurance policies and contracts with emergency service suppliers.

Local Authorities are charged additionally with providing advice and assistance to businesses and voluntary organisations about business continuity management.

Patriot Act and Homeland Defense 2001 (USA)

The USA Patriot Act facilitates information sharing and cooperation among government agencies. The Act removed barriers that prevented the law enforcement, intelligence, and national defence communities from coordinating their work to protect national security. The Act legalises law enforcement officers to conduct investigations in new ways without tipping off suspected terrorists. There has been much discussion about some compromise with civil liberties.

Sarbanes-Oxley 2002 (USA)

The Sarbanes-Oxley Act of 2002 came about due to financial scandals and lack of corporate oversight that resulted in corporate losses in the billions of dollars. These losses produced a domino effect that significantly affected financial markets and investor trust in American companies and stock markets. The Sarbanes-Oxley Act was introduced in 2003 to try to discourage the kind of behaviour that brought about these scandals, ensure better transparency and more effective corporate governance, disclosure, and financial accounting. Sarbanes-Oxley can be separated into three distinct areas of corporate governance where key changes are being be implemented:

- **Legal and regulatory requirements** - Interpretation of the laws

- **Accounting standards and guidance** - Interpretation of accounting rules and requirements

- **Internal operations and management** - Assessment of compliance and management of programs related to improve compliance

Government Agencies During a Crisis

Emergency services

We have already stated that the emergency services' very first and often only immediate concern will be to minimise the number of deaths and injuries. To do this they need to immediately take control of the site, barring any others that do not feed this specific objective. The Police usually take immediate leadership amongst the organisations in controlling all access to the site. Organisations which find themselves within these Police cordons will be denied access, however important they consider their own needs. An urgent business need therefore is to establish how to communicate and gain access to the decision-makers in the command centre.

The Police are likely to establish an outer cordon and an inner one. The immediate outer cordon, following a terrorist incident, for example, can be around a whole area of a city and could occupy a five-mile radius. In the event of a large weather catastrophe such as a hurricane they can demand evacuation over an area of many square miles. As safety is reassured within the outer cordon it will gradually transition into the inner cordon, and this could take hours or days depending on the circumstances and possible threat of a further attack or other safety concern. The inner cordon can stay for weeks or even months, as the area is reinstated. An organisation may be denied access even if their own individual building is safe to use and otherwise operable. This likelihood is vital planning information for a risk manager wishing to store backup data and other information and tools that could be needed urgently after a crisis.

Although control processes vary in different countries, we offer two case studies to demonstrate how they operate. The clear message from both for continuity planners is that they need to gain an understanding of the command and control procedures in whichever country they have exposures and build this information into their continuity planning document. In particular they need to ensure that the crisis managers will know how to make contact with the control rooms of those emergency authorities to gain information and offer help as is needed.

Furthermore, when considering likely scenarios there is a value in thinking further through how each scenario may unfold once it has begun. In a fire example, the Fire and Rescue Services will most likely use water as the primary extinguisher. The organisation may have knowledge of what is in the building that would render the use of water dangerous or indeed further damaging. There may be chemicals or other substances in the building that may place fire fighters at particular risk of explosion or flashback. Using water may cause environmentally damaging runoff into public water supplies. It is in everybody's interest to share this information before the incident.

Case Study 1
United Kingdom

The command and control infrastructure we use elsewhere in this book has its roots in Police and Military crisis management models. Clearly there must be leadership in control and decision-making on site to ensure that fast decisions can be made, priorities are not diluted and that the various teams and agencies do not get in the way of each other. Instant decisions have to be made around such vital matters as keeping access routes clear for ambulances and other emergency vehicles, getting up-to-date information to families and the media, and countless other details including decisions about injured individuals.

The overall crisis management operation is likely to take the form of a Gold control; away from the site where the chief officers and their staff of the Emergency Service organisations cooperate to ensure resources are available to meet the priorities decided. They will ensure overall strategic direction and other crucial needs are in place, such as communications and liaison with other agencies, families, the media and others.

Silver control is on site and located where the overall control and coordination is managed. The Silver commander is the overall on-site incident commander and he or she will ensure that coordination and priorities are maintained.

The Bronze controller will be in control over all of the agencies operating in one area of the incident. This could be, say in the event of a train crash, managing the events around one particular carriage. In this way there is a chain of both command and communication right through from the actual incident itself to the overall strategic command. The players will have been trained within one service and trained also alongside other services that would be playing their part also.

The planning work ensures that the structure is clear and empowered, the communication links are all in place and each is aware of their role. The plans would cover the wider management issues and also the detail that would be necessary to avoid a breakdown in the structure.

Just one detail to illustrate this point would be a standing instruction to the first person on site not to get involved in a rescue but to stand back, assess the situation, report and thus ensure that the full and measured response structure is triggered. This could be an unnatural thing to do had the planning and training not convinced that person that holding back to evaluate and report would be in the much greater interest of all the victims – or potential victims - involved.

Case study 2
EL AL Plane Crash: Schiphol Airport, Amsterdam 1992

A plane owned by El Al took of from Schiphol Airport at around 18.30 on the 4th October 2004. It carried 70 tons of fuel, 114 tons of commercial cargo, three crewmembers, and a passenger. Within a few minutes the captain reported that two engines had failed. After dumping fuel the captain tried to return to Schiphol, failed and crashed into two ten story blocks of flats nearby.

The emergency services response:

Fire service

Fire officers from the local station and the specially equipped service from the airport arrived quickly. Eventually there were more than 300 Fire Department personnel on site. They were hampered by the strength of the fire, the risk of buildings or parts collapsing and explosions from aircraft parts and gas mains. The latter was eventually sealed off by gas company personnel. The most serious seats of fire were extinguished four hours after the crash.

Police

The first officers arrived at 18.44. In the early minutes however, large numbers of people had streamed towards the crash site before an effective police cordon could be established. The police had established an early command post in a local Police station by 20.06 and by 20.30 there were sufficient officers to begin to clear the area and establish an outer cordon around the flats. Eventually 500 Police Officers were needed and they included motor cyclists, mounted officers and the riot squad. Major traffic jams hampered emergency vehicles.

Ambulance Service

The first Ambulance set off at 18.37; not arriving until 18.48. There were many rumours amongst the news agencies about large death tolls and diversions caused by a rumour about a disco in one of the buildings. At 22.00 medical teams had very little to do and several ambulances were withdrawn.

Hospitals

The designated hospital had a disaster plan and this was put into operation at 19.14. Only 12 bodies had been recovered by 21.40 and 27 slightly injured people were taken to the Hospital. A problem was that there was an influx of volunteers, many on their own initiative and this created a surplus. There were a constant stream of City officials and other department heads causing the medical department to comment: 'The problem with disasters is that so many people want to get involved. The Health inspector arrived at the Central Ambulance Station just over an hour after the first alarm had been raised, followed by the Director General for Public Health and the Chief Health Inspector. Personnel doing the work saw the presence of these VIPs as an extra burden. Some felt it hindered their performance.'(7)

Local Authority

The mayor declared the crash to be a disaster at 18.51 and thus triggered the Amsterdam disaster plan. He went into the coordination centre under the City Hall. Key personnel there included the Fire Chief, the Police Chief, the Deputy Director of the Municipal Medical and Health Department, the Director General of the Municipal Social Services Department, the Director of the Department of Population Census, and the Head of Information for the City of Amsterdam. Telephones in the vicinity of the crash were not functioning and early activity was mostly trying to get direct communication to the site and get a best possible picture of the scale of the disaster.

Reception Centre

A large number of people needed assistance and the Gaasperdam Sports Centre was opened for this purpose. Other Sports Centres opened on their own initiative causing a fragmentation in the relief work and information. Overnight accommodation was provided in a range of churches, hotels, nursing homes, youth hostels and naval barracks. The Social Services Department made payments to cover cost of living expenses but were hampered by many other people arriving from elsewhere and claiming that they were a victim of the incident.

The National Political Response

In The Hague, the Minister of the Interior opened the National Coordination Centre in case assistance was required. At the same time the North Holland Provincial Authority opened its Crisis Centre in Haarlem. Embassies from those countries whose nationals were resident in that area were seeking information from both these centres. The Israeli Prime Minister announced the setting up of a joint airline-Government commission to investigate the disaster. Queen Beatrix accompanied by her son and a range of cabinet Ministers and members of Amsterdam City Council visited the site on the morning of the 5th October. Fortunately, here in Holland but by no means common in other disasters around the world, they had the foresight to arrange to come all at the same time; and thus minimise the disruption to the emergency work.

Recovery Of The Dead

Recovery operations could not start until the Monday morning after the buildings had been rendered safe. The organisations engaged in this grim task included the Amsterdam Fire Brigade, the Police, regional Fire Brigade units, Civil Defence volunteers, various private contractors, aviation experts and the National Police Identification Team. Only 43 bodies had been recovered by the 8th October against a missing person list of 1600. Credibility in this list was hampered by the fact that many illegal immigrants had been afraid to register that there were friends and relatives missing in this largely immigrant area.

The Role Of Media

There was an instant and massive influx of media personnel, both national and international. They received information from a variety of sources; some of them contradictory. For example, one neighbourhood council held a press conference without reference to the coordination centre. There were even some clashes, some ugly, between journalists and the emergency services. Some camera crews had to be removed by Police.

Summary

The purpose of this very brief summary of this incident is to illustrate that the public services in these disasters have a massive job of coordination and control and the needs of an individual organisation are likely to be put aside while the larger issues are handled. A recovery manager considering the relationships with the emergency services should recognise this realism in the planning. Above all, risk managers should ensure that their own organisations can be contacted 24/7 by these public services if needed and conversely know how they in turn can make contact if there are real values in doing so.

Another example of the value of co-operation between public services and other organisations was after the London Provisional Irish Republican Army (PIRA) bombings. Police had an urgent need to contact individual key holders so they could set about making their buildings safe and secure so that, in turn, the Police would feel comfortable in closing their cordons inwards. The obvious planning demand is to ensure that key holder names and contact numbers are registered beforehand and that in turn the emergency services contact route is inserted into the plan.

Yet another situation where the public authorities' activities could affect an organisation in distress would be when the Police decide that the site of the incident is a 'crime scene.' They would then close all access to the site until their enquiries were complete. This could be for days or even weeks. They may secure items needed by the organisation as evidence for a future criminal court case. Following the London PIRA bombs the Police, once they had satisfied themselves about all human safety, introduced shredders to the streets and set about shredding all the huge volumes of paper that had fallen from windows and was drifting about the streets. The objective was to retain as much as possible the security of sensitive information and reduce the opportunities for later frauds, extortion and other crime.

A similar denial would occur if the Police considered that an area is unsafe (e.g., following an accidental or terrorist-created chemical leakage) and would again set up cordons to deny all access until they had satisfied themselves that the area was safe again. The individual organisation's survival needs, however important to that organisation, would be subsumed by the wider community need. It is important again to remember that the single driver of the emergency services in the first minutes and hours of a wide-ranging disaster will be to save human life. This will drive their own response teams to set out immediately to identify who is dead and alive, leave the former and concentrate on reducing the death toll by putting all their energies into the safety and treatment of those that are still alive. Only when they are satisfied that there is no longer any risk of further injury or death will they begin to consider other issues.

The significant disruption to the wider transport and communications infrastructures for miles around the incident are also a major Police and Public Service challenge; as they are also a challenge to the movements of the individual organisation's own response teams.

If an organisation suffers the death of an employee, or has missing employees, there is the sensitive matter of identifying the dead and then advising the family. This is clearly best for public services to do but there is a need for information sharing with the organisation and an instant need to follow that notification with all the support the organisation feels it can bring to that family.

> *The recovery planning should therefore take on board realism about how long it may be before an individual organisation can gain access to its site, and the organisation's need to work alongside the public authorities. Even before the incident there is a need to understand the potential extent of damage and the demands on them around which their own decisions will then need to be made.*

Other Organisations

Many Public Authorities have developed major crisis plans that will also bring in other organisations that can add value. As illustrated in the Schiphol incident above they may be schools and other public buildings to house people not needing hospitalisation, care organisations to give support such as Red Cross, Red Crescent or other charities. Authorities may decide also to use the media proactively where there is value; and may take over or constrain private companies such as telecommunications services suppliers. Teams of undertakers could be brought in to take control of the body identification process, communications with families and matching personal possessions to those bodies. Local authorities will be brought in to deal with cleanup and making safe roads, buildings and other infrastructures.

It is clear that the range of skills and resources needed during a major incident are both wide and deep and it is vital that the risk managers' organisation sets out to understand both the roles and the pressures of the wider, unfolding scenario. With that insight, and the knowledge of how to keep up to date, hour by hour of what is going on, the organisation is best able to assess their own damage and how that damage may unfold further. It will be much better able to get to know what may have happened already to its own people, as well as its business and how that is likely to unfold over the next hours and weeks. It will be able to take advantage of early use of the services offered (for example, an information centre set up to advise on deaths and injuries). It may also able to add value to those emergency services where needed.

The emergency services may, for example, wish to contact key holders immediately to get them to assist in providing contact information for the families of the dead and injured. Obtaining assurances that these tasks are being covered by the emergency services will enable the organisation to avoid duplication and, not least getting into arenas for which they are not best skilled.

Exercising with Government Bodies

Government agencies and their support organisations in many countries have sophisticated exercising regimes where they not only exercise their own planning but also exercise alongside the other organisations with whom they will work in a real-life crisis. These exercises provide useful learning opportunities. This is not only for the organisations directly involved but also for other organisations that may not be part of the command and control process but nevertheless will find themselves in the middle of it all.

There is a particular value of exercises that bring together the emergency services and those organisations that are not normally considered to be 24/7 emergency response organisations. By nature they do not maintain 24/7-staffed emergency contact suites to the national standards required by the emergency services. This particular value therefore is for the latter type of organisation who, even though they are not so structured can, in some circumstances be critical and urgent parts of the wider recovery.

Case Study

An exercise used a train crash as its scenario and there were many hundreds of walking injured, stressed people and others who needed support and needed removing away from the crash scene.

The planning entailed a call to the Education Authority to open a nearby school for roll calls and minor treatments. Calls were made to the home addresses of seven different senior Local Education Authority personnel before someone was found at home to receive the call.

Some exercises will set out to involve 'civilian' organisations such as the exercise by the United Kingdom's Financial Services Authority we used as a case study in another chapter. That exercise had participants from 32 firms representing retail banks, investment banks, insurance companies, payments organisations and Government bodies of HM Treasury, the Bank of England, and the Financial Services Authority itself. A further fourteen organisations were represented as part of the 'monitor' group. In total 297 people were involved on the day, with a number of additional people participating remotely in support of their firms' representative team.

A Governmental Body As An Essential Service Suppler

An organisation, working through its Business Impact Analysis, may highlight the fact that a Government Department is a critical service supplier on which it has a total dependency. That may be a nationalised supplier of basic needs such as power or water or it may be a Central Bank providing crucial services between the financial companies themselves and their national and international trading counterparties. While the problem of a failing public service may be more difficult to manage – there may be no possible alternatives to trading with that organisation – it is essentially the same problem. Is the dependency critical and urgent? Can the risk managers continue to manage and control their own organisation so that it is still possible to maintain credibility and minimum service levels until the supplier can get its act together again? Are there any options for alternative services - such as generators for urgent, business-critical buildings, for example?

The impact of public service failures is usually widespread. Some Directors have been heard to say that if the problem is wide enough *we do not need to worry.'* The thinking seems to be on the basis that everybody is 'in the same boat' and stakeholders will have to accept the disruption. This misses a crucial issue for competitive industries. This issue is that customers and other stakeholders will still be measuring their organisation on how well they communicate, how concerned they seem to be, and above all how their recovery matches up against their competitors' reactions to the same problem. All these are crucial continuity management issues even when, on the face of it, the wider circumstances are beyond their control.

Summary

It is critical that information is available to the risk manager concerning incidents and likelihoods that could destroy business and harm its people. Partly in response to perceived, increased threat levels in major cities the Governmental Departments have developed their own plans, their coordination and have recognised themselves that there is huge value in public/private cooperation. They have responded to this recognition by sharing with private businesses a controlled amount of risk information and information about their own contingency plans.

Clearly a Government Department is not able to release all its available information. It will not release information that may place a criminal or other terrorist into a more advantageous position. They also see their role to inform but not to alarm. There may also be potential litigation implications around information they are holding.

Another crucial benefit is in taking the time to better understand the agendas and challenges that the emergency services and other public service face in a disaster. That understanding helps the risk manager to plan more effectively for the situation and delays that his or her own organisation is likely to have to face. Understanding these expectations may result in and better and more realistic continuity planning.

1.   The ten certification standards for business continuity practitioners. BCI

2.   Russ Mansford; LAS Commander; The London Resilience team

3.   www.cityoflondon.gov.uk. (>law and Order>security and contingency planning)

4.   www.leslp.gov.uk website

5.   London Emergency Services Liaison Panel; Major Incident Procedure Manual 1.6.

6.   UK Resilience. Cabinet Office. www.ukresilience.info

7.   Rosenthal et al, 1994:32

16

Rehearsals and Exercising of Plans and Risk Decision-Making

Objectives Of This Chapter Are To:

- Discuss the importance of ensuring as much credibility as is possible in catastrophic risk management and continuity planning.

- Consider the values of rehearsal training and exercising of people, and the resources that are expected to be used.

- Understand the use of exercising and rehearsal training as a quality measuring tool for decision- making around risk.

- Understand the importance of exercising plans as a vital check that these plans are still up to date.

- Consider the different types of exercises that are available to the risk and continuity manager and where different styles best meet different requirements.

- Consider guides and standards that are available on exercising; and their use as benchmarking tools.

- Understand the limitations as well as the values of exercising.

The Need For Credibility

Identifying and managing potentially catastrophic exposures is an important issue that deals with human lives and also the very survival of the risk manager's organisation; its jobs, its customers, the trust of its investors and other stakeholders.

Continuity planning is a subject that runs right across conventional organisational boundaries, brings together people who do not normally work together as a team, and has them make decisions that are likely to be implemented in circumstances that are way beyond the participants' normal experience and familiarity. The planning is to be triggered in times when there is likely to be greatly increased stress levels and where normal communication channels, priorities and organisational 'comfort factor' structures have been swept away. It can be also at a time when there are massive, competing, urgencies and new external demands that are again a long way from the participants' usual work style or lifestyle.

It would be a very confident, perhaps arrogant, risk or continuity manager who considers that decisions and plans laid down would work without further effort on ensuring as is best possible that the plans are seen to be meeting these urgent and new needs. Furthermore it is absolutely crucial that all the people who are expected to play a part understand their roles and feel reasonably comfortable with them. It is necessary to ensure that each and every one knows how it will be possible to communicate and how best they will fit alongside all the other participants in the unfolding drama.

One way of reducing the odds on failure is to take the business through, as far as is realistically possible, the sort of scenario that it may one day have to meet in real life. Then, of course, ensure that all the learning points are captured and introduced into further development of the thinking on continuity.

We feel the need to make an important point, at this early stage in the chapter, about the use of the terms 'test' and 'exercise.' The very nature of continuity planning means that there is no obvious right and wrong answer for every aspect. It is, by its very nature, dealing with the unknown. The participants in the exercises will include those who have made decisions and otherwise worked to bring the state of continuity management up to the state it is in at the start of the exercise. To use the expression 'test' implies a pass or failure of these people that would be unjustified and may indeed constrain them from a full and open participation. The expression 'test' also diminishes the atmosphere that exercising is equally about awareness training of the individuals taking part. We therefore strongly prefer the word 'exercise' and will continue to use it in this chapter and elsewhere in the book.

There is a school of thought that one tests the systems and hardware and one exercises the people and the decision making. We have no strong aversion to this particular restricted use of the word 'test.'

Exercising: The Expectations And The Deliverables

Whatever those deliverables are, they do need to be clear and understood by all before the exercise takes place. No exercise can be fully effective if the participants set about getting involved with quite different hopes and expectations from the outcome. This is not least because exercises can set about to cover quite different things. The objective may be one or more individual aspects of the business continuity and recovery planning only, to the quite different needs of technology or infrastructure exercises. It is by no means possible to cover all contingencies in one exercise and thus the objectives, the type of scenario that is being testing – and the necessary limitations of testing one or few scenarios – need to be clear.

The headline objectives; within which individual more detailed objectives are developed could be as listed below:

- Raise awareness of business continuity concepts, opportunities and roles

- Convey the importance of business continuity and gain ownership by potential participants

- Measure the learnings about risk and continuity gained in the exercise against the existing business impact analysis and the recovery plans

- Develop and update work completed prior to the exercise

- Manage expectations amongst all dependencies and observers that are likely to be affected

The individual objectives that are planned for one exercise can be quite specific ones but will most likely fall within or round these generic headings. An example of more specific objectives follows as a case study

---

Case Study
Exercise Objectives

Market wide Business Continuity Exercise November 2004

Exercise leaders: the Financial Services Authority and HM Treasury (United Kingdom)

- To test communications within and between the different parts of the Financial sector, including Trade associations

- To test the communications procedures between the authorities and financial Sector put in place by the tripartite group since the last exercise, such as (using) the conference facility and the enhanced joint website

- To understand how the authorities will acquire the information needed to address the crisis

- To determine what information the authorities are likely to need, what they are likely to do with that information and what information and decisions will be fed back to the financial sector

- To build an awareness of and confidence in the procedures for communication; and

- To identify potential improvements in the existing procedures **(1)**

In effect this exercise has a particular focus and objectives; that of communications. It does not set out to cover all potential difficulties that may emerge from the headline scenario,

---

It is important at this moment to consider again all the objectives and stepping stones that bring about the complete business recovery cycle. Each of those is crucial and they are all interdependent. In other words a failure in one of the stages – say, the one that develops an effective BIA around which further decisions can be made – can be as destructive as failing to ensure that a particular piece of technology is available quickly. The process of exercising therefore has this entire playing field within which to work and in doing so to raise more trust and credibility in the organisations' resilience. The opposite side of the coin is that exercising one of those steps alone does not raise realistically any expectations beyond those in that individual part of the chain only.

This need to understand quite precise outcomes from individual exercises is a single generic issue throughout this chapter.

Case Study

Extract from questionnaire to potential, just-in-time, critical service supplier:

- Do you have continuity planning in place?   yes / no

- Has this been exercised?   yes / no

These questions provide absolutely no useful information at all. What does their continuity planning deliver? Does it assist the survival of the supplier only and ignore the needs of the receiver? Does the exercise really provide reassurance of the entire continuity management chain or just one part? This approach would most certainly not satisfy regulatory or due diligence requirements.

Types Of Continuity Exercising

Exercising falls into two broad headlines and while they critically need to be brought together (see below), we can best discuss them initially under these two categories. This needs to be exercised to ensure that the promised service level agreement can be delivered.

1. The Technology and other facilities managers will most likely have set up contingency procedures and resources to enable them to rebuild an alternate technological, communications, office or factory infrastructure that be brought alive and used very quickly.

2. Keeping an organisation alive throughout a potentially destructive incident, however, is much more than the facilities infrastructure, and of course the wider continuity risk management and continuity planning will reflect this. This deals with the demands on people, the taking control of an organisation in distress, the interface between people and the infrastructures, and the ability to continue to deliver crucial responsibilities. It furthermore verifies that the decisions that have been made on risk, its tolerance and management are credible and complete. This wider continuity management is also about facing up to the new demands that a crisis will bring; not least the vital and immediate need to keep the brand values alive in the face of a whole range of stakeholders concerns and a possible media attack. There is therefore a vital need for a very different type of exercising beyond rebuilding workspaces and technology.

Exercising Of Infrastructure Continuity Plans

Destroyed or inaccessible workspaces and other business support infrastructures may need to be replaced extremely quickly indeed. This timeline may be measured by the BIA in minutes and hours rather than days and weeks. In an extreme case, the replacement infrastructure may need to be ready to be switched in instantaneously so that customers and other stakeholders are not even aware of the switch.

This can happen routinely – for example when all the operatives in a call centre are busy and new calls are automatically diverted to another call centre miles or even countries away. It may happen only once in a lifetime, because a significant incident has damaged the ability of the primary service centre to deliver to its objectives. The concepts are the same, although in the latter case the lack of experience dramatically increases the chance of failure.

The plans developed by infrastructure managers are therefore extremely rigid in the individual steps to be taken and in which order to ensure that all the infrastructure ingredients; the various hardware, software, data and their dependencies are all brought together in time to deliver the holistic service to users. Sourcing of all the ingredients, in time and in the right order, with the skills to make it happen is a critical first layer of need that needs to be exercised.

The purpose of exercising this particular objective is relatively straightforward and that is to be as confident as it is possible to be that the service promises implied in the service level agreements will be delivered exactly as promised.

By 'the promises,' of course, we need to include the all technological and other hardware, the cabling, the software, the data and the people who will need to be available to step in on time to deliver the whole quite precisely as promised. We need to include all factors in their delivery, whether those are internal facilities and people, outsourced suppliers of these services, their own dependencies such as power, water, air conditioning, heating, electricity, safety, security, environmental acceptability and a host of other support infrastructures. We may need to include also any contingency services suppliers with whom the organisation has contracted to supply contingency equipment.

> *We finally need to bring this all together and be reassured that the combination of all these things will be accessible to the organisation's operatives and managers; and will be useable by them in sufficient numbers. They need to be useable by operational staff in such a way that will enable them in turn to deliver their own responsibilities to customers and other stakeholders. A technical recovery plan that does not meet each and every one of these requirements will fail as totally as though the plan does not exist at all.*

An infrastructure recovery exercise will therefore set out physically to trigger the plans that have been laid for getting that contingency equipment in place in time. It will have the objective to prove that processing can be done from the contingency site and contingency equipment within the time promised to operational managers. The exercise will typically create and make live the contingency workspaces and equipment; load software and back up data as applicable and do checks that it is all useable. The exercise will include of course the creation of new workspaces for real people and the adequacy of any communication links that are needed within the organisation and also beyond. The scenarios that will be considered may include:

- A worksite is still accessible and safe but technology failures or other dependencies will mean that contingency services will need to be recreated on-site or remotely. If remotely, then the services will need to be fed back into the primary site from a remote contingency site.

- The worksite is inaccessible or unsafe and so people and infrastructures will need to be moved together to a contingency site – or indeed to two different sites with communication between.

Sadly, many IT exercises are inward-looking and are performed exclusively by the IT department. This takes their eye away from the ball; and that ball is whether the new infrastructure is actually useable by the organisation itself to deliver whatever it is that it needs urgently to deliver. An infrastructure recovery exercise without users is like a plane without wings and is doomed to failure. Users do need to play a part; perhaps by a cross section of the organisation visiting the contingency site and going through some routine processes onto the backup data that has been reinstated, and reporting on its effectiveness. Stress testing or volume testing can be done technologically.

Case Study

An organisation in Ireland had trusted its contingency plan to the technology manager alone. Its thinking was that as a services company it had a vital dependency on the continuity of computer services. The IT manager had contracted to have backups created regularly and had contracted with a contingency service supplier to have a similar machine loaded with software 10 miles away and to be ready within 24 hours.

When asked how many workspaces had been contracted with this supplier the answer was 10. When asked where the other 200 staff were to sit, the response was that he had thought that this was someone else's responsibility and not his. He needed 10 spaces for his own team to ensure that the computers and their peripherals were all working properly.

It would be easy to criticise this technology manager but the real failure lies in the management team above him who had failed to see the wider picture and ensure that all its needs were brought together and achieved.

The need for exercising, whether the contingency equipment is sourced from elsewhere within the same organisation, or provided by external contingency service suppliers, is equally critical. In the event of the former, it is absolutely crucial to ensure that all the hoped-for equipment is still there and free to be used. It is also vital that all the equipment that has been earmarked for possible crisis contingency use is still able to respond to the latest technological levels now being routinely used. It is important also to ensure that data filing and storage systems are still compatible.

Case Study

A risk manager had agreed that office space currently unused in another city would be earmarked for the recovery suite of an urgent, business-critical service division. That space formed part of a group-owned building and was difficult or unable to be let or sold individually. The space therefore provided a low/no cost option for the contingency managers.

When exercising that part of the plan, the contingency managers arrived to find that a project team from another division had 'camped' in the office. The project was a secret business development project with urgent delivery dates and as such would compete enthusiastically for priority use of the area. The secrecy had meant that the 'camping' had not been advertised.

Fortunately this was discovered during an exercise, not in a live, potentially destructive, incident. The learning point of the exercise was that the risk manager saw the need to ensure that when plans are to use internal 'free' spaces that they are formalised internally by the risk department renting the space from the office services department. The internal cost, if allocated, would then be charged back proportionately to those departments protected by such an arrangement.

With that contract (and thus 'ownership') in place, others wishing to use the workspace would need to negotiate with the risk manager and agree conditions that could include immediate departure if predefined circumstances.

Infrastructure plans may be primarily about equipment, technology hardware, software and data but these things cannot possibly be brought together without a human resource and skill base to make it happen. The infrastructure exercises therefore need to include the element of the call-out and to ensure enough depth in the team so that the rebuild can still take place even when some individuals are missing. The plan sectors to be exercised are also are about the legality, compliance and other 'soft' dependencies before the new infrastructures can be used for the purposes intended.

Case Study

An urgent rebuild had begun late on a Friday evening following flood damage to a computer suite. Continuity of services was a critical and urgent requirement for a Monday morning delivery of services. The planners had included the 24/7 contact numbers for the software supplier's technical teams that had routinely been on call for minor disruptions.

The supplier's technical teams were called and asked to give support to the rebuilding into the organisation's pre-agreed contingency office suites. There was shock when the software supplier's teams were unable to help because the purchased software had been licensed only for use in the organisations normal location. The teams felt that they were not authorised to help; but also there were technical protections built into the software that restricted copies being used on other machines. These controls could only be removed with knowledge of the software's primary code numbers.

The legal/sales department of the software suppliers were not on 24/7 call and their home numbers were not known by neither the damaged organisation nor the software supplier's technical service teams. There was damage to the organisation when it was unable to 'open for business' on Monday morning.

There is a useful additional case study that brings out the fact that, however carefully plans are written, they are obviously and by definition written by someone who knows at the time of writing what it is they wish to say! This is not a luxury held by someone else picking up the document; especially when done in time of great stress and urgency.

Case Study

The operators of one of the largest civilian mainframe computer suites in Europe had contracted with IBM to have access to standby equipment that is kept available in one or more of the IBM sites. The contract enabled and indeed demanded four exercises a year; done comfortably over weekends using backup tapes and without disrupting the business itself. These 'tests' were booked months ahead and all teams were booked beforehand to be available. The recovery plan was a very detailed, step-by-step process leading through eventually to service availability.

Tests had begun to be routine and the organisation decided that for one of the tests that their own personnel and the IBM personnel would reverse roles. In other words the 'plan' was simply handed to a suitably skilled IBM employee and the principal's employees were to be observers only as the rebuilding took place. The objective was to become reassured that the rebuilding could take place even if the principal's employees were killed, injured or otherwise not immediately available to interpret the plan. The exposure was felt to be in the individual small team that had developed the plan documentation itself.

It became clear that the highly skilled IBM employees were not able to rebuild the technology without a requesting a number of clarifications from the plan writers.

A useful exercise that (a) brought out the importance of individuals still in this technological world and (b) caused a rewrite of some sections of the plan.

There is a particular aspect of exercising that is worthy of mention at this time: where the continuity plans will depend on a third party supplier of contingency services and equipment. This is summarised by the United Kingdom Financial Services Authority: "... where a site is shared, a firm should evaluate the likelihood and impact of multiple calls on shared resources such as the availability of a third party site due to its use by another." **(2)**

Business Continuity Exercising

We stated above that keeping an organisation alive throughout a potentially destructive incident is much, much more than the facilities infrastructure. The wider continuity risk management and continuity planning will reflect this. The organisation that survives will have coped with the demands on its people. It will have taken control of the unfolding situation, limited damage, managed the interface between people and the infrastructures, and ensured it had the ability still to continue to deliver confidence and other individual and crucial responsibilities. It will also have had cruelly tested by the incident the decisions that had been made on risk, its tolerance and its management.

Exercising these needs can be undertaken in many different ways. The exercise could entail

- Seminars: Also known as workshops, brainstorming or discussion-based events where the scenarios are simply talked through and the views captured for future development work;

- Control post exercises that entail going one step further and position people into their planned control posts during the exercise;

- Table-top exercises: This type of exercise usually goes further and will demand that the participants respond to a scenario and deal with its developments as it unfolds throughout the exercise time- slot. This will not usually entail any disruption of the normal organisation; or,

- Live exercises that will need to make use of and divert normal processes and people from their business-as-normal tasks.

The Home Office in the United Kingdom (3) uses these particular titles for types of exercise but other organisations may categorise using different names.

We add in this book an additional 'exercise' and that is when real live incidents need to be managed through. If we assume that the organisation is lucky enough or well-managed enough to survive, there will always be a host of individual lessons to be learned from the experience. It would be a dreadfully wasted opportunity if these lessons are not 'captured' and their risk and continuity thinking developed further. We will add therefore this fifth category of exercising.

We will now explore each one of these types individually, but throughout it is important to remember that the infrastructure exercising and now business continuity exercising is by no means contained within comfortable, individual silos. Neither are these other types of continuity exercising that we list immediately above. They meet different needs but above all they are interdependent and we will continue to readdress this important message.

Seminars, Workshops, Brainstorming Or Discussion Based Events

There is a clear logic to the fact that the person who understands a particular risk most thoroughly is the local manager or operator of that function. This knowledge can be found at all levels, not just with the key managers. The 'brainstorm' is one way of accessing that understanding. It can be at any level within the organisation. The risk manager will bring together selected managers and employees and facilitate a discussion about risk, consequences and what challenges they envisage in handling threats to business continuity. Occasionally a professional facilitator may be used whose role it is to keep a careful balance between time, the agenda, and the direction of the flow of conversation.

The meeting can be arranged in the style of a normal business meeting with a chairperson (the facilitator) and an agenda. Specific scenarios may be placed before the participants. The participants are then expected to say how these scenarios might unfold, how damaging they might be and how they could, or could not, be managed. The objectives are more often designed towards identifying problems rather than necessarily completing the cycle of problem-solving.

It is vital to document the thoughts generated for action afterwards. It is advisable for any agreed action points to be formally allocated to named individuals and given a time for completion. The person may, of course, be the risk manager or any one of the other participants.

Groups can gain best value if made up of operational staff, with risk professionals joining as advisers. These teams may reflect the operation managers who are responsible for particular functions, or they may be one of the crisis teams that would be brought together in a potential crisis.

These brainstorms and seminars are likely to be used if the organiser wishes to have a wider discussion than one that would evolve from the presentation of one scenario; and such meetings may best be used relatively early in the planning cycle. Nevertheless the event can only add value if all participants understand clear objectives; and thus at least broad parameters for the discussions are set beforehand. The meetings can certainly meet some of the need to raise awareness; and enable potential players in real disasters to begin to understand the principles on continuity adopted by their organisation, as well as the roles they are likely to have to play. Those roles may not be only within their own organisation but down through the supply chain or across industry bodies where there are interdependencies. The interdependencies can be found in all fields, but not least in public services and in mutually dependent fields such as banking and financial services.

Control Post Exercises

These exercises, used often but not exclusively by emergency services teams, have the team leaders and their support staff position themselves into the control rooms that they will normally occupy during an actual incident. The exercise can, in the main, test the adequacy and effectiveness of the communication infrastructures among them.

Table-Top Exercises

These exercises will place before a team an individual scenario for them to decide how they would respond and handle that scenario. The exercises can range from a simple scenario to one that unfolds gradually throughout the exercise period and involve a hundred or more individual inputs. The initial scenario may be no more than a radio news flash or a phone call and the evolving scenarios could involve half-truths, non-truths, rumours and be fed faster than the teams can realistically have enough time for. The idea is to reflect real life as is best achievable without disrupting the organisation's day-to-day affairs.

The demands on the team would be for them to sort out the truths from the half-truths or rumours, identify priorities and to take a view on what needs to be achieved against what is currently achievable; and the information and other resources they would need to deliver that achievement.

Planning A Table-Top Exercise

A table-top exercise is more complex than the ones above and the planning of the objectives, processes and the deliverables needs more care. The process of getting a successful table-top off the ground will entail some quite clear stepping stones. These stepping stones can fall into the following broad headings:

- Be clear what needs to be exercised;
- Obtain approvals and budgets from the Board or the Divisional Manager;
- Decide on the format to be used and the participants needed;
- Establish the availability of the rooms and other resources that may be needed;
- Establish the exercise scenario;
- Prepare introductory documentation to distribute to participants beforehand;
- Prepare any documentation needed for the exercise itself;
- Undertake the exercise;
- Document the learning and the decisions made;
- Send these reports to the participants for their approval that the key areas of the exercise have been captured and that they accept the ownership of the results;
- Ensure any action points are adopted by suitable right personnel; and,
- Revise the risk registers, BIA and recovery plans as needed.

There are likely to be some individual aspects to be covered within this framework. Some examples now follow:

1. *Should the participants be surprised by the exercise or warned that it is to take place and if so; exactly when?*

This is a decision for the culture of the organisation and the objectives to be achieved. The decision to warn or surprise can also be one that best reflects the development of continuity planning in the organisation. A surprise exercise undertaken when the organisation's people are still at an early stage of continuity planning can be less effective than when the planning is much more developed and embedded.

A danger is that, if the participants are not aware beforehand, there can be resentment that the exercise is taking them away from the particular things they had planned to achieve that day. Unexpected exercises that go beyond normal working hours or 'call-outs' could, for example, cause real problems for parents and carers who have important needs to return home on time.. Planned exercises can ensure that more participants are available on the day and have been able to give some thought to the objectives.

A reasonable compromise can be where the chairman or the most senior executive wishes to undertake a surprise exercise and uses a meeting that had been advertised by him or her for another purpose. The chosen participants are therefore on the premises, and together with time booked out of their diary.

Planned exercises enable instructions to be distributed beforehand and the 'ground rules' explained in writing beforehand.

2. *Provision of exercise ground rules and prompts*

These, beyond a general explanation of the objectives, the mechanics and the expected deliverables may include:

- The name of the exercise controller and how that person may be contacted;
- The name of the exercise facilitator and how that person can be contacted;
- How and by whom the exercise learning points are to be recorded;
- Instruction that the exercise must be entirely contained within the rooms allocated and no calls are to be made to other employees, suppliers or third parties;
- Role players will be identified, their roles explained and how to make contact where needed;
- Instruction to leave all documentation in the room after the exercise for shredding;
- Participants will are asked to accept the limitations of the desktop nature of the exercise;
- Warnings that decisions may be needed when other key staff is missing and/or when only part information is known. This is deliberate and will reflect a real-life incident;
- The volumes of information fed in may be excessive and may demand prioritisation and delegation amongst the teams;
- 'Housekeeping' and the facilities that are available during the exercise; and,
- That members will be continually expected to respond to an unfolding scenario and make decisions; but each decisions should include a consideration of each of the underlying ingredients listed below:

Overriding Ingredients And Pointers In Decision Making

- What is the team's own assessment of the potential for damage?

- What steps can be taken now to limit further damage to the organisation?

- What is the view on how further damage could unfold from the information known? Should this be anticipated and steps taken to limit this too?

- In some situations, does this particular team need to get involved at all?

- What decisions would be made and who needs to be told of those decisions?

- Would the team reinvent itself in the light of this experience? Are the numbers and disciplines within the team the best balance of authority, resources and skills that are available?

- What additional needs would they better resource beforehand should the team feel that any of these could not otherwise be accessible within a timescale demanded by business needs?

- What action points need therefore to be allocated to assist further:

- Understanding of the exposures

- More effective risk management

- Improve the recovery planning and resourcing

- An improvement of risk review and recovery plan documentation

- For legal, compliance or other reasons, which decisions and actions need to have minutes taken formally?

---

3. *Should external organisations be present?*

Carefully chosen third parties can provide valuable additional input or may be just observers, valued for their comments and for stimulating discussion during the event or the de-brief afterwards. Other divisions of an organisation – especially dependent ones – may be useful as observers or even as role players. Clearly business continuity exercises may gain from a presence by service support divisions of the organisation such as personnel, legal, marketing, corporate affairs, technology and others. We believe conversely that technology and infrastructure rebuild must have representatives of the users there to ensure their needs are included in the rebuilds.

Emergency service organisations such as the Police or Fire Brigade can bring their own dimension and experience to planning an exercise and can provide actual inputs as the day unfolds. Stakeholders, for example large customers may value an insight into the exercise should the organisation feel that it is yet able to open up to its strengths and potential weaknesses in this way. It is unlikely that any but the most public of exercises will find the media attending to be more use than danger (but see below regarding media role players).

4. *Should the participants be in one team or two?*

If there are sufficient people involved the exercise controller may decide to split the people into two teams. The teams would be in separate rooms and would consider the same scenarios simultaneously. The absence of one skill or manager from one team would reflect the real-life situation that all managers may not be immediately available to handle all challenges. The debrief can then take the form of a discussion between the two teams as to how they decided to respond and deal with the issues that had been raised.

5. *Challenging participants*

In any group of people there will be those who bring particular challenges to the effective running of a team. A common challenge is when the most senior person in the room feels the need to take all decisions and other members feel the need simply to agree. This is dangerous in quite distinct ways. That person may not be available as a real crisis begins to unfold and other team members may have to step in. Even if we assume that that person is the best available manager in normal working conditions they may not be the best equipped, physically or psychologically to be a leader in a stressful, fast-moving crisis. Furthermore, that person's decisions may simply be wrong. There are opportunities in running exercises to develop scenarios at will. A good exercise facilitator will look for such imbalances and ensure that the unfolding scenario will 'remove' that person from 'the scene' and switch from becoming a team player to an observer. This 'removal' could be, for example, by a painful death or injury, or a call to a media interview room!

6. *The Media*

Managing the media is likely to be central to the recovery of a major, customer-driven, organisation and that requirement can evolve just minutes in from the incident itself. No exercise of such circumstances would be complete without a media element. This can take the form of media-related questions to be answered, or if the exercise budget will stretch enough, to having professional media role players as part of the exercise team. These role players can demand statements, radio or television interviews just as the real media would do and their feedback as part of the exercise debrief can very valuable indeed.

Case Study

A major bank undertook an exercise that included professional media consultants filling the role of media reporters. The scenario was a technical failure that meant that credit cards could not be authorised live throughout the whole country. The 'media' demanded a statement and the Corporate Affairs Director responded.

The media team, unknown to the exercise participants, then recorded a video news item outside the building that was around a 'restaurateur' whose hard-earned business was about to be destroyed because people could not pay for their meals after eating. The angry 'victim' waxed strong about the Bank's 'inefficiencies' and failures and ridiculed the statement for being callous and uncaring to small business people like her.

Later in the exercise the controller stopped the discussion 'as it was time for the news programme on television;' stating that the team would, in a real crisis, wish to check news broadcasts as they occurred. The team was astonished to see the created news item on the television set in the room. They saw that further thinking was rapidly needed.

---

7. *Location*

The planner can use any suitable resourced space that is available. It may be a boardroom within the normal office or, if possible at the recovery site. This latter location has the advantage of the players familiarising themselves with the actual site that may be used in a live incident.

8. *Use of the offsite store*

Many business continuity plans include the use of an 'offsite' store or, as sometimes known, 'battle box.' This might be a room, cupboards or portable carrier located away from the site in question. It can be used for storing anything that each department would find useful to them in the early minutes and hours of a crisis. The list of contents can be endless and will start with the overall toolkit of safety wear, torches, radios, copy of plans, staff phone numbers and next of kin, media contact points, stationery and a whole host of other things that might be useful immediately. An important example would be information that could not await the recovery of the technology infrastructures. Whatever is included should be securely stored, accessible and form part of the overall plan maintenance programme. Torches, mobile phones or radios with dead batteries will be useless.

The contents of this store should be brought to the exercise room and made available.

Scenario Setting

The best scenarios are credible ones with which the participants can identify. They are best when they deal quite specifically with the organisation and thus use real names, functions, stakeholders and current business models. Within a broad scenario therefore the exercise controller needs to create a detailed plot that may begin only with a news flash or a telephone call, but then move on progressively through an unfolding scenario of questions and problems posed by people and circumstances with which they are familiar. The controller will build in the flexibility to respond to the team's responses and can have a hundred or more individual inputs ready to deliver.

Clearly therefore the design of the detailed scenarios need input on the detailed design from someone who has an intimate knowledge of the workings of the division to be exercised. That person would recognise the secrecy and would most likely be an observer on the day of the exercise, not a participant on that day.

The background input will be to set the scene, time, weather, market, political and market conditions and whether there is any ongoing audit, project or other relevant development. The first 'live' input may give very little information at all:

Case Studies

First exercise input example I: Telephone call
Time: 8.09 Monday evening 29th November

"Pat, I have just had a call from Group 4. They have been trying to get hold of Brian but he must be out at the moment."

"They had a fire alert on our alarm system to their control room. They cannot raise the security guard but have called the Fire brigade. They can't tell me any more at present or whether it is just a false alarm. What can I do immediately to help?"

First exercise input example 2: Telephone call to office manager

Time: 12.38 Tuesday 4th July

"This is Supt. Jones here. We have information that a person, whom we believe may be a customer, has left an explosive or an incendiary device inside one of your buildings. We are interviewing him now in Stroud Police Station but he is reluctant to admit anything or give us any information as yet."

"Our intelligence is that the person we suspect has the resources to gain access and to offer a significant threat to your building and to your staff. We believe that an explosion may be imminent. We suggest you take this threat seriously and take precautions against injury and damage."

First exercise input example 3: Newsflash: Radio Sheffield
Time: 1600 Friday 23rd. December

"We interrupt for a serious traffic warning: A serious fire has caused the closure of all of Doncaster Road in Sheffield. Police and Fire brigade have closed the road. We do not yet know what is on fire. The Police are unable to estimate when the road can be re-opened. Traffic has been diverted and there are major traffic jams across South Sheffield. We suggest you avoid this area for some hours. We will bring you further reports as they come in."

There is the opportunity when setting the scenario to make a point or two that the participants may not have otherwise considered. For example, a small fire in a cable duct could destroy all voice and data communications across a building of thousands of workplaces. Another example would be that the unfolding scenario includes the fact that the Police have decided that the location is a crime scene. They have denied access for some days even though the building is otherwise accessible and safe to use.

Scenario setting is of course not only about the crisis response. It is an opportunity to exercise some of the decision-making about risk, risk tolerance and management. The many questions and challenges will be from customers, regulators and other stakeholders who have particular needs and concerns. They may relate to current work on desks, urgent needs and reassurances that their investment or contract is going to be honoured. This will be mixed with such phone calls as an extremely worried, probably hysterical mother whose daughter has not yet returned home. "Was she in the building at the time? Where is she now? Is she all right?"

Live Exercises

We describe the next level as live exercises for want of another clear label and because they are usually large scale and involve people playing the part of victims in the unfolding scenario. Actors playing parts can be useful in exercises undertaken by commercial organisations but in the main these types of exercises are undertaken by the emergency services and the organisations that support them during an incident. At the smaller end of the scale, acting parts may be played by people who telephone into the crisis teams with questions and problems to be resolved. At the other end of the scale many hundreds or thousands of people may play a part and there can be significant disruption to what would otherwise be happening on that day.

Case Study
Terror Exercise USA TOPOFF 3: April, 2005

This anti-terrorism exercise, the largest that the USA had ever held, spread as far as Canada and the United Kingdom and exercised planned responses to attacks involving biological and chemical weapons. More than 10,000 people took part in the five-day exercise. The scenario was a simulated biological attack by terrorists in New Jersey, and simultaneously a chemical attack at a port on the coast of Connecticut.

In addition to testing first responders and emergency units, the exercise was meant also to assess intelligence gathering and communication. The scenario entailed, weeks earlier, a CIA agent in Europe receiving a report - clearly labeled as an exercise - about a possible terrorism event. This report included false information, and thus reflected real-life incidents. That information presumably was assessed as it progressed through the intelligence network. Clearly the intelligence agencies would not have been allowed, under any circumstances, to thwart the mock attack.

The exercise was designed also to test how officials communicate with the public, a crucial part of handling any emergency that could involve panic. The media were invited to cover the event, but they were given only limited information. Full exercise briefings were given to a mock news operation. Videos were made and were also fake but experienced reporters were able to question top officials to simulate a real news conference.

The exercise began when a patient appeared at a New Jersey hospital with strange flu-like symptoms. This was determined to be caused by a biological agent. As the first day progressed, thousands of volunteer "patients" appeared at hospitals.

At the same time, officials in New Jersey received a report of a suspicious sport-utility type vehicle parked at Kean University. When the emergency services approached the vehicle they found a hose nozzle sticking out a rear window. It was found to be a commercial sprayer that presumably had been used to disperse a fake biological agent.

In Connecticut, meanwhile, the local emergency responders received a 911 call from a worker at a first aid tent set up at a water festival in New London. People were turning up sick with unusual symptoms and local authorities quickly became suspicious that a chemical agent might be involved. Before they could fully assess what was happening, a van near a parking garage at the festival exploded.

After the explosion and a brief inspection by safety experts, 500 actors walked up to the site and sprawled on the ground, screaming and crying and generally getting into the spirit of the drill. Reporters, state officials, politicians and consultants watched from the hilltop above. ·

On later days the drill shifted to local hospitals, where thousands of mock "patients" appeared in various degrees of medical crisis. Some were treated in emergency rooms and admitted; others underwent triage and outdoor decontamination in parking lots, depending on what officials deemed to be appropriate for them.

Neither real weapons nor biological agents were used, but emergency services and other involved officials responded as though they were being used. Police and emergency workers needed to respond to the situations as they unfolded

The Department of Homeland Security said that both types of attack are plausible but neither was chosen because of any specific intelligence. Officials in both Canada and Britain were involved in the $16 million exercise. This cost was mostly to pay for the overtime costs for local emergency responders and officials. Some 10,000 paid personnel and volunteers participated in total, as well as authorities in Canada and Britain. The exercise was known as TOPOFF 3, for Top Official. TOPOFF 2 was held in May 2003 and involved 8,500 people in the USA and Canada.

US Homeland Security Secretary Michael Chertoff gave a clear message beforehand that is relevant to all exercising.

"The point of this is not to design a simulation that makes us 'look good' because we were able to figure out how to pre-package everything that we wanted to do. The point is to actually drive at the areas where we think there are potential questions or criticisms, to really push there in order to learn more lessons."

Case Study
Lessons Learned From London's Emergency Exercise on the Tube, 7 September 2004

"The emergency exercise at Bank Underground Station carried out on 7 September confirmed that a great deal of work has been done to improve London's capability to respond to major emergencies but identified further areas for action.

"The exercise was designed to enable London's frontline services, fire, police and ambulance, to practise their response to a chemical attack on the Tube.

"Key lessons from the exercise were published today by Alistair Darling, Secretary of State for Transport.

Mr Darling said, "This was an extremely valuable exercise, which allowed us to test the capability and constraints of our emergency services under difficult circumstances. Exercises such as this are also an opportunity to learn and we have identified areas that need furtherdevelopment."

"While some of the conclusions need to remain confidential for reasons of security we are today fulfilling our commitment to make public the key findings that the emergency services and others have identified."

"The exercise found that:

- *A great deal of work has already been done by Government, Emergency Services and the Mayor of London to improve London's capability to respond to emergencies through improved equipment and planning;*

- *There needs to be contingency planning, preparation and funding for responding to large scale emergencies and that this work continues to be given high priority;*

- *Work needs to continue to look at and prepare for alternative rescue plans for difficult environments like the London Underground;*

- *Work needs to continue to improve the ability of those wearing protective suits to be able to communicate under difficult conditions;*

- *Ambulance crews need to be able to provide earlier assessment, care and delivery of specific antidotes to contaminated casualties; and,*

- *We must not underestimate the number of people and specialist equipment required to respond to such emergencies."*

(4)

The Home Secretary, United Kingdom Government issued an Exercise Planners Guide and while this was issued in 1999 as part of the planning for the millennium computer challenges there remain many valuable lessons that are useful in a much wider context. The guide explores the differences between controlled exercises where each step is pre-planned to a much more free play style where the participants themselves are free to move the exercise forward, within only a set of broad parameters and scenarios, in the way they think it will go. There are clearly safety issues to monitor, codewords to ensure all are aware that it is an exercise and that at any time the exercise itself could be overtaken by a real live event that could occur with unfortunate timing. The guide explains the role of the exercise controller, the exercise directors, umpires, observers and ensure that matters such as communications, identification, logging, media participation and briefings are all carefully considered and agreed before the exercise commences.

Exercise Check List

The Home office Exercise Planners guide includes a useful checklist that is reproduced below:

1. Agree on the scenario, extent and aim of the exercise with senior management.

2. Assemble a multi-disciplinary exercise planning team and agree on the objectives for each area to be exercised.

3. Sketch out and then develop the main events of the exercise and associated timetables.

4. Determine and confirm the availability of the outside agencies to be involved, such as the media or voluntary agencies.

5. List the facilities required for the exercise and confirm their availability, e.g., transport, buildings and equipment.

6. Ensure that all communications to be used during the exercise have been tested at some stage prior to the exercise. If a control post or live exercise, test radios, mobile phones, etc. in the locations in which they will be used as near to the date of the exercise as possible.

7. Check that umpires for each stage of the exercise are clearly identified and properly briefed.

8. Ensure that directing staff are clearly identified and properly briefed, and have good independent communications with 'exercise control' throughout the exercise.

9. If the exercise links a number of activities or functions which are dependent on each other, confirm that each has been individually tested beforehand.

10. Ensure that all participants have been briefed.

11. Ensure that all players are aware of the procedures to be followed if a real emergency occurs during the exercise.

12. If spectators are to be invited, including the media, ensure that they are clearly identified and properly marshalled, and arrange for them to be kept informed of the progress of the exercise. Ensure their safety.

13. For the longer exercise, arrange catering and toilet facilities.

14. Ensure that where appropriate outside agencies are indemnified in the event of exercise accident.

15. Warn the local media, emergency services switchboards / controls and any neighbours who might be worried or affected by the exercise. Position "Exercise in Progress" signs if appropriate.

16. Ensure that senior management, directing staff, umpires and key players are aware of the time and location for the 'hot' debrief, and circulate a timetable for a full debrief.

17. Agree and prepare a detailed set of recommendations, each one accompanied by an action addressee and timescale.

18. Prepare a clear and concise summary report of the exercise to distribute to all organisations and groups which took part, together with major recommendations.

19. Discuss with senior management the outcome of the exercise and agree on the future exercise programme.

20. Thank all personnel and outside agencies which took part. **(5)**

Real Live Incidents

Our additional category of 'exercise' beyond the British Home Office definitions is when a real-life incident occurs that puts the organisation under threat. As these incidents unfold, and hopefully, lead to survival, it would be an awful waste if the lessons being learned are not recorded for a debriefing and then incorporated into preparations for any future incident that may occur.

Any disruption, however small, can provide important lessons to be learned. This can include detail matters such as the organisation's infrastructure to be rebuilt *(e.g., Can we do it better? Faster? Do we need to do it faster? Better? Can we design out the cause of the incident or the extent of impact?)*. The lessons can similarly be big ones. Some incidents moved the goal posts of scenario setting. These include the St Mary Axe Bomb in London in 1993, the falling stock prices over some years from the 1990s into the year 2000 and beyond, the Y2K threats, the September 11, 2001 attacks on America, the frequency of Atlantic hurricanes through 2004, the Asian Tsunami in December 2004, the London terrorist bombings in July 2005 and Hurricanes Katrina, Rita and Wilma in August through October, 2005.

Case Study 1
World Trade Center, New York City, New York

There were countless individual lessons emerging from the September 11 attacks on the World Trade Center in New York. Just a couple were that the geographical range of the damage is now likely to be much wider than envisaged beforehand; also the expectation that two separate but related attacks may be made simultaneously. Many multinational organisations with the ability to switch operations across continents found that they were dependent on a small, just-in-time supplier of essential services without that flexibility. Some organisations were already moving into their emergency suites in the other building at the time of the second attack there.

Case Study 2
Tsunami

"At 7.30am, we were informed by our Chennai unit that co-ordinates the logistics for the Car Nicobar base about a massive earthquake near Andamans and Nicobar," Air Chief S Krishnaswamy told the Indian Express today. But communication links went down to the island territories, the Chennai unit could only raise Car Nicobar base on the high frequency set at 7.50am. The last message from Car Nicobar was that the island is sinking and that there is water all over.

"At 8.15am, the Air Chief asked his Assistant Chief of Air staff (Operations) to alert the Defence Ministry. Unaware of its fax goof-up, the IMD, as per routine, sent anther fax to the Disaster Control Room in the Ministry of Home affairs (MHA) at 9.14am. At 10.30, the director of the Control room, T Swami, informed the Cabinet Secretariat Officials. By then the Tsunami had hit the Chennai coastline and another earthquake measuring 7.3 struck 50miles west of Indira point at 9.53am. **(6)**

These vital communication lessons are now being addressed.

Case Study 3
Italian Power Blackout, September 2004

At 3.11, the ETRANS (Swiss Network Operators) operators requested by a phone call for GTRN (the Italian Network Operators) to decrease the control deviation by 300MW. According to ETRANS, GTRN was informed by ETRANS on the trip of the 380kV line Mettlon-Lavargo and the resulting overload of the 380kV line Sils-Soazza, and asked for the control deviation to be reduced by 300MW.

The ETRANS checklist also mentions that this communication be confirmed by fax. The ETRANS fax journal indicates faxes to the GTRN dispatching at 04.34 – 06.05 –06.36 –08.53 – 09.14 – 09.29 and 09.41. According to GTRN the first fax was received only at 09.41. **(7)**

Important communication lessons again.

Case Study 4

A major insurance company suffered significant damage following an IRA bomb attack on Central London. The emergency team leaders were allowed by the Police into the cordoned area to take a look at their damaged building. These leaders saw that there were cracks along the side of their major building, and one that housed their dealing rooms. They then set about their recovery plan on the assumption that the building would be unusable for months and may even have to be pulled down.

A couple of days later they were allowed further personnel into the area and arranged that structural engineers would be part of the group. The Engineers undertook structural tests and were able to report later that the building was sound. It was the cladding only that had moved and the dealing rooms could be made safe for occupancy within a week.

There followed a significant change in the contingency arrangements needed and the time scales for recovery.

A real sadness is when it has become clear that lessons to be learned are not captured and followed up to save future loss, death and injury. Two examples alone are the Foot and Mouth disease epidemics in the United Kingdom, and the lessons on communications which were clearly available from the first attacks on the World Trade Center in New York City in 1993.

Danger Areas

As we state throughout this book, no activity is without its own risks and dangers. Running exercises is no exception. There is a very real risk that the exercise may 'escape' beyond the participants and there have been examples of phone calls to suppliers and other expensive triggering of inappropriate actions or interruption of work. IT exercises could also lead to failure of the very systems that they are seeking to test.

- One such example was when a pre-prepared role player was called during an exercise on the internal phone system. That person was on the phone on another call and the exercise call was automatically diverted to a colleague. The resultant mayhem was distinctly unpleasant.

- An exercise involved military personnel and used Council offices in Nottingham, England. The exercise controller clearly thought he could add drama by setting off a small explosive in a tin box. This certainly had the desired effect, but what was not expected was that a considerable amount of smoke emerged and set off the fire alarm. The poor controller had to watch in embarrassment as many hundreds of council staff trooped past the door on their way to the fire evacuation point.

- An exercise scenario at the BBC involved a bomb near the building and this scenario found itself in the newsroom logs the following morning. Fortunately the news editor checked before broadcasting the incident.

- A Sutton, London, exercise included a real evacuation following a fictitious bomb incident. Hundreds of staff went into the street to find Police cordons in place holding them back while they were handling a real bomb alert further up the street. It was difficult to see who was more confused and alarmed.

- The use of a staff information line in an exercise did not anticipate that there would be a real incident hundreds of miles away and that staff, looking for real information, would hear the exercise scenario and instructions.

- A bomb threat exercise in Regent Street, London had to be evacuated because of a real bomb threat.

- An exercise decision was made that a division is low priority and may need to close down following a particular incident. That decision became public knowledge after a participant talked about his day later in the pub. This created difficult morale and other management challenges.

- The underground tube bombs London in July, 2005 occurred just as the emergency services were exercising with a scenario of suicide bombs on the London underground.

The message that emerges from these incidents is that great care needs to be taken. Clearly, participants need to be made aware of the limitations and dangers; and procedures such as code words for stopping and starting the exercise. Shredding and other controls need to be introduced and participants clearly warned.

There is a further and vital danger. The danger is that one exercise will unrealistically raise expectations and these expectations need to be actively managed. The scenario, by definition, is based on one event or a small number of coinciding events. In the real world the event may be something very different. Furthermore, an exercise that deals with infrastructure rebuilds will not move forward the organisation's important need to deal, professionally, with the media or other wider, and just as important needs

The exercise debriefing and report should state this limitation clearly.

Exercise Regulations And Benchmarking

There is a separate chapter in this book regarding regulations and benchmarking but it is important to remind here that some regulators require exercising to be part of the wider resilience programme. One example is the Financial Services Authority in the United Kingdom. **(8)**

There are risk and continuity market organisations that provide benchmarking tools against which organisations can measure their own exercising. One such example is the Business Continuity Institute. **(9)**

Summary

We set out in this chapter to explain the importance of and where exercising has a place in the wider programme that ensures the organisation's resilience.

There are different ways around which exercising can be designed and undertaken, and the exercise planner will make choices that relate to the particular objectives of the day. There are, however, common denominators such as the need for awareness training, gaining ownership, and as a measuring tool for the decision-making that has previously been taken around risk and survival planning. Exercising can also identify where plans are not up to date.

Exercising is a positive process that is designed to move the risk and continuity work forward and gain further credibility in the risk work and plans that are in place. It is by no means a performance measuring exercise of those previously involved.

The nature of the beast is that, if an exercise brings out a message that all is perfect and no lessons were learned it would raise strong questions about the quality of the exercise itself.

(1) Financial Services Authority, www.fsa.gov.uk

(2) CP142: Section 3A.6 External event and other changes.

(3) Home office: United Kingdom; The Exercise Planners Guide 1999.

(4) www.ukresilience.info/londonprepared/antiterrorism/lessons

(5) Home office: United Kingdom; The Exercise Planners Guide 1999

(6) Indian Express, 30th December 2004

(7) Report of the Investigating Committee

(8) Financial Services Authority in the United Kingdom, www.fsa.gov.uk

(9) Business Continuity Institute, www.thebci.org

17

Maintenance, Benchmarking, Assurance and Audit

Objectives Of This Chapter Are To:

- Review the drivers and options for plan review and maintenance
- Consider the role of benchmarking tools
- Discuss quality assurance and compliance in the context of business continuity management
- Explore the validation of business continuity plans through the processes of internal and external audit
- Know where you are heading

Ferdinand Magellan was a Portuguese navigator who travelled around the world. He died in the Philippines but his crew continued the voyage and many people think it was the greatest navigational feat in history. However when Magellan set off he did not know where he was heading, during his travels he did not know where he was, and when his crew returned they did not know where they had been!

Today's world is rather different and organisations most certainly need to know that the path they are travelling is the one they have chosen, and how well their journey is working out against their plan. Fortunately most organisations operate without major incident, but when and if they do experience an unexpected incident, this is the very last time they should be finding out whether their business continuity plans are up to the task.

Business continuity managers will require a mechanism with indicators to facilitate their assessment of the business continuity performance levels across the scope of the business continuity programme. Indicators can provide the basis from which to make a judgement on performance, provide direction for future programme priorities and the foundation for business continuity managers from which to challenge business and functional units on their self-assessments of performance.

A number of external stakeholders such as customers, investors or regulators will also demand to know how well prepared an organisation is, although their level and focus of interest may vary depending on their stake in the organisation.

Internal and external auditors deliver an independent assessment of an organisation's accounting and reporting practices, business risks, and internal controls. Their goal is to establish audit comfort by determining how well management's system of internal controls is working. To validate their judgement, auditors will need to drill down into an organisation. To do this will require data on which to apply the substantive testing methods they use to achieve this.

To Measure Is To Manage

A factor that emerged from the research conducted in connection with this book is that while business continuity plan exercising and review are adequately addressed in many of the publications and standards available, the subjects of quality assurance and internal audit in this regard are less well covered. Professional standards and guidelines adopted by business continuity and internal audit bodies fail to focus on these issues adequately, even though governments and regulators increasingly stress their importance.

Interestingly, however, while business continuity management has retained attention and interest with the regulatory community across the world, the level of "chatter" on regulatory websites on associated matters, and the degree of urgency with which these are addressed, generally appears to be falling as we move away from the events of 9/11.

But the business continuity manager should beware. Perhaps this is more an indication of the fact that regulators and the network of those they liaise and work with has matured, and that their focus is now more on resilience than reaction. Certainly, the regulators' responsibilities to monitor the performance of their regulatory universe has not diminished, but their level of knowledge has grown and with this a grasp of what type and nature of indicators they require to test the resilience of the industry they regulate and the market within which they operate.

Plan Review and Maintenance - Objectives

We live in a dynamic world. While business divisions within an organisation are expected to produce three- or five-year strategic plans and annual operational plans reflecting their changing environment, it can prove problematic to persuade a Board to recognise similar needs for risk and business continuity management activities. There remains a view in some organisations that once a business continuity plan has been drafted it can be distributed, perhaps rehearsed, and then filed away - job done!

Most organisations are subject to change and people, processes, products, suppliers, markets, geographic spread, politics, social climates and business solutions evolve. Nothing stays the same for very long.

If business continuity management has a mission to reflect the nature, scale and complexity of an organisation, then business continuity plans will need to evolve. Change demands a constant process of review and maintenance to reflect these changes - and to ensure that developments on business continuity solutions are also effectively assessed and harnessed.

"The purpose of the Business Continuity Management (BCM) maintenance process is to ensure that the organisation's BCM competence and capability remains effective, fit-for-purpose and up-to-date to meet the business requirements." **(1)**

The business continuity maintenance programme stress-tests and validates that the organisation remains ready to handle incidents despite the constant changes that all organisations experience. To be effective, as with any other aspect of business continuity, the process for review and maintenance must be clearly documented as part of the business continuity management programme. There need to be clear objectives and milestones, as part of the organisation's normal management processes (rather than as a separate structure that can be forgotten).

A maintenance process should form a component of the business continuity management programme. Each plan owner should be responsible for updating their team business continuity plans and dynamic data such as contact numbers, team tasks, notification and supplier contact details, battle box contents, etc.

Plan sections should be reviewed at frequencies ranging from monthly to annually, in accordance with the schedule laid down in the organisation's plan maintenance guidelines. 'Date of last update' should be clearly displayed at the beginning of each plan to provide an effective review and audit trail.

Business Continuity Management In A Changing Environment

Most of the issues that show up in rehearsals and exercises are the result of internal changes within an organisation such as staff, locations or technology. Indeed, in addition to a regular programme of review, ad hoc reviews may be triggered by change management processes, post-exercise or incident 'learning points' or an audit report.

Senior management buy-in to this process is as important as that required to initiate a programme, yet often proves more difficult to achieve. This will be particularly so if the original programme is built on questionable foundations - for example, the last major incident to affect the organisation, the industry, or the world in general.

As memories fade following an incident so too may enthusiasm and commitment to the subject throughout an organisation. Consequently business continuity managers must be sure to build their programmes on a sustainable basis and not just the last incident in memory. This situation may be one reason why the regulatory "chatter" referred to above has seen some evidence of decline.

In some industries where there is a strong regulatory interest, this fading of attention has been less evident. Here, initiatives do still flourish albeit some have been slow to incubate and deliver.

The Board may need to be gently reminded, perhaps with the assistance of external auditors, that corporate governance and regulatory requirements demand that Board members and the senior executives of organisations take business continuity seriously. The Business Continuity Institute (BCI) definition of business continuity emphasises four principles aimed at safeguarding the interests of an organisation's key stakeholders, reputation, brand and value creating activities:

- The holistic nature of the management process

- Identification of potential impacts that might threaten an organisation

- Provision of a framework for building resilience

- Provision of capability for an effective response.

All of these principles should be considered parts of a review programme as the whole of an organisation's business continuity competence and capability should be maintained. This should consequently embrace the strategies, Business Impact Analysis and Risk Assessment and is a critical distinction to an approach which only seeks to review plans.

Plan Review and Maintenance - Outcomes

Little is documented in the public domain as to how an organisation should conduct a review and what tools might be deployed. In essence, a review and maintenance process should be a mirror image of the initial programme and the business continuity programme cycle should be followed. This said, the scale and pace of internal and external change that an organisation has experienced should be a driver for the degree and emphasis of review. Significant change - including that resulting from an invocation, significant near-miss, breach in resilience, merger, outsourcing project, new product development or when "industry good practice or standards" are adopted - are all examples of change that should impact on the scope of the review.

An incident or near-miss provides a unique opportunity to assess whether the plans follow a logical sequence, format and structure:

- Were plans accessible and up-to-date?

- Did the teams come together as planned?

- Did team members understand their roles and responsibilities?

- Were teams competent in their response?

- Did the plans work and interface at all levels ("Gold, Silver and Bronze" - see Chapter Ten)

- Did alternative work areas respond - and were they available to planned timescales?

- Did assumptions made in the Business Impact Analysis (BIA) about the environment in which the organisation operates hold true - have time imperatives changed since the last review?

If an organisation operates in a regulated environment then this too may impact on the priorities of the review. Most regulators adopt as part of their business plans industry priorities which will be based on the regulators' perception of planning priorities - often based on post-incident reaction or the maturity of the industry generally. An organisation, while needing to react to these priorities and absorb them within their own programme, must remember that the regulator is working to a mandate delivered by its governing authority and as such may be different in emphasis to that of the organisation.

Regulators also have to implement and maintain their own programme for business continuity and all organisations regulated should be aware of their regulator's plans and how these should dovetail with those of their own.

To ensure that an entire organisation is reviewed at some time, and especially if an organisation is multi-territory, multi-business-line or significant in size, an organisation can be sub-divided into operational units or territorial units and different stages of the business continuity cycle reviewed for each unit segment within which they operate. Changes in this environment may also impact on the review. This approach can ensure that over a targeted period of time through a rolling programme, the whole organisation can be reviewed against the complete cycle.

However, an organisation may have sub-divisions at different stages of maturity in the business continuity programme. To underpin the rolling approach to review, an organisation may identify a number of core capabilities which are considered to be minimum requirements, whatever stage of a programme each sub-division is at. For example:

- Crisis Management (Response) Teams

- Business Impact Analyses

- Risk assessment
- Critical IT applications recovery plans
- Cascade process
- Battle Boxes
- Employee emergency help lines

If there are mission-critical processes, products or suppliers then these elements of the organisation may require a review on a more frequent basis. Material suppliers and outsource providers (especially those that are time-critical) should provide evidence of review and maintenance to the standards agreed in the contract. As will be recalled from Chapter One, a product or service can be outsourced but the responsibility for management cannot. Consequently, required reporting should be to the standards of the ceding organisation.

The adequacy and availability of external services and solutions that might be required by an organisation to support a business continuity invocation and recovery should also be included in this process; for example, loss adjusters, asset recovery and restoration, specialist security, recovery sites and associated subcontractors. If the review reveals any perceived inadequacies, these should be analysed and as agreed result in amendments to the business continuity policy, supporting standards and plans. As agreed, changes should be included as actions and implemented as part of the maintenance action plan. The action plan should include training, awareness and communication needs.

PAS 56: 2003 (2)

The outcomes from the business continuity management maintenance process should include the following, clearly defined, documented and signed-off by the organisation's executive or senior management:

a) Business continuity management monitoring and maintenance programme;

b) Maintenance report (including recommendations);

c) Business continuity management maintenance report action plan;

d) Due diligence reports to the effect that the business continuity management competence and capability of suppliers (internal or outsourced providers) of management care agreements, their dependencies, and recovery suppliers is effective, up-to-date and fit-for-purpose (as defined in contractual terms and condition or Service Level Agreements);

e) Effective, up-to-date and fit-for-purpose business continuity plans, crisis management strategies and solutions concerning the organisation's management care agreements.

A programme review should be documented and the results reported to the Board or its nominated group (for example the Risk Committee) as part of the overall governance and associated reporting processes. The report should validate whether the current business continuity policy and framework are appropriate and relevant.

Following agreement, updated, amended and changed business continuity management policy, strategies, solutions, processes and plans should be distributed to key stakeholders under the formal change (version) control process of the business continuity programme.

Benchmarking - A Case for Continuous Measurement

Benchmarking is about making comparisons with other organisations and then learning the lessons that those comparisons present. Organisations may take this broad definition and adapt it to their own language and to meet their own strategic and operational planning objectives: "Benchmarking is the continuous process of measuring products, services and practices against the toughest competitors or those companies recognised as industry leaders (best in class)." **(3)**

In practice, benchmarking usually encompasses:

- Regularly comparing aspects of performance (functions or processes) with best practitioners;
- Identifying gaps in performance;
- Seeking fresh approaches to bring about improvements in performance;
- Following through with implementing improvements; and
- Following up by monitoring progress and reviewing the benefits.

Benchmarking should be considered as a versatile tool that can be applied in a variety of ways. Before an organisation starts out on a route of benchmarking it should be very clear on what their objectives are and their expectations of the deliverables, as these affect the methodology to be used. Standard benchmarking terms include:

- Strategic
- Performance
- Process
- Functional or Generic
- Internal
- External
- International

All of these types of benchmarking can have a role to play in business continuity management and the business continuity management programme:

Strategic Benchmarking is used where organisations seek to improve their overall performance by examining the long-term strategies and general approaches that have enabled high-performers to succeed. This can be used when an organisation commences or reviews its overall strategic approach to business continuity.

Performance Benchmarking is used where organisations consider their positions in relation to performance characteristics of key products and services. In business continuity this approach is most often used when industry comparisons are drawn through surveys conducted by professional or trade associations (which preserve confidentiality), or regulatory bodies to assist them to assess achievement and target against their own objectives. Relevant regulatory web sites hold the results of a number of these benchmarking exercises and can provide helpful information when investigating examples of what others perceive to be best practices.

Process Benchmarking is used when the focus is on improving specific, critical processes and operations. Benchmarking partners are sought from best practice organisations that perform similar work or deliver similar services. In business continuity, process benchmarking may involve producing process maps to facilitate comparison and analysis and generally what are short term improvements. Functional Benchmarking or Generic Benchmarking is used when organisations benchmark with partners drawn from different business sectors or areas of activity to find ways of improving similar functions or work processes. This sort of benchmarking can lead to innovation and dramatic improvements.

Internal Benchmarking involves seeking partners from within the same organisation, for example, from business units located in different functional or geographic areas. The main advantages of internal benchmarking is the ease of access to sensitive data and information and the ability to benchmark against standards and measures derived from those common to the organisation. There may be fewer barriers to implementation as practises may be relatively easy to transfer across the same organisation. However, real innovation may be lacking and best-in-class performance is more likely to be found through external benchmarking.

External Benchmarking involves seeking outside organisations that are known to be best–in-class. External benchmarking provides opportunities for learning from those who are considered to be at the leading edge, although not every best practice solution can or should be transferred to others. In addition, this type of benchmarking may take up more time and resource to ensure the comparability of data and information, the credibility of the findings and the development of sound recommendations. External learning may be slower because of the 'not-invented-here' syndrome. (Although one might expect that it would be quicker, as you learn from the skills and mistakes of others.).

International Benchmarking is used where partners are sought from other countries because best practitioners are located elsewhere in the world or there are too few benchmarking partners within the same country to produce valid results. Globalisation and advances in information technology are increasing opportunities for international projects. However, these could take more time and resources to set up and implement and the results may need careful analysis due to national differences. For business continuity management this approach will be helpful for those practitioners either operating in territories where good practice is emerging or where they have subsidiaries in such environments.

Benchmarking - The Process

There is no standard approach to benchmarking in terms of phases or steps to take, as essentially benchmarking takes the steps taken in any project or programme, namely:

- Planning
- Collecting data and information
- Analysing the findings
- Recommendations
- Implementation
- Monitoring and reviewing

Planning involves identification of the subject, definition of the objectives for the study and the criteria that will be used to assess success. At this stage the benchmarking approach should be selected and the potential internal or external partners. This phase should conclude with the creation of a project plan supported by a communication strategy and suitable resource, signed off by relevant management.

Collecting data and information involves compilation of information and data on performance. A mutual understanding about the procedures to be followed must be developed with the partners and, as necessary, a "Benchmarking Protocol." Questions and terminology together with performance measures to be used must be developed and agreed.

The schedule of questions will be distributed to each partner along with information and data collected by the chosen method; for example, interviews, site visits, telephone, fax and e-mail. Finally, results will require collation and analysis. An example of a benchmarking questionnaire can be found in Appendix A. Analysing the findings will involve the production of the findings with tables, charts and graphs to support the analysis.

Gaps in performance between the organisation being analysed and better performers should be identified and examined. Where necessary, measures used may need to be normalised through the application of correction factors to take account of reasons for differences in performance other than inefficiencies. Findings should be validated with the business continuity management community of the organisation prior to consideration of recommendations for action and potential change.

Recommendations may follow from analysis and those considered desirable and feasible tabled to the organisation's business continuity Executive or Steering Group. Once initial agreement has been secured, support of key business continuity stakeholders should be gained and the changes agreed for implementation.

The implementation phase will involve making the changes and keeping those engaged through the stakeholder process informed of progress.

Monitoring and reviewing is essential to ensure that the results of the improvements are being achieved. As necessary key business continuity performance objectives should be adjusted to reflect the changes made to the programme. Finally, going forward, benchmarking needs should be assessed and requirements built into the programme.

Do's And Don'ts Of Benchmarking

- Do learn from others who have built up experience applying benchmarking in a comparable way.

- Don't benchmark for the sake of it; focusing entirely on comparisons of performance measures rather than the processes and activities that enable the achievement of good practice;

- Don't expect that benchmarking will be quick or easy;

- Don't spend too much time on one part of the process, particularly at the expense of other key parts;

- Don't expect to find benchmarking partners comparable in all respects to your organisation;

- Don't expect to ask for information and data without being prepared to share it with others.

- Don't expect organisations to share information that is commercially sensitive.

- Do agree to abide by an agreed benchmarking "code of conduct," which can help to avoid problems over confidentiality of information

---

Independent Oversight

In some of its activities a Board will reply on the advice of internal oversight functions. This may range from internal audit, compliance, risk management or business continuity management. These functions must be supported by the Board, adequately resourced, provided with the authority to conduct independent assurance and provided with a route to report their findings directly to the Board. These functions will help the Board to validate whether the system of controls is working and to ensure that the performance of an organisation is being reliably reported to its stakeholders.

Quality Assurance - Key Performance Indicators As Measures Of Success

The output of the Business Impact Analysis (BIA and risk assessment processes should be a suite of key performance (KPIs) - or key risk indicators (KRIs) - the scores of which are judged to provide an organisation with the ability to track how well its business continuity management programme is performing.

These indicators should assess performance at each stage of the business continuity lifecycle and be derived from a suite of questions and metrics designed to challenge the competence and capability of an organisation.

In terms of what constitutes good performance, there will be a number of evaluation criteria driven by the stage of business continuity management in the organisation's programme lifecycle, as well as customer, legal and regulatory requirements. An organisation should consider which indicators it wishes to use for measurement; and then incorporate others that meet assurance requirements and incorporate these as supplements to the main reporting suite.

The Securities and Exchange Commission (SEC) examination of a firm's business continuity planning includes:

- Senior management involvement;
- Adequacy of resources;
- Review and update of the plan;
- Employee training;
- Testing;
- Coverage of critical areas;
- Backup facilities;
- Coverage of third party vendors and major counterparties and customers;
- Short-term and long term strategies;
- Communication alternatives; and
- Data backup timing and capacity.

SEC (4)

If each measure in the overall matrix of measures is coded, combinations of the measures may be clustered into different groupings to meet a variety of reporting and compliance requirements including:

- International standards; e.g., ISO17799
- Regional standards; e.g., Standards Australia and BSI PAS 56
- Regulatory guidelines; e.g., The UK Financial Services Authority (FSA) Handbook

- Corporate Governance Guidelines; e.g., Corporate Governance Guidelines - Office of the Superintendent of Financial Institutions - Canada

- Professional guidelines; e.g., Business Continuity Institute (BCI) Good Practice Guidelines

- National Fire Protection Association (US) 1600 for emergency management and business continuity

- Internal standards

- Industry benchmarks

- Customer contracts and service level agreements

- Outsource providers and key suppliers contracts and service level agreements

Measures can be structured and collected in a number of ways. A questionnaire comprising twenty questions addressing each element of the business continuity management lifecycle and using a sliding scale of answers depending on the degree of compliance, will provide a good indication of performance. Customers may set minimum standards of performance, which may be contractual. Global and local legal and regulatory guidelines relevant to an organisation must be considered.

Whatever core and local suite of Key Performance Indicators (KPIs) are determined, these can form the basis for evidence of regulatory and legal compliance. In this regard, the business continuity manager should liaise closely with those in dedicated legal or regulatory departments - often aligned to or located as part of the risk management function. Remember, that the drivers for regulators may not totally coincide with those of an organisation and consequently inward-looking assessment tools may be insufficient.

On April 7, 2003, the Federal Reserve, OCC and SEC issued the "Interagency Paper on Sound Practices to Strengthen the Resilience of the U.S. Financial System." (5). The paper identified three new business continuity objectives for all financial institutions with special importance in the post-9/11 risk environment. It also identified four sound practices to ensure the resilience of the U.S. financial system. These practices focus on minimizing the immediate systemic effects of a wide-scale disruption on critical financial markets. The three business continuity objectives are:

- Rapid recovery and timely resumption of critical operations following a wide-scale disruption;

- Rapid recovery and timely resumption of critical operations following the loss or inaccessibility of staff in at least one major operation location; and

- A high level of confidence, through ongoing use or robust testing, that critical internal and external continuity arrangements are effective and compatible.

The Paper also identified four broad sound practices for core clearing and settlement organizations and firms that play significant roles in critical financial markets.

The SEC objectives are of interest and relevant but do not sufficiently emphasise the need for organisations and industries to preserve information and other intellectual assets.

Annex B of PAS 56, reproduced with kind permission of the British Standards Institute (BSI) at **Appendix A**, provides a wealth of ideas for the design of indicators. These questions have been designed to reflect the stages of business continuity management to form part of a process of self-assessment process or by an auditor as part of an audit programme.

All questions carry an equal value and weighting.

PAS 56 warns "... the questions themselves do not provide a quality assurance audit. Quality assurance auditing requires the assistance of a professional business continuity management practitioner and may involve a further, rigorous quality assurance review, verification and validation (accreditation) process." **(6)**

The UK Financial Services Authority (FSA) View On Compliance (7)

A firm should:

1. As appropriate, regularly report to the relevant level of management its operational exposures loss experience (including if possible cumulative losses) and authorised deviations from the firm's operational risk policy

2. Engage in exception-based escalation to management of unauthorised deviation from the firm's operational risk policy where set, likely or actual breaches in predefined thresholds for operational exposures and losses significant increases to the firm's exposure to operational risk or alternations to its operational risk profile

---

The examples below also provide an illustrative sample of the type of questions that might be posed addressing responsibility, governance, assessment of performance at each stage of planning. This is not intended to be exhaustive.

Business Continuity Management

Self Assessment Questionnaire

Period of Assessment ....

Function ....

Completed by ....

Date ....

Number	Assessment	Score*
	Responsibility And Ownership	
1	The CEO is responsible for business continuity management	
2	There is a documented management structure in place at organisation level, which includes the appointment of business/country/support function business continuity leaders and addresses each operation, with clearly defined roles and responsibilities for the delivery and management of business continuity	
3	Managers and employees have been briefed in the last twelve months and understand what will be involved in a site incident recovery, where they will recover to and what will be expected of them.	
	Governance And Reporting	
1	Appropriate governance and reporting procedures to monitor business continuity capability at business/country/support Function level are in place	
2	Governance and reporting procedures and their output are documented	
3	3 Business continuity is a standing agenda item on Board meetings or equivalent	
	Planning Process And Plan Scope	

1	All planning is based on the 'worst case' scenario and: a) documented risk assessment b) for site and IT planning a Business Impact Analysis (BIA) which involves business units/departments in its preparation	
2	Site level planning - recovery priorities for business-critical processes/units and vital records are identified; Recovery Time Objective (RTO) and Recovery Point Objective (RPO) established and documented	
3	Site level planning - alternative sites used for work areas are located at least 5 miles/8km away from the primary site, and have maintained Uninterrupted Power Supply (UPS), standby generators and diverse routing for communications (data and voice)	
	Review	
1	All plans undergo a complete review involving reviewing plans against the organisation, revisiting risk assessments (and BIA and recovery strategies for site plans and site-based IT recovery	
2	Details on all people involved in an invocation and the invocation processes are reviewed for key internal/external recovery providers, i.e., work area, on-site and off-site IT recovery.	
3	Process is in place to ensure plans and teams are reviewed: a) following exercises where deficiencies are identified b) following near-misses c) where the pace of change is aggressive	
	Testing And Incidents	
1	A documented annual testing programme is in operation which tests all key levels of plans, e.g., country, site, IT	
2	The annual testing programme covers a representative selection of business-critical units and processes, and tests the following components against RTO/RPO.	

3	All testing is documented – covering aims, methodology, results, remedial actions as required, timescales and ownership, learning points and next steps	
	Outsourced Services and Key Suppliers	
1	Outsourced functions meet the organisation's other core ownership and management organisation requirements	
2	Documented governance and reporting procedures to monitor the business continuity capability of outsourced functions are in place	
3	Outsourced function plans specifically detail a notification and escalation process and contain the appropriate team contact details	
	<ul><li>Results</li><li>Key Performance indictors (KPIs)</li><li>Charts of actual and comparative performance</li><li>Conversion of scores into "RAG" (Red/Amber/Green) or "Traffic light" matrices</li><li>Recommendations</li><li>Remedial action plans with time scales and assignment of responsibility</li></ul> *(* yes = 4; mainly = 3; largely = 2; partial = 1; no = 0)*	

The Audit Committee As Part Of The Control Environment

A Board of an organisation will often exercise the requirement to deliver their responsibilities for establishing effective and independent oversight through the appointment of an audit (or risk management) committee. Audit committees may have a blend of statutory and Board-assigned responsibilities.

The audit committee should review the annual statements of an organisation, evaluate and approve the internal control procedures, and review those who provide independent oversight to discuss the effectiveness of the organisation's internal controls and reporting practices.

The audit committee should also ensure that the audit plan is risk-based, covers all relevant activities over a measurable cycle, and that the work between internal and external auditors is coordinated.

While still comparatively rare, if an audit function is wholly or partially outsourced the audit committee must ensure that their responsibilities extend to embrace governance of the outsourced capability.

The audit committee's operating environment should include:

- Operation with independence

- A charter that addresses membership, meeting frequency and core agenda items

- Unlimited access to internal and external auditors, senior management, employees and relevant information

- Approval of policies and practices that constitute an organisation's control environment

- Approval of policies and practices for the reporting of risk management and audit, including assurance on the competence of those providing audit services

- Criteria for the non-audit work that an organisation's external auditor might provide, e.g., consultancy - including that for business continuity management

- Provision to the Board of status reports on audit plan performance, including ongoing reports from internal and external auditors on actions agreed, with clear indication of responsibility and timescales for delivery

Towards A Better Understanding

An audit is established to understand how management across an organisation run the business and manage risk. Scoped and delivered effectively, an audit should not be perceived as a threat but as an opportunity to add value to an organisation. This can be achieved by the audit providing a better understanding of the full range of business risks faced and whether those risks pose threats to the achievement of business objectives. This approach can provide greater comfort than looking purely at the financial statements in isolation, and may be used to reflect an organisation's true performance.

> *"Auditable activities consist of those subjects, units, or systems which are capable of being defined and evaluated. Auditable activities may include: policies, procedures, and practices; cost centres, profit centres, and investment centres; general ledger account balances; information systems (manual and computerised); major contracts and programs.*
>
> *"Further, organisational units such as product or service lines; functions such as information technology, purchasing, marketing, production, finance, accounting, and human resources; transaction systems for activities such as sales, collection, production, treasury, payroll, and capital assets; financial statements; and, laws and regulations should be considered."*
>
> *SIAS No. 14, (the old red book). Glossary – "Auditable Activities" (8)*

Audits can be conducted by internal and external audit teams. Typically in most larger organisations, and especially in those that are publicly listed, it will be a requirement for external audits to be undertaken as a means of verification of the publicly reported statement of accounts and supporting performance.

Legislation, notably that found in the US through the Sarbanes-Oxley Act, (9) has resulted in a further toughening of the reporting and sign-off requirements of the Board of companies and as a consequence, additional responsibilities for the risk and business continuity managers and internal and external auditors.

In the matrix of management responsibilities of an organisation, the key word associated with audit is that of *independence*.

Essentially any audit, whether conducted by internal or external auditors, should deliver an independent assessment of an organisation's accounting and reporting practices, business risks, and internal controls. An audit should determine how well management's internal controls mitigate the risks of material misstatement in the financial statements.

The Definition and "Universe" Or Scope of an Audit

Audits can be classified on the basis of particular areas or "universe" in which the audit work is performed, but agreement as to usable definitions of the nature of an audit has been difficult to reach by the audit community. Generally accepted terms (10) include:

- **Compliance** - evaluation compliance with laws, regulations, ethical standards or similar reviews

- **Financial** - evaluating internal accounting controls, financial information and related reports

- **Integrated** - covering business units or processes, across business operations, finance, and information technology, using teams or individuals who have the necessary range of auditing skills.

- **Operational** - evaluating controls, processes, and effectiveness, other than those covered under financial audits, including assessment and implementation of process improvement.

- **Systems/IT** - evaluating controls and operations in computer facilities, networks, systems, applications, etc.

- Depending on the approach that an organisation takes to the internal auditing of its operations, the scope of an internal audit may embrace one or more of the above defined areas.

Audit and Business Continuity Management

The business continuity audit should be designed to ensure that an organisation has an effective business continuity capability. The scope of a business continuity audit may include most of the audit areas defined above and therefore it is unlikely that any one auditor will have the skills set to undertake such an audit in isolation of third party specialists.

Consequently, while the audit process can be designed by an organisation's internal auditor or external auditor, the advice and services of external professional business continuity practitioners (not otherwise engaged in the business continuity programme activities of the organisation) working under the supervision of the auditor, may be called upon.

A business continuity audit has five key functions (11):

1. To validate compliance with an organisation's business continuity management policies and standards

2. To review an organisation's business continuity management solutions.

3. To validate an organisation's business continuity plans.

4. To verify that appropriate exercising and maintenance activities are taking place

5. To highlight deficiencies and issues and ensure their resolution.

The frequency of a business continuity audit and the scope of an audit should be considered in line with the fundamental principles of business continuity management. Specifically, the audit should reflect the nature, scale and complexity of an organisation, the risks and critical processes and the location and dependencies of these.

An annual programme for audit should be scoped as part of the business continuity programme. However, the scope may be subject to change driven by internal or external events and changes which impact on the organisation.

But whatever the scope of the internal audit, this should not replace ongoing self-assessment and performance monitoring. This should be carried out more frequently by the business continuity planning "owners," facilitated by the business continuity manager and overseen by the business continuity Executive or Steering Group, as applicable. There will be further oversights by the organisation's Risk and Audit Committees, and ultimately the Board or its governance equivalent.

The business continuity management audit should form an impartial review against defined standards and policies and provide an indication of how effective business continuity is as a means of internal control, and what action might be required to achieve a fully effective performance.

There are a number of ways in which this assurance of the control environment might be achieved.

As with any other management process, it is not a requirement for the auditor to replicate the competence required to manage the capability of business continuity, but it is a requirement that the auditor should have a sufficient level of competence to undertake the audit of those who are engaged in the business continuity management process and to offer an objective opinion.

The audit should examine how the business continuity programme has been established, the policies, practices and standards that are embraced, the effectiveness of the programme against these and how effectiveness is being monitored and reported. The audit should consequently establish whether the business continuity programme is achieving the agreed objectives and the evidence for this.

Competence and capability in business continuity management and the standards and guidelines that organisations are required to observe are continually evolving. An audit must reflect this environment and assess whether policies and standards are appropriate for the nature, scale and complexity of an organisation.

An audit may be conducted at a number of levels, from an assessment of the plans to an assessment of the competence and capability of the business continuity function. Assurance of the business continuity capability might include which standards an organisation has chosen to observe and why, and the suitability of these in the context of an organisation's internal and external environment, including customer base, supplier and outsource provider dependencies, and regulatory and legal requirements.

"The business continuity management audit, like business continuity planning, implementation and maintenance, is concerned with a complex process and requires interaction with a wide range of managerial and operational roles from both a business and technical perspective." **(12)**

The Audit Process

The business continuity management audit should include a plan that addresses:

- The type of audit to be carried out, e.g., compliance, project management/control, feasibility study, due diligence or investigative;
- Audit objectives, i.e., outcomes and deliverables. The audit objectives may in part be driven and governed or restricted by legal or regulatory requirements. This includes key issues of high priority;

- Any external standards or benchmarks deployed, e.g., PAS 56. (The audit framework may be governed or restricted by legal or regulatory requirements or guidelines);

- Definition of the audit scope including:

  - The corporate governance, compliance or other issues to be audited;

  - The area/department/site of an organisation to be audited;

- Definition of the audit approach;

- The auditing activities that will be undertaken, e.g., questionnaires, face-to-face interview, document review, solution review;

- Activity timetable and due dates;

- Audit evaluation criteria;

- The requirement for specific subject expertise or third party assistance to conduct the audit.

The audit should compile and summarise interview notes, questionnaires and other sources of information. Gaps in content and level of information gathered, and conduct of further or follow-up interviews should be identified.

Relevant primary information and documentation should be identified and gathered such as Business Impact Analyses (BIAs) together with interview data and other sources, e.g., walkthrough, physical inspection and sampling.

Secondary sources of data such as relevant standards, regulatory guidelines, industry good practice guidelines and customer service level agreements should be gathered to validate preliminary audit findings.

Risk weightings consistent with those used generally by an organisation should be used to distinguish between acceptable and unacceptable risk findings - using a scale of indicators based on rating criteria.

A draft audit report should be produced for discussion with key stakeholders. Following consideration of the draft report an agreed audit opinion report should be published incorporating recommendations. A summary of where differences of opinion persist and why, should form a section within the final report. The audit report should provide clear priorities for remedial attention and action, based upon perceived importance in the context of the audit objectives.

A remedial action plan should be agreed including timescales for implementation. This should form part of ongoing business continuity management maintenance and monitoring processes.

Summary

"Any governance framework should ensure that timely and accurate disclosure is made on all material matters regarding an entity, including the ownership, governance, financial situation and performance of the entity". **(13)**

Internal controls of an organisation encompass the policies, processes, culture, tasks, and other aspects of an organisation that support the achievement of an organisation's objectives. *"They facilitate the efficiency of operations, contribute to effective risk management, assist compliance with applicable laws and regulations, and strengthen capacity to respond appropriately to business opportunities."* **(14)**

All of the energy and effort expended in delivering a business continuity management programme can be wasted if in the event a plan is called upon to perform, it fails to deliver. While reviewing, maintaining, exercising, challenging and auditing a business continuity management programme is no guarantee of success, obtaining reasonable assurance that business continuity is operating within the control framework agreed provides an indication of likely plan relevance and success.

Bibliography

1. British Standards Institute (BSI) PAS 56, www.bsi-global.com

2. British Standards Institute (BSI) PAS 56, www.bsi-global.com

3. Benchmarking - www.benchmarking.gov.uk/about_bench/types.asp

4. Securities and Exchange Commission (SEC), www.sec.gov

5. Securities and Exchange Commission (SEC), www.sec.gov

6. British Standards Institute (BSI) PAS 56, www.bsi-global.com

7. The Financial services Authority (FSA), www.fsa.gov.uk

8. SIAS No. 14, (the old red book). Glossary – "Auditable Activities"

9. Sarbanes Oxley Act – 2002, www.sec.gov/spotlight/sarbanes-oxley.htm.

10. Institute of Internal Auditors England and Wales, www.theiia.org

11. Institute of Internal Auditors England and Wales , www.theiia.org

12. Business Continuity Institute (BCI) Good Practice Guide (GPG)

13. Good governance principles - Standards Australia - 2004

14. Corporate Governance Guidelines - Office of the Superintendent of Financial Institutions - Canada

18

Developing a Plan: Putting Theory Into Practice

Objectives Of This Chapter:
- Examine the purpose of a plan

- Explain the plan components

- Outline the stages of an incident and how plan design can address these

- Consider the differing needs of the small, medium and large organisation

- Review specialized planning needs from call centre to board-level crisis

- Examine team characteristics at various positions within the an organisation's plan framework

- Review support services and suppliers

- Evaluate the role of software

- Consider where Business Continuity Management is heading as a discipline both independently and as part of Risk Management

> *"Plans are nothing. Planning is everything."*
>
> Napoleon

THE PURPOSE OF A PLAN

Before You Start Writing ...

In this book we have provided a view on the relationship between business continuity and risk management. We have travelled through issues as diverse as business impact analysis, culture, outsourcing and audit and arrived at the point where this knowledge can be harnessed and the production of a programme and plans may begin.

Before the pen touches paper, the business continuity strategy should be in place. This will articulate the responsibilities and ownership for business continuity within the organisation; where the business continuity programme needs to be and why; who the stakeholders are and their needs and expectations; and, the look and feel of the business continuity programme, and its overall capability.

To achieve Board support a roadmap for implementation will set out the order of events in the programme, including what will happen first, who will roll out the programme and how they will do this. Business today is notoriously short-term, so while a business continuity programme is a long term investment, details of any early or 'quick wins' should be a top priority. But a word of warning: too often, the 'quick win' enables a director to report back to the Board that they have 'fixed' business continuity management. Caution should be exercised and that short-term gains must not replace long term goals.

In a regulated organisation, business continuity performance will form part of the regulator's risk assessment process. While business continuity should always form part of a Board agenda, operating within a regulated environment will guaranteed this is the case (1).

The programme will include the suite of performance indicators to be used and the reporting that will take place to enable the Board to know how well the programme is performing. This will include compliance with any customer or regulatory-driven indicators including performance improvement requirements.

And how long should the process of implementing a programme take from start to finish? This is an impossible question to answer as all organisations will be different. However, the longer it takes to deliver a programme, the sooner the plans will require updating.

GENERAL PRINCIPLES

The Role and Profile of The Planner

As with any aspect of business, it is important to ensure that roles and responsibilities within a business continuity programme are clearly defined and that the people involved are competent and assigned appropriate responsibilities.

The business continuity manager and those who draft business continuity plans may not automatically form part of the teams that use them. It takes a different set of skills to lead the design of a business continuity programme and to draft effective plans than it does to lead the invocation and application of them. Some individuals may have the full range of skills required for each of these responsibilities, but many will not.

The Purpose and Scope of A Plan

The existence of plans in isolation does not demonstrate a Business Continuity Management competence or capability, although the presence of a current plan which has been produced by an organisation does suggest a degree of capability.

The purpose of a business continuity plan is to identify the actions necessary and the resources required as far as is possible, to enable an organisation to manage a potential threat or actual interruption to its business, whatever the cause.

Predefined procedures and solutions to recover from different scenarios should be designed and embedded in a plan. However, these should not be so prescriptive that they assume a rigidity which prevents modification to deal effectively with an incident. Actions outlined in a plan should not attempt to cover every eventuality. All incidents will be different and, as an incident unfolds circumstances may change - opportunities may open up or barriers may be created, either of which could render a predetermined response no longer the most effective mechanism or path to recovery.

How big should an ideal plan be? While plans designed to address the recovery of information technology systems might typically be quite detailed and follow a relatively well-defined process, no plan should be of such size that it is unwieldy or difficult to follow in use. For example, if the action to take following an incident first appears a significant way through the document, then almost certainly it contains material that belongs elsewhere. Following an incident, most team leaders faced with the choice of a detailed plan which attempts to address every conceivable incident supported by an adequately resourced and rehearsed team, and a higher-level plan based on realistic scenarios supported by an empowered and exercised team, would probably pick the latter.

A debate continues as to whether an organisation should focus and plan for the unthinkable event or those of less impact but higher probability. This is an issue for each organisation to resolve. Perhaps the answer is that consideration of the unthinkable event should form part of scenario management and consideration of the more predictable event should form part of the risk assessment.

The time subsequently dedicated to the production of plans should be proportionate to the risks and the severity of these evaluated as part of these processes. Based on the aftermath of events such as the 2004 Asia Tsunami and Hurricane Katrina in the U.S. in 2005, it is increasingly necessary for every organisation to evaluate "unthinkable" worst-case scenarios. If an organisation wishes to have fully addressed its position within the landscape of government and local authority plan arrangements, consideration of worst-case scenarios will inevitably be involved.

Whatever the final risk profile, regulators will almost certainly expect to see all levels of 'material' incidents addressed by the organisations they regulate.

The Planning Language

Language used in plans should be familiar, simple and jargon-free. If business continuity management language and procedures stray too far from the day-to-day approach in an organisation, then plans are likely to be harder to communicate and less effective to use.

"When writing plans, a common error is to include tasks for a recovery process that are not actually part of that process, or department's normal working approach. Identify who would deal with that particular item in normal working, and ensure that it is part of their plan. There can still be a reference to that item in the recovery plan, but not as a specific action, but a confirmation the action is, or has, been taken." **(2)**

Where relevant, the use of commonly accepted industry terms, including those offered by business continuity professional associations, standards bodies and regulators will help ensure consistent communication with stakeholders. It is probable that stakeholders will use the same language.

A Place To Meet

All plan teams will require somewhere to meet. The first choice for any team meeting should be a room at the business-as-usual site.

At least two alternative locations with 24/7 access should be identified at a distance sufficiently far away from the business-as-usual site so as to be accessible in the event of a major incident around which an exclusion zone may be erected.

Any site used must have effective, pre-assigned communications. Team members may wish to attend meetings from a distance and others may be called in as part of the decision making process.

The location of all potential meeting sites must be clearly stated, and publicised in all plans.

Location, Location, Location

During an incident, a number of locations may be required for plan teams on-site and off-site. Key characteristics of any site include:

- 24/7 accessibility

- Relevant security

- Sufficient space and facilities and ad hoc team members/support

- Suitable distance from a potential incident (evacuation for a hurricane, a major flood, terrorist event and a fire will vary)

- Alternate locations

- Equipment and information to support response and recovery will be required

- Communication about locations including how to contact them

- Facilities for the press as appropriate

THE PLANNING MATRIX

The business continuity management infrastructure of an organisation will contain a number of plans.

Plans will document the response and continuity strategies of an organisation to all stages of an incident, from perceived threat to invocation and response. They will apply to all levels of an organisation and across all business units, support functions and territories and establish an infrastructure for incident command and control.

A document providing an overview of an organisation's plan infrastructure, including command and control management, is essential. This should set out each type of plan, how they interface, the notification, escalation and invocation processes and provide an explanation of how on-going communications will be managed.

A one-page summary with a simple diagram or flowchart embracing this information could form a useful introduction to every plan. The message will be further underlined if the summary is endorsed and signed by the Chief Executive or equivalent. Whatever approach is taken, the objective remains to ensure that there is a means of communicating an organisation's plan infrastructure as well as who is making decisions at each level and incident stage, thereby avoiding plan and team duplication, contradiction, confusion and potential failure.

THE PLAN INFRASTRUCTURE

There are a number of different models that Business Continuity planners can call upon to use as guides to building a Business Continuity infrastructure for an organisation. However there is no generally accepted blueprint. Every organisation is different and any plan infrastructure should be designed to suit the scale, nature and complexity of an organisation and the environment within which it operates - including legal and regulatory requirements.

One model of incident response borrowed from UK Emergency Services shows three tiers of incident response often referred to as Gold, Silver and Bronze. **(3)**

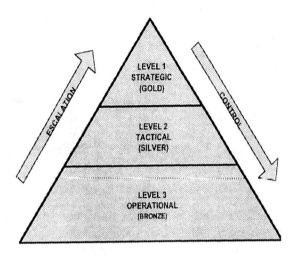

Strategic Level: Crisis Management Plan

This defines how the strategic issues of a crisis affecting an organisation would be addressed and managed by relevant senior executives. This may be when the incident is not entirely within the scope of the Business Continuity Plan and include crises that do not result from interruptions such as a hostile takeover or media exposure.

The media response to any incident is usually managed through a Crisis Management plan although some organisations may manage the media under the Business Continuity Plan. Plan objectives are to:

- Ensure the recovery process is focused and coordinated.
- Set objectives and especially priorities.
- Authorise and instruct the Silver Control team.
- Authorize and control financials.
- Advise the Shareholder.
- Control media statements.
- Arbitrate priorities and cooperation across business functions where necessary.
- Monitor the recovery process.

Tactical: Business Continuity Plan:

This plan addresses business disruption, interruption or loss from the initial response to the point at which normal business operations are resumed. The plan is based upon the agreed Business

Continuity Strategies and provides procedures and processes for both the business continuity and resource recovery teams. In particular the plans allocate roles and their accountability, responsibility and authority. The plans must also detail the interfaces and the principles for dealing with a number of external players in the response such as recovery services suppliers and emergency services.

This team will be created by the Gold team. It is likely to be a small team comprising representatives of the local management and other personnel who will contribute directly to the recovery process. These may include the managers of Group Risk, Human Resources, Finance, Facilities, Production, Distribution, Sales, Corporate Affairs, Office Services, Technology, etc.

The function of Silver control will be the recreation of the office, manufacturing and services environment within which business managers can recommence operation.

Operational: Business Unit and Functional Unit Resumption Plan:

The responsibilities of the most senior managers available from each department and function are to continue managing their business units and meet stakeholder needs as best they can within the environment that the Silver team is able to create for them. Bronze team members will also act as a communication channel between all staff, segments of customers and suppliers and, as needed, to the Silver and Gold teams.

The function of Silver control will be the recreation of the office, manufacturing and services environment within which business managers can recommence operation. For the business these plans will provide for resumption of normal business capabilities. For functions such as Facilities and IT which are managing an organisation's infrastructure, plans will provide a structure for restoring existing services or for providing alternative support facilities.

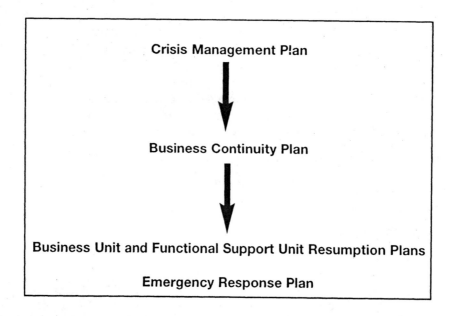

While the three levels provide a suitable model for a medium-sized organisation with a single site, a smaller organisation may have a single, hands-on management group with both tactical and strategic responsibilities. However it is still important that this group addresses the strategic issues despite the pressing issues of a tactical response.

For multiple site organisations a variety of model options exist, for example:

- A response team at each site with a central Business Continuity 'flying squad'
- A Business Continuity team at each major site with a central Crisis Management Team
- Plans at a national level with limited Board involvement unless global reputation is threatened

THE CRISIS MANAGEMENT PLAN

PAS 56 describes Crisis Management as a *"Process by which an organisation manages the wider impact of any incident until it is either under control or contained without impact to the organisation or until the business continuity plan is invoked."* **(4)**

The purpose of a Crisis Management Plan is to provide a documented framework to enable an organisation to manage any crisis event regardless of cause including those where no Business Continuity response is appropriate and beyond those involving tangible assets (people or property) at site level. For example an incident that:

- Is media-related
- Involves the injury or death of an employee off-site
- Concerns the failure of a key supplier or outsource provider
- Involves major fraud
- Relates to a significant systems failure including virus
- Relates to a product defect or recall
- Is of wide geographic impact affecting the external operating environment
- Affects an organisation's ability to fulfil legal or regulatory requirements
- Presents a threat to an organisation's reputation

Many of these risks will be recognised from earlier discussions in this book on key risks (notably Chapter One). The identification of this level of potential crises might consequently be cross-referenced to an organisation's high-level risk assessment.

A Crisis Management Plan might also be required where an organisation operates across geographic boundaries and therefore embraces incidents where more than one country, time zone, business or trading division, may be affected, and where high-level coordination is essential.

Circumstances, actions and communications at this level require tight management, and decisions may be of such materiality that they could affect the future viability of an organisation and should only be taken with central authority.

Plan Structure

The outcomes of the Crisis Management Planning process include:

- A Crisis Management Plan that can support the role of an organisation's Crisis Management team during a crisis event. As all crises are different the Crisis Management Plan should be a set of components and resources which may be useful and will depend on the nature and complexity of an organisation. At a minimum, a plan should contain:.

- A summary of an organisation's infrastructure of plans and how they fit together;

- Definitions of what scenarios might constitute a crisis - potentially linked to an organisation's appetite or tolerance for risk;

- A list of senior managers covering all business units, support functions and territories with at least one alternate and contact information, from which a Crisis Management Team might be formed;

- Other key internal and external contact information;

- Operational locations for the team both on and away from business-as-usual sites;

- A suite of key messages (this may be contained in a separate Crisis Communications Plan);

- Demonstration of preparation for effective crisis management to the media, markets, customers, stakeholders and regulators;

- Compliance with the law;

- Compliance with regulatory requirements; and

- Compliance with client requirements including those of a contractual nature.

CRISIS MANAGEMENT PLAN – CONTENTS

SECTION 1

Page Header

- Document classification in line with an organisation's classification policy e.g. "company confidential"

Page Footer

- Version control reference and date

- Page number

Front Page

- Title

- Document classification in line with an organisation's classification policy

- Version control including version number, date, change author and change details

- Distribution List

- Table of Contents

- Document Ownership

- Date of next plan review

SECTION 2

Overview of Business Continuity Management Plan infrastructure within the organisation

Crisis Management Scope, Levels and Escalation

Crisis Management Process Flowchart (Appendix)

Evaluation and categorisation framework (Appendix)

Roles

- A Crisis Management Team and its composition may vary in size throughout a crisis based on the circumstances of the crisis and the level of, skills, knowledge and expertise required to manage it and its resolution. This may include internal and external individuals and/or organisations.

- The Crisis Management Team may also be supported by a Crisis Communications Team and/or a support team to provide facilities

SECTION 3

Emergency Procedures (Site Plans only).

- Building Evacuation - reference where they can be found.

- Invacuation (if building previously surveyed and appropriate location identified) - reference where they can be found.

- Bomb Threat and similar scenarios - reference where they can be found.

- Evacuation points - including alternate or off-site.

- Dispersal of staff and visitors

SECTION 4

Notification process and/or flowchart

Invocation process and/or flowchart

Escalation process and/or flowchart

Call out/information (call tree) cascade process and/or flowchart (Appendix).

SECTION 5

Crisis Management Team Manager and alternates

Crisis Management Team and alternates

Membership of Crisis Management support Team/s and alternates

SECTION 6

Location and contact details of 'on-site' and 'off-site' command centres (including non-city or metropolitan areas where appropriate)

Map and directions to 'off-site' command centre location

Command centre resource list

Battle box/bag - location and contents

SECTION 7

Contacts: External

Contacts: Internal

Subject Experts, e.g., product, service, system

SECTION 8

Tasks:

- Mandatory tasks
- Discretionary tasks
- Task completion tracking process
- Across the organisation's business areas (where appropriate)

SECTION 9

Supporting Information

- Staff welfare and counselling
- Media and public relations
- Health and Safety
- Finance
- Legal Advice
- Insurance
- Invocation of specialist Crisis Management services (intra-organisation or external provider)
- Communications, e.g., free-phone number details
- Schedule of Critical Business Activities or support activities (Business function and Site Plans only)
- Internal briefings (preformatted agenda located with Section 10)

SECTION 10

Templates

- Evaluation and categorisation

- Meetings agenda
- Internal briefings
- Crisis decision and action log
- Crisis task list status report
- Telephone messages
- Action or task worksheet
- Incident Control Sheets

APPENDICES

- Contracts and Service Level Agreements
- Evaluation Categorisation Framework
- Cascade information, internal and external

In organisations where a Risk Committee exists, as long as members of that Committee have the required seniority and exhibit the desired characteristics for effective performance in crisis situations, the responsibilities of Committee members might include membership of the Crisis Management team.

But whatever the source of membership, the Crisis Management Team should be thought of as a "Crisis Pool" with the scenario of an incident driving the specific make-up of the Crisis Management Team. A major computer virus may not require the support of the Human Resources Director and an incident involving employee death may not require the support of the Information Technology Director.

Notification, Escalation and Invocation

A member of a Crisis Management team should ask the following questions when faced with deciding t whether an organisation is facing a potential or an actual crisis situation:

- Has an incident happened already?
- What has caused the incident?
- What is the current status?
- If there is a potential incident how likely is an actual incident to happen?
- Is the situation stable or likely to develop further?
- How might the incident unfold?
- Do we know the facts or are we speculating?
- What are or would be the implications for the organisation – e.g., damage to reputation?

Depending on the assessment, the Crisis Management team could be called to action either on identification of an incident or well before an incident becomes a crisis, i.e., when it is still an issue or contained incident.

These definitions may be helpful:

- **Issues**: Usually a subject of ongoing debate which might occasionally 'peak' as attention is focused at an industry, country or global level, e.g., an increasing shortage of fuel, the growth of a virus, a change in tropical storm frequency forecasts or a variation in criminal or terrorist activity.

- **Incidents**: Isolated or contained incidents which, although brief or controllable in themselves have the potential to develop into a crisis, especially if unmanaged or mismanaged, e.g., a small fire or burglary, or outbreak of illness at a key site including that of a supplier.

- Crisis: Any situation which has the possibility to escalate, broaden or pose a significant threat to the reputation, operations or business performance of the organisation; e.g., a financial crisis, significant fraud, significant legal or regulatory breach, major accident/fire/explosion at a key location, loss of or threat to life, major breach or failure of IT systems.

Communication

Depending on the scale and complexity of an organisation, it might be considered appropriate to prepare a separate Crisis Communications plan. The objective of such a plan would be to focus on media, employee and other stakeholder communications. While communication was explored in depth in Chapter Seven, it is worth reflecting here on the importance of having clear lines of communication to and from an organisation to the media, employees and other stakeholders following an incident.

Media

To ensure that media-related issues are correctly handled, at least two or more individuals at every site and plan level should be appointed as media representatives, documented as such in the plans and suitably trained. Plans should indicate that contact with the media should be avoided other than through those nominated. (Sometimes it may be necessary to set up entire media interview rooms with space and communications for dozens, even hundreds of media personnel).

While not part of the plan, prepared communication and press release templates can be drafted and retained by those with this responsibility for use at short notice. The style of communication for certain events can be established, for example advice to customers on product recalls, alternative products and service arrangements, including alternative trading locations. This type of preparation can be undertaken without the added pressure of an incident or when precious communications resource is otherwise diverted. However any pre-prepared materials must never be placed in the hands of "gifted amateurs" and should only be part of response preparation for the communications professional.

The plan will identify a trained person with deputies who will require immediate to the incident and who will then draft, in the light of what precisely is then known, communications that are relevant. Any materials prepared in advance will require revision. The content, style, frequency and audiences of communications will change as the incident scenario develops.

Whatever the message, all messages should consistently present an organisation's mission, principals and core values.

It is vital to draw trained spokespersons forward into events quickly. Employees should be advised to desist from talking with the media (because they may not be fully informed, may have incorrect information, or may view issues from only their own dimension). However this cannot be allowed to create a vacuum and employees must urgently be advised to where they should direct enquiries. 24/7.

Employees

A message recorded immediately after the incident using a prearranged telephone number can provide information about an incident and guidance to employees on whether and when they should return to work.

A more interactive response might involve a call centre manned by staff who support a number of businesses using scripted responses which can be amended quickly and effectively.

These services can be provided in-house or by third-party suppliers - but whatever solution is deployed, this should be in place and ready for invocation at any time.

Details of these lines and how and by whom they may be invoked should be embedded within the plan. Pre-drafted messages can be prepared and held in readiness should these be required at short notice, although these could be included as plan appendices.

However, care should be exercised when applying such drafts and as with external communications, only messages that are appropriate to the situation and audience and which have been suitably fine-tuned should be used.

Emergency Control Centre

If an off-site location is required, then this should have been pre-selected and included in the plan. Requirements might include:

- Accessibility 24/7
- Location of sufficient distance from an incident so as to be available
- Backup battle box or bag
- Access to IT, telephones email, mobiles, etc.
- Acceptable security

Task List for A Crisis Management Team:

Site-related Incident, e.g. fire, flood, denial of access

Following plan invocation a team might follow a task list such as that set out below:

- Incident notification and escalation procedures invoked to the team Chair.
- Team convenes at Emergency control centre

  - appoint Chair

  - appoint administrator to log all activity into incident event log
- Establish the facts
- Establish the scale

  - nature and number of casualties

  - extent of loss, damage or access to premises

  - time before site re-entry
- Assess impact on business

  - can critical business functions continue at usual premises?
- Identify whether the incident requires business recovery procedures including back-up site
- If business cannot continue at the incident site then the business continuity plan need to be invoked.

  - invoke the business continuity plan and assign a person in the team, to act as coordinator

 - decide whether the Crisis Management team requires to remain in place and if so what the constitution of the team should be based on the nature, scale and complexity of the incident.
- Determine escalation strategy upwards into the organisation

Task List For A Crisis Management Team:

Non Site-related Incident e.g. fraud, employee death, threat to reputation, product recall

Following plan invocation a team might follow a task list such as that set out below:

- Team convenes at Emergency control centre

    - appoint Chair

    - appoint administrator to log all activity into incident event log

- Establish the facts

- Establish the nature and scale of the incident

- Assess impact on business

- Identify whether the incident requires business recovery procedures or specialist procedures

    - invoke the business continuity plan and assign a person in the team, to act as coordinator

    - decide whether the Crisis Management team is required to remain in place and if so what the constitution of the team should be based on the nature, scale and complexity of the incident.

- Consider whether an external expert is required to either form part of the team, act externally to the team or to be retained on standby

- Determine escalation strategy upwards into the organisation

---

How Ready is Your Company?

CEO Questions in the US:

- Has your senior management made contact with those involved at both the local and national levels in the National Response Plan and the National Incident Management System?

- Are you registered with "CEO COM LINK" so that you can receive direct, rapid information and guidance about a threat or an attack?

- Are your employees drilled and ready to respond to an emergency?

- Are your backup systems in place and ready for operations?

(5)

The Relationship Between the Crisis Management Plan and the Business Continuity Plan

The Crisis Management Plan does not address, nor is the team responsible for, business recovery efforts or the logistics of these, which more properly reside with the Business Continuity Plan and team. Further, this plan or team is not responsible for operational business unit or support unit recovery and resumption, which more properly resides with the Business Unit and Support Function Plans and teams, addressed below.

THE BUSINESS CONTINUITY PLAN

The Business Continuity Institute defines a Business Continuity Plan as *"a documented collection of procedures and information that is developed, compiled and maintained in readiness for use in an incident."* **(6)**

The Business Continuity Plan pulls together the response of an entire organisation to a disruptive incident. Those using the plan should be able to:
* analyse information received from those responding to the incident concerning the impact
* select and deploy appropriate strategies from those available in the plan
* direct the resumption of business units according to agreed priorities.

The components and content of a Business Continuity Plan will vary from organisation to organisation and will have a different level of detail based on the culture of the organisation and the technical complexity of the solutions. But the fundamental purpose of the plan remains the same: to provide a documented, tactical framework and response to enable an organisation to resume all of its business processes (or, as a minimum those required most rapidly) within the timescales identified by the Business Impact Analysis (BIA). Consequently, plans should not be drafted until this stage of the planning process has been completed.

A matrix can be developed whereby business and support needs based on output from the risk assessment and the BIA are subdivided into categories ranging from the essential, to the preferable, to the nonessential.

The Benchmarking tools we considered in Chapter Seventeen provide a good source of ideas on what plan headlines might be considered.

In larger organisations, Business Continuity Plan elements might be produced as plans in a modular format. This will enable relevant sections to be provided to teams on a need–to-know basis, although all teams should be trained in where their plans fit into the overall plan matrix or framework. Some individual business units may require a plan with a specific customer orientation, or a set of contractual standards to recover the relevant business infrastructure.

Whatever the structure, all plans should be action-oriented and easy to reference at speed.

As a minimum, teams should be prepared to deal with situations such as the following which might arise from an incident:

* The business is moved to another location but the technology that supports it continues at its usual location

* The business runs from its usual location but either computer or telecommunications operate from a different site

* Both the business and the technology are operating from different locations and they may all be at different sites

* Partial disruption of either a site or technology - e.g., loss of a single floor or service in a multi-floor, multi-service site

* Denial of site access

* Denial of site services, e.g., power or water

- The business runs from its usual site but a key supplier fails, e.g., component manufacturer or outsource service provider
- The business runs from its usual site but a product is faulty and needs to be recalled
- The business runs from its usual site but employees are ill and unable to work
- Business as usual is operating but a major non-IT system failure is detected, e.g., fraud

Responsibilities might include:

- Coordination of the business unit and support function Business Resumption Teams
- Reporting up to the Crisis Management Team
- Management of the internal and external communications strategy
- Contact with government, local authorities and regulators as instructed by the Crisis Management Team
- Internal and external communications as instructed by the Crisis Management Team

---

BUSINESS CONTINUITY PLAN - CONTENTS

A Business Continuity Plan incorporates a number of key elements which include:
- Solutions
- Time based objectives
- RTOs - Recovery Time Objectives
- RPOs - Recovery Point Objectives
- The infrastructure of Plans within the organisation
- Tasks and activities required to achieve time-based objectives based on scenarios
- Procedures or processes
- Industry/organisation information
- Teams
- Meeting points and emergency centres
- Key suppliers
- Key contacts
- Content and location of battle bags, boxes or rooms
- Relevant information not contained in the plan and how to access this

---

BUSINESS CONTINUITY PLAN - DEVELOPMENT - KEY STEPS

- Appoint an owner for the BC Plan (or each plan for multiple sites)
- Define the objectives and scope of the plan with reference to the organisational strategy and BCM Policy
- Develop and approve a planning process and timetabled programme
- Create a planning team to carry out the plan development
- Decide the structure, format, components and content of the plan
- Determine the strategies which the plan will document and what will be documented in other plans
- Determine the circumstances that are beyond the scope of the BCP
- Gather information to populate the plan
- Draft the plan
- Circulate the draft of the plan for consultation and review
- Gather feedback from consultation process
- Amend the plan as appropriate.
- Test the plan using a desktop exercise
- Schedule ongoing exercising and maintenance of the plan to maintain current state. Some information within a Business Continuity Plan such as contact details will require monthly or quarterly review. Other information should be formally reviewed annually and tested through exercising. Other triggers leading to a review include a significant change in technology or telecommunications, a major business process or supplier change, a significant change in staff and a change in the supplier of BCM solutions

(7)

The Benchmarking tools we considered in Chapter Seventeen provide a good source of ideas on what plan headlines might be considered.

A Business Continuity Plan should be modular in design so that separate sections can be supplied to teams on a need-to-know basis. Regularly changing information such as contact details should be kept in appendices at the back of the plan which can more easily be amended, with job titles rather than names held in the text of the document.

A variety of software products are available to assist in building and maintaining a Business Continuity Plan, although the use of these is not essential. However, where these are used, packages should dovetail with the overall IT strategy of the organisation..

Whatever the planning solution, there must be a clearly defined and documented control and change management process used for the production, update and distribution of the Plan.

BUSINESS RESUMPTION PLANS

Depending on the complexity of an organisation, the Business Continuity Plan may be supplemented by more detailed plans for specific responses, business units, support units, or equipment such as that concerning information technology, machinery, locations providing unique products, key components or services, key suppliers, outsource partners or work area recovery sites.

Teams which operate at this level will be drawn together as part of the Bronze response, thereby providing a link into the Silver and Gold teams. These links will ensure that recovery and associated communications will be seamless.

The Risk Assessment and BIA should identify the requirement for these plans, assess criticality and drive plan prioritisation and needs. However as a minimum the following should be considered:

- An Emergency Response Plan for site-specific response, evacuation or in-vacuation
- Business Unit Resumption Plans to resume functions within predefined timescales
- Support Unit Resumption Plans to resume support functions within predefined timescales including those driven by the priorities of business unit recovery

The requirements for technology-specific resumption plans are addressed elsewhere in this book, (Chapter Eleven and Seventeen) and are further expanded on later in this Chapter.

Emergency Response Plan
- An Emergency Response Plan should address:
    - Relevant roles and responsibilities of the team
    - Building Evacuation and In-vacuation plans
    - Details relating to shared sites, e.g., where the landlord is a third party
    - Response to bomb or other specific threats including terrorist or activist threats
    - Dispersal of staff, contractors and visitors
    - Evacuation and assembly points
    - Salvage resources and contracted assistance
    - Environmental issues including the release of restricted substances
    - Escalation circumstances
    - Escalation procedures

Business Unit Resumption Plan
- A Business Unit Resumption Plan should address:
    - Escalation criteria
    - Escalation procedure
    - Resumption Plan for each business unit
    - Key clients
    - Consideration of time sensitivities. For example, priorities may change due to seasonal business patterns and priorities

Support Unit Resumption Plan
- A Support Unit Resumption Plan should address:
    - Escalation criteria
    - Escalation procedure
    - Resumption plan for each support function

These plans identify teams with responsibilities in specific areas such as Human Resources, Facilities Management, Health, Safety and Security, Risk Management, Business Continuity Management, Information Technology, Legal and Finance.

Support plans might include a number of incident-specific and generic check lists.

The support recovery plan team's responsibilities include:
- Recovering the support function's own needs

- People well-being and welfare issues

- Implementing third-party support services such as employee communication and assistance telephone lines

- Implementing and managing cascade contact processes

- Asset salvage and protection

- Identification and fulfilment of business unit recovery needs

- Deciding which work-area options will be used and whether third-party support services should be invoked - including work area

- Setting up work-area recovery locations for customer users of the support function

- Recovery of vital records

- Replacing equipment

- Arranging inventory and raw material replacements

- Allocated supplier management tasks - including transport and catering

- Organising stationery and supplies

- Internal communications in partnership with the Business Continuity and Crisis Management Teams

- External communications - including local authorities, emergency services, and health, safety and environmental authorities - in partnership with the Crisis Management Team

---

Human Resources: Resumption Plan
- Welfare issues

- Health and Safety legal liabilities

- Procedure for accounting for staff

- Procedure for contacting staff

- Counselling and rehabilitation resources

(8)

Suppliers

Suppliers referred to here include those whose support might be required in the first hours following an incident. A variety of contracts might be offered from one of guaranteed delivery to one of 'best efforts.' All suppliers should be noted in the Plan together with contact details and the means of invocation. Contracts and service level agreements should be stored in the battle box or bag away from the primary work location. This type of contractual arrangement might include:

Security

Security required following an incident might be outside business–as-usual experience. Securing a site and exercising site control of an already damaged site that might be vulnerable to theft and further damage could be critical. An organisation does not want to find an already testing situation further exacerbated by the removal of employee's personal effects, confidential documents, IT equipment, stock, work in progress, etc.

Post-incident arrangements may require urgent enhancement concerning the number of security personnel, manning hours and skill levels. There can be a further advantage in using security personnel who are unfamiliar with employees and managers. They may find it easier to exercise the level of control required and to say 'no' to those who are unauthorised to be on site.

The same considerations apply to any temporary sites used post incident.

Health and Environment

A crisis situation involving people may involve compliance with health and safety, legal and regulatory requirements; for example, timely notification of death or injury of employees. An organisation should be aware of these needs and able to respond with suitably qualified support. If, for example, a crisis leads to the release of emissions into the environment of substances that are controlled such as asbestos, chemicals or inert gases, these must be reported to the appropriate authorities, contained and managed. External expertise may be required quickly. In addition to harm to people and damage to the environment, failure to manage emissions properly can lead to prosecution and damage to reputation.

Loss Adjusters and Loss Assessors

Loss adjusters usually assist in the quantification and management of an insured loss. An adjuster of choice may even be identified and appointed in advance by an organisation with the agreement of an insurer and consequently their brief is to support the recovery from an incident to the extent of any insured losses or damage.

An organisation has a wider need for the loss adjuster's skills and knowledge. These are to assist in getting the organisation back into business, to reinstate intellectual assets, to reinstate brand and wider confidences levels amongst a range of different stakeholders - much of which is often uninsured.

The organisation therefore has an additional need for specialist recovery skills and may invite the adjuster to become a full or part-time member of a recovery team. It is possible for an adjuster to deliver on both roles but this distinction is important.

When loss adjusters are appointed by an insurer they will act on an impartial basis. They will take instructions to appoint further support suppliers and services (e.g., salvage specialists, quantity surveyors) from the insured organisation and will take a coordinating role. Loss adjusters can be aware of significant external events and resources and the detail attaching to these before individual organisations. This may be a key factor when precious recovery support suppliers are in demand and those quick to appoint are first to secure these services - even where contracts to supply exist.

An organisation must be sure to keep its own priorities for survival at the top of the response and recovery list, and balance these priorities with those of an insured nature. If, for example, invocation of a third-party work-area recovery facility or site is required, it is beneficial to make this invocation with the knowledge and support of the adjuster as the insurer may be asked to pay the subsequent bill as part of an insurance claim. Such decisions need to be taken quickly and remain those of an organisation rather than of its insurer or loss adjuster.

Salvage Experts

As part of the risk assessment and business impact analysis an organisation should identify what type of salvage supplier might be required and where. Part of planning preparation should concern the evaluation of salvage needs and a tendering and pre-appointment process - notably if specialist services are required to support machinery or document recovery or restoration, which may be in short supply following an incident.

Property

An organisation must establish where critical workstations might be moved and sourced if an incident occurs. External property advisers can assist in the identification and selection of other temporary accommodations and accommodations for salvage recovery or a new site in the event that a business-as-usual site is unavailable. It is difficult to retain a list of potential property on an ongoing basis and it is probably more feasible to have an idea of what might be required by way of square footage and infrastructure for each site's recovery with a good agent on hand to assist when needed.

It is estimated that to house salvage from the average office, approximately 60% of the business-as-usual space will be required for asset storage, salvage recovery and preparation for return to the business as part of business resumption.

The above list is not exhaustive and there will be other players involved who should be considered, pre-appointed, embedded in plans and made familiar with their roles. These might include architects, quantity surveyors, accountants and lawyers as well as industry-specific experts, all of whom may be difficult to secure at a fair price after an incident; especially if an incident has a significant geographic or industry reach.

Employee and Family Support and Post-Trauma Care

The primary concern following an incident should be the well-being of employees and the comfort and safety of their families: this may involve evacuation, first aid, hospital treatment of employees and the consideration of and delivery of bad news to their families. This is a specialist area and there are service providers in most countries who can provide professional support using suitably qualified personnel who can access further specific skills, such as those concerned with the treatment of post-incident trauma.

As with employee hotlines, services for the treatment and counselling of employees should be pre-tendered and contact details pre-assigned. Details of these services and how and by whom they may be invoked should be embedded within the plans at all levels. This should include any high-level plan summaries or guidelines provided to employees.

The anticipated local role of emergency services including the police in this regard should be understood and documented in the plan as part of the relevant check list.

THE STAGES OF AN INCIDENT AND THE IMPACT ON PLANNING

All Plans should clearly establish the response expected of each Plan and team during every phase of an incident. The path of an incident is rarely linear, nor does it typically follow a neat sequence of events.

Several teams may need to operate in concert with one another. This is why the roles and responsibilities of each Plan and team should not excessively overlap and why the overall plan architecture and respective responsibilities must be clearly identified, defined and communicated to all.

It is unlikely that any one team will be able to satisfy the blend of skills and experience required in all situations. The nature and scale of an incident and how this emerges will determine what plans should be invoked, what teams should be brought together, whether any supplementary teams should be created or specialist advisors brought in.

Teams with a specific focus may be required, such as those dealing with sensitive, people-related issues, salvage-specific recovery or the management of an associated insurance claim.

This process must be carefully coordinated and managed.

While most incidents follow a timeline, not all incidents occur as sudden and unforeseen events. An emerging issue can lead to an incident. When detected as an outcome of early-warning mechanisms or through sensitivity monitoring, an organisation's response may need to change as a situation unfolds. Examples of this type of issue include the emergence of SARS or avian flu, the development of national or regional fuel shortages, or the impending disruption that might arise from an approaching tropical storm.

In such situations, enhanced monitoring and communication is essential. The issue needs to be closely watched and different emergent scenarios and responses considered. All stakeholders should be reminded of an organisation's plans, where they are, that they should be observed and that each individual has a role with a set of responsibilities. As an issue escalates into an incident, the response might only ever concern the implementation of such preparations, with relevant plan teams placed on standby.

In most situations, pre-planned, preventative measures or defensive action might be taken. For example:

- Pandemic such as Avian Flu or SARS: reduction in travel and especially travel off-shore, heightened hygiene arrangements, selective vaccination, contingency plans for home working.
- Fuel shortages: restocking of fuel supplies for generators, enhanced arrangements for remote communications, e.g., videoconferencing, contingency plans for home working.
- Impending tropical storm: relocation of key services and people to a safe haven before the storm hits, fixing down assets at vulnerable sites, escalation of support requirements including food supplies, notification of potential invocation to suppliers such as third party work areas.

While this might vary depending on the scale and nature of an impending event, oversight of this activity would usually form a responsibility of the relevant Crisis Management teams.

Emergency Response covers the immediate response and stabilising of a situation following a sudden and unforeseen or gradually occurring incident; including damage limitation.

It is critical that all concerned understand in advance the roles, responsibilities and powers of the emergency services in an incident and the procedures for the command and control of an incident. We have addressed this elsewhere the concept of Gold, Silver and Bronze teams, but in summary, the procedure must include:

- Liaison with the emergency services
- Ensuring the safety and welfare of staff.

Any incident should be recorded as soon as possible in a log of events, with actions established and maintained. This need not be a complex document and simply cover headings of:

- Date
- Time
- Activity
- Decision
- Responsibility.

There is no set pattern for the timeline or associated activities following an incident - every incident will be different. A more or less standardised approach can increase efficiency and recordkeeping, which will be important during the post-event assessment and subsequent audits.

However, there are a number of broad phases that most incidents travel through up until recovery has been achieved and declared. And even then, there may be a 'tail' of actions and care that might journey well beyond recovery until 'business as usual' can be assumed.

Are these plans invoked as part of a continuum or can they operate in parallel? To a degree this should not overly concern or tax the thinking of the risk manager nor business continuity manager. What an organisation must do is to plot its own timeline for managing an incident and how notification, escalation and response would work most effectively. The keys are an open mind together with flexibility in approach and solution, as there is no blueprint for how this should be done.

Using a range of scenarios, an organisation should assess how it would respond as well as who would respond. Then they should design their business continuity programme around this using, where possible, terminology and practices which are familiar. Forced reactions that are out of step managerially or culturally are unlikely to succeed.

But whatever approach is taken, an organisation must move from crisis to regain control as soon as possible. While there is no single blueprint, typically an incident - especially one confined to a single site - may involve a series of baton passes from team to team as an incident develops. In the vast majority of situations, events will not pass beyond Emergency Response - an incident will be minor or even a false alarm, teams will stand down and business will resume with the minimum of disruption. Where an incident is for real, primary responsibility will be delegated to recovery teams over a period of time (generally as an incident unfolds), with any Crisis Management team moving into a position of high-level control and oversight.

CASE STUDY

The Manchester Bombing

Following the Bombing in 1996 the insurance company Royal & SunAlliance formed a Crisis Management Team which met at an Emergency Control Site in the city centre:

- At the close of the first meeting of the Crisis Management Team on Day One, the meeting formally noted the renaming of the team to the Control Management Team. It was agreed that this team would meet the following day, at an out-of-city company site and would be significantly downsized to comprise only those who were required to exercise ongoing oversight and control of the recovery.

- Business Unit teams for each business channel or client market segment and functional support area were formed at each recovery location (two locations were required due to the size of the incident).

- The Chief Executive remained in London and continued to run business as usual and act as the senior representative and face of the company to the outside world. (This was particularly relevant as the company was completing the most significant merger in its operating history at the time and already attracting significant media and customer interest).

Two weeks into the recovery three sub-teams were formed by the Control Management Team. These operated across both recovery locations:

- **People**: managing post-trauma management working under the guidance of an external expert

- **Salvage and insurance claim**: managing site salvage recovery, loss adjusters, quantity surveyors, architects and insurers

- **Property**: managing the procurement and coordination of interim and permanent replacement sites for returning the business to the city and the sale of the site devastated by the bomb

The sub-teams continued to operate after business as usual had been resumed in the city centre and managed run-off issues for a period which varied by team but for up to a further two years.

CASE STUDY

The World Trade Center - 9/11: Thinking the Unthinkable

Business Continuity Management in a Global Organisation

As the second aircraft hit the Twin Towers, the organisation reacted at three locations:

- **Manhattan** - as news of the incident broke the Emergency Response Plans and Crisis Management Plans at the two sites were invoked. Priorities were survival, information and communication. The Manhattan Crisis Management team responded to the crisis and took overall control on the ground. Denied exit, employees remained on site and the Crisis Management Team exercised leadership, maintaining contact with the U.S. headquarters as local means of communication, (primarily cell phones and email) permitted. Once those affected gained some appreciation of what had taken place, the main priority moved to tracking down the whereabouts of employees. It was also vital to respond to concerns expressed by employees on site regarding family members who may have been touched by the event, and to respond to families trying to reach those trapped in Manhattan and to those unable to get home.

- **U.S. Headquarters** - as those in Manhattan grappled with the reality of the sequence of events, those watching the TV screens elsewhere quickly realised that they had a major incident without precedent affecting their people and locations in Manhattan. Concern circulated regarding other actions against the US outside Manhattan and the picture was far from clear with reports about missing aircraft still coming in. The Country Crisis Management Plan was invoked. The central switchboard was flooded with calls coming in from concerned colleagues, relatives, business partners and the Global headquarters. Related email traffic reached an all-time high. Priorities were to make contact with the Manhattan Crisis Management Team and to offer support, continue to gather information and to communicate with employees, family and stakeholders across the US, and to the global headquarters in London. The Crisis Management Team in the US Headquarters maintained overall responsibility and activated other Plans and teams to support the team in Manhattan. Throughout the days that followed, the US headquarters team played a coordinating role towards the team on site in Manhattan and group head office in London.

- **London** - as those in the US headquarters watched events unfold on television, so too did those watching television in London. Concurrent to the invocation of the US headquarters Crisis Management Plan, the Global Crisis Management Plan was invoked and the team moved into action. Calls were already coming in from concerned colleagues, business partners, financial markets and regulators. Priorities were the offer of support to Manhattan via the U.S. headquarters, continued gathering of information, and communication with employees globally outside the U.S. and stakeholders outside the U.S. including London-based markets and regulators. All contact with Manhattan was retained via the U.S. headquarters team allowing Manhattan to focus on local issues without interference or distraction.

The priorities of each team were consequently driven by the nature of the day's events, their proximity to what very quickly became a major disaster, the type of response required and the questions each faced. Subsequent examination of how the Plans and teams interfaced and how effective the overall response has been revealed communication as a primary area of perceived disappointment.

A debrief in which the Manhattan, U.S. and UK teams took part revealed that the team in the U.S. headquarters experienced a sense of frustration with the team in London. Calls received for financial status were viewed as premature and uncaring. London was facing intense market and media questioning concerning corporate health and survival - questions to which answers could not be denied nor unreasonably delayed. Was this a question of cultural difference or insensitivity to each others needs? The general view was that rehearsal of plans at all levels and on an integrated basis might have improved the understanding of the role of each team and what their relative issues might have been.

SPECIALIST SUPPORT RESUMPTION PLANS

Work Area Recovery Plan

Work area recovery plans should identify the teams required, responsibilities, resources and the actions to be taken regarding the relocation of business or support functions to alternative working environments.

We have addressed elsewhere the options for recovery, but the point to recall here is that there may be more than one option or combination of options for site recovery. The recovery solution chosen will depend on the circumstances of an incident, the area affected, site access and the likely speed of recovery.

The teams must be sufficiently skilled and the solutions documented and available must be sufficiently flexible to facilitate a recovery that is appropriate for the recovery required.

This plan is where details of third-party site recovery options and how they may be invoked and accessed should be found. However, the plan is not the location for significant details of third-party sites. This information, such as floor plans, desk layouts, general facilities and the contract is more properly located in the battle box or bag stored in an offsite store.

Work area coordinator responsibilities include:

- Liaison with the facility owner to ensure availability to specification

- Assurance that all predefined equipment and facilities are available

- Agreement of frequency and methods of update to other teams

- Security management

- Arrangements for catering, transport and hotel accommodation

- Cleaning and waste removal

- Stationery and equipment management including cheques and suitable access

- Guidance and communication for staff on site

- Management of the site receiving salvaged items

- Notification of suppliers and deliveries regarding the new location

---

Technology Recovery Plan

Technology plans, sometimes called Contingency or Disaster Recovery (DR) plans, should include strategies for desk tops and portable systems, servers, web sites, local area networks (LANs), wide area networks (WANs), voice communications, distributed systems, mainframe systems, and specialist needs such as those associated with e-commerce and outsource providers. For the purposes of technology continuity, an IT system is "… *identified by defining boundaries around a set of processes, communications, storage and related resources (an architecture)"* (9). All the components of a system need not be physically connected, e.g., a group of standalone PCs.

Technology is an area where documentation for recovery should be included within a plan but is often not. Too frequently, technology managers will hold recovery details in their heads rather than document them, assuming that test documentation will suffice in a live situation. This will fail in the event the relevant manager is unavailable to 'download' their knowledge.

Further, where an organisation operates to industry or professional standards or trades in a regulated environment, this approach will not reach the standards for documentation required and as such may be treated as noncompliant. As already discussed, a regulator will consider that if a planning activity - including IT - is not documented, then it does not happen.

In some organisations the roles of business continuity manager and technology continuity manager have separate reporting lines and may therefore not operate in the same functional team. Whatever the structure, the technology business continuity manager and the enterprise business continuity manager must work closely together to ensure that at some stage in the business continuity programme, the processes of planning come together as a single framework under an umbrella policy using consistent standards and language. This interface will work to ensure that technology plans meet the needs of the business in terms of recovery time objectives and the cost of these, rather than allow technology plans to be developed in isolation.

The technology business continuity management process is basically the same as the non-technology process and should involve an understanding of the business. This includes conducting business impact analyses (BIAs); looking at different strategies for response and recovery; establishing a business continuity culture across the technology function; and, rigorous processes for testing and review. Having followed this process, the technology continuity manager should scope the matrix of technology continuity plans and ensure that for each component a technology coordinator is appointed. Above all, the technology and other infrastructure plans should be driven by the precise operational needs that have been established by operational directors. Furthermore, these operational directors need to sign off a service level agreement (SLA) with the infrastructure managers that establishes clear expectations –and limits - of the continuity of infrastructure delivery.

It will be the role of the technology coordinator to produce the technology plan assigned within the overall boundaries defined. Fundamentally the steps involved in developing and implementing plans for technology recovery are no different to that for any other type of plan.

A technology plan will typically address at least one of the following:

- Restoring IT operations at an alternate location

- Recovering IT operations using alternate equipment

- Performing some or all of the affected business processes using non-IT (manual) means (for short term periods)

Broadly, two types of technology plan might be required:

- **Contingency** - These plans should be developed for each major application and general support system, consequently creating multiple plans that will form part of an organisation's overall business continuity programme and planning framework.

- **Disaster Recovery** - As implied by its name this plan relates to potential catastrophic events that deny access to a system or facility for a significant period of time relative to an organisation's recovery time objectives.

"Catastrophic" will vary depending on the nature of the business. For example, an outage of a week for an internet-based business might be catastrophic but not necessarily so for other types of business that might find the outage serious but not terminal.

These two types of plan are not mutually exclusive and may overlap. Contingency is more often likely to involve site-based situations requiring localised support and recovery rather than wholesale movement of mainframe or server farm capabilities where a disaster recovery situation will apply.

A technology plan should follow the overall approach to planning in an organisation in terms of scope and plan document layout but might include:

- Business operational requirements

- Technology operational requirements

- Security requirements

- Technical procedures

- Hardware, software and other types of equipment

- Connectivity specifications and requirements

- Names and contact information of the team

- Names and contact details of vendors including alternate and offsite vendors point of contact

- Alternate and offsite facilities

- Vital records (electronic and hard copy)

As with other plans, action-oriented check lists will provide an approach for recovery that is simple to follow and unambiguous.

Recovery Process For A LAN Recovery Team

These procedures are followed for recovering a file from backup tapes. The LAN recovery team is responsible for reloading all critical files necessary to continue production.

- Identify file and date from file ifs to be recovered …. [time]

- Identify tape using tape log book …. [time]

- If tape is not in tape library request tape from recovery facility, complete with authorising signature …. [time]

- When tape is received log date and time …. [time]

- Place tape in drive and begin recovery process …. [time]

- When file is recovered notify LAN recovery coordinator …. [time]

(10)

Technology planning is also no different in that where possible information should be located in plan appendices or in relevant battle boxes or bags. Appendices might include:

- Standard operating procedures

- Equipment and system requirements - including an inventory

- Vendor and supplier contracts and service level agreements

- Alternate site description and location

- The BIAs by recovery time phase

Call Centre Plan

Call centre resources within an organisation may operate from one or more sites.

In the case of the failure of a single call centre that offers a unique service that cannot be replicated elsewhere within an organisation, recovery alternatives are limited. A firm may choose to have incoming calls diverted to a bureau or agency that would answer the telephone and take messages, but this offers little interaction. Consequently, recovery will most often be to a dedicated, in-house site or more likely to a third-party service or work-area provider.

If punitive service level agreements are in place with one or more customers, the notification and escalation processes in the plan may need to be especially sensitive.

If an organisation has a number of call centres, then a plan could offer recovery through a virtual solution utilising techniques similar to those of business-as-usual, when call flows peak and trough, and may be moved between call centres to find those offering the greatest levels of capacity.

TEAM CHARACTERISTICS AND REQUIREMENTS

All those individuals named in plan teams should have at least one alternate team member, with home, office and remote contact information indicated for all. All plans should indicate who the chair and alternate chair of the team are, how the plan is to be invoked, and by whom. Sitting in reserve to ensure 24/7 coverage in the event of invocation, consideration should be given to a third or even fourth alternate to ensure coverage and effective plan operation.

Details of suppliers, support services or resources required to underpin the plan should be included with applicable contact information.

Whatever the scope of responsibilities which exist for a team, certain characteristics are consistent. This team may be the initial face of an organisation to the outside world - whether this be to the media or to a regulator.

They must feel and be empowered to take the decisions required to deliver their responsibilities. Constant referral back up the managerial line for authority may slow down and limit the effectiveness of a response.

Any initial assessment of an incident will demand a relevant level of understanding of the issues involved and whether escalation beyond the team in control is required.

The DNA of effective teams was addressed in greater depth as part of Chapter Twelve but as a reminder, the dynamics of any successful team include:

- Strong organisational leader
- Competence and skills mix suitable for a crisis
- Right membership for the level of materiality of a crisis
- Optimum size between four and ten
- Empowered and that authorisation is communicated group wide.
- Strong team alternates
- Rehearsed against scenarios
- Rehearsed with other planning teams.

The chair of the team might not be the most senior team member on a day-to-day basis and should be selected for the qualities that may be required in the event of invocation. Some managers faced with disaster respond very differently than their demeanour during business as usual - rehearsal is essential to ensure that not only the team is fit to function, but that its leader is fit to lead.

We should not overlook the CEO. The invocation process must embrace them and they must be prepared and trained to step up to the task. The media may demand their involvement. However, the fundamental role of a CEO remains the leadership of an organisation rather than taking control of each crisis or recovery situation.

The Role of the CEO

The CEO's role includes:

- Direct, ongoing involvement in the crisis preparedness and response process

- Direct and frequent endorsement to all stakeholders of the importance of crisis preparedness

- Readiness to immediately serve as the primary spokesperson

When actual crisis strikes, the CEO's role often includes serving as:

- An active participant in strategy discussions

- The 'commander in chief' approving primary strategies and major decisions

- Spokesperson for the company

- Chief morale builder

(11)

PLANNING SOFTWARE

The use of software for business continuity planning has prompted many debates among business continuity professionals as well as other business managers.

The first myth to explode is that continuity software is a necessity to achieve an effective business continuity programme. The knowledge of an organisation cannot be replaced by software.

Many organisations produce effective plans able to respond when required without the use of a specifically designed software package. Today's standard word processing, email, database and spreadsheet software applications offer opportunities to support the business continuity management process and the production, review and updating of plans. On the other hand, using some of these applications could make it more difficult to achieve consistency across plans with reliable, up-to-date information, especially when this is embedded in more than one plan.

The expression 'continuity software' is used generically, yet it can mean several things. One of the first obstacles facing potential software users is the myriad of packages available and working through what they can do to support the process. A classification **(12)** which attempts to provide a description of the different types is outlined below:

- **Plan Development, Maintenance and Testing** - These assist with the development and maintenance of all forms of plan (business continuity, disaster recovery, and crisis management) and the scheduling and conduct of testing.

- **Incident Management and Interactive Testing** - Interactive tools used at time of incident or during testing to automate recording and monitoring of actions taken.

- **Data Gathering, Analysis and Presentation** - These are used to design questionnaires and surveys to gather key information and to provide the means for analysing and presenting the results.

- **Automated Call-Out and Notification** - Tools that send out phone calls, e-mails and faxes to call out key personnel and provide the means for recording information back from them.

- **Risk Analysis and Dependency Modelling** - These provide the means for performing a structured risk analysis using questionnaires or dependency-modelling techniques.

While the smaller organisation could probably deliver a business continuity plan without specific software, how can a large organisation with many business lines, departments and locations possibly achieve standards of plan integrity and quality (and performance indicators with evidence of performance) without a specially designed computer application?

If the answer to this question is that they cannot, then this begs a second question of why then, have so many large organisations tried to use continuity software and failed?

Perhaps the source of an answer rests more with ineffective implementation rather than inadequacy of software. Most organisations underestimate the level of effort that is required to implement a continuity package. Specialist packages have been produced by developers with specific approaches and intentions in mind and if these are not clearly understood, or they are incompatible with the nature, style or culture of an organisation, there will be a mismatch.

Organisations often approach the use of software as an alternative to having a comprehensive business continuity framework and programme. Software will not replace the needs for these nor will it remove the need to observe the business continuity cycle. Moreover, software cannot make informed business decisions nor commit to specific continuity strategies. At the point of purchase, the work required by an organisation to specify and customise software is nearly always underestimated and the need for oversight, management control and maintenance overlooked. Software cannot do anything without commitment from an organisation. The majority of users demand packages that are capable of producing reports and plans in the shape, manner and form of their choosing. 'Ownership of plans' is often quoted as a prerequisite for software to work, yet the more customisation that is allowed, the more complicated it becomes to set up continuity software and the more work is needed at the outset.

This said, all the fault should not rest with the user. The business continuity and computer press have carried many articles about continuity software released while insufficiently tested and with problems that seem to have taken a long time to resolve.

The important step for an organisation to take is to determine whether or not software will help in the achievement of its aims. If it is agreed that software will help, then consideration needs to be given as to whether to use generic software or continuity software. An organisation should scope the functionality it requires and match this against the specifications of relevant products. Compatibility with the overall software strategy of an organisation, support available internally and externally, language needs, and the potential requirement for flexibility to strip down functionality for the smaller business unit, together with the software maintenance and upgrade commitments and cost, are all considerations to avoid an expensive mistake.

WHAT PLANS SHOULD NOT CONTAIN

Plans should be brief and focussed and only contain essential information. Too often plans start with a long preamble about an organisation's risk and business continuity management philosophy and approach to planning, with the information that is required to help a team respond to an incident located too far into the body of the document.

Those who might need to use a plan, often at unsociable hours, should be able to do so easily and without the burden of working through interesting but irrelevant information for the circumstances. Plans should start at the right pace - and if there is the need to make a statement that says "If this plan is being accessed for invocation go to page ...." - then the plan is not starting at the right place.

Information about an organisation's business continuity policy or standards should be located in an organisation's planning guide or 'bible,' communications and training materials. And if those who respond to an incident have a need to read this type of document for the first time after an incident has occurred, then training, education and rehearsal has been inadequate - this is too late!

WHERE NEXT?

At we write this book, there is ongoing discussion and debate concerning the future of Business Continuity Management, its relationship with Risk Management as part of the Governance and Risk Framework of organisations and specifically with Operational Risk Management. Rarely does a relevant conference take place without this as a key topic of interest.

There are two main schools of thought which appear to vary depending on one's professional persuasion.

First, the view that Business Continuity Management is an umbrella under which many other risk-related disciplines sit with Business Continuity Management as the uniting force. Second, that Business Continuity Management is closely related to Risk Management but as a subordinate control mechanism. If there is a close 'risk relative,' then Operational Risk is the one most commonly quoted.

The world's regulators and standards-setters appear to favour the latter although, as always, there are exceptions to this rule and what is set today will surely change tomorrow. Risk and Business Continuity Management are part of a fast-moving professional world.

But if one respects that each subject attracts its own specific set of professional competencies and skills, which are related but sufficiently distinct to demand separate training, education and qualification, then perhaps we should celebrate the differences and embrace the compatibilities.

'Risk Federations' are surfacing and these will involve practitioners from a number of risk-related professions. Working together is the key to success; 'vive la difference' celebrates 'la même chose.'

SUMMARY

> *Picture the scene: a business continuity management training video shows the chairman of a Crisis Management Team at the site of a major incident. Red in the face- not from the stress of the incident but from carrying the weight of an enormous binder holding the Crisis Management plan - we can guess the result. Confusion reigns as pages are turned, papers dropped and the right page proves elusive for some considerable time...*

Plans should not attempt to provide a solution for every eventuality - they are documents to guide and inform and establish options that may be useful to the crisis managers. A number of realistic scenarios addressing potential key risks and material business impacts; details or pre-arranged suppliers; and, a qualified and well-rehearsed team that can be readily contacted are the primary components. Plans should be fit for the purpose and reflect the business or support unit whose needs they have been designed to meet.

So we complete the circle. Business continuity management is "...*a holistic management process that identifies potential impacts that threaten an organisation and provides a framework for building resilience and the capability for an effective response that safeguards the interests of its key stakeholders, reputation, brand and value-creating activities.*" Business continuity plans are the end result of the process, and if the management process has been followed effectively, then the business continuity manager should arrive at their destination with the information required for an organisation to deliver effective and efficient business continuity plans.

But did we say arrive? Of course, producing plans is *not* the end of the journey - the journey will continue as organisations and the environment within which they operate evolve and change.

Bibliography

1. Continuity Forum - Mark Carey - 2005

2. The Firm Risk Assessment Framework - Financial Services Authority (FSA) - 2003

3. The Business Continuity Institute God Practice Guide www.thebci.org - 2005

4. Guide to Business Continuity Management - British Standards Institution (BSI) PAS 56 - 2003

5. Good Practice Guidelines - The Business Continuity Institute (BCI) - 2005

6. UK Resilience www.ukresilience - 2004

7   Evacuation Planning www.mi5.gov.uk - 2004

8. The Business Continuity Institute God Practice Guide www.thebci.org - 2005

9.   National Institute of Standards and Technology (NIST) - 2002

10. National Institute of Standards and Technology (NIST) - 2002

11. Committed to Protecting America: A Private Sector Crisis Preparedness Guide (2005)

12 Malcolm Cornish - Marsh - 2005

Appendix A

British Standard PAS 56
Guide to Business Continuity Management
Annex B: BCM Evaluation Criteria

PUBLICLY AVAILABLE SPECIFICATION PAS 56:2003
ICS 03.100.01
The Business Continuity Institute
© BSI 24 March 2003, Excerpted With Permission.

Annex B: BCM Evaluation Criteria

B.1 General

The evaluation criteria described in B.2 to B.7 are based on a set of core questions that reflect the six stages of the BCM lifecycle. They can be used either as part of a self assessment process or by an auditor as part of a formal audit.

The evaluation criteria have been designed to facilitate a multi-stage assessment of an organization's business continuity and crisis management competence and capability, and can be used as benchmark comparators.

All questions are of equal value and weighting.

NOTE The questions themselves do not provide a quality assurance audit. Quality assurance auditing requires the assistance of a professional BCM practitioner, and may involve a further, rigorous quality assurance review, verification and validation (accreditation) process.

The aim of the evaluation process is to:

- provide a consistent BCM good practice benchmark;
- enable and inform the identification of an organization's BCM KPIs [*Key Performance Indicators*];
- identify gaps in an organization's BCM competence and capability;
- demonstrate and provide evidence that the organization is discharging its legal, regulatory and corporate governance accountability and responsibilities.

B.2 BCM Programme Management

B.2.1 Management
   • Does the organization have a clearly defined, documented and approved management process to manage its BCM programme?

   • Does the organization use PAS 56 as an integral part of its BCM programme?

   • Does the organization's BCM programme management process achieve the outcomes of BCM programme management as set out in 5.2.3?

   • Does the organization's BCM programme clearly identify and comply with current regulatory, legal and the organization's BCM policy and principle requirements?

   • Are professionally qualified BCM practitioners involved in the implementation of the organization's BCM programme?

   • Have the overall organizational accountability and responsibilities for the management of the organization's BCM programme been clearly defined and documented?

   • Has the organization successfully demonstrated its BCM (including crisis management) competence and capability via exercising, rehearsal and testing or invocation?

   • Does the organization's BCM programme incorporate the allocation of dedicated resources and finance as a part of the annual budget development and management process?

   • Does the management of the organization's BCM programme focus upon the organization's MCAs [*Mission Critical Activities*] at a product and service level?

   • Is the management of the organization's BCM programme based upon an E2E approach in the context of product and service delivery?

   • Does the management of the organization's BCM programme provide assurance that suppliers (internal and/or outsourced providers) of the organization's MCAs have an effective, up-to-date and fit-for-purpose BCM capability?

   • Does the organization have a Management Information System (MIS) to monitor and provide regular reports concerning the status of BCM within the organization?

B.2.2 BCM policy
   • Does the organization have a clearly defined, documented and approved BCM policy?

   • Does the organization's BCM policy include the BCM principles set out in 4.1?

   • Does organization's BCM policy achieve the outcomes of a BCM policy as set out in 5.3.3?

   • Does the organization's BCM policy enable corporate governance, the discharge of its responsibilities and satisfaction of its legal and regulatory obligations?

   • Does the organization's BCM policy provide for a clearly defined, documented and approved set of BCM guidelines and minimum standards?

   • Does the organization's BCM policy provide for a clearly defined, documented and approved independent audit process including frequency and triggers of the organization's BCM capability (not just plans)?

   • Does the organization's BCM policy provide for the verification and validation of the effectiveness and fit-for-purpose BCM capability of the suppliers (internal and/or outsourced providers) of its MCAs?

B.2.3 BCM Assurance
- Does the organization have a clearly defined, documented and approved BCM assurance management process and frequency (cycle)?

- Does the organization's BCM assurance process achieve the outcomes of a BCM assurance process as set out in 5.4.3?

- Does the organization have a set of clearly defined, documented and approved KPIs (objectives, targets and standards) for BCM?

- Does the organization have a clearly defined and documented monitoring, evaluation and review process for its BCM KPIs?

- Does the organization's BCM assurance process provide clearly defined, documented and approved management information assurance reports?

- Does the organization's BCM assurance process provide clearly defined, approved, prioritized and documented remedial action plan(s) to implement the agreed recommendations of the assurance report?

B.3 Understanding Your Business

B.3.1 Business impact analysis
- Has the organization adopted a clearly defined and documented standard BIA process?

- Does the organization's BIA process achieve the outcomes of a BIA as set out in 6.2.3?

- Was the current BIA completed within the last 12 months?

- Was the current BIA conducted in an E2E business service or product context?

- Has the organization clearly identified, defined and documented its MCAs (including outsourcing of products and services)?

- Has the organization clearly defined and documented the RTO, RPO and LBC for its MCAs (products and services)?

- Does the BIA identify resource recovery requirements?

- Does the organization have a process to ensure that a BIA is carried out as a part of all project and change management including new developments of (and major changes to) IT systems, services and their sourcing?

B.3.2 Risk assessment
- Does the organization have a clearly defined, documented and approved risk management strategy?

- Does the organization's risk assessment process achieve the outcomes of a risk assessment as set out in 6.3.3?

- Does the organization have a clearly defined, documented and approved standard process to carry out an operational risk assessment?

- Does the organization have a clearly defined and documented process to ensure the approved risk methodology, tools, techniques and criteria are consistently applied?

- Does the organization have a clearly defined, documented and approved organization risk appetite benchmark, including the acceptance of residual risk?

- Has a risk assessment been completed within the last 12 months in respect of the organization's MCAs?

- Has the organization identified its own organizational and industry systemic risks?

- Has the organization identified its areas of high risk concentration e.g. one building/site with several MCAs?

- Has the organization introduced risk management controls (an action plan) to eliminate, mitigate, reduce, transfer the effects of identified key threats, vulnerabilities, exposures or liabilities to MCAs?

B.4 BCM Strategies

B.4.1 Organization BCM strategy
- Does the organization have a clearly defined, documented and approved organization BCM strategy?

- Does the organization BCM strategy achieve the outcomes of an organization BCM strategy as set out in 7.2.3?

- Is the organization's BCM strategy clearly linked to, aligned to and supporting the overall strategic aims and business strategies or plan of the organization?

- Does the organization have a clearly defined, documented and approved BCM framework?

- Has the organization identified key roles, responsibilities and authorities within its organization BCM strategy?

B.4.2 Process level (systemic) BCM strategy
- Does the organization have a clearly defined, documented and approved process level BCM strategy?

- Does the organization's process level BCM strategy achieve the outcomes of a process level BCM strategy as set out in 7.3.3?

- Has the organization identified key roles, accountabilities, responsibilities and authorities within its process level BCM strategy?

- Has the selected process level BCM strategy(ies) been fully evaluated to ensure it is fit-for-purpose and capable of working within the required timescales?

B.4.3 Resource recovery BCM strategy
- Does the organization have a clearly defined, documented and approved resource recovery BCM strategy?

- Does the resource recovery BCM strategy incorporate the resource recovery requirement from the BIA?

- Does the organization's resource recovery BCM strategy achieve the outcomes of a resource recovery BCM strategy as set out in 7.4.3?

- Have the key roles, accountabilities, responsibilities and authorities within the resource recovery BCM strategy been clearly defined and documented?

- Has the resource recovery strategy been fully evaluated to ensure it is fit-for-purpose and capable of working within the required timescales?

- Have both technical (e.g. IT, telecommunications, WAR [*Work Area Recovery*], specialist services) and nontechnical (e.g. people and equipment) issues been considered within the resource recovery BCM strategy?

- Has the internal sourcing and outsourcing of products and services been included within the resource recovery BCM strategy?

B.5 Developing and Implementing BCM Plans

B.5.1 Business continuity plan

B.5.1.1 General
- Does the organization have a clearly defined, up-to-date, fit-for-purpose and approved BCP(s) for all its MCAs?
- Does the BCP reflect the most up-to-date BIA, business impact resource recovery requirements and RA?
- Does the BCP establish a clearly predefined BCM response (solutions, resumption and recovery) following a business disruption, interruption or loss of the organization's MCAs from the initial response to the point at which normal business operations are resumed?

B.5.1.2 BCM planning
- Does the organization have a clearly defined, documented and approved BCM planning process framework?
- Does the organization's BCM planning process achieve the outcomes of the BCM planning process set out in 8.2.3?
- Is the organization's BCM planning process primarily concerned with its MCAs?
- Is the planning process coordinated with the organization's service or product sourcing (outsourcing and internal sourcing) providers?
- Is the organization's BCM planning process integrated and coordinated with other parts of the organization e.g. geographically (departments, sites, etc.)?
- Are CP templates, frameworks, sample plans or minimum standards available for reference and to provide a standardized BCM planning approach?

B.5.1.3 Emergency BCM response procedures
- Does the BCP provide a clearly defined, up-to-date and fit-for-purpose BCM emergency response?
- Does the BCP provide a clearly defined process to ensure there are links to other organizations e.g. emergency services, or suppliers that may be involved in the recovery and restoration process?

B.5.1.4 Notification, invocation and escalation
- Does the BCP have a clearly defined and structured up-to-date and fit-for-purpose BCM notification, invocation and escalation process?
- Has the effective capability of the notification, invocation and escalation process been demonstrated and proven via exercising and/or invocation?

B.5.1.5 Roles, accountability, responsibility and authority
- Is the role of organization's executive or senior management during a BCM incident clearly defined, approved and documented?
- Does the BCP clearly define the BCM roles and their accountability, responsibility and authority?
- Has each BCP role been assigned to a principal and an alternate individual, should the principal be incapacitated or otherwise unavailable?

B.5.1.6 Key supporting information
- Does the BCP contain either mandatory instructions, advice, process, procedure or guidelines concerning key supporting information?

B.5.1.7 People issues
- Does the BCP contain either mandatory instructions, advice, process, procedure or guidelines concerning casualties and fatalities?

- Does the BCP contain mandatory instructions, advice, process, procedure or guidelines concerning confidential staff counselling and staff welfare, e.g. consideration of personal belongings, travel and relocation issues?

B.5.1.8 Communication
- Does the BCP contain mandatory instructions, advice, process, procedure or guidelines concerning internal and external communications?

B.5.1.9 Documentation, forms and checklists
- Does the BCP have an up-to-date task list that clearly identifies both mandatory and discretionary tasks together with the individuals accountable or responsible for their completion within an allocated timeframe?

- Does the BCP provide an auditable process for tracking and recording the completion of the BCP task list after the plan has been invoked and any additional on-going tasks?

- Does the BCP provide up-to-date (internal and external) contact lists (e.g. for key and alternate staff, suppliers, stakeholders, etc.)?

- Has a current list of key service providers, suppliers and other third-party sourcing contacts been identified and documented within the BCP?

- Does the BCP provide a situation management and decision log template?

B.5.1.10 External bodies and organizations
- Has an Emergency Services Liaison Officer been appointed?

- Have statutory/regulatory/official agencies been identified and included in the organization's BCM planning process?

- Does the BCP provide clearly defined coordination procedures for local authorities, service utilities and other relevant public authorities?B.5.1.11 Media and public relations

- Does the BCP provide a clearly defined process for dealing with the media and public relations during a BCM situation?

B.5.2 Resource recovery and solutions plan

B.5.2.1 General
- Have the "owners" of the organization's MCAs and dependencies developed and implemented BCM solutions within their BCM strategy or plan to achieve the RTO [*Recovery Time Objective*], RPO [*Recovery Point Objective*] and LBC [*Level of Business Continuity*] of their MCAs?

- Does the resource recovery and solutions plan achieve the resource recovery and solutions plan outcomes as set out in 8.3.3?

B.5.2.2 Insurance
- Are all BCM insurance policies and their coverage limits reviewed regularly for adequacy and cost benefit?

B.5.2.3 People
- Does the BCP clearly identify key members of staff (according to their skills, knowledge, organizational role and experience) and a process or strategy to ensure their availability?

B.5.2.4 Work area recovery (WAR)

- Has a WAR strategy for MCAs and their support activities been developed and documented within the BCP?

- Is the WAR site located at least 800 metres (based on a large vehicle bomb) from the site of the incident, so as not to be affected by the same incident?

- Is the level of specialist service support required to enable the use of the WAR site and its services clearly identified within a service contract or SLA?

B.5.2.5 Information technology

- Has an information technology resumption and recovery strategy for MCAs and their dependencies been developed and clearly documented within the BCP?

- Does the BCP clearly identify that the technical recovery site is located at least 800 metres (based on a large vehicle bomb) from the site of the incident, so as not to be affected by the same incident?

- Have the business owners of the MCAs and the technical and/or specialist third party service providers successfully tested the resumption and/or recovery of the IT systems?

B.5.2.6 IT software

- Does the BCP provide a clear inventory of all IT systems software necessary for the BCM of MCAs to achieve their BCM RTO, RPO and LBC objectives?

- Does the BCP provide clear details of specialist software configuration(s) and a process for its restoration, including licensing arrangements?

- Have arrangements been made to place specialist software in escrow?

- Have the business owners of the MCAs and technical and/or specialist third party service providers successfully tested the resumption and/or recovery of the IT software systems?

B.5.2.7 Telecommunications

- Has a telecommunications recovery strategy for MCAs been developed and clearly defined within the BCP?

- Have the business owners of the MCAs and suppliers and/or specialist third party service providers successfully tested the resumption and/or recovery of the telecommunications systems?

B.5.2.8 Data

- Does the organization have clearly defined backup procedures for all applications, hardware and data (both electronic and paper, e.g. records, unique records or documents) necessary to support MCAs?

- Does the organization have clearly defined recovery and restoration processes and procedures in place for all data (both electronic and paper , e.g. records, unique records or documents) necessary to support MCAs?

- Have the business owners of the MCAs, technical staff, WAR providers and specialist third-party data storage providers successfully tested the recovery and restoration of vital records (both electronic and paper)necessary to support MCAs?

- Can vital records (both electronic and paper) necessary to support MCAs and their dependencies be recovered simultaneously at more than one WAR site if required?

B.5.2.9 Equipment

- Does the BCP provide clear details and a list of equipment e.g. photocopier, manufacturing machinery, etc. needed for MCAs?

B.5.2.10 BCM service providers

- Is the level of specialist BCM service required to enable the use of a WAR site or other services clearly identified and documented within the service contract and/or SLA, and a copy placed in the BCP?

- Does the BCP provide clear details and a process for the initiation and progressing of recovery, restoration and salvage service by specialist BCM service suppliers?

B.5.2.11 Security

- Do the BCM solutions within the BCP have appropriate physical security and environmental controls?

B.5.2.12 Business processes

- Does the BCP provide clear details and a process for recovering MCA work in progress?
  - Does the BCP provide clear details and a process concerning work backlog processing?

  - Does the BCP provide clear details and a process for the provision of manual operations and fallback solutions and related activities to achieve MCA RTOs and RPOs wherever gaps exist between IT resumption and/or recovery capabilities and BCM needs?

B.5.2.13 Change management

- Does the organization have a clearly defined change control process to ensure BCM requirements and selected BCM solutions are maintained in an up-to-date and fit-for-purpose status?

B.5.2.14 Sourcing (internal and outsourcing)

- Does the organization maintain a schedule of its sourced (internal or outsourced) MCAs?

- Does the organization's BCM policy clearly define that an outsourced or internal provider of MCAs should have a verifiable, fit-for-purpose and demonstrated BCM capability?

- Does the organization have a clearly defined due diligence process to verify and validate that outsourced or internal providers of MCAs have a fit-for-purpose and demonstrated BCM capability in respect of each MCA?

- Does the organization have a clearly defined and documented structure to "relationship manage" any sourcing of its MCAs?

- Does the organization have a supplier exit strategy or plan, i.e. the capability to switch the provision of the MCA to another outsourcer or to internal provision, to cover the complete failure of any contract or SLA for each of its sourced MCAs?

- Does the sourcing contract and/or SLA of the organization's sourced MCAs include a right by the organization to audit the BCM capability and resilience of the supplier against predefined and agreed BCM standards (e.g. within RTOs, RPOs and to the minimum LBC)?

- As a part of the organization's due diligence process of the sourcing of its MCAs, does the organization regularly receive certified copies of the supplier's own internal BCM exercising reports and action plans?

B.5.3 Crisis Management

B.5.3.1 Crisis management planning

- Does the organization have a clearly defined, documented and approved crisis management framework?

- Are professionally qualified crisis management practitioners involved in the planning process?

B.5.3.2 Crisis management plans
- Does the organization have a clearly defined, up-to-date, fit-for-purpose and approved crisis management plan (CMP)?

- Does the organization's CMP achieve the outcomes of a CMP as set out in 8.4.3?

B.5.3.3 Emergency procedures
- Does the CMP clearly set out and document emergency evacuation procedures; other staff and building safety procedures; evacuation and assembly points for different types of incident (e.g. fire or bomb) and their testing programme?

B.5.3.4 Control and coordination centres
- Does the CMP provide a clearly defined control and coordination organization structure to manage an incident?

- Has the effective capability of the control and coordination centre(s) been demonstrated and proven via exercising and/or invocation?

B.5.3.5 Notification, invocation and escalation
- Does the CMP have a structured up-to-date, fit-for-purpose and approved incident notification, invocation and escalation process?

- Has the effective capability of the notification, invocation and escalation process been demonstrated and proven via exercising and/or invocation?

B.5.3.6 Roles, accountability, responsibility and authority
- Is the role of the organization's executive or senior management during an incident clearly defined, agreed and documented?

- Does the CMP clearly define the organization's crisis management roles, accountabilities, responsibilities and authorities?

- Has each CMP role been assigned to a principal and an alternate individual should the principal be incapacitated or otherwise unavailable during an incident?

B.5.3.7 Key supporting information
- Does the CMP contain either mandatory instructions, advice, process, procedure or guidelines concerning key supporting information?

B.5.3.8 People issues
- Does the CMP contain either mandatory instructions, advice, process, procedure or guidelines concerning casualties and fatalities?

- Does the CMP contain either mandatory instructions, advice, process, procedure or guidelines concerning confidential staff counselling and staff welfare, e.g. consideration of personal belongings, travel and relocation issues?

B.5.3.9 Communication
- Does the CMP contain mandatory instructions, advice, process, procedure or guidelines concerning internal and external communications?

B.5.3.10 Documentation, forms and checklists
- Does the CMP have an up-to-date task list that clearly identifies both mandatory and discretionary tasks together with the roles accountable or responsible for their completion with an allocated timeframe?

- Does the CMP provide an auditable process for tracking and recording the completion of the CMP task list(s) after the plan has been invoked?

- Does the CMP provide up-to-date (internal and external) contact lists (e.g. for key and alternate staff, suppliers, stakeholders)?

- Does the CMP provide a crisis management and decision log template?

B.5.3.11 External bodies and organizations
- Has an individual been clearly identified and appointed to the role of emergency services liaison officer within the CMP?

- Does the CMP provide clearly defined and documented coordination procedures for local authorities, utility services and other relevant public authorities?

B.5.3.12 Media and public relations
- Does the CMP contain a clearly defined media and public relations strategy and plan?

- Does the CMP clearly identify and unambiguously describe stakeholders and interest groups?

B.6   Building and Embedding a BCM Culture

- Does the organization have a clearly defined, published and approved BCM vision and policy statement?

- Does the organization's awareness, training and cultural development programme achieve the outcomes set out in 9.1.3?

- Have the BCM policy, principles and programme been communicated throughout the organization?

- Does the organization's executive or senior and middle management proactively demonstrate its support and strong commitment to the organization's BCM vision, policy and programme?

- Are the implementation and maintenance of the organization's BCM policy and principles strictly monitored and evaluated?

- Are BCM roles, accountabilities, responsibilities and authorities clearly defined and documented within job descriptions at all levels of the organization?

- Is BCM integrated with the organization's reward and recognition system?

- Is BCM integrated with the organization's performance management and appraisal system?

- Does the organization have clearly defined and documented KPIs for BCM?

- Is BCM an integral part of the organization's change management process?

- Is BCM integral part of the organization's project management process?

- Does the organization have a formal BCM awareness or induction training programme for all new and existing managers and staff?

B.7   Exercising, Maintenance and Audit

B.7.1 Exercising
- Doesgramme?

- Does the organization's BCM exercising programme achieve the outcomes of a BCM exercising programme as set out in 10.1.3?

- Is a "live" exercise(MCA) run in a "business as usual" context for one week every six months at the WAR location?

- Is the six monthly "live" BCM exercise coordinated, integrated and linked with other organizations' stakeholders and regulators?

- Does the organization have a clearly defined, documented and approved standardized exercise contract that must be approved and signed-off by the exercise sponsor and other participants prior to each scheduled exercise?

- Does the organization's exercising, rehearsal and testing programme provide for various methods, types and techniques of exercising, rehearsal and testing?

- Does the frequency of BCM and crisis management exercising, rehearsal and testing reflect the nature, scale, complexity, culture and operating environment of the organization?

- Does the organization use professionally qualified practitioners to plan and facilitate BCM and crisis management exercises, rehearsals and tests?

- Does the organization provide clearly defined, documented and approved exercising, rehearsal and testing guidelines?

- Does the organization have a clearly defined, documented and approved process to verify that the business continuity competence and capability is being exercised in line with the organization's BCM exercising programme?

- Does the organization have a clearly defined, documented and approved process to provide a standardized post-exercise, rehearsal and/or testing evaluation report?

- Does the organization have a clearly defined and documented post exercise process to provide an approved, prioritized, time-scaled action plan to implement lessons learned, changes and amendments as identified within the recommendations of the post-exercise report?

B.7.2 Maintenance

- Does the organization have a clearly defined, documented and approved BCM maintenance cycle and programme?

- Does organization's BCM maintenance programme achieve the outcomes of a BCM maintenance programme as set out in 10.2.3?

- Does the organization's BCM maintenance programme cover the whole of the organization's BCM capability and not solely BCP(s)?

- Does the frequency of the BCM management maintenance programme reflect the nature, scale, complexity and culture of the organization including its operating environment, risk profile and risk appetite?

- Does the organization have a clearly defined, documented and approved process for escalating BCM non-compliance issues as highlighted by individuals, exercising reports, assurance report and/or audit findings or situations?

- Does the organization have a clearly defined and documented BCM maintenance process to ensure the BCM competence and capability of sourcing suppliers (internal or outsourced providers) of MCAs is effective and fit-for-purpose (as defined in contractual terms and conditions or SLAs [*Service Level Agreements*])?

- Does the organization have a clearly defined, documented and approved BCM maintenance process to ensure the BCM competence and capability of suppliers of BCM specialist services (internal or outsourced providers) concerning the organization's MCAs is effective and fit-for-purpose (as defined in contractual terms and conditions or SLAs)?

- Is there a clearly defined, documented and approved process within the BCM and CMP to provide an approved and time-scaled action plan to implement lessons learned, changes and amendments to the organization's BCM and/or crisis management capability as identified within either a BCM or crisis management exercise, audit or assurance report?

- Does the organization's BCM and crisis management maintenance process provide a clearly defined, documented and approved procedure to ensure that all changes to the BCM strategy and/or BCP are reflected in the BCM exercising, training and awareness programmes?

B.7.3 Audit

- Does the organization have a clearly defined, documented and approved BCM audit cycle and programme?

- Does organization's BCM audit process achieve the outcomes of a BCM audit process as set out in 10.3.3?

- Does the organization's audit policy clearly define the minimum level of frequency and the triggers at which the organization's BCM and crisis management capability should be audited?

- Are the terms of reference and details of a BCM audit clearly defined and documented in the audit contract?

- Does the audit contract clearly identify any external or other professional assistance needed to perform the audit?

- Is a prioritized and signed-off audit opinion report produced after each audit?

- Is a prioritized and signed-off BCM or crisis management action plan to address issues identified during an audit prepared and implemented after each audit, with a specific timescale?

GLOSSARY OF RISK AND BUSINESS CONTINUITY TERMS

Alternate site
A site held in readiness for use to maintain the continuity of the critical processes of an organisation. Alternate sites may be 'cold,' 'warm' or 'hot.' This type of site is also known as a Recovery, Work Area Recovery or Fall Back site.

Assembly area
The designated area at which employees, visitors and contractors assemble if evacuated from a building or site. The fire risk assembly area location may be different than the bomb risk evacuation point and options for the latter may include a predetermined location inside the building.

Asset
Useful or valuable thing or person, property, activity or process owned by a person or organisation. There are four types of asset: physical (e.g., buildings, equipment and stock), financial (e.g., currency, bank deposits and shares), intellectual (e.g., goodwill, brand and reputation) and human (e.g., employees).

Assurance
The activity and process whereby an organisation can verify and validate its business continuity management capability.

Audit
The process by which procedures and documentation are measured against pre-agreed standards. An audit is established to understand how management runs the business and manages risk. An audit may be conducted by teams internal or external to an organisation.

Backup
A copy of files and programmes made to facilitate technology recovery.

Battle box/bag
A container in which information and equipment (e.g., floor layouts, staff lists, torch, radio, stationery, contracts, details of alternate sites) is stored to be available at short notice to Emergency Response or Crisis Management teams.

Benchmarking
The continuous process of measuring products, services and practices against competitors or those organisations and standards that are recognised as industry or profession leaders.

Bronze control
The operational level at which control over all of the agencies in one area of an incident at the site of an incident is exercised. This is to ensure that there is a chain of command and communication from an incident to the overall strategic command. See also Silver Control and Gold Control.

Business Continuity Management (BCM)	A holistic management process that identifies potential impacts that threaten an organisation, and provides a framework for building resilience and the capability for an effective response that safeguards the interests of its key stakeholders, reputation, brand and value-creating activities.
Business Continuity Management framework	The structure required to deliver an organisation's business continuity strategy including policies, standards, practises, tools, techniques, performance indicators, scenarios and the process for quality assurance and audit.
Business Continuity Management policy	The document that sets out an organisation's business continuity vision, mission, values, overall goals and objectives. Usually agreed by the Board and signed by the Chief Executive or equivalent.
Business Continuity Management strategy	The mechanism by which an organisation's business continuity policy is delivered.
Business Continuity Management life-cycle	The set of activities and processes divided into stages that are necessary to manage business continuity.
Business Continuity Institute (BCI)	The institute of professional business continuity managers (www.thebci.org)
Business Continuity plan (BCP)	A collection of information and procedures developed, documented, reviewed, tested and maintained in readiness for use in the event of an emergency, event or crisis.
Business Impact Analysis (BIA)	(also, Business Impact Assessment) The process by which an organisation assesses the qualitative and quantitative impacts, effects and losses that might result following an emergency, event or crisis. The findings of a BIA are used to make decisions concerning business continuity management strategy and solutions
Business interruption	A discontinuity in an organisation's operations that might lead to the invocation of the business continuity plan.
Business Recovery plan	The plan that addresses the actions required and the processes to be followed by specific business unit and support-function teams as part of a recovery.
Business Resumption Plan	The plan that addresses the actions required and the processes to be followed by a specific business unit to resume business.
Call Tree	A structured cascade process that enables a list of personnel to be contacted as part of a communication or plan invocation process.
Campus	The buildings of one organisation that are geographically grouped together.
Cascade System	A system where a call tree is invoked and one person contacts others who in turn initiate further calls as necessary. This process can be operated manually in-house, using an automated system, or by a third-party call centre. Used for plan invocation or communication.
Cold site	A site equipped with data or work area capability to facilitate a technology installation and the personnel required to resume critical business operations, but which does not have some or all of the technology required on-site. See also Hot Site and Warm Site.
Command centre	The facility used by the Crisis Management Team and/or the Business Continuity Management Team following an Emergency Response. This may

be on-site if the usual site is unaffected or off-site if the usual site is inoperable.

Compliance	The process whereby an organisation achieves an assessment of assurance against internal or external standards of performance, rules and guidelines. Often used in a regulatory context.
Contingency planning	An expression that is sometimes used as an alternative to aspects of business continuity planning.
Control	Any action that reduces the probability of a risk occurring or reduces its impact if it does occur.
Control environment	The overall set of controls in place for an organisation.
Control framework	The structure required to deliver the control environment including policy, standards, practise, tools, techniques, performance indicators, scenarios and the process for quality assurance and audit.
Cordon	The boundary line of a zone that is determined, reinforced and exclusively managed by the emergency services and from which all unauthorised personnel are excluded for a period determined by those in command. Also known as an Exclusion Zone. There are often outer and inner cordons with the former reducing back to the inner cordon as safety is assured in the wider area.
Corporate governance	Oversight mechanisms including the processes, structures and information used for directing and overseeing the management of an organisation.
Cost-benefit analysis	A process conducted after the risk assessment and business impact analysis that concerns the financial and operational assessment of different strategic business continuity management options. The analysis balances the whole cost of each option against the perceived savings.
Counselling	The process of helping those people affected directly or indirectly (and in some cases the families of those involved) at times of crisis to manage their reactions.
Crisis	An incident or a perception that threatens the operations, personnel, shareholder value or stakeholders, brand, reputation; or, the operational or strategic goals of an organisation.
Crisis Management plan	The plan that provides a documented framework to enable an organisation to manage in a structured way any event regardless of cause that has the potential to evolve into a crisis..
Critical	Usually applied to a resource or process that must be kept operational or reinstated as soon as possible following an incident to ensure operational survival.
Critical data point	The point to which data must be restored in order to achieve recovery objectives.
Damage assessment	The process of assessing all potential damage following an incident to the organisation, its people and other stakeholders,
Data mirroring	A process whereby critical data is copied instantaneously to another location so that it is constantly accessible. Also referred to as Data Shadowing.

Data protection	Requirements including those of a statutory nature to manage personal data in a manner that does not threaten or disadvantage the person or organisation to which it refers.
Decision point	The latest moment at which the decision to invoke emergency response or crisis procedures has to be taken in order to ensure the continuity of critical processes.
Denial of access	The inability of an organisation to access or occupy its normal working environment.
Dependency	The reliance directly or indirectly of one activity or process upon another. Also referred to as Mission-Critical Activities.
Disaster	The plan for processing critical applications in the event of a major Recovery planhardware or software failure or destruction of facilities. Also referred to as the Systems Recovery Plan or Technology Recovery Plan.
Disruption	An unplanned event that causes the general system or major application to be inoperable for an unacceptable length of time.
Diverse routing	The routing of information through split or duplicate cable facilities
E-commerce	A business that operates by virtual means, by interconnecting computers through networks and notably the internet.
Electronic vaulting	The transfer of data to an offsite storage facility, typically using an electronic communications link.
Emergency	An actual or impending situation that may cause loss of life or injury; loss of or damage to an asset, reputation and brand; or, interruption to usual business operations of a level or nature as defined.
Emergency Coordinator	Responsible for the overall response following an emergency.
Emergency data services	Remote capture and storage of electronic data such as journaling, vaulting, and data shadowing or mirroring.
Emergency Marshal	Responsible for allocated parts of a site following an emergency including coordination of the evacuation of all personnel from the site and reporting the results to the Emergency Coordinator.
Emergency Response	The immediate reaction to an incident.
Emergency Services	Usually refers to the police, fire brigade and ambulance services; and where introduced, military and other support.
Enterprise risk management	A process applied in strategy-setting and across an enterprise designed to Identify potential events that may affect the entity, to manage risks that are beyond the risk appetite of an entity. Also known as Integrated Risk Management or Holistic Risk Management.
Escalation	The process by which an incident is communicated upwards through the incident reporting chain of an organisation.
Exercise	A way of testing part of a Business Continuity Plan. Most likely to involve simulation of an event in which participants role-play against a number of scenarios in order to improve awareness, critically assess what the issues are prior to a real invocation and to develop further the process of business continuity management.

Fire Marshal	Responsible for allocated parts of a site following an emergency specifically concerning fire or explosion, including coordination of the evacuation of all employees, visitors and contractors from the site and reporting the results to the Emergency Coordinator. A similar role to an Emergency Marshal.
First Aid Officers	Responsible for allocated parts of a site following an emergency including evacuation of employees, visitors and contractors as directed, treatment of casualties and accompanying casualties to hospital or home.
Gap analysis	A survey with the objective to identify the differences between the current state of business continuity plans and the required future state of business continuity plans. Also known as a Current/future state analysis.
Gold control	The operational level at which overall control of an incident is exercised. See also Bronze Control and Silver Control.
Hazard	A source of potential harm or a situation with a potential to cause loss.
Hot site	A site already equipped with data or work area capability to facilitate a technology installation or the personnel required to resume critical business operations at immediate notice. See also Cold Site and Warm site.
Hot standby	A term that is usually reserved for technology recovery. An alternate means of processing that minimises downtime so that no loss of processing occurs. Usually involves the use of a standby site that is permanently connected to business users and is often used to record transactions in tandem with the primary system.
Impact	The actual or potential size of a loss if a risk occurs. Measurement may be qualitative (e.g. high, medium, low) or quantitative (on personnel, finances, operations or responsibilities).
Incident	Any event that may or may not evolve into to a business interruption, disruption, loss and/or a crisis.
Information security	The securing or safeguarding of all sensitive information, electronic or otherwise, which is owned or under the control of an organisation.
Infrastructure	A building and all of its support services.
Insurance	A contract to finance the cost of risk. In consideration of the premium paid the insurer will pay to the insured the contracted amount in the event of a named loss.
Invocation	The act by which a business continuity process is formally started. The term is also often used to refer to the act of using a service such as work-area recovery, including that offered by a third-party provider.
Lead time	The time it takes for a supplier to make equipment or a service available to users.
Line re-routing	A facility offered by telephone service providers to re-route dedicated telephone lines to back-up or other sites.
Loss Adjuster	A professional who assists in the evaluation and management of an insured loss and the response to that loss. An Adjuster may be pre-appointed by an organisation to become one of the business continuity management team members.

Loss Assessor	A professional employed by an organisation to assist in the management of a loss, including an insured loss. An Assessor may be pre-appointed and form part of one or more of the relevant business continuity management plan teams.
Maximum acceptable outage (MAO)	The timeframe during which a recovery must become effective before an outage compromises the ability of an organisation to achieve its critical objectives.
Mission-critical activities	The critical operations and/or business activities without which the organisation would quickly be unable to achieve its business objectives. Also known as Critical Service.
Mobile standby	A transportable operating environment complete with office equipment and supporting technology. Can also comprise portable capability for technology including telecommunications.
Operational risk	The possibility of direct or indirect loss resulting from inadequate or failed internal processes, people and systems; or, from external events.
Organisation	An enterprise, corporate entity, firm, partnership, establishment, public authority, government body, department or agency, a business or a charity.
Outage	The period of time that a service, system, process or business function is, or is expected to be, unusable or inaccessible.
Outsourcing	The transfer of a business function or functions to an external or internal service provider over a set period of time, during which the service provider performs a defined service within agreed limits of discretion for a price.
Plan maintenance	The management process of keeping an organisation's business continuity management competence and capability up to date, fit for purpose and effective.
Post-traumatic disorder (PTSD	Caused where a person has witnessed or confronted an incident that stress involved actual or threatened death or serious injury, or threat to the physical integrity of self or others, and the person's response involved intense fear, helplessness or horror.
Pre-positioned	Physical assets stored at an offsite location to be used in business or upport recovery operations.
Preventative	Controls put in place to manage a risk and to prevent an interruption to business.
Prioritisation	The order in which Mission-Critical activities and their dependencies are addressed following invocation of a business continuity plan.
Probability	The chance of a risk occurring.
Project management	The techniques and tools required to describe, control and deliver a series of activities with given deliverables, timeframes and budgets.
Qualitative assessment	A form of assessment that analyses the general structures and systems currently in place. A descriptive methodology, which typically involves risk mapping and risk matrices. These assessments do not involve numeric or other quantitative measures.

Quantitative assessment	A form of assessment that analyses the actual or estimated numbers and values involved. This type of methodology typically applies mathematical and statistical techniques and modelling.
Reciprocal agreement Objective (RPO)	An agreement that allows organisations to support each other in various ways.
Recoverable loss	Financial losses due to an invocation that may be recovered in the future e.g., through insurance, other contract or via an action in tort against a third party.
Recovery Point	The point in time to which work should be restored following the invocation of a business continuity plan that interrupts business.
Recovery Time Objective (RTO)	An output from the BIA that identifies the time by which Mission-critical Activities or their dependencies must be recovered. Also known as Maximum Tolerable Downtime.
Reputation	Failure to meet stakeholders' reasonable expectations of an organisation's performance and behaviour.
Resilience	The ability of an organisation to continue critical activities and to absorb loss and other damage throughout an otherwise disruptive incident.
Risk	The combination of the probability of an event and its consequences.
Risk Appetite or Tolerance	The defined level of risk and impact that is considered by an organisation to be acceptable from an operational, cost or responsibility view point. Also known as Risk Tolerance.
Risk categories	The clustering of risk types into groupings of risks with similar cause of loss or issue e.g., people, systems, process, environmental or external events.
Risk control	The part of the risk management process that concerns implementation of policies, processes, tools and techniques that accept, eliminate, remove or transfer risk; or, establish business continuity processes. Controls may be of a preventative, detective or post-event nature.
Risk effects	The clustering of risk types into groupings of risks with similar effects in case of a loss e.g., asset loss, compensation, mandated payout or fine.
Risk evaluation	The process of comparing actual risk levels with previously established risk criteria. As a result of this comparison, risks can be prioritised for further action.
Risk events	The clustering of risk types into groupings of risks with similar events e.g., transactional, crime, ethics, accidents, human resource issues or business.
Risk identification	The process of identifying what can happen, why, when and how.
Risk management	Establishment of culture, processes and structures to manage potential opportunities and adverse effects
Risk profile	The collection of risks that an organisation faces organised by severity.
Risk profiling	The systematic process by which all the risks and associated controls relating to an organisation are identified, assessed by severity and documented.
Risk retention	The level of risk and impact to operations, finances, responsibilities and people that is accepted by the organisation.

Risk transfer	The treatment or control of risk through sharing the burden of loss or benefit of gain for a risk with another party. Transfer can be carried out for example through insurance contracts, other financial instruments and the use of third parties such as outsource providers and suppliers. Risk transfer can create new or modify existing risks.
Risk treatment	The selection and implementation of options for managing risk.
Roll call	The process of ensuring that all employees, visitors and contractors have been safely evacuated and accounted for following the evacuation of a building or site.
Roll Call Marshals	Those responsible at an assembly area for the identification and safety of personnel including the identification and reporting of those unaccounted for.
Salvage	The value of the remaining damaged and undamaged assets following an incident.
Scenarios	Probable events and their consequences.
Service level agreement (SLA)	A formal agreement between an internal or external service provider and an organisation which covers the nature, quality, availability, scope and response of the service provider. The SLA should address business as usual as well as expectations and situations following a potentially damaging incident and risk scenarios.
Silver control	Silver control is the level at which the overall control and coordination of a site is managed. The Silver commander is the overall on-site incident commander and will ensure that the coordination and priorities are maintained. See also Bronze Control and Gold Control.
Single point of failure	The only (single) source of a critical service, activity and/or process in the supply or delivery chain.
Speculative risk	A risk where a director or manager chooses to place money or other resources at risk. The objective of using risk capital in this way would be to make a profit or other gain.
Stand down	Notification that that the formal response to an incident has concluded.
Standby service	The provision of relevant recovery facilities.
Statutory services	Those services with responsibilities that are laid down by law such as the police, fire services and ambulance.
Structured walkthrough	A type of exercise in which team members physically implement and verbally review each step of a plan to assess its effectiveness and to identify constraints, issues and improvements.
Supplier	An individual or entity that provides goods or services to an organisation.
Supplier management	The effective management of a supplier relationship and the associated activities from both a contractual and performance perspective and from a strategic perspective, to ensure the appropriate relationship management model is applied to the given supplier.
Syndication ratio	The number of times that a third-party work area recovery facility is sold to different concurrent customers.
System denial	A failure of the technology system for a period sufficient to impact on an organisation's business activities.

System restore	The procedures necessary to get a system into an operable condition where it is possible for operational staff to proceed to deliver normal processing from the application software, hardware and data.
Systemic risk	The risk that the failure of a participant or part of a process, system, industry or market to meet its obligations in such a way that will cause other participants to fail to meet their obligations when due, causing significant liquidity or other problems. The implication is a threat to the stability of the whole process, system, industry or market.
Tabletop exercise	A scenario-based method of testing plans, procedures and people without disrupting normal operations.
Task list	Defined mandatory and discretionary tasks allocated to teams or individual roles within plans.
Technology Recovery Plan	The plan for processing critical technology applications in the event of a major hardware or software failure or the destruction of facilities on which they depend. Also referred to as the Systems Recovery Plan or Disaster Recovery Plan.
Technology system	A technology system is identified by defining boundaries around a set of processes, communications, storage and related resources (an architecture) All the components of a system need not be physically connected, e.g., a group of standalone PCs.
Telecommunications	The science and technology of communications at a distance by electronic transmission of impulses, such as by telegraph, telephone, radio or television. It is the foundation for the Internet and all of the emerging activities surrounding the Internet's activities. Telecommunications is the transmission of information by wire, radio, optical cable, electromagnetic, or other means.
Test	An activity in which part of a business continuity plan is followed to ensure that the plan contains the appropriate information and produces the desired result.
Tolerance threshold	The maximum period of time during which an organisation can afford to be without a Mission-Critical Activity or its dependencies.
Uninterrupted power supply (UPS)	Equipment that offers short-term protection against power surges and failures. UPS typically allows enough power for critical systems to be powered down plus a degree of supply to emergency lighting, and for transition to a longer-term backup power supply such as a generator if available.
Utilities	Organisations providing essential services such as gas, electricity and water.
Virus	An unauthorised computer programme that enters a computer system and then propagates itself into other computers via networks and/or discs or otherwise causes damage or loss of operability.
Warm site	A site which is completely or partially equipped with hardware, software, communications capability and asset infrastructure to support the continuation of business within a short time scale. See also Hot Site and Cold Site.
Work area facility	A pre-designated space provided with all the equipment needed to enable work to continue to provide at least urgent and critical deliveries of products and services.

Work Area Recovery Plan	The Plan that provides a documented framework to enable an organisation to take up occupancy of a work area facility.
Zone	A region or area characterised by a common feature or quality that should be considered in business continuity plans e.g. a high risk concentration of organisation or Mission Critical Activities in an area.

Other Helpful Glossaries

The Business Continuity Institute Glossary of General Business Continuity Management Terms
http://www.thebci.org/Glossary.pdf

The Disaster Recovery Institute International and Disaster Recovery Journal Business Continuity Glossary
http://www.thebci.org/Glossary.pdf

The Disaster Recovery Institute International Glossary of Terms
http://www.drii.org/displaycommon.cfm?an=3

US Federal Emergency Management Agency: FEMA Acronyms, Abbreviations and Terms
http://www.fema.gov/preparedness/faat.shtm

All Hands Community Glossary of Terms and Definitions
http://www.all-hands.net/pn/modules.php?op=modload&name=pn_glossary&file=index

Binomial International Common Disaster Recovery / Business Continuity Terms
http://www.binomial.com/resources/glossary.php

ABOUT THE AUTHORS

JULIA GRAHAM
FCII FBCI MIRM CHARTERED INSURER

Julia Graham worked in the insurance industry for 30 years in a variety of managerial roles including marketing, underwriting and operations. In the early 1990s she set up the first in-house Risk Management capability for the multi-national insurance company Royal Insurance. In 1996, following the Manchester bombing, Julia led the recovery team for the Royal Insurance business in Manchester, one of the most severely affected locations in Manchester and working environment for more than 600 employees.

Julia went on to become the Group Risk Manager for Royal & SunAlliance with global responsibility for operational and strategic risk. This role included the responsibility for establishing policy and good practice for business continuity management across the organisation. In addition to the Manchester bomb recovery which touched aspects of post-trauma, asset recovery and insurance claims management, Julia has practical experience of recovery situations including those touched by asset damage, SARS, employee death, kidnap for ransom, The World Trade Center and the bombings in London July 2005.

An enthusiast for the risk profession, Julia has experience in a number of industry governance roles as an officer of local and national Chartered Insurance Institute committees, the Council of AIRMIC (the UK association for insurance and risk managers), the Board of the BCI (Business Continuity Institute), the Board of the ifs (The Institute of Financial Services) and the UK Advisory Board for SunGard.

A resident of the UK Julia has worked in all continents of the world and is a regular author of risk management articles. Her conference speaking engagements have included the US, Australia, New Zealand, the UK, Continental Europe and Asia.

In 2004 Julia took up a position with the global legal services organisation DLA Piper Rudnick Gray Cary as Chief Risk Officer. One of the world's leading legal organisations, Julia's role covers all aspects of risk management, including operational risk and business continuity management. DLA Piper is a rapidly expanding organisation and at the time of publication, Julia's role embraced 23 countries and more than 50 cities.

Julia is currently the chair of the team assisting the British Standards Institution (BSI) in creating a British and International Standard for risk management.

Julia is a Fellow of the Chartered Insurance Institute, a Fellow of the Business Continuity Institute, a Member of the Institute of Risk Management and a Chartered Insurer.

ABOUT THE AUTHORS

DAVID KAYE
FRSA FCII FBCI MIRM CHARTERED INSURER

David Kaye has spent much of his working life resident, and with bottom-line responsibility, for multi-million pound insurance and financial services businesses in the United Kingdom, Holland, Caribbean and the Far East. A two-year secondment to work with a Police Service reporting to the Chief Constable added further valuable and wide ranging experiences.

Prior to becoming a management consultant, David was a Divisional Director within the multinational group of companies and carried the Group responsibility worldwide for operational risk and continuity planning. In this role David evaluated and managed risk, and also developed and exercised continuity plans. He was required on numerous occasions to implement those plans and lead the response following potentially business-destroying damage by IRA bombs, and by numerous other natural and manmade disasters around the world.

David therefore brings to this book a mixture of wide international experience, a track record of achievements at Board level and as CEO, and also a deep experience of the international world of business risk and its consequences. He currently writes, lectures and provides guidance on matters of risk and business continuity to a wide range of business and public service clients around the world.

He has lived in six different countries, worked in twenty six, and has lead workshops or addressed public and corporate audiences on Business Risk in seventeen. He is the current author of the Chartered Insurance Institute's examination textbook on Risk Management. The Institute of Risk Management has appointed David to the new role of lead examiner on business continuity risks.

Many articles on risk and related subjects have been published by the Geneva Association and many other magazines and professional bodies. David is currently a member of the team assisting the British Standards Institute in creating a British and International Standard for Continuity risk management and has assisted other industry bodies in a variety of ways.

David is a Fellow of the Chartered Insurance Institute, A Fellow of the Royal Society of Arts, a Fellow of the Business Continuity Institute, a Member of the Institute of Risk Management and a Chartered Insurer.

RISK MANAGEMENT APPROACH TO BUSINESS CONTINUITY:
ALIGNING BUSINESS CONTINUITY WITH CORPORATE GOVERNANCE
By Julia Graham, FCII, FBCI MIRM and David Kaye, FCII FBCI MIRM FRSA

ISBN 1-931332-36-3

REGISTRATION AND *FREE* CD-ROM

If you purchased this book <u>other than</u> directly from Rothstein Associates, please fill out and return this form to register for future updates, and for your complimentary CD-ROM containing THE ROTHSTEIN CATALOG ON DISASTER RECOVERY. (*If you purchased this book directly from Rothstein Associates – The Rothstein Catalog On Disaster Recovery – you are automatically registered; be sure to let us know if your address changes*).

To qualify for future updates and receive your complimentary CD, please fill out this form <u>completely</u> and return it by fax to 203.740.7401, email to <u>info@rothstein.com,</u> or mail to the address below.

PRODUCT: <u>RISK MANAGEMENT APPROACH TO BUSINESS CONTINUITY</u>
ISBN 1-931332-36-3

First Name _____ Last Name _____

Company/Organization _____

Department/Mail Station _____ Title _____

Street Address _____

City _____ State/Province _____

Zip/Postal Code _____ Country _____

Email address _____ Phone _____

Where Purchased _____ Purchase Date _____

Check here for a complimentary subscription to our email newsletter, BUSINESS SURVIVAL™: BUSINESS CONTINUITY FOR KEY DECISION-MAKERS (*be sure to include your email address above!*) ☐

Check here if you would like to receive a complimentary CD-ROM containing THE ROTHSTEIN CATALOGS ON DISASTER RECOVERY, the industry's principal source for hundreds of books, software tools, videos and research reports since 1989. ☐

THE ROTHSTEIN CATALOG ON DISASTER RECOVERY
ROTHSTEIN ASSOCIATES INC.
4 Arapaho Rd.
Brookfield, Connecticut 06804-3104 USA
203.740.7444   Fax 203.740.7401
<u>info@rothstein.com</u>

www.rothstein.com

CPSIA information can be obtained
at www.ICGtesting.com
Printed in the USA
FFOW01n0959150814
6808FF